THE INTELLIGENT WOMAN'S GUIDE TO SOCIALISM & CAPITALISM

THE INTELLIGENT WOMAN'S GUIDE TO SOCIALISM & CAPITALISM

George Bernard Shaw

Welcome Rain Publishers
NEW YORK

The Library of Congress has cataloged this book as follows:
Shaw, George Bernard, 1856–1950.
The intelligent woman's guide to socialism and capitalism
Reprint. Originally published: Brentano's Publishers, 1928.
Includes index.
1. Socialism. 2. Capitalism. #. Communism. 4. Fascism. I. Title.
HX72.S42

ISBN 978-1-56649-0-535

Printed in the USA

TO

MY SISTER-IN-LAW

MARY STEWART CHOLMONDELY

THE INTELLIGENT WOMAN TO WHOSE QUESTION
THIS BOOK IS THE BEST ANSWER I CAN MAKE

A FOREWORD FOR AMERICAN READERS

I have never been in America; therefore I am free from the delusion, commonly entertained by the people who happen to have been born there, that they know all about it, and that America is their country in the same sense that Ireland is my country by birth, and England my country by adoption and conquest. You, dear madam, are an American in the sense that I am a European, except that the American States have a language in common and are federated, and the European states are still on the tower of Babel and are separated by tariff fortifications. When I hear people asking why America does not join the League of Nations I have to point out to them that America *is* a League of Nations, and sealed the covenant of her solidity as such by her blood more than sixty years ago, whereas the affair at Geneva is not a League of Nations at all, but only a so far unsuccessful attempt to coax Europe to form one at the suggestion of a late American President, with the result that the British Secretary of State for Foreign Affairs makes occasional trips to Geneva, and, on returning, reassures the British House of Commons by declaring that in spite of all Woodrow-Wilsonic temptations to combine with other nations he remains an Englishman first, last, and all the time; that the British Empire comes before everything with him; and that it is on this understanding and this alone that he consents to discuss with foreigners any little matters in which he can oblige them without detriment to the said reserved interests. And this attitude seems to us in England so natural, so obvious, so completely a matter of course, that the newspapers discuss the details of Mr Chamberlain's report of his trip without a word about the patriotic exordium which reduces England's membership of the League to absurdity.

Now your disadvantage in belonging to a league of nations instead of to a nation is that if you belong to New York or Massachusetts, and know anything beyond the two mile radius of which you are the centre, you probably know much more of England, France, and Italy than you do of Texas or Arizona, though you are expected, as an American, to know all about America. Yet I never met an American who knew anything about America except the bits she had actually set eyes on or felt with her boots; and even of that she could hardly see the wood for the trees. By comparison I may be said to know almost all about America. I am far enough off to get a good general view, and, never having assumed, as the natives do, that a knowledge of America is my intuitional birthright, I have made enquiries, read books, availed myself of the fact that I seem to be personally an irresistible magnet for every wandering American, and even gathered something from the recklessly confidential letters which every American lady who has done anything unconventional feels obliged to write me as a testimony to the ruinous efficacy of my books and plays. I could and should have drawn all the instances in this book from American life were it not that America is such a fool's paradise that no American would have believed a word of them, and I should have been held up, in exact proportion to my accuracy and actuality, as a grossly ignorant and prejudiced Britisher, defaming the happy West as ludicrously as the capitalist West defames Russia. What I tell you of England you will believe. What I could tell you of America might provoke you to call on me with a gun. Also it would lead you to class me as a bitter enemy to America, whereas I assure you that though I do not adore your country with the passion professed by English visitors at public banquets when you have overwhelmed them with your reckless hospitality, I give it a good deal of my best attention as a very interesting if still very doubtful experiment in civilization.

But this much I will permit myself to say. Do not imagine that because at this moment certain classes of American workmen are buying bathtubs and Ford cars, and investing in building societies and the like the money that they formerly spent in the saloons, that America is doing as well as can be expected. If you were at this moment a miner's wife in South Wales you would be half starving; but the wife of a Colorado miner might think you very lucky in having nothing more violent than half starving to endure. The sweated women workers in the tenements of your big cities are told that in America anyone can make a fortune who wants to. Here we spare them that mockery, at least. You must take it from me, without driving me to comparisons that between nations wound as personalities do between individuals, that Capitalism is the same everywhere, and that if you look for its evils at home you will miss nothing of them except perhaps some of the socialistic defences which European States have been forced to set up against their worst extremities.

In truth it is odd that this book should not have been written by an American. Its thesis is the hopelessness of our attempts to build up a stable civilization with units of unequal income; and it was in America that this inequality first became monstrous not only in money but in its complete and avowed dissociation from character, rank, and the public responsibility traditionally attached to rank. On the eastern shores of the Atlantic the money makers formed a middle class between the proletariat, or manual working class, and the aristocracy, or governing class. Thus labor was provided for; business was provided for; and government was provided for; and it was possible to allow and even encourage the middle class to make money without regard to public interests, as these were the business of the aristocracy.

In America, however, the aristocracy was abolished; and the only controlling and directing force left was business, with nothing to restrain it in its pursuit of money except the business necessity for maintaining property in land and capital and enforcing contracts, the business prudence which perceives that it would be ruinous to kill outright the proletarian goose that lays the golden eggs, and the fear of insurrection. There was no longer a king and an aristocratic governing class to say to the tradesman "Never mind the public interest: that is our business: yours is to get as rich as you can, incidentally giving employment to the proletariat and increasing our rent rolls". All that remained was the tradition of unscrupulous irresponsibility in business; and when the American millionaires first began to astonish Europe with their wealth it was possible for the most notorious of them, in the course of an enquiry into the proceedings of a Trust with which he was connected, to reply to a criticism as to the effect of his business policy on the public with a simple "Damn the public!". Had he been a middle class man in a country where there was a governing class outside and above business, or a monarch with a council in the same position, or even a State Church, his answer would have been entirely in order apart from its verbal profanity. Duly bowdlerized it would have run "I am a man of business, not a ruler and a lawgiver. The public interest is not my job: I do not presume to meddle with it. My sole function is to make as much money as I can". Queen Elizabeth would have applauded such an attitude as socially sound and highly becoming: nothing angered her more than presumptuous attempts on the part of common persons to concern themselves with *her* business of high politics.

When America got rid of monarchs and prelates and popes and British cabinets and the like, and plunged into the grand republican experiment which has become the rule instead of the exception in Europe since the war swept all the emperors into the dustbin of history, she raised the middle classes to the top of the social structure and thus delivered its civilization into their hands without ennobling their traditions. Naturally they raced for money, for more money, and still more money, and damned the public when they were not doping it with advertisements which were by tacit agreement exempted from the law against obtaining money by false pretences or practising medicine without qualifications. It is true that they were forced to govern as well by the impossibility of maintaining civilization without government; but their government was limited and corrupted by their principle of letting nothing stand in the way of their getting rich quickly. And the ablest of them at that game (which has no attraction for the ability that plays the higher games by which finally civilization must live) soon became rich at a rate that made the European middle classes envious. In my youth I heard little of great men arising in America—not that America did not produce them, but that her money masters were more apt to persecute than to advertize them—but I heard much of the great fortunes that were being made there. Vanderbilt, Jay Gould, Carnegie, Rockefeller became famous by bringing our civilization to the point to which Crassus and the other millionaire contemporaries of Sulla and Julius Cæsar brought the civilization of ancient republican Rome just before it set up Emperor idolatry as a resting place on the road to ruin. Nowadays we have multimillionaires everywhere; but they began in America; and that is why I wonder this book of mine was not written in America by an American fifty years ago. Henry George had a shot at it: indeed it was his oratory (to which I was exposed for fortyfive minutes fortyfive years ago by pure chance) that called my attention to it; but though George impressed his generation with the outrageous misdistribution of income resulting from the apparently innocent institution of private property in land, he left untouched the positive problem of how else income was to be distributed, and what the nation was to do with the rent of its land when it was nationalized, thus leaving the question very much where it had been left a century earlier by the controversy between Voltaire and the elder Mirabeau, except for the stupendous series of new illustrations furnished by the growth of the great cities of the United States. Still, America can claim that in this book I am doing no more than finishing Henry George's job.

Finally, I have been asked whether there are any intelligent women in America. There must be; for politically the men there are such futile gossips that the United States could not possibly carry on unless there were some sort of practical intelligence back of them. But I will let you into a secret which bears on this point. By this book I shall get at the American men through the American women. In America as in England every male citizen is supposed to understand politics and economics and finance and diplomacy and all the rest of a democratic voter's business on the strength of a Fundamentalist education that excites the public scorn of the Sioux chiefs who have seen their country taken from them by palefaced lunatics. He is ashamed to expose the depths of his ignorance by asking elementary questions; and I dare not insult him by volunteering the missing information. But he has no objection to my talking to his wife as to one who knows nothing of these matters: quite the contrary. And if he should chance to overhear——!!!

G. B. S.

CONWAY, NORTH WALES
17th April 1928

TABLE OF CONTENTS

4

NO WEALTH WITHOUT WORK

As a nation lives from hand to mouth there must be continuous productive labor or there will be no food to distribute. But though everyone must eat, everyone need not work, because under modern conditions each of us can produce much more than enough to support one person. If everyone worked everyone would have a good deal of leisure. But it is possible to arrange that some people shall do all the work and have no leisure in order that others should have all leisure and no work. These two extremes are represented by complete Socialism and complete Slavery. Serfdom and Feudalism and Capitalism are intermediate stages. The continual struggle of persons and classes to alter the allotment of the labor task and the distribution of wealth and leisure in their own favor is the key to the history of revolutions. Enormous increase of the stakes in this game through modern discoveries and inventions. . . . PAGE 9

5

COMMUNISM

Communism must be considered without personal, political, or religious prejudice as a plan of distribution like any other. It was the plan of the apostles, and is universally practised in the family. It is indispensable in modern cities. All services and commodities which are paid for by a common fund and are at the disposal of everyone indiscriminately are examples of communism in practice. Roads and bridges, armies and navies, street lighting and paving, policemen, dustmen, and sanitary inspectors are familiar and obvious instances. 11

6

LIMITS TO COMMUNISM

Communism is so satisfactory and unquestioned as far as it has gone that those who are conscious of it may ask why everything should not be communized. Reasons why this cannot be done. Communism is applicable only to commodities and services which, being necessary or useful to everybody, enjoy general moral approval. It can be extended to matters in which the citizens are willing to give and take, as when the oarsman pays rates for a cricket pitch in consideration of the cricketer paying rates for the lake. But services as to which there is any serious difference of opinion, such as church services, and commodities which some people believe to be deleterious, such as alcoholic liquors, are excluded from the scope of Communism. Surreptitious communism is necessary in the case of science, and of learning generally, because the ordinary citizen does not understand their importance sufficiently to be willing to pay for their endowment. Governments are therefore obliged to endow them without

16

EUGENICS

Effect of distribution on the quality of people as human beings. The problem of breeding the nation. In breeding animals the problem is simple though the art is uncertain and difficult, because the animal is bred for some single specific purpose, such as the provision of food or for racing or haulage. The stockbreeder knows exactly what sort of animal is wanted. Nobody can say what sort of human being is wanted. It is not enough to say that certain sorts are not wanted. The stockbreeders' methods are therefore not applicable: the keeper of a human stud farm, if such a thing were established by a mad professor of eugenics, would not know what to aim at or how to begin. We are therefore thrown back on natural sexual attraction as our only guide. Sexual attraction in human beings is not promiscuous: it is always specific: we choose our mates. But this choice is defeated by inequality of income, which restricts our choice to members of our own class: that is, persons with similar incomes or no incomes. Resultant prevalence of bad breeding and domestic unhappiness. The most vital condition of good distribution is that it shall widen the field of sexual selection to the extent of making the nation completely intermarriageable. Only equality of income can do this. PAGE 53

17

THE COURTS OF LAW

Though Justice should not be a respecter of persons, the courts must respect persons if they have different incomes. Trial by jury is trial by a jury of peers, not only the peers of the accused but of the accusers and of the whole body of citizens. This is in practice impossible in a civilized society of persons with unequal incomes, as the person with a large income has not the same interests and privileges as the person with a small one. As access to the courts of justice costs money the poor are cut off from them by their poverty or terrorized by the threats of the rich to drag them there. The abuses of divorce and alimony. Sale of husbands and wives. Blackmail. Abuses in the criminal courts. Corruption of the law itself at its source in Parliament by the rich majority there. Severity of the laws against theft practised by the poor on the rich. Complete exemption of the crime of rich idling, which is the form of theft practised by the rich on the poor. Inequality of income thus effects a divorce of law from justice, leading to an anarchic disrespect for the law and a general suspicion of the good faith of lawyers. . . 56

18

THE IDLE RICH

Idleness does not mean inactivity. Over-exertion and "rest cures" of the rich. Their dangerous and exhausting sports. The flapper dances

paid class or are thrown out into an unpaid vagrancy; but the rule is that each class either keeps its economic level or rises and falls as a class, its internal equality being maintained at every level. As people are put so they will stay. Equality of income, far from being a novelty, is an established practice, and the only possible one as between working individuals in organized industry. The problem is therefore not one of its introduction, but of its extension from the classes to the whole community. . . . . PAGE 68

22

MERIT AND MONEY

Equality of income has the advantage of securing promotion by merit. When there is inequality of income all merits are overshadowed by the merit of having a large income, which is not a merit at all. Huge incomes are inherited by nincompoops or made by cunning traders in vice or credulity; whilst persons of genuine merit are belittled by the contrast between their pence and the pounds of fools and profiteers. The person with a thousand a year inevitably takes precedence of the person with a hundred in popular consideration, no matter how completely this may reverse their order of merit. Between persons of equal income there can be no eminence except that of personal merit. Hence the naturally eminent are the chief preachers of equality, and are always bitterly opposed by the naturally ordinary or inferior people who have the larger shares of the national income. 70

23

INCENTIVE

It is urged against equality that unless a person can earn more than another by working harder she will not work harder or longer. The reply is that it is neither fair nor desirable that she should work harder or longer. In factory and machine industry extra exertion is not possible: collective work goes on at the engine's speed and stops when the engine stops. The incentive of extra pay does not appeal to the slacker, whose object is to avoid work at any cost. The cure for that is direct compulsion. What is needed is an incentive to the community as a whole to choose a high standard of living rather than a lazy and degraded one, all standards being possible. Inequality of income is not merely useless for this purpose, but defeats it. The problem of the Dirty Work. On examination we discover that as it is done mostly by the worst paid people it is not provided for at present by the incentive of extra pay. We discover also that some of the very dirtiest work is done by professional persons of gentle nurture without exceptional incomes. The objection to dirty work is really an objection to work that carries a stigma of social inferiority. The really effective incentive to work is our needs, which are equal, and include leisure. 72

38

DOLES, DEPOPULATION, AND PARASITIC PARADISES

Investments of our capital abroad bring in gratuitous imports as interest. The expenditure of this tribute gives employment. It is, however, parasitic employment. The employees may be more pampered than productive employees; and this, combined with the disappearance of manufacturing towns and their replacement by attractive residential resorts, may produce an air of increased prosperity and refinement in all classes; but it does not provide suitable employment for the rougher workers discharged by the discarded factories, who have to be got rid of by Assisted Emigration or kept quiet by doles. If the process were unchecked England would become a country of luxurious hotels and pleasure cities inhabited by wealthy hotel guests and hotel servants with their retinue of importers and distributors, all completely dependent on foreign tribute from countries which might at any moment tax the incomes of absentee capitalists to extinction, and leave us to starve. . . . PAGE 145

39

FOREIGN TRADE AND THE FLAG

Only freshly saved capital can be exported. The capital consumed in the establishment of mines, railways, and fixed industrial plant cannot be shipped abroad. When the home market supplied by them dries up through change or exhaustion of demand, the plant must either close down or seek markets abroad. This is the beginning of foreign trade. Trade with civilized nations is hampered by foreign protective duties or by the competition of the manufacturers on the spot. Undeveloped countries which have no tariffs and no manufactures are the most lucrative markets; but the ships' crews and cargoes must be defended against massacre and plunder by the natives. This leads to the establishment of trading stations where British law is enforced. The annexation of the station makes it an outpost of the British Empire; and its boundary becomes a frontier. The policing of the frontier soon necessitates the inclusion of the lawless district beyond the frontier; and thus the empire grows without premeditation until its centre shifts to the other side of the earth. . 150

40

EMPIRES IN COLLISION

Collision of the expanding empires. Fashoda incidents. The German demand for a place in the sun. The war of 1914-18. Expansion of professional soldiering into conscription. The strains set up automatically by the pressure of capitalistic commerce, and not the depravity of human nature, are the causes of modern wars. Its horrors are therefore not a

attempt to force them on the whole Capitalist class simultaneously by a tax on capital must fail. The income of the capitalist is real: her capital, once invested, is imaginary, as it has been consumed in the act of converting it into aids to labor. Death Duties, nominally taxes on capital, are not really so, and are as objectionable in practice as they are unsound in theory. Insanity of estimates of the wealth of the country in terms of capital values. . . . . PAGE 225

52

THE MONEY MARKET

The Money Market is not a market for the sale and purchase of spare money, but for its hire. Difference between hiring and borrowing. Payment for the hire of spare money is called in business interest, and in old-fashioned economic treatises "the reward of abstinence". In the case of spare cash in the money market the obligation of the owner to the hirer is as great as that of the hirer to the owner, since capital not hired perishes by natural decay. Negative interest. The real business of the money market is to sell incomes for lump sums of spare ready money. Enormous rates of interest paid by the poor. The Bank Rate. Lending to companies. Limited liability. Varieties of shares and debentures. Jobbers and brokers. The connection of Stock Exchange transactions with industry is mostly only nominal. Warnings. Bogus companies. Genuine companies which are smoked out. "Coming in on the third reconstruction." Perils of enterprise, of public spirit, of conscience, and of imaginative foresight. 231

53

SPECULATION

Risk of becoming a gambler's wife. Selling and buying imaginary shares for phantom prices. How this is possible. Settling day on the Stock Exchange. Fluctuations. Bulls, bears, and stags. Contango and Backwardation. Cornering the bears. The losses risked are only net, not gross. Cover. Bucket shops. Unreality of the transactions. An extraordinary daily waste of human energy, audacity, and cunning. . . 239

54

BANKING

Spare money for business purposes is mostly hired from bankers. Overdrafts. Discounted bills of exchange. The Bank Rate. How the bankers get the spare money they deal in. Customers must not draw their balances simultaneously. The word credit. Credit is not capital: it is a purely abstract opinion formed by a bank manager as to the ability of a customer to repay an advance of goods. Credit, like invested capital, is a phantom category. Its confusion with real capital is a dangerous delusion of the

tion of capital and yet left the world with less income to distribute than before, a veiled repudiation of at least part of the debt is inevitable. Our method of repudiation is to redistribute income as between the holders of War Loan and the other capitalists. But as the huge borrowing and confiscation of capital that was feasible when the Government had war employment ready for an unlimited number of proletarians leaves them destitute now that the Government has demobilized them without providing peace employment, the capitalists have now to pay doles in addition to finding the money to pay themselves their own interest. PAGE 289

64

NATIONAL DEBT REDEMPTION LEVIES

Though taxation of capital is nonsensical, all proposals in that form are not necessarily impracticable. A Capitalist Government could, without requiring ready money or disturbing the Stock Exchange or the Bank Rate, cancel the domestic part of the National Debt to relieve private industry from taxation by veiling the repudiation as a levy on capital values and accepting loan and share scrip at face value in payment. Illustration. The objection to such a procedure is that levies, as distinguished from established annual taxes, are raids on private property. As such, they upset the sense of security which is essential to social stability, and are extremely demoralizing to Governments when once they are accepted as legitimate precedents. A raiding Chancellor of the Exchequer would be a very undesirable one. The regular routine of taxation of income and compensated nationalizations is available and preferable. . . 294

65

THE CONSTRUCTIVE PROBLEM SOLVED

Recapitulation. The difficulty of applying the constructive program of Socialism lies not in the practical but in the metaphysical part of the business: the will to equality. When the Government finally acquires a virtually complete control of the national income it will have the power to distribute it unequally; and this possibility may enlist, and has to a certain extent already enlisted, the most determined opponents of Socialism on the side of its constructive political machinery. Thus Socialism ignorantly pursued may lead to State Capitalism instead of to State Socialism, the same road leading to both until the final distributive stage is reached. The solution of the constructive problem of Socialism does not allay the terrors of the alarmists who understand neither problem nor solution, and connect nothing with the word Socialism except red ruin and the breaking up of laws. Some examination of the effect of Socialism on institutions other than economic must therefore be appended. 297

66

SHAM SOCIALISM

The War, by shewing how a Government can confiscate the incomes of one set of citizens and hand them over to another set with or without the intention of equalizing distribution or nationalizing industries or services, shewed also how any predominant class, trade, or clique which can nobble our Cabinet Ministers can use the power of the State for selfish ends by measures disguised as reforms or political necessities. All retrogressions and blunders, like all genuine reforms, are lucrative to somebody, and so never lack plausible advocates. Illustrative cases of exploitation of the rates and taxes and of private benevolence by Capitalism and Trade Unionism. Public parks, endowed schools, garden cities, and subsidies. The Government subsidy to the coal owners in 1925 not Socialistic nor even Capitalistic, but simply unbusinesslike. Poplarism. Mischief done by subsidies and doles. Subsidies plus Poplarism burn the candle at both ends. The danger of conscious and deliberate exploitation of the coercive and confiscatory powers of the Government by private or sectional interests is greatly increased by the modern American practice of employing first-rate brains as such in industrial enterprise. The American Trade Unions are following this example. Surprising results. What its adoption by English Trade Unions will mean. Socialists will still have to insist on equalization of income to prevent Capitalist big business and the aristocracy of Trade Unionism controlling Collectivist Governments for their private ends. . . . . PAGE 299

67

CAPITALISM IN PERPETUAL MOTION

Nothing stays put. Literal Conservatism impossible. Human society is like a glacier, apparently stationary, always in motion, always changing. To understand the changes that are happening, and the others that are coming, it is necessary to understand the changes that have gone before. Examples of every phase in economic evolution still survive and can be studied from life. Without such study we are liable to be misguided and corrupted or exasperated. Those adventures of Capitalism in pursuit of profits which took the form of thrilling exploits by extraordinary individuals with no sordid aims are narrated as the splendid history of our race. On the other hand, the more shameful episodes in that pursuit may be imputed to the greed of capitalists instead of to the ferocity and bigotry of their agents. Both views may be discounted as special pleadings. A capitalist may accidentally be a genius just as she may be a fool or a criminal. But a capitalist as such is only a person with spare money and a legal right to withhold it from the hungry. No special ability or quality of any sort beyond ordinary prudence and selfishness is involved in the

capitalist's function: the solicitor and stockbroker, the banker and employer, will carry the capital to the proletarians and see that when consuming it they replace it with interest. The most intelligent woman can do no better than invest her money, which does far more good when invested than when spent in charity. But the employers and financiers who exploit her capital are pressed by the exhaustion of home markets and old industries to finance adventurous and experimental geniuses who explore and invent and conquer. They cannot concern themselves with the effect of these enterprises on the world or even on the nation provided they bring back money to the shareholders. Capital, to save itself from rotting, has to be ruthless in its ceaseless search for investment; and mere Conservatism is of no avail against this iron necessity. Its chartered companies. It adds India, Borneo, Rhodesia to the white Englishman's burden of its naval and military defence. It may yet shift our capital from Middlesex to Asia or West Africa. Our helplessness in such an event. No need to pack up yet; but we must get rid of static conceptions of civilization and geography. . . . . PAGE 308

68

THE RUNAWAY CAR OF CAPITALISM

Controlled motion is a good thing; but the motion of Capital is uncontrollable and dangerous. As the future of civilization depends on Governments gaining control of the forces that are running away with Capitalism an understanding of them is necessary. Very few people do understand them. The Government does not: neither do the voters. The difference between Governments and governed. The Governments know the need for government and want to govern. The governed have no such knowledge: they resent government and desire freedom. This resentment, which is the central weakness of Democracy, was not of great importance when the people had no votes, as under Queen Elizabeth and Cromwell. But when great extensions of government and taxation came to be required to control and supplant Capitalism, bourgeois Democracy produced an increase of electoral resistance to government; and proletarian Democracy has continued the bourgeois tradition. The resultant paralysis of Parliament has produced a demand for dictatorships; and Europe has begun to clamor for political disciplinarians. Between our inability to govern well and our unwillingness to be governed at all, we furnish examples of the abuses of power and the horrors of liberty without ascertaining the limits of either. 314

69

THE NATURAL LIMIT TO LIBERTY

We are not born free: Nature is the supreme tyrant, and in our latitudes a hard taskmaster. Commercial progress has been at root nothing

70

RENT OF ABILITY

The proper social use of brains. Methods of making exceptional personal talents lucrative. When the talents are popular, as in the case of artists, surgeons, sports champions and the like, they involve hard work and confer no political or industrial power. As their lucrativeness is a function of their scarcity their power to enrich their possessors is not formidable and is controllable by taxation. Occasional freak incomes would not matter if equality of income were general. Impossibility of living more expensively than the richest class. Millionaires give away money for this reason. Special case of the talent for exploitation, which is a real social danger. Its forms. Administrative ability. The ability to exercise authority and enforce discipline. Both are indispensable in industry and in all organized activities. When tactfully exercised they are not unpopular, as most of us like to be saved the trouble of thinking for ourselves and so are not averse from being directed. Authority and subordination in themselves are never unpopular; but Capitalism, by creating class differences and associating authority with insolence, destroys the social equality which is indispensable to voluntary subordination. Scolding, slave driving, cursing, kicking, and slacking. Reluctance to obey commanders who are trusted and liked is less likely to give trouble

than reluctance to command. Fortunately, persons of exceptional ability do not need any special inducement to exercise it. Instances of their failure in subordinate employment. In our socialized services they do not demand excessive incomes. The demand of the real lady or gentleman. Both are compelled to act as cads in capitalist commerce, in which organizers and financiers, by reason of their special cunning, are able to extort prodigious shares of the country's output as "rent of ability." The meaning of rent. It cannot be abolished but it can be nationalized. Futility of recriminations as to indispensability between employers and employed. The talent of the exploiter is as indispensable to the landlord and capitalist as to the proletarian. Directed labor is indispensable to all three. Nationalization and equalization socializes rent of ability as well as rent of land and capital by defeating its private appropriation. PAGE 331

71

PARTY POLITICS

The steps to Socialism will not necessarily be taken by Socialist Governments. Many of them may be taken, as some already have, by anti-Socialist Cabinets. The growth of the Labor Party and the enormous electoral preponderance of the proletarian electorate promises a complete Labor conquest of the House of Commons. In that case the victorious Labor Party would split into several irreconcilable groups and make parliamentary government impossible unless it contained a unanimous Socialist majority of members really clear in their minds as to what Socialism exactly means. Precedent in the Long Parliament. The danger is not peculiar to Labor. Any political party obtaining complete possession of Parliament may go to pieces and end in a dictatorship. The Conservative triumph produced by the anti-Russian scare of 1924 made it almost impossible to hold the party together. Large majorities in Parliament, far from enabling Cabinets to do what they like, destroy their cohesion and enfeeble their party. Demoralization of Parliament during the period of large majorities brought in by the South African war. Concealment of preparations for the war of 1914-18. Parliamentary value of the fact that Socialism cannot be shaken by political storms and changes. 343

72

THE PARTY SYSTEM

Popular ignorance of what the term Party System really means. Enslavement of voters by the system, in and out of Parliament. Its advantage is that if the House of Commons has good leaders the quality of the rank and file does not matter. How it was introduced as a war measure by William III. Under it the upshot of the General Elections is determined not by the staunch party voters but by the floating body of

in the nursery. Comte's law of the three stages of belief. Tendency of parents, voters, elected persons, and governments to impose their religions, customs, names, institutions, and even their languages on everyone by force. Such substitutions may be progressive. Toleration is incompatible with complete sectarian conviction: the historic tolerations were only armistices or exhaustions after drawn battles. Examples of modern bigotry. Toleration is impossible as between Capitalism and Socialism. It is therefore necessary to demonstrate that a Labor Party can neither establish Socialism by exterminating its opponents, nor its opponents avert it by exterminating the Socialists. . . . . PAGE 359

75

REVOLUTIONS

Difference between revolutions and elections or ordinary reforms. Revolutions transfer political power from one faction or leader to another by violence or the threat of violence. Examples from English history. The transfer of political power from our capitalists to our proletarians has already taken place in form but not in substance, because, as our proletariat is half parasitic on Capitalism, and only half productive and self-supporting, half the proletarians are on the side of Capitalism. "Ye are many: they are few" is a dangerously misleading slogan. Consciousness of their formidable proletarian backing may embolden the capitalists to refuse to accept a parliamentary decision on any issue which involves a serious encroachment of Socialism on Private Property. The case of Ireland, and the simultaneous post-war repudiations of parliamentary supremacy in several continental countries forbid us to dismiss this possibility as unlikely. But whether our political decisions are made by votes or by blood and iron the mere decisions to make changes and the overruling of their opponents cannot effect any changes except nominal ones. The Russian Revolution effected a complete change from absolute monarchy to proletarian republicanism and proclaimed the substitution of Communism for Capitalism; but the victorious Communists found themselves obliged to fall back on Capitalism and do their best to control it. Their difficulties were greatly increased by the destruction involved by violent revolution. Communism can spread only as a development of existing economic civilization and must be thrown back by any sudden overthrow of it. "The inevitability of gradualness" does not imply any inevitability of peaceful change; but Socialists will be strongly opposed to civil war if their opponents do not force it on them by repudiating peaceful methods, because though civil war may clear the way it can bring the goal no nearer. The lesson of history on this point. The French Revolution and the *mot* of Fouquier Tinville. Socialism must therefore be discussed on its own merits as an order of society apart from the methods by which the necessary political power to establish it may be attained. 370

highly civilized society under a Government with a highly trained civil service and an elaborate code of laws, fortified by general moral approval. The process of its establishment will necessarily be dangerously slow rather than dangerously quick; for we are not educated to be Socialists: we teach children that Socialism is wicked. The material advantages of the steps towards Socialism are, however, biassing proletarian parents, who are in a huge majority, more and more in favor of the movement towards Socialism. This tendency is helped by the moral revolt against the cruelty of Capitalism in its operation and the sordidness of its principle. In a Socialist State economic selfishness would probably stand on the moral level now occupied by cardsharping instead of being held up as the key to social eminence. . . . . . PAGE 391

79

SOCIALISM AND LIBERTY

Nervous dread of over-regulation produced by the endless inspections and restrictions needed to protect the proletariat from unbridled Capitalist exploitation. These would have no sense in a Socialist state. Examples. Preoccupation of the police with the enforcement of private property rights and with the crimes and disorder caused by poverty. The drink question. Drink the great anæsthetic. Artificial happiness indispensable under Capitalism. Dutch courage. Drugs. Compulsory prophylactics as substitutes for sanitation. Direct restrictions of liberty by private property. "The right to roam." Deer forests and sheep runs. Existing liberties which Socialism would abolish. The liberty to be idle. Nonsense about capital and not labor being source of wealth. The case of patents and copyrights. Unofficial tyrannies. Fashion. Estate rules. The value of conventionality. 393

80

SOCIALISM AND MARRIAGE

Socialists apt to forget that people object to new liberties more than to new laws. Marriage varies from frontier to frontier. Civil marriage. Religious and communist celibacy, or the negation of marriage. Socialism has nothing to do with these varieties, as equality of income applies impartially to them all. Why there is nevertheless a rooted belief that Socialism will alter marriage. The legend of Russian "nationalization of women". Where women and children are economically dependent on husbands and fathers marriage is slavery for wives and home a prison for children. Socialism, by making them economically independent, would break the chain and open the prison door. Probable results. Improvement in domestic manners. The State should intervene to divorce separated couples, thus abolishing the present power of the parties to enforce a

82

SOCIALISM AND THE CHURCHES

Will a Socialist State tolerate a Church? This question must be discussed objectively. Survey of the age-long struggle between Church and State for the control of political and social institutions. The Inquisition and the Star Chamber. Theocracy has not lost its power. Mormon Theocracy. Christian Science. Both have come into conflict with the secular government. New Churches capture secular Governments by denying that they are Churches. The persecutions and fanaticisms of today rage in the name of Science. The avowed Church of Christ Scientist *versus* the masked Church of Jenner and Pasteur, Scientists. Tests for public office, governing bodies, and professions. Church of England tests broken by the English people refusing to remain in one Church. The Quakers. Admission to Parliament of Dissenters, then of Jews, finally of Atheists, leading to civil marriage and burial and the substitution of civil registration of birth for baptism, leaves the State in the grip of pseudo-scientific orthodoxy. Extravagances of this new faith in America and the new European republics. The assets of religion are also the assets of science. The masses, indifferent to both, are ungovernable without an inculcated faith (the official second nature). Modern conflicts between secular authority and Church doctrine. Cremation. Rights of animals. Use of cathedrals. The Russian situation: the State tolerating the Church whilst denouncing its teaching as dope. Such contemptuously tolerant anti-clericalism is necessarily transient: positive teaching being indispensable. Subjective religion. Courage. Redskin ideals. Man as hunter-warrior with Woman as everything else. Political uselessness of ferocity and sportsmanship. Fighting men cowardly and lazy as thinkers. Women anxious lest Socialism should attack their religion. It need not do so unless inequality of income is part of their religion. But they must beware of attempts to constitute Socialism as a Catholic Church with an infallible prophet and Savior. The Moscow Third International is essentially such a Church, with Karl Marx as its prophet. It must come into conflict with the Soviet and be mastered by it. We need not, however, repudiate its doctrine and vituperate its prophet on that account any more than we need repudiate the teaching of Christ and vilify his character when we insist that the State and not the Church shall govern England. The merits of Marx. . . . . PAGE 429

83

CURRENT CONFUSIONS

The Intelligent Woman must resist the impulse to intervene in conversational bickerings and letters to the Press about Socialism and Capitalism by people who understand neither. Meaningless vituperation and general misuse of nomenclature. Politicians misname themselves as well as oneanother. Self-contradictory names such as Communist-Anarchist. Real distinctions. Dircet Action *versus* Fabianism. Poor Man's Capitalism: its forms. It often masquerades as Socialism. The assumption of the name Communist by the cruder sort of Direct-Actionists produces the anomaly of a Labor Party expelling Communists whilst advocating Communist legislation. Fascism, produced by impatient disgust with Parliament as an institution, is common to the extreme Right and the extreme Left. Methods of Direct Action. The General Strike. Its absurdity. Its futility as a preventive of war. Pacifism. Supernational social organization. Empires and Commonwealths. Confusions as to Democracy. Proletarian jealousy of official power. Resultant autocracy in the Trade Unions. Labor leaders more arbitrary than Peers, and much more cynical as to working class political capacity than middle class and aristocratic idealists. Democracy in practice has never been democratic; and the millennial hopes based on every extension of the franchise, from the Reform Bill of 1832 to Votes for Women, have been disappointed. The reaction. Discipline for everybody and votes for nobody. Why women should stick resolutely to their votes. Proportional Representation opposed by the Labor Party. Need for a scientific test of political capacity. Those who use democracy as a stepping stone to political power oppose it as a dangerous nuisance when they get there. Its real object is to establish a genuine aristocracy. To do this we must first ascertain which are the aristocrats; and it is here that popular voting fails. Mrs Everybody votes for Mrs Somebody only to discover that she has elected Mrs Noisy Nobody.

84

PERORATION

A last word. Danger of discouragement through excessive sympathy. Public evils are fortunately not millionfold evils. Suffering is not cumulative; but waste is; and the Socialist revolt is against waste. Honor, health, and joy of heart are impossible under Capitalism: rich and poor are alike detestable: both must cease to exist. Our need for neighbors whose interests do not compete with ours is against the principle of Capitalism. Waiting for dead men's shoes. The professions. Husband hunting. The social friction is intense: Capitalism puts sand instead of oil in all the bearings of our machinery. The remonstrance of the optimist. Natural kindliness. Capitalism itself was better-intentioned in its inception than early Christianity. Goodwill is not enough: it is dangerous until it finds the right way. Unreasoning sentiment an unsafe guide. We believe what we want to believe: if a pecuniary bias is given to our activities it will corrupt them in institution, teaching, and practice until the best intentioned citizens will know no honest methods and doctrines. In our search

xlv

APPENDIX

THE INTELLIGENT WOMAN'S GUIDE TO SOCIALISM AND CAPITALISM

I

A CLOSED QUESTION OPENS

IT would be easy, dear madam, to refer you to the many books on modern Socialism which have been published since it became a respectable constitutional question in this country in the eighteen-eighties. But I strongly advise you not to read a line of them until you and your friends have discussed for yourselves how wealth should be distributed in a respectable civilized country, and arrived at the best conclusion you can.

For Socialism is nothing but an opinion held by some people on that point. Their opinion is not necessarily better than your opinion or anyone else's. How much should you have and how much should your neighbors have? What is your own answer?

As it is not a settled question, you must clear your mind of the fancy with which we all begin as children, that the institutions under which we live, including our legal ways of distributing income and allowing people to own things, are natural, like the weather. They are not. Because they exist everywhere in our little world, we take it for granted that they have always existed and must always exist, and that they are self-acting. That is a dangerous mistake. They are in fact transient makeshifts; and many of them would not be obeyed, even by well-meaning people, if there were not a policeman within call and a prison within reach. They are being changed continually by Parliament, because we are never satisfied with them. Sometimes they are scrapped for new ones; sometimes they are altered; sometimes they are simply done away with as nuisances. The new ones have to be stretched in the law courts to make them fit, or to prevent them fitting too well if the judges happen to dislike them. There is no end to this scrapping and altering and innovating. New laws are made to compel people to do things they never dreamt of doing before (buying insurance stamps, for instance). Old laws are repealed to allow people to do what they used to be punished for doing (marrying their deceased wives' sisters and husbands' brothers, for example). Laws that are not repealed are amended and amended and amended like a child's knickers until there is hardly a shred of the first stuff left. At the elections some candidates get votes by promising to make new laws or to get rid of old ones, and others by promising to keep things just as they are. This is impossible. Things will not stay as they are.

Changes that nobody ever believed possible take place in a few generations. Children nowadays think that spending nine years in school, old-age and widows' pensions, votes for women, and short-skirted ladies in Parliament or pleading in barristers' wigs in the courts, are part of the order of Nature, and always were and ever shall be; but their greatgrandmothers would have set down anyone who told them that such things were coming as mad, and anyone who wanted them to come as wicked.

When studying how the wealth we produce every year should be shared among us, we must not be like either the children or the greatgrandmothers. We must bear constantly in mind that our shares are being changed almost every day on one point or another whilst Parliament is sitting, and that before we die the sharing will be different, for better or worse, from the sharing of today, just as the sharing of today differs from the nineteenth century sharing more than Queen Victoria could have believed possible. The moment you begin to think of our present sharing as a fixture, you become a fossil. Every change in our laws takes money, directly or indirectly, out of somebody's pocket (perhaps yours) and puts it into somebody else's. This is why one set of politicians demands each change and another set opposes it.

So what you have to consider is not whether there will be great changes or not (for changes there certainly will be) but what changes you and your friends think, after consideration and discussion, would make the world a better place to live in, and what changes you ought to resist as disastrous to yourself and everyone else. Every opinion you arrive at in this way will become a driving force as part of the public opinion which in the long run must be at the back of all the changes if they are to abide, and at the back of the policemen and jailers who have to enforce them, right or wrong, once they are made the law of the land.

It is important that you should have opinions of your own on this subject. Never forget that the old law of the natural philosophers, that Nature abhors a vacuum, is true of the human head. There is no such thing as an empty head, though there are heads so impervious to new ideas that they are for all mental purposes solid, like billiard balls. I know that you have not that sort of head, because, if you had, you would not be reading this book. Therefore I warn you that if you leave the smallest corner of your head vacant for a moment, other people's opinions will rush in from all quarters, from advertisements, from newspapers, from books and pamphlets, from gossip, from political speeches, from plays and pictures—and, you will add, from this book!

Well, of course I do not deny it. When I urge you to think for yourself (as all our nurses and mothers and schoolmistresses do even though they clout our heads the moment our conclusions differ from theirs) I do not mean that you should shut your eyes to everyone else's opinions. I myself, though I am by way of being a professional thinker, have to content myself with second-hand opinions on a great many most important subjects on which I can neither form an opinion of my own nor criticize the opinions I take from others. I take the opinion of the Astronomer Royal as to when it is twelve o'clock; and if I am in a strange town I take the opinion of the first person I meet in the street as to the way to the railway station. If I go to law I have to consent to the absurd but necessary dogma that the king can do no wrong. Otherwise trains would be no use to me, and lawsuits could never be finally settled. We should never arrive anywhere or do anything if we did not believe what we are told by people who ought to know better than ourselves, and agree to stand by certain dogmas of the infallibility of authorities whom we nevertheless know to be fallible. Thus on most subjects we are forced by our ignorance to proceed with closed minds in spite of all exhortations to think boldly for ourselves, and be, above all things, original.

St Paul, a rash and not very deep man, as his contempt for women shews, cried "Prove all things: hold fast that which is good". He forgot that it is quite impossible for one woman to prove all things: she has not the time even if she had the knowledge. For a busy woman there are no Open Questions: everything is settled except the weather; and even that is settled enough for her to buy the right clothes for summer and winter.

Why, then, did St Paul give a counsel which he must have known to be impracticable if he ever thought about it for five minutes?

The explanation is that the Settled Questions are never really settled, because the answers to them are never complete and final truths. We make laws and institutions because we cannot live in society without them. We cannot make perfect institutions because we are not perfect ourselves. Even if we could make perfect institutions, we could not make eternal and universal ones, because the conditions change, and the laws and institutions that work well with fifty enclosed nuns in a convent would be impossible in a nation of forty million people at large. So we have to do the best we can at the moment, leaving posterity free to do better if it can. When we have made our laws in this makeshift way, the questions they concern are settled for the moment only. And in politics the moment may be twelve months or twelve hundred years, a mere breathing space or a whole epoch.

Consequently there come crises in history when questions that have been closed for centuries suddenly yawn wide open. It was in the teeth of one of these terrible yawns that St Paul cried that there are no closed questions, that we must think out everything for ourselves all over again. In his Jewish world nothing was more sacred than the law of Moses, and nothing more indispensable than the rite of circumcision. All law and all religion seemed to depend on them; yet St Paul had to ask the Jews to throw over the law of Moses for the contrary law of Christ, declaring that circumcision did not matter, as it was baptism that was essential to salvation. How could he help preaching the open mind and the inner light as against all laws and institutions whatever?

You are now in the position of the congregations of St Paul. We are all in it today. A question that has been practically closed for a whole epoch, the question of the distribution of wealth and the nature of property, has suddenly yawned wide open before us; and we all have to open our closed minds accordingly.

When I say that it has opened suddenly, I am not forgetting that it never has been closed completely for thoughtful people whose business it was to criticize institutions. Hundreds of years before St Paul was born, prophets crying in the wilderness had protested against the abominations that were rampant under the

Mosaic law, and prophesied a Savior who would redeem us from its inhumanity. I am not forgetting either that for hundreds of years past our own prophets, whom we call poets or philosophers or divines, have been protesting against the division of the nation into rich and poor, idle and overworked. But there comes finally a moment at which the question that has been kept ajar only by persecuted prophets for a few disciples springs wide open for everybody; and the persecuted prophets with their tiny congregations of cranks grow suddenly into formidable parliamentary Oppositions which presently become powerful Governments.

Langland and Latimer and Sir Thomas More, John Bunyan and George Fox, Goldsmith and Crabbe and Shelley, Carlyle and Ruskin and Morris, with many brave and faithful preachers, in the Churches and out of them, of whom you have never heard, were our English prophets. They kept the question open for those who had some spark of their inspiration; but prosaic everyday women and men paid no attention until, within my lifetime and yours, quite suddenly ordinary politicians, sitting on the front benches of the House of Commons and of all the European legislatures, with vast and rapidly growing bodies of ordinary respectable voters behind them, began clamoring that the existing distribution of wealth is so anomalous, monstrous, ridiculous, and unbearably mischievous, that it must be radically changed if civilization is to be saved from the wreck to which all the older civilizations we know of were brought by this very evil.

That is why you must approach the question as an unsettled one, with your mind as open as you can get it. And it is from my own experience in dealing with such questions that I strongly advise you not to wait for a readymade answer from me or anyone else, but to try first to solve the problem for yourself in your own way. For even if you solve it all wrong, you will become not only intensely interested in it, but much better able to understand and appreciate the right solution when it comes along.

2

DIVIDING-UP

EVERYBODY knows now that Socialism is a proposal to divide-up the income of the country in a new way. What you perhaps have not noticed is that the income of the country is being divided-up every day and even every minute at present, and must continue to be divided-up every day as long as there are two people left on earth to divide it. The only possible difference of opinion is not as to whether it shall be divided or not, but as to how much each person should have, and on what conditions he should be allowed to have it. St Paul said "He that will not work, neither shall he eat"; but as he was only a man with a low opinion of women, he forgot the babies. Babies cannot work, and are shockingly greedy; but if they were not fed there would soon be nobody left alive in the world. So that will not do.

Some people imagine that because they can save money the wealth of the world can be stored up. Stuff and nonsense. Most of the wealth that keeps us alive will not last a week. The world lives from hand to mouth. A drawingroom poker will last a lifetime; but we cannot live by eating drawingroom pokers; and though we do all we can to make our food keep by putting eggs into water-glass, tinning salmon, freezing mutton, and turning milk into dry goods, the hard fact remains that unless most of our food is eaten within a few days of its being baked or killed it will go stale or rotten, and choke or poison us. Even our clothes will not last very long if we work hard in them; and there is the washing. You may put india-rubber patches on your boot soles to prevent the soles wearing out; but then the patches will wear out.

Every year must bring its own fresh harvest and its new generations of sheep and cattle: we cannot live on what is left of last year's harvest; and as next year's does not yet exist, we must live in the main on this year's, making things and using them up, sowing and reaping, brewing and baking, breeding and butchering (unless we are vegetarians like myself), soiling and washing, or else dying of dirt and starvation. What is called saving is only making bargains for the future. For instance, if I bake a hundred and one loaves of bread, I can eat no more than the odd one; and I cannot save the rest, because they will be uneatable in a week. All I can do is to bargain with somebody who wants a hundred loaves to be eaten on the spot by himself and his family and persons in his employment, that if I give my hundred spare loaves to him he will give me, say, five new loaves to eat every year in future. But that is not saving up the loaves. It is only a bargain between two parties: one who wants to provide for the future, and another who wants to spend heavily in the present. Consequently I cannot save until I find somebody else who wants to spend. The notion that we could all save together is silly: the truth is that only a few well-off people who have more than they need can afford to provide for their future in this way; and they could not do it were there not others spending more than they possess. Peter must spend what Paul saves, or Paul's savings will go rotten. Between the two nothing is saved. The nation as a whole must make its bread and eat it as it goes along. A nation which stopped working would be dead in a fortnight even if every man, woman, and child in it had houses and lands and a million of money in the savings bank. When you see the rich man's wife (or anyone else's wife) shaking her head over the thriftlessness of the poor because they do not all save, pity the lady's ignorance; but do not irritate the poor by repeating her nonsense to them.

3
HOW MUCH FOR EACH?

YOU now realize that a great baking and making and serving and counting must take place every day; and that when the loaves and other things are made they must be divided-up immediately, each of us getting her or his legally appointed share. What should that share be? How much is each of us to have; and why is each of us to have that much and neither more nor less? If the hardworking widow with six children is getting two loaves a week whilst some idle and dissolute young bachelor is wasting enough every day to feed six working families for a month, is that a sensible way of dividing-up? Would it not be better to give more to the widow and less to the bachelor? These questions do not settle themselves: they have to be settled by law. If the widow takes one of the bachelor's loaves the police will put her in prison, and send her children to the workhouse. They do that because there is a law that her share is only two loaves. That law can be repealed or altered by parliament if the people desire it and vote accordingly. Most people, when they learn this, think the law ought to be altered. When they read in the papers that an American widow left with one baby boy, and an allowance of one hundred and fifty pounds a week to bring him up on, went to the courts to complain that it was not enough, and had the allowance increased to two hundred, whilst other widows who had worked hard early and late all their lives, and brought up large families, were ending their days in the workhouse, they feel that there is something monstrously unjust and wicked and stupid in such a dividing-up, and that it must be changed. They get it changed a little by taking back some of the rich American widow's share in taxes, and giving it to the poor in old-age pensions and widows' pensions and unemployment doles and "free" elementary education and other things. But if the American widow still has more than a hundred pounds a week for the keep of her baby boy, and a large income for herself besides, whilst the poor widow at the other end of the town has only ten shillings a week pension between her and the workhouse, the difference is still so unfair that we hardly notice the change. Everybody wants a fairer division except the people who get the best of it; and as they are only one in ten of the population, and many of them recognize the injustice of their own position, we may take it that there is a general dissatisfaction with the existing daily division of wealth, and a general intention to alter it as soon as possible among those who realize that it can be altered.

But you cannot alter anything unless you know what you want to alter it to. It is no use saying that it is scandalous that Mrs A. should have a thousand pounds a day and poor Mrs B. only half a crown. If you want the law altered you must be prepared to say how much you think Mrs A. should have, and how much Mrs B. should have. And that is where the real trouble begins. We are all ready to say that Mrs B. ought to have more, and Mrs A. less; but when we are asked to say exactly how much more and how much less, some say one thing; others say another; and most of us have nothing to say at all except perhaps that Mrs A. ought to be ashamed of herself or that it serves Mrs B. right.

People who have never thought about the matter say that the honest way is to let everyone have what she has the money to pay for, just as at present. But that does not get us out of the difficulty. It only sets us asking how the money is to be allotted. Money is only a bit of paper or a bit of metal that gives its owner a lawful claim to so much bread or beer or diamonds or motor-cars or what not. We cannot eat money, nor drink money, nor wear money. It is the goods that money can buy that are being divided-up when money is divided-up. Everything is reckoned in money; and when the law gives Mrs B. her ten shillings when she is seventy years old and young Master A. his three thousand shillings before he is seven minutes old, the law is dividing-up the loaves and fishes, the clothes and houses, the motor-cars and perambulators between them as if it were handing out these articles directly instead of handing out the money that buys them.

4
NO WEALTH WITHOUT WORK

BEFORE there can be any wealth to divide-up, there must be labor at work. There can be no loaves without farmers and bakers. There are a few little islands thousands of miles away where men and women can lie basking in the sun and live on the cocoa-nuts the monkeys throw down to them. But for us there is no such possibility. Without incessant daily labor we should starve. If anyone is idle someone else must be working for both or there would be nothing for either of them to eat. That was why St Paul said "If a man will not work neither shall he eat". The burden of labor is imposed on us by Nature, and has to be divided-up as well as the wealth it produces.

But the two divisions need not correspond to oneanother. One person can produce much more than enough to feed herself. Otherwise the young children could not be fed; and the old people who are past work would starve. Many a woman with nothing to help her but her two hands has brought up a family on her own earnings, and kept her aged parents into the bargain, besides making rent for a ground landlord as well. And with the help of water power, steam power, electric power, and modern machinery, labor can be so organized that one woman can turn out more than a thousand women could turn out 150 years ago.

This saving of labor by harnessing machines to natural forces, like wind and water and the heat latent in coal, produces leisure, which also has to be divided-up. If one person's labor for ten hours can support ten persons for a day, the ten can arrange in several different ways. They can put the ten hours' work on one person and let the other nine have all the leisure as well as free rations. Or they can each do one hour's work a day and each have nine hours leisure. Or they can have anything between these extremes. They can also arrange that three of them shall work ten hours a day each, producing enough for thirty people, so that the other seven will not only have nothing to do, but will be able to eat enough for fourteen and to keep thirteen servants to wait on them and keep the three up to their work into the bargain.

Another possible arrangement would be that they should all work much longer every day than was necessary to keep them, on condition that they were not required to work until they were fully grown and well educated, and were allowed to stop working and amuse themselves for the rest of their lives when they were fifty. Scores of different arrangements are possible between out-and-out slavery and an equitable division of labor, leisure, and wealth. Slavery, Serfdom, Feudalism, Capitalism, Socialism, Communism are all at bottom different arrangements of this division. Revolutionary history is the history of the effects of a continual struggle by persons and classes to alter the arrangement in their own favor. But for the moment we had better stick to the question of dividing-up the income the labor produces; for the utmost difference you can make between one person and another in respect of their labor or leisure is as nothing compared to the enormous difference you can make in their incomes by modern methods and machines. You cannot put more than 24 hours into a rich man's day; but you can put 24 million pounds into his pocket without asking him to lift his little finger for it.

5
COMMUNISM

IF I have made this clear to you, will you try to make up your mind how you would like to see the income of your country divided-up day by day? Do not run to the Socialists or the Capitalists, or to your favorite newspaper, to make up your mind for you: they will only unsettle and bewilder you when they are not intentionally misleading you. Think it out for yourself. Conceive yourself as a national trustee with the entire income of the country placed in your hands to be distributed so as to produce the greatest social wellbeing for everybody in the country.

By the way, you had better leave your own share and that of your children and relations and friends out of the question, lest your personal feelings upset your judgment. Some women would say "I never think of anyone else: I dont know anyone else". But that will never do in settling social questions. Capitalism and Socialism are not schemes for distributing wealth in one lady's circle only, but for distributing wealth to everybody; and as the quantity to be distributed every year is limited, if Mrs Dickson's child, or her sister's child, or her dearest and oldest friend gets more, Mrs Johnson's child or sister's child or dearest friend must get less. Mrs Dickson must forget not only herself and her family and friends, but her class. She must imagine herself for the moment a sort of angel acting for God, without any earthly interests and affections to corrupt her integrity, concerned solely with the task of deciding how much everybody should have out of the national income for the sake of the world's greatest possible welfare and the greatest possible good of the world's soul.

Of course I know that none of us can really do this; but we must get as near it as we can. I know also that there are few things more irritating than the glibness with which people tell us to think for ourselves when they know quite well that our minds are mostly herd minds, with only a scrap of individual mind on top. I am even prepared to be told that when you paid the price of this book you were paying me to think for you. But I can no more do that than I can eat your dinner for you. What I can do is to cook your mental dinner for you by putting you in possession of the thinking that has been done already on the subject by myself and others, so that you may be saved the time and trouble and disappointment of trying to find your way down blind alleys that have been thoroughly explored, and found to be no-thoroughfares.

Here, then, are some plans that have been tried or proposed.

Let us begin with the simplest: the family plan of the apostles and their followers. Among them everybody threw all that she or he had into a common stock; and each took from it what she or he needed. The obligation to do this was so sacred that when Ananias and Sapphira kept back something for themselves, St Peter struck them dead for "lying to the Holy Ghost".

This plan, which is Communism in its primitive purity, is practised to this day in small religious communities where the people live together and are all known to one another. But it is not so simple for big populations where the people do not live together and do not know each other. Even in the family we practise it only partially; for though the father gives part of his earnings to the mother, and the children do the same when they are earning anything, and the mother buys food and places it before all of them to partake in common, yet they all keep some of their earnings back for their separate use; so that family life is not pure Communism, but partly Communism and partly separate property. Each member of the family does what Ananias and Sapphira did; but they need not tell lies about it (though they sometimes do) because it is understood between them that the children are to keep back something for pocket money, the father for beer and tobacco, and the mother for her clothes if there is any left.

Besides, family Communism does not extend to the people next door. Every house has its own separate meals; and the people in the other houses do not contribute to it, and have no right to share it. There are, however, exceptions to this in modern cities. Though each family buys its own beer separately, they all get their water communistically. They pay what they call a water rate into a common fund to pay for a constant supply to every house; and they all draw as much or as little water as they need.

In the same way they pay for the lighting of the streets, for paving them, for policemen to patrol them, for bridges across the rivers, and for the removal and destruction of dustbin refuse.

Nobody thinks of saying "I never go out after dark; I have never called a policeman in my life; I have no business on the other side of the river and never cross the bridge; and therefore I will not help to pay the cost of these things". Everybody knows that town life could not exist without lighting and paving and bridges and police and sanitation, and that a bedridden invalid who never leaves the house, or a blind man whose darkness no street lamp can dispel, is as dependent on these public services for daily supplies of food and for safety and health as any healthy person. And this is as true of the army and navy as of the police force, of a lighthouse as of a street lamp, of a Town Hall as of the Houses of Parliament: they are all paid for out of the common stock made up by our rates and taxes; and they are for the benefit of everybody indiscriminately. In short, they are Communistic.

When we pay our rates to keep up this Communism we do not, like the apostles, throw all we have into the common stock: we make a contribution according to our means; and our means are judged by the value of the house we live in. But those who pay low contributions have just the same use of the public services as those who pay high ones; and strangers and vagrants who do not pay any contributions at all enjoy them equally. Young and old, prince and pauper, virtuous and vicious, black and white and yellow, thrifty and wasteful, drunk and sober, tinker, tailor, soldier, sailor, rich man, poor man, beggarman and thief, all have the same use and enjoyment of these communistic conveniences and services which cost so much to keep up. And it works perfectly. Nobody dreams of proposing that people should not be allowed to walk down the street without paying and producing a certificate of character from two respectable householders. Yet the street costs more than any of the places you pay to go into, such as theatres, or any of the places where you have to be introduced, like clubs.

6

LIMITS TO COMMUNISM

WOULD you ever have supposed from reading the newspapers that Communism, instead of being a wicked invention of Russian revolutionaries and British and American desperadoes, is a highly respectable way of sharing our wealth, sanctioned and practised by the apostles, and an indispensable part of our own daily life and civilization? The more Communism, the more civilization. We could not get on without it, and are continually extending it. We could give up some of it if we liked. We could put turnpike gates on the roads and make everybody pay for passing along them: indeed we may still see the little toll houses where the old turnpike gates used to be. We could abolish the street lamps, and hire men with torches to light us through the streets at night: are not the extinguishers formerly used by hired linkmen still to be seen on old-fashioned railings? We could even hire policemen and soldiers by the job to protect us, and then disband the police force and the army. But we take good care to do nothing of the sort. In spite of the way people grumble about their rates and taxes they get better value for them than for all the other money they spend. To find a bridge built for us to cross the river without having to think about it or pay anyone for it is such a matter of course to us that some of us come to think, like the children, that bridges are provided by nature, and cost nothing. But if the bridges were allowed to fall down, and we had to find out for ourselves how to cross the river by fording it or swimming it or hiring a boat, we should soon realize what a blessed thing Communism is, and not grudge the few shillings that each of us has to pay the rate collector for the upkeep of the bridge. In fact we might come to think Communism such a splendid thing that everything ought to be communized.

But this would not work. The reason a bridge can be communized is that everyone either uses the bridge or benefits by it. It may be taken as a rule that whatever is used by everybody or benefits everybody can be communized. Roads, bridges, street lighting, and water supply are communized as a matter of course in cities, though in villages and country places people have to buy and carry lanterns on dark nights and get their water from their own wells. There is no reason why bread should not be communized: it would be an inestimable benefit to everybody if there were no such thing in the country as a hungry child, and no housekeeper had to think of the cost of providing bread for the household. Railways could be communized. You can amuse yourself by thinking of lots of other services that would benefit everyone, and therefore could and should be communized.

Only, you will be stopped when you come to services that are not useful to everyone. We communize water as a matter of course; but what about beer? What would a teetotaller say if he were asked to pay rates or taxes to enable his neighbors to have as much beer as they want for the asking? He would have a double objection: first, that he would be paying for something he does not use; and second, that in his opinion beer, far from being a good thing, causes ill-health, crime, drunkenness, and so forth. He would go to prison rather than pay rates for such a purpose.

The most striking example of this difficulty is the Church. The Church of England is a great communistic institution: its property is held in trust for God; its temples and services are open to everybody; and its bishops sit in Parliament as peers of the realm. Yet, because we are not all agreed as to the doctrines of the Church of England, and many of us think that a communion table with candles on it is too like a Roman Catholic altar, we have been forced to make the Church rate a voluntary one: that is, you may pay it or not as you please. And when the Education Act of 1902 gave some public money to Church schools, many people refused to pay their rates, and allowed their furniture to be sold year after year, sooner than allow a penny of theirs to go to the Church. Thus you see that if you propose to communize something that is not used or at least approved of by everybody, you will be asking for trouble. We all use roads and bridges, and agree that they are useful and necessary things; but we differ about religion and temperance and playgoing, and quarrel fiercely over our differences. That is why we communize roads and bridges without any complaint or refusal to pay rates, but have masses of voters against us at once when we attempt to communize any particular form of public worship, or to deal with beer or spirits as we deal with water, and as we should deal with milk if we had sense enough to value the nation's health.

This difficulty can be got round to some extent by give-and-take between the people who want different things. For instance, there are some people who care for flowers and do not care for music, and others who care for games and boating and care neither for flowers nor music. But these differently minded people do not object to paying rates for the upkeep of a public park with flower-beds, cricket pitches, a lake for boating and swimming, and a band. Laura will not object to pay for what Beatrice wants if Beatrice does not object to pay for what Laura wants.

Also there are many things that only a few people understand or use which nevertheless everybody pays for because without them we should have no learning, no books, no pictures, no high civilization. We have public galleries of the best pictures and statues, public libraries of the best books, public observatories in which astronomers watch the stars and mathematicians make abstruse calculations, public laboratories in which scientific men are supposed to add to our knowledge of the universe. These institutions cost a great deal of money to which we all have to contribute. Many of us never enter a gallery or a museum or a library even when we live within easy reach of them; and not one person in ten is interested in astronomy or mathematics or physical science; but we all have a general notion that these things are necessary; and so we do not object to pay for them.

Besides, many of us do not know that we pay for them: we think we get them as kind presents from somebody. In this way a good deal of Communism has been established without our knowing anything about it. This is shewn by our way of speaking about communized things as free. Because we can enter the National Gallery or the British Museum or the cathedrals without paying at the doors, some of us seem to think that they grew by the roadside like wildflowers. But they cost us a great deal of money from week to week. The British Museum has to be swept and dusted and scrubbed more than any private house, because so many more people tramp through it with mud on their boots. The salaries of the learned gentlemen who are in charge of it are a trifle compared with the cost of keeping it tidy. In the same way a public park needs more gardeners than a private one, and has to be weeded and mown and watered and sown and so forth at a great cost in wages and seeds and garden implements. We get nothing for nothing; and if we do not pay every time we go into these places, we pay in rates and taxes. The poorest tramp, though he may escape rent and rates by sleeping out, pays whenever he buys tobacco, because he pays about eight times as much for the tobacco as it costs to grow and put on the market; and the Government gets the difference to spend on public purposes: that is, to maintain Communism. And the poorest woman pays in the same way, without knowing it, whenever she buys an article of food that is taxed. If she knew that she was stinting herself to pay the salary of the Astronomer Royal, or to buy another picture for the National Gallery, she might vote against the Government at the next election for making her do it; but as she does not know, she only grumbles about the high prices of food, and thinks they are all due to bad harvests or hard times or strikes or anything else that must be put up with. She might not grudge what she has to pay for the King and Queen; but if she knew that she was paying the wages of the thousands of charwomen who scrub the stone staircases in the Houses of Parliament and other great public buildings, she would not get much satisfaction out of helping to support them better than she can afford to support herself.

We see then that some of the Communism we practise is imposed on us without our consent: we pay for it without knowing what we are doing. But, in the main, Communism deals with things that are either used by all of us or necessary to all of us, whether we are educated enough to understand the necessity or not.

Now let us get back to the things as to which tastes differ. We have already seen that Church of England services and beer and wine and spirits and intoxicants of all sorts are considered necessary to life by some people, and pernicious and poisonous by others. We are not agreed even about tea and meat. But there are many things that no one sees any harm in; yet everybody does not want them. Ask a woman what little present she would like; and one woman will choose a pet dog, another a gramophone. A studious girl will ask for a microscope when an active girl will ask for a motor bicycle. Indoor people want books and pictures and pianos: outdoor people want guns and fishing-rods and horses and motor cars. To communize these things in the way that we communize roads and bridges would be ridiculously wasteful. If you made enough gramophones and bred enough pet dogs to supply every woman with both, or enough microscopes and motor bicycles to provide one each for every girl, you would have heaps of them left on your hands by the women and girls who did not want them and would not find house room for them. They could not even sell them, because everybody who wanted one would have one already. They would go into the dustbin.

There is only one way out of this difficulty. Instead of giving people things you must give them money and let them buy what they like with it. Instead of giving Mrs Smith, who wants a gramophone, a gramophone and a pet dog as well, costing, say, five pounds apiece, and giving Mrs Jones, who wants a pet dog, a pet dog and a gramophone as well, with the certainty that Mrs Smith will drive her pet dog out of her house and Mrs Jones will throw her gramophone into the dustbin, so that the ten pounds they cost will be wasted, you can simply give Mrs Smith and Mrs Jones five pounds apiece. Then Mrs Smith buys a gramophone; Mrs Jones buys a pet dog; and both live happily ever after. And, of course, you will take care not to manufacture more gramophones or breed more dogs than are needed to satisfy them.

That is the use of money: it enables us to get what we want instead of what other people think we want. When a young lady is married, her friends give her wedding presents instead of giving her money; and the consequence is that she finds herself loaded up with six fish-slices, seven or eight travelling clocks, and not a single pair of silk stockings. If her friends had the sense to give her money (I always do), and she had the sense to take it (she always does), she would have one fish-slice, one travelling clock (if she wanted such a thing), and plenty of stockings. Money is the most convenient thing in the world: we could not possibly do without it. We are told that the love of money is the root of all evil; but money itself is one of the most useful contrivances ever invented: it is not its fault that some people are foolish or miserly enough to be fonder of it than of their own souls.

You now see that the great dividing-up of things that has to take place year by year, quarter by quarter, month by month, week by week, day by day, hour by hour, and even minute by minute, though some of it can be done by the ancient simple family communism of the apostles, or by the modern ratepayers' communism of the roads and bridges and street lamps and so forth, must in the main take the form of a dividing-up of money. And as this throws you back again on the old questions: how much is each of us to have? what is my fair share? what is your fair share? and why? Communism has only partly solved the problem for you; so we must have another shot at it.

7
SEVEN WAYS PROPOSED

A PLAN which has often been proposed, and which seems very plausible to the working classes, is to let every person have that part of the wealth of the country which she has herself produced by her work (the feminine pronoun here includes the masculine). Others say let us all get what we deserve; so that the idle and dissolute and weak shall have nothing and perish, and the good and industrious and energetic shall have all and survive. Some believe in "the good old rule, the simple plan, that they shall take who have the power, and they shall keep who can", though they seldom confess it nowadays. Some say let the common people get enough to keep them alive in that state of life to which it has pleased God to call them; and let the gentry take the rest, though that, too, is not now said so openly as it was in the eighteenth century. Some say let us divide ourselves into classes; and let the division be equal in each class though unequal between the classes; so that laborers shall get thirty shillings a week, skilled workers three or four pounds, bishops two thousand five hundred a year, judges five thousand, archbishops fifteen thousand, and their wives what they can get out of them. Others say simply let us go on as we are.

What the Socialists say is that none of these plans will work well, and that the only satisfactory plan is to give everybody an equal share no matter what sort of person she is, or how old she is, or what sort of work she does, or who or what her father was.

If this, or any of the other plans, happens to startle and scandalize you, please do not blame me or throw my book into the fire. I am only telling you the different plans that have been proposed and to some extent actually tried. You are not bound to approve of any of them; and you are quite free to propose a better plan than any of them if you can think one out. But you are not free to dismiss it from your mind as none of your business. It is a question of your food and lodging, and therefore part of your life. If you do not settle it for yourself, the people who are encouraging you to neglect it will settle it for you; and you may depend on it they will take care of their own shares and not of yours, in which case you may find yourself some day without any share at all.

I have seen that happen very cruelly during my own lifetime. In the country where I was born, which is within an hour's run of England at the nearest point, many ladies of high social standing and gentle breeding, who thought that this question did not concern them because they were well off for the moment, ended very pitiably in the workhouse. They felt that bitterly, and hated those who had brought it about; but they never understood why it happened. Had they understood from the beginning how and why it might happen, they might have averted it, instead of, as they did, doing everything in their power to hasten their own ruin.

You may very easily share their fate unless you take care to understand what is happening. The world is changing very quickly, as it was around them when they thought it as fixed as the mountains. It is changing much more quickly around you; and I promise you that if you will be patient enough to finish this book (think of all the patience it has cost me to finish it instead of writing plays!) you will come out with much more knowledge of how things are changing, and what your risks and prospects are, than you are likely to have learnt from your schoolbooks.

Therefore I am going to take all these plans for you one after another, and examine them chapter by chapter until you know pretty well all that is to be said for and against them.

8

TO EACH WHAT SHE PRODUCES

THE first plan: that of giving to every person exactly what he or she has made by his or her labor, seems fair; but when we try to put it into practice we discover, first, that it is quite impossible to find out how much each person has produced, and, second, that a great deal of the world's work is neither producing material things nor altering the things that Nature produces, but doing services of one sort or another.

When a farmer and his laborers sow and reap a field of wheat nobody on earth can say how much of the wheat each of them has grown. When a machine in a factory turns out pins by the million nobody can say how many pins are due to the labor of the person who minds the machine, or the person who invented it, or the engineers who made it, to say nothing of all the other persons employed about the factory. The clearest case in the world of a person producing something herself by her own painful, prolonged, and risky labor is that of a woman who produces a baby; but then she cannot live on the baby: the baby lives greedily on her.

Robinson Crusoe on his desert island could have claimed that the boats and shelters and fences he made with the materials supplied by Nature belonged to him because they were the fruit of nobody's labor but his own; but when he returned to civilization he could not have laid his hand on a chair or table in his house which was not the work of dozens of men: foresters who had planted the trees, woodmen who had felled them, lumbermen and bargemen and sailors and porters who had moved them, sawyers who had sawn them into planks and scantlings, upholsterers and joiners who had fashioned them into tables and chairs, not to mention the merchants who had conducted all the business involved in these transactions, and the makers of the shops and ships and all the rest of it. Anyone who thinks about it for a few minutes must see that trying to divide-up by giving each worker exactly what she or he has produced is like trying to give every drop of rain in a heavy shower exactly the quantity of water it adds to the supply in your cistern. It just cannot be done.

What can be done is to pay every person according to the time she or he spends at the work. Time is something that can be measured in figures. It is quite easy to pay a worker twice as much for two hours work as for one. There are people who will work for sixpence an hour, people who will work for eighteenpence an hour, people who will work for two guineas an hour, people who will work for a hundred and fifty guineas an hour. These prices depend on how many competitors there are in the trade looking for the work, and whether the people who want it done are rich or poor. You pay a sempstress a shilling to sew for an hour, or a laborer to chop wood, when there are plenty of unemployed sempstresses and laborers starving for a job, each of them trying to induce you to give it to her or him rather than to the next applicant by offering to do it at a price that will barely keep body and soul together. You pay a popular actress two or three hundred pounds a week, or a famous opera singer as much a night, because the public will pay more than that to hear her. You pay a famous surgeon a hundred and fifty guineas to cut out your appendix, or a famous barrister the same to plead for you, because there are so few famous surgeons or barristers, and so many patients and clients offering them large sums to work for them rather than for you. This is called settling the price of a worker's time, or rather letting it settle itself, by supply and demand.

Unfortunately, supply and demand may produce undesirable results. A division in which one woman gets a shilling and another three thousand shillings for an hour of work has no moral sense in it: it is just something that happens, and that ought not to happen. A child with an interesting face and pretty ways, and some talent for acting, may, by working for the films, earn a hundred times as much as its mother can earn by drudging at an ordinary trade. What is worse, a pretty girl can earn by vice far more than her plain sister can earn as an honest wife and mother.

Besides, it is not so easy to measure the time spent on a piece of work as it seems at first. Paying a laborer twice as much for two hours work as for one is as simple as twice one are two; but when you have to divide between an opera singer and her dresser, or an unskilled laborer and a doctor, you find that you cannot tell how much time you have to allow for. The dresser and the laborer are doing what any ablebodied person can do without long study or apprenticeship. The doctor has to spend six years in study and training, on top of a good general education, to qualify himself to do his work. He claims that six years of unpaid work are behind every minute of his attendance at your bedside. A skilled workman may claim in the same way that seven years of apprenticeship are behind every stroke of his hammer. The opera singer has had to spend a long time learning her parts, even when, as sometimes happens, she has never learnt to sing. Everybody acknowledges that this makes a difference; but nobody can measure exactly what the difference is, either in time or money.

The same difficulty arises in attempting to compare the value of the work of a clever woman with that of a stupid one. You may think that the work of the clever woman is worth more; but when you are asked how much more in pounds, shillings, and pence you have to give it up and fall back on supply and demand, confessing that the difference cannot be measured in money.

In these examples I have mixed up making things with doing services; but I must now emphasize this distinction, because thoughtless people are apt to think a brickmaker more of a producer than a clergyman. When a village carpenter makes a gate to keep cattle out of a field of wheat, he has something solid in his hand which he can claim for his own until the farmer pays him for it. But when a village boy makes a noise to keep the birds off he has nothing to shew, though the noise is just as necessary as the gate. The postman does not make anything: he only delivers letters and parcels. The policeman does not make anything; and the soldier not only does not make things: he destroys them. The doctor makes pills sometimes; but that is not his real business, which is to tell you when you ought to take pills, and what pills to take, unless indeed he has the good sense to tell you not to take them at all, and you have the good sense to believe him when he is giving you good advice instead of bad. The lawyer does not make anything substantial, nor the clergyman, nor the member of Parliament, nor the domestic servant (though she sometimes breaks things), nor the Queen or King, nor an actor. When their work is done they have nothing in hand that can be weighed or measured: nothing that the maker can keep from others until she is paid for it. They are all in service: in domestic service like the housemaid, or in commercial service like the shop assistant, or in Government service like the postman, or in State service like the King; and all of us who have fullsize consciences consider ourselves in what some of us call the service of God.

And then, beside the persons who make the substantial things there must be persons to find out how they should be made. Beside the persons who do things there must be persons who know how they should be done, and decide when they should be done, and how much they should be done. In simple village life both the making or the doing and the thinking may be done by the same person when he is a blacksmith, carpenter, or builder; but in big cities and highly civilized countries this is impossible: one set of people has to make and do whilst another set of people thinks and decides what, when, how much, and by whom.

Our villages would be improved by a little of this division of labor; for it is a great disadvantage in country life that a farmer is expected to do so many different things: he has not only to grow crops and raise stock (two separate arts to begin with, and difficult ones too), but to be a man of business, keeping complicated accounts and selling his crops and his cattle, which is a different sort of job, needing a different sort of man. And, as if this were not enough, he has to keep his dwelling house as part of his business; so that he is expected to be a professional man, a man of business, and a sort of country gentleman all at once; and the consequence is that farming is all a muddle: the good farmer is poor because he is a bad man of business; the good man of business is poor because he is a bad farmer; and both of them are often bad husbands because their work is not separate from their home, and they bring all their worries into the house with them instead of locking them up in a city office and thinking no more about them until they go back there next morning. In a city business one set of men does the manual work; another set keeps the accounts; another chooses the markets for buying and selling; and all of them leave their work behind them when they go home.

The same trouble is found in a woman's housekeeping. She is expected to do too many different things. She may be a very good housekeeper and a very bad cook. In a French town this would not matter, because the whole family would take all the meals that require any serious cooking in the nearest restaurant; but in the country the woman must do both the housekeeping and the cooking unless she can afford to keep a cook. She may be both a good housekeeper and a good cook, but be unable to manage children; and here again, if she cannot afford a capable nurse, she has to do the thing she does badly along with the things she does well, and has her life muddled and spoilt accordingly. It is a mercy both to her and the children that the school (which is a bit of Communism) takes them off her hands for most of the day. It is clear that the woman who is helped out by servants or by restaurants and schools has a much better chance in life than the woman who is expected to do three very different things at once.

Perhaps the greatest social service that can be rendered by anybody to the country and to mankind is to bring up a family. But here again, because there is nothing to sell, there is a very general disposition to regard a married woman's work as no work at all, and to take it as a matter of course that she should not be paid for it. A man gets higher wages than a woman because he is supposed to have a family to support; yet if he spends the extra money in drink or betting, the woman has no remedy against him if she is married to him. But if she is his hired housekeeper she can recover her wages at law. And the married man is in the same predicament. When his wife spends the housekeeping money in drink he has no remedy, though he could have a hired housekeeper imprisoned for theft if she did the very same thing.

Now with these examples in mind, how can an Intelligent Woman settle what her time is worth in money compared to her husband's? Imagine her husband looking at it as a matter of business, and saying "I can hire a housekeeper for so much, and a nursemaid for so much, and a cook for so much, and a pretty lady to keep company with for so much; and if I add up all this the total will be what a wife is worth; but it is more than I can afford to pay"! Imagine her hiring a husband by the hour, like a taxi cab!

Yet the income of the country has to be divided-up between husbands and wives just as it has between strangers; and as most of us are husbands and wives, any plan for dividing-up that breaks down when it is applied to husbands and wives breaks in the middle and is no use. The old plan of giving the man everything, and leaving the woman to get what she could out of him, led to such abuses that it had to be altered by the Married Women's Property Acts, under which a rich woman with a poor husband can keep all her property to herself whilst her husband is imprisoned for life for not paying her taxes. But as nine families out of ten have no property, they have to make the best of what the husband can earn at his trade; and here we have the strangest muddles: the wife getting nothing of her own, and the bigger children making a few shillings a week and having the difference between it and a living wage made up by the father's wage; so that the people who are employing the children cheaply are really sweating the father, who is perhaps being sweated badly enough by his own employer. Of this, more later on.

Try to straighten out this muddle on the plan of giving the woman and the children and the man what they produce each by their own work, or what their time is worth in money to the country; and you will find the plan nonsensical and impossible. Nobody but a lunatic would attempt to put it into practice.

9
TO EACH WHAT SHE DESERVES

THE second plan we have to examine is that of giving to each person what she deserves. Many people, especially those who are comfortably off, think that this is what happens at present: that the industrious and sober and thrifty are never in want, and that poverty is due to idleness, improvidence, drink, betting, dishonesty, and bad character generally. They can point to the fact that a laborer whose character is bad finds it more difficult to get employment than one whose character is good; that a farmer or country gentleman who gambles and bets heavily, and mortgages his land to live wastefully and extravagantly, is soon reduced to poverty; and that a man of business who is lazy and does not attend to it becomes bankrupt. But this proves nothing but that you cannot eat your cake and have it too: it does not prove that your share of the cake was a fair one. It shews that certain vices and weaknesses make us poor; but it forgets that certain other vices make us rich. People who are hard, grasping, selfish, cruel, and always ready to take advantage of their neighbors, become very rich if they are clever enough not to overreach themselves. On the other hand, people who are generous, public-spirited, friendly, and not always thinking of the main chance, stay poor when they are born poor unless they have extraordinary talents. Also, as things are today, some are born poor and others are born with silver spoons in their mouths: that is to say, they are divided into rich and poor before they are old enough to have any character at all. The notion that our present system distributes wealth according to merit, even roughly, may be dismissed at once as ridiculous. Everyone can see that it generally has the contrary effect: it makes a few idle people very rich, and a great many hardworking people very poor.

On this, Intelligent Lady, your first thought may be that if wealth is not distributed according to merit, it ought to be; and that we should at once set to work to alter our laws so that in future the good people shall be rich in proportion to their goodness and the bad people poor in proportion to their badness. There are several objections to this; but the very first one settles the question for good and all. It is, that the proposal is impossible. How are you going to measure anyone's merit in money? Choose any pair of human beings you like, male or female, and see whether you can decide how much each of them should have on her or his merits. If you live in the country, take the village blacksmith and the village clergyman, or the village washerwoman and the village schoolmistress, to begin with. At present the clergyman often gets less pay than the blacksmith: it is only in some villages he gets more. But never mind what they get at present: you are trying whether you can set up a new order of things in which each will get what he deserves. You need not fix a sum of money for them: all you have to do is to settle the proportion between them. Is the blacksmith to have as much as the clergyman? or twice as much as the clergyman? or half as much as the clergyman? or how much more or less? It is no use saying that one ought to have more and the other less: you must be prepared to say exactly how much more or less in calculable proportion.

Well, think it out. The clergyman has had a college education;

but that is not any merit on his part: he owes it to his father; so you cannot allow him anything for that. But through it he is able to read the New Testament in Greek; so that he can do something the blacksmith cannot do. On the other hand, the blacksmith can make a horse-shoe, which the parson cannot. How many verses of the Greek Testament are worth one horse-shoe? You have only to ask the silly question to see that nobody can answer it.

Since measuring their merits is no use, why not try to measure their faults? Suppose the blacksmith swears a good deal, and gets drunk occasionally! Everybody in the village knows this; but the parson has to keep his faults to himself. His wife knows them; but she will not tell you what they are if she knows that you intend to cut off some of his pay for them. You know that as he is only a mortal human being he must have some faults; but you cannot find them out. However, suppose he has some faults that you can find out! Suppose he has what you call an unfortunate manner; that he is a hypocrite; that he is a snob; that he cares more for sport and fashionable society than for religion! Does that make him as bad as the blacksmith, or twice as bad, or twice and a quarter as bad, or only half as bad? In other words, if the blacksmith is to have a shilling, is the parson to have a shilling also, or is he to have sixpence, or fivepence and one-third, or two shillings? Clearly these are fools' questions: the moment they bring us down from moral generalities to business particulars it becomes plain to every sensible person that no relation can be established between human qualities, good or bad, and sums of money, large or small. It may seem scandalous that a prize-fighter, for hitting another prize-fighter so hard at Wembley that he fell down and could not rise within ten seconds, received the same sum that was paid to the Archbishop of Canterbury for acting as Primate of the Church of England for nine months; but none of those who cry out against the scandal can express any better in money the difference between the two. Not one of the persons who think that the prize-fighter should get less than the Archbishop can say how much less. What the prize-fighter got for his six or seven minutes boxing would pay a judge's salary for two years; and we are all agreed that nothing could be more ridiculous, and that any system of distributing wealth which leads to such absurdities must be wrong. But to suppose that it could be changed by any possible calculation that an ounce of archbishop or three ounces of judge is worth a pound of prize-fighter would be sillier still. You can find out how many candles are worth a pound of butter in the market on any particular day; but when you try to estimate the worth of human souls the utmost you can say is that they are all of equal value before the throne of God. And that will not help you in the least to settle how much money they should have. You must simply give it up, and admit that distributing money according to merit is beyond mortal measurement and judgment.

10

TO EACH WHAT SHE CAN GRAB

THE third plan: that of letting everyone have what she can lay her hands on, would produce a world in which there would be no peace and no security. If we were all equally strong and cunning we should all have an equal chance; but in a world where there are children and old people and invalids, and where able-bodied adults of the same age and strength vary greatly in greediness and wickedness, it would never do: we should get tired of it in no time. Even pirate crews and bands of robbers prefer a peaceful settled understanding as to the division of their plunder to the Kilkenny cat plan.

Among ourselves, though robbery and violence are forbidden, we still allow business to be conducted on the principle of letting everyone make what he can out of it without considering anyone but himself. A shopkeeper or a coal merchant may not pick your pocket; but he may overcharge you as much as he likes. Everyone is free in business to get as much and give as little for his money as he can induce his customers to put up with. House rent can be raised without any regard to the cost of the houses or the poverty of the tenant. But this freedom produces such bad results that new laws are continually being made to restrain it; and even when it is a necessary part of our freedom to spend our money and use our possessions as seems best to us, we still have to settle how much money and what possessions we should be given to start with. This distribution must be made according to some law or other. Anarchy (absence of law) will not work. We must go on with our search for a righteous and practicable law.

II
OLIGARCHY

THE fourth plan is to take one person in every ten (say), and make her rich without working by making the other nine work hard and long every day, giving them only enough of what they make to keep them alive and enable them to bring up families to continue their slavery when they grow old and die. This is roughly what happens at present, as one-tenth of the English people own nine-tenths of all the property in the country, whilst most of the other nine-tenths have no property, and live from week to week on wages barely sufficient to support them in a very poor way. The advantage claimed for this plan is that it provides us with a gentry: that is, with a class of rich people able to cultivate themselves by an expensive education; so that they become qualified to govern the country and make and maintain its laws; to organize and officer the army for national defence; to patronize and keep alive learning, science, art, literature, philosophy, religion, and all the institutions that distinguish great civilizations from mere groups of villages; to raise magnificent buildings, dress splendidly, impose awe on the unruly, and set an example of good manners and fine living. Most important of all, as men of business think, by giving them much more than they need spend, we enable them to save those great sums of spare money that are called capital, and are spent in making railways, mines, factories full of machinery, and all the other contrivances by which wealth is produced in great quantities.

This plan, which is called Oligarchy, is the old English plan of dividing us into gentry living by property and common people living by work: the plan of the few rich and the many poor. It has worked for a long time, and is still working. And it is evident that if the incomes of the rich were taken from them and divided among the poor as we stand at present, the poor would be only very little less poor; the supply of capital would cease because nobody could afford to save; the country houses would fall into ruins; and learning and science and art and literature and all the rest of what we call culture would perish. That is why so many people support the present system, and stand by the gentry although they themselves are poor. They see that if ten women can produce only £110 a year each by their labor, it may be wiser for nine of them to be content with £50 apiece, and make the other one an educated lady, mistress, and ruler by giving her £500 a year without any obligation to work at all, or any inducement to work except the hope of finding how to make their work more fruitful for her own benefit, rather than to insist on having £110 a year each. Though we make this sort of arrangement at present because we are forced to, and indeed mostly without knowing that we are making it, yet it is conceivable that if we understood what we were doing and were free to carry it out or not as we thought best, we might still do it for the sake of having a gentry to keep up finer things in the world than a miserable crowd all equally poor, and all tied to primitive manual labor.

But the abuses that arise from this plan are so terrible that the world is becoming set against it. If we decide to go on with it, the first step is to settle who is to be the tenth person: the lady. How is that to be decided? True, we could begin by drawing lots; and after that the gentry could intermarry and be succeeded by their firstborns. But the mischief of it is that when we at last got our gentry established we should have no guarantee that they would do any of the things we intended them to do and paid them to do. With the best intentions, the gentry govern the country very badly because they are so far removed from the common people that they do not understand their needs. They use their power to make themselves still richer by forcing the common people to work still harder and accept still less. They spend enormous sums on sport and entertainment, gluttony and ostentation, and very little on science and art and learning. They produce poverty on a vast scale by withdrawing labor from production to waste it in superfluous menial service. They either shirk military duties or turn the army into a fashionable retinue for themselves and an instrument of oppression at home and conquest abroad. They corrupt the teaching in the universities and schools to glorify themselves and hide their misdeeds. They do the same with the Church. They try to keep the common people poor and ignorant and servile so as to make themselves more indispensable. At last their duties have to be taken out of their hands and discharged by Parliament, by the Civil Service, by the War Office and the Admiralty, by city corporations, by Poor Law Guardians, by County and Parish and District Councils, by salaried servants and Boards of paid directors, by societies and institutions of all kinds depending on taxation or on public subscription.

When this occurs, as it actually has occurred, all the cultural and political reasons for the maintenance of a gentry vanish. It always does occur when city life grows up and takes the place of country life. When a peeress resides on her estates in a part of the country where life is still very simple, and the nearest thing to a town is a village ten miles from the railway station, the people look to her ladyship for everything that is not produced by their daily toil. She represents all the splendor and greatness and romance of civilization, and does a good deal for them which they would not know how to do for themselves. In this way a Highland clan, before Scotland became civilized, always had a chief. The clansmen willingly gave him the lion's share of such land and goods as they could come by, or of the plunder they took in their raids. They did this because they could not fight successfully without a leader, and could not live together without a lawgiver. Their chief was to them what Moses was to the Israelites in the desert. The Highland chief was practically a king in his clan, just as the peeress is a queen on her estates. Loyalty to him was instinctive.

But when a Highland chief walked into a city he had less power than the first police constable he met: in fact it sometimes happened that the police constable took him in charge, and the city authorities hanged him. When the peeress leaves her estate and goes up to London for the season, she becomes a nobody except to her personal acquaintances. Everything that she does for her people in the country is done in London by paid public servants of all sorts; and when she leaves the country and settles in America or on the Continent to evade British income tax she is not missed in London: everything goes on just as before. But her tenants, who have to earn the money she spends abroad, get nothing by her, and revile her as a fugitive and an Absentee.

Small wonder then that Oligarchy is no longer consented to willingly. A great deal of the money the oligarchs get is now taken back from them by taxation and death duties; so that the old families are being reduced very rapidly to the level of ordinary citizens; and when their estates are gone, as they will be after a few generations more of our present heavy death duties, their titles will only make their poverty ridiculous. Already many of their most famous country houses are occupied either by rich business families of quite ordinary quality, or by Co-operative Societies as Convalescent Homes or places for conference and recreation, or as hotels or schools or lunatic asylums.

You must therefore face the fact that in a civilization like ours, where most of the population lives in cities; where railways, motor cars, posts, telegraphs, telephones, gramophones and radio have brought city ways and city culture into the country; and where even the smallest village has its parish meeting and its communal policeman, the old reasons for making a few people very rich whilst all the others work hard for a bare subsistence have passed away. The plan no longer works, even in the Highlands.

Still, there is one reason left for maintaining a class of excessively rich people at the expense of the rest; and business men consider it the strongest reason of all. That reason is that it provides capital by giving some people more money than they can easily spend; so that they can save money (capital is saved money) without any privation. The argument is that if income were more equally distributed, we should all have so little that we should spend all our incomes, and nothing would be saved to make machinery and build factories and construct railways and dig mines and so forth. Now it is certainly necessary to high civilization that these savings should be made; but it would be hard to imagine a more wasteful way of bringing it about.

To begin with, it is very important that there should be no saving until there has been sufficient spending: spending comes first. A nation which makes steam engines before its little children have enough milk to make their legs strong enough to carry them is making a fool's choice. Yet this is just what we do by this plan of making a few rich and the masses poor. Again, even if we put the steam engine before the milk, our plan gives us no security that we shall get the steam engine, or, if we get it, that it will be set up in our country. Just as a great deal of the money that was given to the country gentlemen of England on the chance of their encouraging art and science was spent by them on cockfighting and horse-racing; so a shocking proportion of the money we give our oligarchs on the chance of their investing it as capital is spent by them in self-indulgence. Of the very rich it may be said that they do not begin to save until they can spend no more, and that they are continually inventing new and expensive extravagances that would have been impossible a hundred years ago. When their income outruns their extravagance so far that they must use it as capital or throw it away, there is nothing to prevent them investing it in South America, in South Africa, in Russia, or in China, though we cannot get our own slums cleaned up for want of capital kept in and applied to our own country. Hundreds of millions of pounds are sent abroad every year in this way; and we complain of the competition of foreigners whilst we allow our capitalists to provide them at our expense with the very machinery with which they are taking our industries from us.

Of course the capitalists plead that we are none the poorer, because the interest on their capital comes back into this country from the countries in which they have invested it; and as they invest it abroad only because they get more interest abroad than at home, they assure us that we are actually the richer for their export of capital, because it enables them to spend more at home and thus give British workers more employment. But we have no guarantee that they will spend it at home: they are as likely to spend it in Monte Carlo, Madeira, Egypt, or where not? And when they do spend it at home and give us employment, we have to ask what sort of employment? When our farms and mills and cloth factories are all ruined by our importing our food and cloth from abroad instead of making them ourselves, it is not enough for our capitalists to shew us that instead of the farms we have the best golf courses in the world; instead of mills and factories splendid hotels; instead of engineers and shipwrights and bakers and carpenters and weavers, waiters and chambermaids, valets and ladies' maids, gamekeepers and butlers and so forth, all better paid and more elegantly dressed than the productive workers they have replaced. We have to consider what sort of position we shall be in when our workers are as incapable of supporting themselves and us as the idle rich themselves. Suppose the foreign countries stop our supplies either by a revolution followed by flat repudiation of their capitalistic debts, as in Russia, or by taxing and supertaxing incomes derived from investments, what will become of us then? What is becoming of us now as taxation of income spreads more and more in foreign countries? The English servant may still be able to boast that England can put a more brilliant polish on a multi-millionaire's boots than any foreigner can; but what use will that be to us when the multi-millionaire is an expropriated or taxed-out pauper with no boots to have polished?

We shall have to go into this question of capital more particularly later on; but for the purposes of this chapter it is enough to shew that the plan of depending on oligarchy for our national capital is not only wasteful on the face of it, but dangerous with a danger that increases with every political development in the world. The only plea left for it is that there is no other way of doing it. But that will not hold water for a moment. The Government can, and to a considerable extent actually does, check personal expenditure and enforce the use of part of our incomes as capital, far less capriciously and more efficiently than our oligarchy does. It can nationalize banking, as we shall see presently. This leaves oligarchy without its sole economic excuse.

12

DISTRIBUTION BY CLASS

NOW for the fifth plan, which is, that though everybody should work, society should be divided into as many classes as there are different sorts of work, and that the different classes should receive different payment for their work: for instance, the dustmen and scavengers and scullery-maids and charwomen and ragpickers should receive less than the doctors and clergymen and teachers and opera singers and professional ladies generally, and that these should receive less than the judges and prime ministers and kings and queens.

You will tell me that this is just what we have at present. Certainly it happens so in many cases; but there is no law that people employed in different sorts of work should be paid more or less than oneanother. We are accustomed to think that schoolmistresses and clergymen and doctors, being educated ladies and gentlemen, must be paid more than illiterate persons who work with their hands for weekly wages; but at the present time an engine driver, making no pretension to be a gentleman, or to have had a college education, is paid more than many clergymen and some doctors; and a schoolmistress or governess is very lucky indeed when she is as well off as a firstrate cook. Some of our most famous physicians have had to struggle pitiably against insufficient means until they were forty or fifty; and many a parson has brought up a family on a stipend of seventy pounds a year. You must therefore be on your guard against the common mistake of supposing that we need nowadays pay more for gentility and education than for bodily strength and natural cunning, or that we always do pay more. Very learned men often make little money or none; and gentility without property may prove rather a disadvantage than otherwise to a man who wants to earn a living. Most of the great fortunes are made in trade or finance, often by men without any advantages of birth or education. Some of the great poverties have been those of saints, or of geniuses whose greatness was not recognized until they were dead.

You must also get rid of the notion (if you have it: if not, forgive me for suspecting you of it) that it costs some workers more than others to live. The same allowance of food that will keep a laborer in health will keep a king. Many laborers eat and drink much more than the King does; and all of them wear out their clothes much faster. Our King is not rich as riches go nowadays. Mr Rockefeller probably regards His Majesty as a poor man, because Mr Rockefeller not only has much more money, but is under no obligation to spend it in keeping up a great establishment: that is, spending it on other people. But if you could find out how much the King and Mr Rockefeller spend on their own personal needs and satisfaction, you would find it came to no more than is now spent by any other two persons in reasonably comfortable circumstances. If you doubled the King's allowance he would not eat twice as much, drink twice as much, sleep twice as soundly, build a new house twice as big as Buckingham Palace, or marry another queen and set up two families instead of one. The late Mr Carnegie, when his thousands grew to hundreds of thousands and his hundreds of thousands to millions, gave his money away in heaps because he already had everything he cared for that money could buy for himself or his household.

Then, it may be asked, why do we give some men more than they need and some less? The answer is that for the most part we do not give it to them: they get it because we have not arranged what anyone shall get, but have left it to chance and grab. But in the case of the King and other public dignitaries we have arranged that they shall have handsome incomes because we intend that they shall be specially respected and deferred to. Yet experience shews that authority is not proportionate to income. No person in Europe is approached with such awe as the Pope; but nobody thinks of the Pope as a rich man: sometimes his parents and brothers and sisters are very humble people, and he himself is poorer than his tailor or grocer. The captain of a liner sits at table every day with scores of people who could afford to throw his pay into the sea and not miss it; yet his authority is so absolute that the most insolent passenger dares not treat him disrespectfully. The village rector may not have a fifth of the income of his farmer churchwarden. The colonel of a regiment may be the poorest man at the mess table: everyone of his subalterns may have far more than double his income; but he is their superior in authority for all that. Money is not the secret of command.

Those who exercise personal authority among us are by no means our richest people. Millionaires in expensive cars obey policemen. In our social scale noblemen take precedence of country gentlemen, country gentlemen take precedence of professional men, professional men of traders, wholesale traders of retail traders, retail traders of skilled workmen, and skilled workmen of laborers; but if social precedence were according to income all this would be completely upset; for the tradesmen would take precedence of everybody; and the Pope and the King would have to touch their hats to distillers and pork packers.

When we speak of the power of the rich, we are speaking of a very real thing, because a rich man can discharge anyone in his employment who displeases him, and can take away his custom from any tradesman who is disrespectful to him. But the advantage a man gets by his power to ruin another is a quite different thing from the authority that is necessary to maintain law and order in society. You may obey the highwayman who puts a pistol to your head and demands your money or your life. Similarly you may obey the landlord who orders you to pay more rent or take yourself and your brats into the street. But that is not obedience to authority: it is submission to a threat. Real authority has nothing to do with money; and it is in fact exercised by persons who, from the King to the village constable, are poorer than many of the people who obey their orders.

13
LAISSER-FAIRE

AND now, what about leaving things just as they are? That is just what most people vote for doing. Even when they dont like what they are accustomed to, they dread change, lest it should make matters worse. They are what they call Conservative, though it is only fair to add that no Conservative statesman in his senses ever pretends (except perhaps occasionally at election times, when nobody ever tells the truth) that you can conserve things by simply letting them alone.

It seems the easiest plan and the safest; but as a matter of hard fact it is not only difficult but impossible. When Joshua told the sun to stand still on Gibeon, and the moon in the valley of Ajalon, for a trifle of twentyfour hours, he was modest in comparison with those who imagine that the world will stay put if they take care not to wake it up. And he knew he was asking for a miracle.

It is not that things as they are are so bad that nobody who knows how bad they are will agree to leave them as they are; for the reply to that may be that if they dont like them they must lump them, because there seems to be no way of changing them. The real difficulty is that things will not stay as they are, no matter how careful you are not to meddle with them. You might as well give up dusting your rooms and expect to find them this time next year just as they are now. You might as well leave the cat asleep on the hearthrug and assume that you would find her there, and not in the dairy, when you came back from church.

The truth is that things change much faster and more dangerously when they are let alone than when they are carefully looked after. Within the last hundred and fifty years the most astounding changes have taken place in this very business that we are dealing with (the production and distribution of the national income) just because what was everybody's business was nobody's business, and it was let run wild. The introduction of machinery driven by steam, and later on of electric power distributed from house to house like water or gas, and the invention of engines that not only draw trains along the ground and ships over and under the sea, but carry us and our goods flying through the air, has increased our power to produce wealth and get through our work easily and quickly to such an extent that there is no longer any need for any of us to be poor. A labor-saving house with gas stoves, electric light, a telephone, a vacuum cleaner, and a wireless set, gives only a faint notion of a modern factory full of automatic machines. If we each took our turn and did our bit in peace as we had to do during the war, all the necessary feeding and clothing and housing and lighting could be done handsomely by less than half our present day's work, leaving the other half free for art and science and learning and playing and roaming and experimenting and recreation of all sorts.

This is a new state of things: a change that has come upon us when we thought we were leaving things just as they were. And the consequence of our not attending to it and guiding and arranging it for the good of the country is that it has actually left the poor much worse off than they used to be when there was no machinery at all, and people had to be more careful of pence than they now are of shillings; whilst the rich have become rich out of all reason, and the people who should be employed in making bread for the hungry and clothes for the naked, or building houses for the homeless, are wasting their labor in providing service and luxuries for idle rich people who are not in the old sense of the words either gentle or noble, and whose idleness and frivolity and extravagance set a most corrupting moral example.

Also it has produced two and a half revolutions in political power, by which the employers have overthrown the landed gentry, the financiers have overthrown the employers, and the Trade Unions have half overthrown the financiers. I shall explain this fully later on; meanwhile, you have seen enough of its effects in the rise of the Labor Party to take my word for it that politics will not stand still any more than industry merely because millions of timid old-fashioned people vote at every election for what they call Conservatism: that is, for shutting our eyes and opening our mouths.

If King Alfred had been told that the time would come in England when one idle family would have five big houses and a steam yacht to live in whilst hard-working people were living six in a room, and half starving at that, he would have said that God would never allow such things to happen except in a very wicked nation. Well, we have left God out of the question and allowed it to happen, not through wickedness, but through letting things alone and fancying that they would let themselves alone.

Have you noticed, by the way, that we no longer speak of letting things alone in the old-fashioned way? We speak of letting them slide; and this is a great advance in good sense; for it shews that we at last see that they slide instead of staying put; and it implies that letting them slide is a feckless sort of conduct. So you must rule out once for all the notion of leaving things as they are in the expectation that they will stay where they are. They wont. All we can do in that line is to sit idly and wonder what will happen next. And this is not like sitting on the bank of the stream waiting for the water to go by. It is like sitting idly in a carriage when the horse is running away. You can excuse it by saying "What else can I do?"; but your impotence will not avert a smash. People in that predicament must all think hard of some way of getting control of the horse, and meanwhile do all they can to keep the carriage right side up and out of the ditch.

The policy of letting things alone, in the practical sense that the Government should never interfere with business or go into business itself, is called Laisser-faire by economists and politicians. It has broken down so completely in practice that it is now discredited; but it was all the fashion in politics a hundred years ago, and is still influentially advocated by men of business and their backers who naturally would like to be allowed to make money as they please without regard to the interests of the public.

14
HOW MUCH IS ENOUGH?

WE seem now to have disposed of all the plans except the Socialist one. Before grappling with that, may I call your attention to something that happened in our examination of most of the others. We were trying to find out a sound plan of distributing money; and every time we proposed to distribute it according to personal merit or achievement or dignity or individual quality of any sort the plan reduced itself to absurdity. When we tried to establish a relation between money and work we were beaten: it could not be done. When we tried to establish a relation between money and character we were beaten. When we tried to establish a relation between money and the dignity that gives authority we were beaten. And when we gave it up as a bad job and thought of leaving things as they are we found that they would not stay as they are.

Let us then consider for a moment what any plan must do to be acceptable. And first, as everybody except the Franciscan Friars and the Poor Clares will say that no plan will be acceptable unless it abolishes poverty (and even Franciscan poverty must be voluntary and not compelled) let us study poverty for a moment.

It is generally agreed that poverty is a very uncomfortable misfortune for the individual who happens to be poor. But poor people, when they are not suffering from acute hunger and severe cold, are not more unhappy than rich people: they are often much happier. You can easily find people who are ten times as rich at sixty as they were at twenty; but not one of them will tell you that they are ten times as happy. All the thoughtful ones will assure you that happiness and unhappiness are constitutional, and have nothing to do with money. Money can cure hunger: it cannot cure unhappiness. Food can satisfy the appetite, but not the soul. A famous German Socialist, Ferdinand Lassalle, said that what beat him in his efforts to stir up the poor to revolt against poverty was their wantlessness. They were not, of course, content: nobody is; but they were not discontented enough to take any serious trouble to change their condition. It may seem a fine thing to a poor woman to have a large house, plenty of servants, dozens of dresses, a lovely complexion and beautifully dressed hair. But the rich woman who has these things often spends a good deal of her time travelling in rough places to get away from them. To have to spend two or three hours a day washing and dressing and brushing and combing and changing and being messed about generally by a lady's maid is not on the face of it a happier lot than to have only five minutes to spend on such fatigues, as the soldiers call them. Servants are so troublesome that many ladies can hardly talk about anything else when they get together. A drunken man is happier than a sober one: that is why unhappy people take to drink. There are drugs that will make you ecstatically happy whilst ruining your body and soul. It is our quality that matters: take care of that, and our happiness will take care of itself. People of the right sort are never easy until they get things straight; but they are too healthy and too much taken up with their occupations to bother about happiness. Modern poverty is not the poverty that was blest in the Sermon on the Mount: the objection to it is not that it makes people unhappy, but that it degrades them; and the fact that they can be quite as happy in their degradation as their betters are in their exaltation makes it worse. When Shakespear's king said

Then happy low, lie down:
Uneasy lies the head that wears a crown,

he forgot that happiness is no excuse for lowness. The divine spark in us flashes up against being bribed to submit to degradation by mere happiness, which a pig or a drunkard can achieve.

Such poverty as we have today in all our great cities degrades the poor, and infects with its degradation the whole neighborhood in which they live. And whatever can degrade a neighborhood can degrade a country and a continent and finally the whole civilized world, which is only a large neighborhood. Its bad effects cannot be escaped by the rich. When poverty produces outbreaks of virulent infectious disease, as it always does sooner or later, the rich catch the disease and see their children die of it. When it produces crime and violence the rich go in fear of both, and are put to a good deal of expense to protect their persons and property. When it produces bad manners and bad language the children of the rich pick them up no matter how carefully they are secluded; and such seclusion as they get does them more harm than good. If poor and pretty young women find, as they do, that they can make more money by vice than by honest work, they will poison the blood of rich young men who, when they marry, will infect their wives and children, and cause them all sorts of bodily troubles, sometimes ending in disfigurement and blindness and death, and always doing them more or less mischief. The old notion that people can "keep themselves to themselves" and not be touched by what is happening to their neighbors, or even to the people who live a hundred miles off, is a most dangerous mistake. The saying that we are members one of another is not a mere pious formula to be repeated in church without any meaning: it is a literal truth; for though the rich end of the town can avoid living with the poor end, it cannot avoid dying with it when the plague comes. People will be able to keep themselves to themselves as much as they please when they have made an end of poverty; but until then they will not be able to shut out the sights and sounds and smells of poverty from their daily walks, nor to feel sure from day to day that its most violent and fatal evils will not reach them through their strongest police guards.

Besides, as long as poverty remains possible we shall never be sure that it will not overtake ourselves. If we dig a pit for others we may fall into it: if we leave a precipice unfenced our children may fall over it when they are playing. We see the most innocent and respectable families falling into the unfenced pit of poverty every day; and how do we know that it will not be our turn next?

It is perhaps the greatest folly of which a nation can be guilty to attempt to use poverty as a sort of punishment for offences that it does not send people to prison for. It is easy to say of a lazy man "Oh, let him be poor: it serves him right for being lazy: it will teach him a lesson". In saying so we are ourselves too lazy to think a little before we lay down the law. We cannot afford to have poor people anyhow, whether they be lazy or busy, drunken or sober, virtuous or vicious, thrifty or careless, wise or foolish. If they deserve to suffer let them be made to suffer in some other way; for mere poverty will not hurt them half as much as it will hurt their innocent neighbors. It is a public nuisance as well as a private misfortune. Its toleration is a national crime.

We must therefore take it as an indispensable condition of a sound distribution of wealth that everyone must have a share sufficient to keep her or him from poverty. This is not altogether new. Ever since the days of Queen Elizabeth it has been the law of England that nobody must be abandoned to destitution. If anyone, however undeserving, applies for relief to the Guardians of the Poor as a destitute person, the Guardians must feed and clothe and house that person. They may do it reluctantly and unkindly; they may attach to the relief the most unpleasant and degrading conditions they can think of; they may set the pauper to hateful useless work if he is able-bodied, and have him sent to prison if he refuses to do it; the shelter they give him may be that of a horrible general workhouse in which the old and the young, the sound and the diseased, the innocent girl and lad and the hardened prostitute and tramp are herded together promiscuously to contaminate one another; they can attach a social stigma to the relief by taking away the pauper's vote (if he has one), and making him incapable of filling certain public offices or being elected to certain public authorities; they may, in short, drive the deserving and respectable poor to endure any extremity rather than ask for relief; but they must relieve the destitute willy nilly if they do ask for it. To that extent the law of England is at its root a Communistic law. All the harshnesses and wickednesses with which it is carried out are gross mistakes, because instead of saving the country from the degradation of poverty they actually make poverty more degrading than it need be; but still, the principle is there. Queen Elizabeth said that nobody must die of starvation and exposure. We, after the terrible experience we have had of the effects of poverty on the whole nation, rich or poor, must go further and say that nobody must be poor. As we divide-up our wealth day by day the first charge on it must be enough for everybody to be fairly respectable and well-to-do. If they do anything or leave anything undone that gives ground for saying that they do not deserve it, let them be restrained from doing it or compelled to do it in whatever way we restrain or compel evildoers of any other sort; but do not let them, as poor people, make everyone else suffer for their shortcomings.

Granted that people should not on any account be allowed to be poor, we have still to consider whether they should be allowed to be rich. When poverty is gone, shall we tolerate luxury and extravagance? This is a poser, because it is much easier to say what poverty is than what luxury is. When a woman is hungry, or ragged, or has not at least one properly furnished room all to herself to sleep in, then she is clearly suffering from poverty. When the infant mortality in one district is much greater than in another; when the average age of death for fully grown persons in it falls far short of the scriptural threescore-and-ten; when the average weight of the children who survive is below that reached by well-fed and well-cared-for children, then you can say confidently that the people in that district are suffering from poverty. But suffering from riches is not so easily measured. That rich people do suffer a great deal is plain enough to anyone who has an intimate knowledge of their lives. They are so unhealthy that they are always running after cures and surgical operations of one sort or another. When they are not really ill they imagine they are. They are worried by their property, by their servants, by their poor relations, by their investments, by the need for keeping up their social position, and, when they have several children, by the impossibility of leaving these children enough to enable them to live as they have been brought up to live; for we must not forget that if a married couple with fifty thousand a year have five children, they can leave only ten thousand a year to each after bringing them up to live at the rate of fifty thousand, and launching them into the sort of society that lives at that rate, the result being that unless these children can make rich marriages they live beyond their incomes (not knowing how to live more cheaply) and are presently head over ears in debt. They hand on their costly habits and rich friends and debts to their children with very little else; so that the trouble becomes worse and worse from generation to generation; and this is how we meet everywhere with ladies and gentlemen who have no means of keeping up their position, and are therefore much more miserable than the common poor.

Perhaps you know some well-off families who do not seem to

suffer from their riches. They do not overeat themselves; they find occupations to keep themselves in health; they do not worry about their position; they put their money into safe investments and are content with a low rate of interest; and they bring up their children to live simply and do useful work. But this means that they do not live like rich people at all, and might therefore just as well have ordinary incomes. The general run of rich people do not know what to do with themselves; and the end of it is that they have to join a round of social duties and pleasures mostly manufactured by West End shopkeepers, and so tedious that at the end of a fashionable season the rich are more worn out than their servants and tradesmen. They may have no taste for sport; but they are forced by their social position to go to the great race meetings and ride to hounds. They may have no taste for music; but they have to go to the Opera and to the fashionable concerts. They may not dress as they please nor do what they please. Because they are rich they must do what all the other rich people are doing, there being nothing else for them to do except work, which would immediately reduce them to the condition of ordinary people. So, as they cannot do what they like, they must contrive to like what they do, and imagine that they are having a splendid time of it when they are in fact being bored by their amusements, humbugged by their doctors, pillaged by their tradesmen, and forced to console themselves unamiably for being snubbed by richer people by snubbing poorer people.

To escape this boredom, the able and energetic spirits go into Parliament or into the diplomatic service or into the army, or manage and develop their estates and investments instead of leaving them to solicitors and stockbrokers and agents, or explore unknown countries with great hardship and risk to themselves, with the result that their lives are not different from the lives of the people who have to do these things for a living. Thus riches are thrown away on them; and if it were not for the continual dread of falling into poverty which haunts us all at present they would refuse to be bothered with much property. The only people who get any special satisfaction out of being richer than others are those who enjoy being idle, and like to fancy that they are better than their neighbors and be treated as if they were. But no country can afford to pamper snobbery. Laziness and vanity are not virtues to be encouraged: they are vices to be suppressed. Besides, the desire to be idle and lazy and able to order poor people about could not be satisfied, even if it were right to satisfy it, if there were no poor people to order about. What we should have would be, not poor people and rich people, but simply people with enough and people with more than enough. And that brings up at last the knotty question, what is enough?

In Shakespear's famous play, King Lear and his daughters have an argument about this. His idea of enough is having a hundred knights to wait on him. His eldest daughter thinks that fifty would be enough. Her sister does not see what he wants with any knights at all when her servants can do all he needs for him. Lear retorts that if she cuts life down to what cannot be done without, she had better throw away her fine clothes, as she would be warmer in a blanket. And to this she has no answer. Nobody can say what is enough. What is enough for a gipsy is not enough for a lady; and what is enough for one lady leaves another very discontented. When once you get above the poverty line there is no reason why you should stop there. With modern machinery we can produce much more than enough to feed, clothe, and house us decently. There is no end to the number of new things we can get into the habit of using, or to the improvements we can make in the things we already use. Our grandmothers managed to get on without gas cookers, electric light, motor cars, and telephones; but today these things are no longer curiosities and luxuries: they are matter-of-course necessities; and nobody who cannot afford them is considered well-off.

In the same way the standard of education and culture has risen. Nowadays a parlormaid as ignorant as Queen Victoria was when she came to the throne would be classed as mentally defective. As Queen Victoria managed to get on very well in spite of her ignorance it cannot be said that the knowledge in which the parlormaid has the advantage of her is a necessity of civilized life any more than a telephone is; but civilized life and highly civilized life are different: what is enough for one is not enough for the other. Take a half-civilized girl into a house; and though she may be stronger and more willing and goodnatured than many highly civilized girls are, she will smash everything that will not stand the roughest handling. She will be unable to take or send written messages; and as to understanding or using such civilized contrivances as watches, baths, sewing machines, and electric heaters and sweepers, you will be fortunate if you can induce her to turn off a tap instead of leaving the water running. And your civilized maid who can be trusted with all these things would be like a bull in a china shop if she were let loose in the laboratories where highly trained scientific workers use machines and instruments of such delicacy that their movements are as invisible as that of the hour hands of our clocks, handling and controlling poisons and explosives of the most dangerous kind; or in the operating rooms where surgeons have to do things in which a slip of the hand might prove fatal. If every housemaid had the delicacy of touch, the knowledge, and the patience that are needed in the laboratories and operating theatres (where they are unfortunately not always forthcoming), the most wonderful changes could be made in our housekeeping: we could not only have the present work done much more quickly, perfectly, and cleanly, but we could do a great deal that is now quite impossible.

Now it costs more to educate and train a laboratory worker than a housemaid, and more to train a housemaid than to catch a savage. What is enough in one case is not enough in another. Therefore to ask baldly how much is enough to live on is to ask an unanswerable question. It all depends on what sort of life you propose to live. What is enough for the life of a tramp is not enough for a highly civilized life, with its personal refinements and its atmosphere of music, art, literature, religion, science, and philosophy. Of these things we can never have enough: there is always something new to be discovered and something old to be bettered. In short, there is no such thing as enough civilization, though there may be enough of any particular thing like bread or boots at any particular moment. If being poor means wanting something more and something better than we have—and it is hard to say what else feeling poor means—then we shall always feel poor no matter how much money we have, because, though we may have enough of this thing or of that thing, we shall never have enough of everything. Consequently if it be proposed to give some people enough, and others more than enough, the scheme will break down; for all the money will be used up before anybody will be content. Nobody will stop asking for more for the sake of setting up and maintaining a fancy class of pampered persons who, after all, will be even more discontented than their poorer neighbors.

The only way out of this difficulty is to give everybody the same, which is the Socialist solution of the distribution problem. But you may tell me that you are prepared to swallow this difficulty rather than swallow Socialism. Most of us begin like that. What converts us is the discovery of the terrible array of evils around us and dangers in front of us which we dare not ignore. You may be unable to see any beauty in equality of income. But the least idealistic woman can see the disasters of inequality when the evils with which she is herself in daily conflict are traced to it; and I am now going to shew you the connexion.

15
WHAT WE SHOULD BUY FIRST

TO test the effects of our unequal division of the nation's income on our national institutions and on the life and prosperity of the whole people we must view the industry of the country, and see how it is affected by inequality of income. We must view one by one the institution of marriage, the working of the courts of justice, the honesty of our Houses of Parliament, the spiritual independence of the Church, the usefulness of our schools, and the quality of our newspapers, and consider how each of them is dependent on the way in which money is distributed.

Beginning with industry, we are at once plunged into what we call political economy, to distinguish it from the domestic economy with which we are all only too familiar. Men find political economy a dry and difficult subject: they shirk it as they shirk housekeeping; yet it means nothing more abstruse than the art of managing a country as a housekeeper manages a house. If the men shirk it the women must tackle it. The nation has a certain income to manage on just as a housekeeper has; and the problem is how to spend that income to the greatest general advantage.

Now the first thing a housekeeper has to settle is what things are wanted most, and what things can be done without at a pinch. This means that the housekeeper must settle the order in which things are desirable. For example, if, when there is not enough food in the house, she goes out and spends all her money on a bottle of scent and an imitation pearl necklace, she will be called a vain and silly woman and a bad mother. But a stateswoman would call her simply a bad economist: one who does not know what should come first when money has to be spent. No woman is fit to have charge of a household who has not sense and self-control enough to see that food and clothing and housing and firing come first, and that bottles of scent and pearl necklaces, imitation or real, come a long way afterwards. Even in the jeweller's shop a wrist watch comes before a necklace as being more useful. I am not saying that pretty things are not useful: they are very useful and quite right in their proper order; but they do not come first. A Bible may be a very proper present to give to a child; but to give a starving child a Bible instead of a piece of bread and a cup of milk would be the act of a lunatic. A woman's mind is more wonderful than her flesh; but if her flesh is not fed her mind will perish, whereas if you feed her flesh her mind will take care of itself and of her flesh as well. Food comes first.

Think of the whole country as a big household, and the whole nation as a big family, which is what they really are. What do we see? Half-fed, badly clothed, abominably housed children all over the place; and the money that should go to feed and clothe and house them properly being spent in millions on bottles of scent, pearl necklaces, pet dogs, racing motor cars, January strawberries that taste like corks, and all sorts of extravagances. One sister of the national family has a single pair of leaking boots that keep her sniffing all through the winter, and no handkerchief to wipe her nose with. Another has forty pairs of high-heeled shoes and dozens of handkerchiefs. A little brother is trying to grow up on a penn'orth of food a day, and is breaking his mother's heart and wearing out her patience by asking continually for more, whilst a big brother, spending five or six pounds on his dinner at a fashionable hotel, followed by supper at a night club, is in the doctor's hands because he is eating and drinking too much.

Now this is shockingly bad political economy. When thoughtless people are asked to explain it they say "Oh, the woman with the forty shoes and the man drinking at the night club got their money from their father who made a fortune by speculating in rubber; and the girl with the broken boots, and the troublesome boy whose mother has just clouted his head, are only riffraff from the slums". That is true; but it does not alter the fact that the nation that spends money on champagne before it has provided enough milk for its babies, or gives dainty meals to Sealyham terriers and Alsatian wolf-hounds and Pekingese dogs whilst the infant mortality rate shews that its children are dying by thousands from insufficient nourishment, is a badly managed, silly, vain, stupid, ignorant nation, and will go to the bad in the long run no matter how hard it tries to conceal its real condition from itself by counting the pearl necklaces and Pekingese dogs as wealth, and thinking itself three times as rich as before when all the pet dogs have litters of six puppies a couple. The only way in which a nation can make itself wealthy and prosperous is by good housekeeping: that is, by providing for its wants in the order of their importance, and allowing no money to be wasted on whims and luxuries until necessities have been thoroughly served.

But it is no use blaming the owners of the dogs. All these mischievous absurdities exist, not because any sane person ever wanted them to exist, but because they must occur whenever some families are very much richer than others. The rich man, who, as husband and father, drags the woman with him, begins as every one else begins, by buying food, clothing, and a roof to shelter them. The poor man does the same. But when the poor man has spent all he can afford on these necessaries, he is still short of them: his food is insufficient; his clothes are old and dirty; his lodging is a single room or part of one, and unwholesome even at that. But when the rich man has fed himself, and dressed himself, and housed himself as sumptuously as possible, he has still plenty of money left to indulge his tastes and fancies and make a show in the world. Whilst the poor man says "I want more bread, more clothes, and a better house for my family; but I cannot pay for them", the rich man says "I want a fleet of motor cars, a yacht, diamonds and pearls for my wife and daughters, and a shooting-box in Scotland. Money is no object: I can pay and overpay for them ten times over". Naturally men of business set to work at once to have the cars and the yacht made, the diamonds dug out in Africa, the pearls fished for, and the shooting lodge built, paying no attention to the poor man with his crying needs and empty pockets.

To put the same thing in another way, the poor man needs to have labor employed in making the things he is short of: that is, in baking, weaving, tailoring, and plain building; but he cannot pay the master bakers and weavers enough to enable them to pay the wages of such labor. The rich man meanwhile is offering money enough to provide good wages for all the work required to please him. All the people who take his money may be working hard; but their work is pampering people who have too much instead of feeding people who have too little; therefore it is misapplied and wasted, keeping the country poor and even making it poorer for the sake of keeping a few people rich.

It is no excuse for such a state of things that the rich give employment. There is no merit in giving employment: a murderer gives employment to the hangman; and a motorist who runs over a child gives employment to an ambulance porter, a doctor, an undertaker, a clergyman, a mourning-dressmaker, a hearse driver, a gravedigger: in short, to so many worthy people that when he ends by killing himself it seems ungrateful not to erect a statue to him as a public benefactor. The money with which the rich give the wrong sort of employment would give the right sort of employment if it were equally distributed; for then there would be no money offered for motor cars and diamonds until everyone was fed, clothed, and lodged, nor any wages offered to men and women to leave useful employments and become servants to idlers. There would be less ostentation, less idleness, less wastefulness, less uselessness; but there would be more food, more clothing, better houses, more security, more health, more virtue: in a word, more real prosperity.

16
EUGENICS

THE question has been asked, would the masses be any better for having more money? One's first impulse on hearing such a silly question is to take the lady who asks it by the shoulders and give her a violent shaking. If a fully fed, presentably clothed, decently housed, fairly literate and cultivated and gently mannered family is not better than a half-starved, ragged, frowsy, overcrowded one, there is no meaning in words.

Still, let us not lose our tempers. A well-fed, clean, decently lodged woman is better than one trying to live on tea and rashers in dirty clothes in a verminous garret. But so is a well-fed clean sow better than a hungry dirty one. She is a sow all the same; and you cannot make a silk purse out of her ear. If the common women of the future were to be no better than our rich ladies today, even at their best, the improvement would leave us deeply dissatisfied. And that dissatisfaction would be a divine dissatisfaction. Let us consider, then, what effect equality of income would have on the quality of our people as human beings.

There are some who say that if you want better people you must breed them as carefully as you breed thoroughbred horses and pedigree boars. No doubt you must; but there are two difficulties. First, you cannot very well mate men and women as you mate bulls and cows, stallions and mares, boars and sows, without giving them any choice in the matter. Second, even if you could, you would not know how to do it, because you would not know what sort of human being you wanted to breed. In the case of a horse or a pig the matter is very simple: you want either a very fast horse for racing or a very strong horse for drawing loads; and in the case of the pig you want simply plenty of bacon. And yet, simple as that is, any breeder of these animals will tell you that he has a great many failures no matter how careful he is.

The moment you ask yourself what sort of child you want, beyond preferring a boy or a girl, you have to confess that you do not know. At best you can mention a few sorts that you dont want: for instance, you dont want cripples, deaf mutes, blind, imbecile, epileptic, or drunken children. But even these you do not know how to avoid as there is often nothing visibly wrong with the parents of such unfortunates. When you turn from what you dont want to what you do want you may say that you want good children; but a good child means only a child that gives its parents no trouble; and some very useful men and women have been very troublesome children. Energetic, imaginative, enterprising, brave children are never out of mischief from their parents' point of view. And grown-up geniuses are seldom liked until they are dead. Considering that we poisoned Socrates, crucified Christ, and burnt Joan of Arc amid popular applause, because, after a trial by responsible lawyers and Churchmen, we decided that they were too wicked to be allowed to live, we can hardly set up to be judges of goodness or to have any sincere liking for it.

Even if we were willing to trust any political authority to select our husbands and wives for us with a view to improving the race, the officials would be hopelessly puzzled as to how to select. They might begin with some rough idea of preventing the marriage of persons with any taint of consumption or madness or syphilis or addiction to drugs or drink in their families; but that would end in nobody being married at all, as there is practically no family quite free from such taints. As to moral excellence, what model would they take as desirable? St Francis, George Fox, William Penn, John Wesley, and George Washington? or Alexander, Caesar, Napoleon, and Bismarck? It takes all sorts to make a world; and the notion of a Government department trying to make out how many different types were necessary, and how many persons of each type, and proceeding to breed them by appropriate marriages, is amusing but not practicable. There is nothing for it but to let people choose their mates for themselves, and trust to Nature to produce a good result.

"Just as we do at present, in fact," some will say. But that is just what we do not do at present. How much choice has anyone among us when the time comes to choose a mate? Nature may point out a woman's mate to her by making her fall in love at first sight with the man who would be the best mate for her; but unless that man happens to have about the same income as her father, he is out of her class and out of her reach, whether above her or below her. She finds she must marry, not the man she likes, but the man she can get; and he is not often the same man.

The man is in the same predicament. We all know by instinct that it is unnatural to marry for money or social position instead of for love; yet we have arranged matters so that we must all marry more or less for money or social position or both. It is easy to say to Miss Smith or Miss Jones "Follow the promptings of your heart, my dear; and marry the dustman or marry the duke, whichever you prefer". But she cannot marry the dustman; and the duke cannot marry her; because they and their relatives have not the same manners and habits; and people with different manners and habits cannot live together. And it is difference of income that makes difference of manners and habits. Miss Smith and Miss Jones have finally to make up their minds to like what they can get, because they can very seldom get what they like; and it is safe to say that in the great majority of marriages at present Nature has very little part in the choice compared to circumstances. Unsuitable marriages, unhappy homes, ugly children are terribly common; because the young woman who ought to have all the unmarried young men in the country open to her choice, with dozens of other strings to her bow in the event of her first choice not feeling a reciprocal attraction, finds that in fact she has to choose between two or three in her own class, and has to allow herself to be much petted and tempted by physical endearments, or made desperate by neglect, before she can persuade herself that she really loves the one she dislikes least.

Under such circumstances we shall never get a well-bred race; and it is all the fault of inequality of income. If every family were brought up at the same cost, we should all have the same habits, manners, culture, and refinement; and the dustman's daughter could marry the duke's son as easily as a stockbroker's son now marries a bank manager's daughter. Nobody would marry for money, because there would be no money to be gained or lost by marriage. No woman would have to turn her back on a man she loved because he was poor, or be herself passed by for the same reason. All the disappointments would be natural and inevitable disappointments; and there would be plenty of alternatives and consolations. If the race did not improve under these circumstances, it must be unimprovable. And even if it be so, the gain in happiness by getting rid of the heartbreak that now makes the world, and especially its women, so miserable, would make the equalization of income worth while even if all the other arguments for it did not exist.

17
THE COURTS OF LAW

WHEN we come to the courts of law the hopeless incompatibility of inequality of income with justice is so plain that you must have been struck by it if you ever notice such things. The very first condition of legal justice is that it shall be no respecter of persons; that it shall hold the balance impartially between the laborer's wife and the millionairess; and that no person shall be deprived of life or liberty except by the verdict of a jury of her peers, meaning her equals. Now no laborer is ever tried by a jury of his peers: he is tried by a jury of ratepayers who have a very strong class prejudice against him because they have larger incomes, and consider themselves better men on that account. Even a rich man tried by a common jury has to reckon with their envy as well as their subservience to wealth. Thus it is a common saying with us that there is one law for the rich and another for the poor. This is not strictly true: the law is the same for everybody: it is the incomes that need changing. The civil law by which contracts are enforced, and redress given for slanders and injuries that are not dealt with by the police, requires so much legal knowledge and artistic eloquence to set it in motion that an ordinary woman with no legal knowledge or eloquence can get the benefit of it only by employing lawyers whom she has to pay very highly, which means, of course, that the rich woman can afford to go to law and the poor woman cannot. The rich woman can terrorize the poor woman by threatening to go to law with her if her demands are not complied with. She can disregard the poor woman's rights, and tell her that if she is dissatisfied she can take her complaint into court, knowing very well that her victim's poverty and ignorance will prevent her from obtaining proper legal advice and protection. When a rich woman takes a fancy to a poor woman's husband, and persuades him to abandon her, she can practically buy him by starving the abandoned wife into divorcing him for a sufficient allowance. In America, where the wife can sue for damages, the price of the divorce is higher: that is all. When the abandoned wife cannot be starved into the divorce court she can stand out for an exorbitant price before setting her husband free to remarry; and an abandoned husband can sell out likewise. Men and women now trap one another into marriage with this object to such an extent that in some States the word alimony has come to mean simply blackmail. Mind: I am not disparaging either divorce or alimony. What is wrong is that any woman should by mere superiority of income be able to make another woman's husband much more comfortable than his wife can, or that any man should be able to offer another man's wife luxuries that her husband cannot afford: in short, that money should have any weight whatever either in contracting or dissolving a marriage.

The criminal law, though we read murder trials and the like so eagerly, is less important than the civil law, because only a few exceptional people commit crimes, whilst we all marry and make civil contracts. Besides, the police set the criminal law in motion without charging the injured party anything. Nevertheless, rich prisoners are favored by being able to spend large sums in engaging famous barristers to plead for them, hunting up evidence all over the country or indeed over the world, bribing or intimidating witnesses, and exhausting every possible form of appeal and method of delay. We are fond of pointing to American cases of rich men at large who would have been hanged or electrocuted if they had been poor. But who knows how many poor people are in prison in England who might have been acquitted if they could have spent a few hundred pounds on their defence?

The laws themselves are contaminated at their very source by being made by rich men. Nominally all adult men and women are eligible to sit in Parliament and make laws if they can persuade enough people to vote for them. Something has been done of late years to make it possible for poor persons to avail themselves of this right. Members of Parliament now receive salaries; and certain election expenses formerly borne by the candidate are now public charges. But the candidate must put down £150 to start with; and it still costs from five hundred to a thousand pounds to contest a parliamentary election. Even when the candidate is successful, the salary of four hundred a year, which carries with it no pension and no prospects when the seat is lost (as it may be at the next election) is not sufficient for the sort of life in London a member of Parliament is obliged to lead. This gives the rich such an advantage that though the poor are in a nine-to-one majority in the country their representatives are in a minority in Parliament; and most of the time of Parliament is taken up, not by discussing what is best for the nation, and passing laws accordingly, but by the class struggle set up by the rich majority trying to maintain and extend its privileges against the poor minority trying to curtail or abolish them. That is, in pure waste of it.

By far the most unjust and mischievous privilege claimed by the rich is the privilege to be idle with complete legal impunity; and unfortunately they have established this privilege so firmly that we take it as a matter of course, and even venerate it as the mark of a real lady or gentleman, without ever considering that a person who consumes goods or accepts services without producing equivalent goods or performing equivalent services in return inflicts on the country precisely the same injury as a thief does: in fact, that is what theft means. We do not dream of allowing people to murder, kidnap, break into houses, sink, burn, and destroy at sea or on land, or claim exemption from military service, merely because they have inherited a landed estate or a thousand a year from some industrious ancestor; yet we tolerate idling, which does more harm in one year than all the legally punishable crimes in the world in ten. The rich, through their majority in Parliament, punish with ruthless severity such forms of theft as burglary, forgery, embezzlement, pocket-picking, larceny, and highway robbery, whilst they exempt rich idling, and even hold it up as a highly honorable way of life, thereby teaching our children that working for a livelihood is inferior, derogatory, and disgraceful. To live like a drone on the labor and service of others is to be a lady or a gentleman: to enrich the country by labor and service is to be base, lowly, vulgar, contemptible, fed and clothed and lodged on the assumption that anything is good enough for hewers of wood and drawers of water. This is nothing else than an attempt to turn the order of Nature upside down, and to take "Evil: be thou my good" as the national motto. If we persist in it, it must finally bring upon us another of those wrecks of civilization in which all the great empires in the past have crashed. Yet nothing can prevent this happening where income is unequally distributed, because the laws will inevitably be made by the rich; and the law that all must work, which should come before every other law, is a law that the rich never make.

18

THE IDLE RICH

DO not let yourself be put out at this point by the fact that people with large unearned incomes are by no means always loafing or lolling. The energetic ones often over-exert themselves, and have to take "rest cures" to recover. Those who try to make life one long holiday find that they need a holiday from that too. Idling is so unnatural and boresome that the world of the idle rich, as they are called, is a world of ceaseless activities of the most fatiguing kind. You may find on old bookshelves a forgotten nineteenth century book in which a Victorian lady of fashion defended herself against the charge of idleness by describing her daily routine of fashion both as hostess and visitor in London. I would cheerfully sweep a crossing rather than be condemned to it. In the country, sport is so elaborately organized that every month in the year has its special variety: the necessary fishes and birds and animals are so carefully bred and preserved for the purpose that there is always something to be killed. Risks and exposures and athletic feats of which the poor in towns know nothing are matters of course in the country house, where broken collar bones are hardly exceptional enough to be classed as accidents. If sports fail there are always games: ski-ing and tobogganing, polo, tennis, skating on artificial ice, and so forth, involving much more exhausting physical exercise than many poor women would care to face. A young lady, after a day of such exercise, will, between dinner and bedtime, dance a longer distance than the postman walks. In fact the only people who are disgustingly idle are the children of those who have just become rich, the new rich as they are called. As these unfortunate fortunates have had neither the athletic training nor the social discipline of the old rich, with whom what we call high life is a skilled art needing a stern apprenticeship, they do not know what to do with themselves; and their resourceless loafing and consumption of chocolate creams, cigarets, cocktails, and the sillier sort of novels and illustrated papers whilst they drift about in motor cars from one big hotel to another, is pitiable. But in the next generation they either relapse into poverty or go to school with the class they can now afford to belong to, and acquire its accomplishments, its discipline, and its manners.

But beside this Spartan routine invented to employ people who have not to work for their living, and which, you will notice, is a survival of the old tribal order in which the braves hunted and fought whilst the squaws did the domestic work, there is the necessary public work which must be done by a governing class if it is to keep all political power in its own hands. By not paying for this work, or paying so little for it that nobody without an unearned income can afford to undertake it, and by attaching to the upper division of the civil service examination tests that only expensively educated persons can pass, this work is kept in the hands of the rich. That is the explanation of the otherwise unaccountable way in which the proprietary class has opposed every attempt to attach sufficient salaries to parliamentary work to make those who do it self-supporting, although the proprietors themselves were the holders of the main parliamentary posts. Though they officered the army, they did everything they could to make it impossible for an officer to live on his pay. Though they contested every parliamentary seat, they opposed the public payment of members of Parliament and their election expenses. Though they regarded the diplomatic service as a preserve for their younger sons, they attached to it the condition that no youth should be eligible for it without a private income of four hundred a year. They fought, and still fight, against making government a self-supporting occupation, because the effect would be to throw it open to the unpropertied, and destroy their own monopoly of it.

But as the work of government must be done, they must do it

themselves if they will not let other people do it. Consequently you find rich men working in Parliament, in diplomacy, in the army, in the magistracy, and on local public bodies, to say nothing of the management of their own estates. Men so working cannot accurately be called the idle rich. Unfortunately they do all this governing work with a bias in favour of the privilege of their class to be idle. From the point of view of the public good, it would be far better if they amused themselves like most of their class, and left the work of governing to be done by well-paid officials and ministers whose interests were those of the nation as a whole.

The stamina of the women of the idle class was formerly maintained by their work in childbearing and family housekeeping. But at present many of them resort to contraception (called birth control) not to regulate the number of their children and the time of their birth, but to avoid bearing any children at all. Hotel life, or life in service flats, or the delegation of household management to professional ladies who are practically private hotel managers, is more and more substituted for old-fashioned domestic housekeeping. If this were an ordinary division of labor to enable a woman to devote herself entirely to a professional career of some sort, it would be defensible; for many women, as you must often have noticed, have no aptitude for domestic work, and are as much out of place in the kitchen and nursery as all men are conventionally supposed to be; but when you have women with unearned and excessive incomes its possibility involves an equal possibility of complete uselessness and self-indulgence, of which many rich women, knowing no better, take the fullest advantage.

There are always a few cases in which exceptional men and women with sufficient unearned income to maintain them handsomely without a stroke of work are found working harder than most of those who have to do it for a living, and spending most of their money on attempts to better the world. Florence Nightingale organized the hospital work of the Crimean war, including the knocking of some sense into the heads of the army medical staff, and much disgusting and dangerous drudgery in the wards, when she had the means to live comfortably at home doing nothing. John Ruskin published accounts of how he had spent his comfortable income and what work he had done, to shew that he, at least, was an honest worker and a faithful administrator of the part of the national income that had fallen to his lot. This was so little understood that people concluded that he must have gone out of his mind; and as he afterwards did, like Dean Swift, succumb to the melancholia and exasperation induced by the wickedness and stupidity of capitalistic civilization, they joyfully persuaded themselves that they had been quite right about him.

But when every possible qualification of the words Idle Rich has been made, and it is fully understood that idle does not mean doing nothing (which is impossible), but doing nothing useful, and continually consuming without producing, the term applies to the class, numbering at the extreme outside one-tenth of the population, to maintain whom in their idleness the other nine-tenths are kept in a condition of slavery so complete that their slavery is not even legalized as such: hunger keeps them sufficiently in order without imposing on their masters any of those obligations which make slaves so expensive to their owners. What is more, any attempt on the part of a rich woman to do a stroke of ordinary work for the sake of her health would be bitterly resented by the poor because, from their point of view, she would be a rich woman meanly doing a poor woman out of a job.

And now comes the crowning irony of it all, which many intelligent women to whom irony means nothing will prefer to call the judgment of God. When we have conferred on these people the coveted privilege of having plenty of money and nothing to do (our idiotic receipt for perfect happiness and perfect freedom) we find that we have made them so wretched and unhealthy that instead of doing nothing they are always doing something "to keep themselves fit" for doing nothing; and instead of doing what they like, they bind themselves to a laborious routine of what they call society and pleasure which you could not impose on a parlormaid without receiving notice instantly, or on a Trappist without driving him to turn atheist to escape from it. Only one part of it, the Red Indian part, the frank return to primitive life, the hunting and shooting and country life, is bearable; and one has to be by nature half a savage to enjoy that continually. So much for the exertions of the idle rich!

19
CHURCH, SCHOOL, AND PRESS

JUST as Parliament and the Courts are captured by the rich, so is the Church. The average parson does not teach honesty and equality in the village school: he teaches deference to the merely rich, and calls that loyalty and religion. He is the ally of the squire, who, as magistrate, administers the laws made in the interests of the rich by the parliament of rich men, and calls that justice. The villagers, having no experience of any other sort of religion or law, soon lose all respect for both, and become merely cynical. They may touch their hats and curtsey respectfully; but they whisper to oneanother that the squire, no matter how kind his wife may be at Christmas by way of ransom, is a despoiler and oppressor of the poor, and the parson a hypocrite. In revolutions, it is the respectful peasants who burn the country houses and parsonages, and rush to the cathedrals to deface the statues, shatter the stained windows, and wreck the organ.

By the way, you may know parsons who are not like that. At least I do. There are always men and women who will stand out against injustice, no matter how prosperous and well-spoken-of it may be. But the result is that they are ill-spoken-of themselves in the most influential quarters. Our society must be judged, not by its few rebels, but by its millions of obedient subjects.

The same corruption reaches the children in all our schools. Schoolmasters who teach their pupils such vital elementary truths about their duty to their country as that they should despise and pursue as criminals all able-bodied adults who do not by personal service pull their weight in the social boat, are dismissed from their employment, and sometimes prosecuted for sedition. And from this elementary morality up to the most abstruse and philosophic teaching in the universities, the same corruption extends. Science becomes a propaganda of quack cures, manufactured by companies in which the rich hold shares, for the diseases of the poor who need only better food and sanitary houses, and of the rich who need only useful occupation, to keep them both in health. Political economy becomes an impudent demonstration that the wages of the poor cannot be raised; that without the idle rich we should perish for lack of capital and employment; and that if the poor would take care to have fewer children everything would be for the best in the worst of all possible worlds.

Thus the poor are kept poor by their ignorance; and those whose parents are too well-off to make it possible to keep them ignorant, and who receive what is called a complete education, are taught so many flat lies that their false knowledge is more dangerous than the untutored natural wit of savages. We all blame the ex-Kaiser for banishing from the German schools and universities all teachers who did not teach that history, science, and religion all prove that the rule of the house of Hohenzollern: that is, of his own rich family, is the highest form of government possible to mankind; but we do the same thing ourselves, except that the worship of rich idleness in general is substituted for the worship of the Hohenzollern family in particular, though the Hohenzollerns have family traditions (including the learning of a common craft by every man of them) which make them much more responsible than any Tom or Dick who may happen to have made a huge fortune in business.

As people get their opinions so largely from the newspapers they read, the corruption of the schools would not matter so much if the Press were free. But the Press is not free. As it costs at least quarter of a million of money to establish a daily newspaper in London, the newspapers are owned by rich men. And they depend on the advertisements of other rich men. Editors and journalists who express opinions in print that are opposed to the interests of the rich are dismissed and replaced by subservient ones. The newspapers therefore must continue the work begun by the schools and colleges; so that only the strongest and most independent and original minds can escape from the mass of false doctrine that is impressed on them by the combined and incessant suggestion and persuasion of Parliament, the law-courts, the Church, the schools, and the Press. We are all brought up wrongheaded to keep us willing slaves instead of rebellious ones.

What makes this so hard to discover and to believe is that the false teaching is mixed up with a great deal of truth, because up to a certain point the interests of the rich are the same as the interests of everybody else. It is only where their interests differ from those of their neighbors that the deception begins. For example, the rich dread railway accidents as much as the poor; consequently the law on railway accidents, the sermons about railway accidents, the school teaching about railway accidents, and the newspaper articles about them are all quite honestly directed to the purpose of preventing railway accidents. But when anyone suggests that there would be fewer railway accidents if the railwaymen worked fewer hours and had better wages, or that in the division of the railway fares between the shareholders and the workers the shareholders should get less and the workers more, or that railway travelling would be safer if the railways were in the hands of the nation like the posts and the telegraphs, there is an immediate outcry in the Press and in Parliament against such suggestions, coupled with denunciations of those who make them as Bolsheviks or whatever other epithet may be in fashion for the moment as a term of the most infamous discredit.

20
WHY WE PUT UP WITH IT

YOU may ask why not only the rich but the poor put up with all this, and even passionately defend it as an entirely beneficial public morality. I can only say that the defence is not unanimous: it is always being attacked at one point or another by public-spirited reformers and by persons whose wrongs are unbearable. But taking it in the lump I should say that the evil of the corruption and falsification of law, religion, education, and public opinion is so enormous that the minds of ordinary people are unable to grasp it, whereas they easily and eagerly grasp the petty benefits with which it is associated. The rich are very charitable: they understand that they have to pay ransom for their riches. The simple and decent village woman whose husband is a woodman or gardener or gamekeeper, and whose daughters are being taught manners as domestic servants in the country house, sees in the lord of the manor only a kind gentleman who gives employment, and whose wife gives clothes and blankets and little comforts for the sick, and presides over the Cottage Hospital and all the little shows and sports and well-meant activities that relieve the monotony of toil, and rob illness of some of its terrors. Even in the towns, where the rich and poor do not know oneanother, the lavish expenditure of the rich is always popular. It provides much that people enjoy looking at and gossiping about. The tradesman is proud of having rich customers, and the servant of serving in a rich house. At the public entertainments of the rich there are cheap seats for the poor. Ordinary thoughtless people like all this finery. They will read eagerly about it, and look with interest at the pictures of it in the illustrated papers, whereas when they read that the percentage of children dying under the age of five years has risen or fallen, it means nothing to them but dry statistics which make the paper dull. It is only when people learn to ask "Is this good for all of us all the time as well as amusing to me for five minutes?" that they are on the way to understand how one fashionably dressed woman may cost the life of ten babies.

Even then it seems to them that the alternative to having the fashionably dressed rich ladies is that all women are to be dowdy. They need not be afraid. At present nine women out of ten are dowdy. With a reasonable distribution of income every one of the ten could afford to look her best. That no woman should have diamonds until all women have decent clothes is a sensible rule, though it may not appeal to a woman who would like to have diamonds herself and does not care a rap whether other women are well-dressed or not. She may even derive a certain gratification from seeing other women worse dressed than herself. But the inevitable end of that littleness of mind, that secret satisfaction in the misfortunes of others which the Germans call *Schadenfreude* (we have no word for it), is that sooner or later a revolution breaks out as it did in Russia; the diamonds go to the pawnbroker, who refuses to advance any money on them because nobody can afford diamonds any longer; and the fine ladies have to wear old clothes and cheaper and worse readymades until there is nothing left for them to wear. Only, as this does not happen all at once, the thoughtless do not believe that the police will ever let it come; and the littlehearted do not care whether it comes or not, provided it does not come until they are dead.

Another thing that makes us cling to this lottery with huge money prizes is the dream that we may become rich by some chance. We read of uncles in Australia dying and leaving £100,000 to a laborer or a charwoman who never knew of his existence. We hear of somebody no better off than ourselves winning the Calcutta Sweep. Such dreams would be destroyed by an equal distribution of income. And people cling all the more to dreams when they are too poor even to back horses! They forget the million losses in their longing for the one gain that the million unlucky ones have to pay for.

Poor women who have too much natural good sense to indulge in these gambler's dreams often make sacrifices in the hope that education will enable their sons to rise from the slough of poverty; and some men with an exceptional degree of the particular sort of cleverness that wins scholarships owe their promotion to their mothers. But exceptional cases, dazzling as some of them are, hold out no hope to ordinary people; for the world consists of ordinary people: indeed that is the meaning of the word ordinary. The ordinary rich woman's child and the ordinary poor woman's child may be born with equally able brains; but by the time they begin life as grown men the rich woman's son has acquired the speech, manners, personal habits, culture, and instruction without which all the higher employments are closed to him; whilst the poor woman's son is not presentable enough to get any job which brings him into contact with refined people. In this way a great deal of the brain power of the country is wasted and spoiled; for Nature does not care a rap for rich and poor. For instance, she does not give everybody the ability to do managing work. Perhaps one in twenty is as far as she goes. But she does not pick out the children of the rich to receive her capricious gifts. If in every two hundred people there are only twenty rich, her gift of management will fall to nine poor children and one rich one. But if the rich can cultivate the gift and the poor cannot, then nine-tenths of the nation's natural supply of managing ability will be lost to it; and to make up the deficiency many of the managing posts will be filled up by pigheaded people only because they happen to have the habit of ordering poor people about.

21
POSITIVE REASONS FOR EQUALITY

SO far, we have not found one great national institution that escapes the evil effects of a division of the people into rich and poor: that is, of inequality of income. I could take you further; but we should only fare worse. I could shew you how rich officers and poor soldiers and sailors create disaffection in the army and navy; how disloyalty is rampant because the relation between the royal family and the bulk of the nation is the relation between one rich family and millions of poor ones; how what we call peace is really a state of civil war between rich and poor conducted by disastrous strikes; how envy and rebellion and class resentments are chronic moral diseases with us. But if I attempted this you would presently exclaim "Oh, for goodness' sake dont tell me everything or we shall never have done". And you would be quite right. If I have not convinced you by this time that there are overwhelming reasons of State against inequality of income, I shall begin to think that you dislike me.

Besides, we must get on to the positive reasons for the Socialist plan of an equal division. I am specially interested in it because it is my favorite plan. You had therefore better watch me carefully to see that I play fairly when I am helping you to examine what there is to be said for equality of income over and above that there is to be said against inequality of income.

First, equal division is not only a possible plan, but one which has been tested by long experience. The great bulk of the daily work of the civilized world is done, and always has been done, and always must be done, by bodies of persons receiving equal pay whether they are tall or short, fair or dark, quick or slow, young or getting on in years, teetotallers or beer drinkers, Protestants or Catholics, married or single, short tempered or sweet tempered, pious or worldly: in short, without the slightest regard to the differences that make one person unlike another. In every trade there is a standard wage; in every public service there is a standard pay; and in every profession the fees are fixed with a view to enable the man who follows the profession to live according to a certain standard of respectability which is the same for the whole profession. The pay of the policeman and soldier and postman, the wages of the laborer and carpenter and mason, the salary of the judge and the member of Parliament, may differ, some of them getting less than a hundred a year and others five thousand; but all the soldiers get the same, all the judges get the same, all the members of Parliament get the same; and if you ask a doctor why his fee is half a crown or five shillings, or a guinea or three guineas, or whatever it may be, instead of five shillings or ten shillings, or two guineas or six guineas or a thousand guineas, he can give you no better reason than that he is asking what all the other doctors ask, and that they ask it because they find they cannot keep up their position on less.

Therefore when some inconsiderate person repeats like a parrot that if you gave everybody the same money, before a year was out you would have rich and poor again just as before, all you have to do is to tell him to look round him and see millions of people who get the same money and remain in the same position all their lives without any such change taking place. The cases in which poor men become rich are most exceptional; and though the cases in which rich men become poor are commoner, they also are accidents and not ordinary everyday circumstances. The rule is that workers of the same rank and calling are paid alike, and that they neither sink below their condition nor rise above it. No matter how unlike they are to oneanother, you can pay one of them two and sixpence and the other half a crown with the assurance that as they are put so they will stay, though here and there a great rogue or a great genius may surprise you by becoming much richer or much poorer than the rest. Jesus complained that he was poorer than the foxes and birds, as they had their holes and nests whilst he had not a house to shelter him; and Napoleon became an emperor; but we need take no more account of such extraordinary persons in forming our general plan than a maker of readymade clothes takes of giants and dwarfs in his price list. You may with the utmost confidence take it as settled by practical experience that if we could succeed in distributing income equally to all the inhabitants of the country, there would be no more tendency on their part to divide into rich and poor than there is at present for postmen to divide into beggars and millionaires. The only novelty proposed is that the postmen should get as much as the postmasters, and the postmasters no less than anybody else. If we find, as we do, that it answers to give all judges the same income, and all navy captains the same income, why should we go on giving judges five times as much as navy captains? That is what the navy captain would like to know; and if you tell him that if he were given as much as the judge he would be just as poor as before at the end of a year he will use language unfit for the ears of anyone but a pirate. So be careful how you say such things.

Equal distribution is then quite possible and practicable, not only momentarily but permanently. It is also simple and intelligible. It gets rid of all squabbling as to how much each person should have. It is already in operation and familiar over great masses of human beings. And it has the tremendous advantage of securing promotion by merit for the more capable.

22
MERIT AND MONEY

THAT last sentence may puzzle even the most Intelligent Woman if she has never before given her mind seriously to the subject; so I had better enlarge on it a little.

Nothing hides the difference in merit between one person and another so much as differences in income. Take for example a grateful nation making a parliamentary grant of twenty thousand pounds to a great explorer, or a great discoverer, or a great military commander (I have to make my example a man: women get only statues after their death). Before he has walked half way down the street on his way home to tell his wife about it he may meet some notorious fool or scandalous libertine, or some quite ordinary character, who has not merely twenty thousand pounds but twenty thousand a year or more. The great man's twenty thousand pounds will bring him in only a thousand a year; and with this he finds himself in our society regarded as "a poor devil" by tradesmen and financiers and quacks who are ten times as rich because they have never in their lives done anything but make money for themselves with entire selfishness, possibly by trading in the vices or on the credulity of their fellow-countrymen. It is a monstrous thing that a man who, by exercising a low sort of cunning, has managed to grab three or four millions of money selling bad whiskey, or forestalling the wheat harvest and selling it at three times its cost, or providing silly newspapers and magazines for the circulation of lying advertisements, should be honored and deferred to and waited on and returned to Parliament and finally made a peer of the realm, whilst men who have exercised their noblest faculties or risked their lives in the furtherance of human knowledge and welfare should be belittled by the contrast between their pence and the grabbers' pounds.

Only where there is pecuniary equality can the distinction of merit stand out. Titles, dignities, reputations do more harm than good if they can be bought with money. Queen Victoria shewed her practical common sense when she said that she would not give a title to anyone who had not money enough to keep it up; but the result was that the titles went to the richest, not to the best. Between persons of unequal income all other distinctions are thrown into the background. The woman with a thousand a year inevitably takes precedence of women with only a hundred, no matter how inferior she may be to them; and she can give her children advantages qualifying them for higher employments than those open to poor children of equal or greater natural capacity.

Between persons of equal income there is no social distinction except the distinction of merit. Money is nothing: character, conduct, and capacity are everything. Instead of all the workers being levelled down to low wage standards and all the rich levelled up to fashionable income standards, everybody under a system of equal incomes would find her and his own natural level. There would be great people and ordinary people and little people; but the great would always be those who had done great things, and never the idiots whose mothers had spoiled them and whose fathers had left them a hundred thousand a year; and the little would be persons of small minds and mean characters, and not poor persons who had never had a chance. That is why idiots are always in favor of inequality of income (their only chance of eminence), and the really great in favour of equality.

23
INCENTIVE

WHEN we come to the objections to equal division of income we find that most of them come to no more than this: that we are not accustomed to it, and have taken unequal division between classes so much for granted that we have never thought any other state of things possible, not to mention that the teachers and preachers appointed for us by the rich governing class have carefully hammered into us from our childhood that it is wicked and foolish to question the right of some people to be much better off than others.

Still, there are other objections. So many of them have been already disposed of in our examination of the schemes for unequal distribution that we need deal now with two only.

The first is that unless a woman were allowed to get more money than another she would have no incentive to work harder.

One answer to this is that nobody wants her to work harder than another at the national task. On the contrary, it is desirable that the burden of work, without which there could be no income to divide, should be shared equally by the workers. If those who are never happy unless they are working insist on putting in extra work to please themselves, they must not pretend that this is a painful sacrifice for which they should be paid; and, anyhow, they can always work off their superfluous energy on their hobbies.

On the other hand, there are people who grudge every moment they have to spend in working. That is no excuse for letting them off their share. Anyone who does less than her share of work, and yet takes her full share of the wealth produced by work, is a thief, and should be dealt with as any other sort of thief is dealt with.

But Weary Willie may say that he hates work, and is quite willing to take less, and be poor and dirty and ragged or even naked for the sake of getting off with less work. But that, as we have seen, cannot be allowed: voluntary poverty is just as mischievous socially as involuntary poverty: decent nations must insist on their citizens leading decent lives, doing their full share of the nation's work, and taking their full share of its income. When Weary Willie has done his bit he can be as lazy as he likes. He will have plenty of leisure to lie on his back and listen to the birds, or watch his more impetuous neighbors working furiously at their hobbies, which may be sport, exploration, literature, the arts, the sciences, or any of the activities which we pursue for their own sakes when our material needs are satisfied. But poverty and social irresponsibility will be forbidden luxuries. Poor Willie will have to submit, not to compulsory poverty as at present, but to the compulsory well-being which he dreads still more.

However, there are mechanical difficulties in the way of freedom to work more or less than others in general national production. Such work is not nowadays separate individual work: it is organized associated work, carried on in great factories and offices in which work begins and ends at fixed hours. Our clothes, for instance, are mostly washed in steam laundries in which all the operations which used to be performed by one woman with her own tub, mangle, and ironing board are divided among groups of women using machinery and buildings which none of them could use single-handed even if she could afford to buy them, assisted by men operating a steam power plant. If some of these women or men were to offer to come an hour earlier or stay two hours later for extra wages the reply would be that such an arrangement was impossible, as they could do nothing without the co-operation of the rest. The machinery would not work for them unless the engine was going. It is a case of all or nobody.

In short, associated work and factory work: that is to say, the sort of work that makes it possible for our great modern civilized populations to exist, would be impossible if every worker could begin when she liked and leave off when she liked. In many factories the pace is set for the lazy and energetic alike by the engine. The railway service would not be of much use if the engine driver and the guard were to stop the train to look at a football match when they felt inclined that way. Casual people are useless in modern industry; and the other sort: those who want to work longer and harder than the rest, find that they cannot do it except in comparatively solitary occupations. Even in domestic service, where the difference between the unpunctual slacker and sloven and the model servant is very perceptible, the routine of the household keeps everybody up to a certain mark below which a servant is discharged as unemployable. And the slacker neither accepts lower wages nor can be cured by higher.

No external incentive is needed to make first-rate workers do the best work they can: their trouble is that they can seldom make a living by it. First-rate work is done at present under the greatest discouragement. There is the impossibility of getting paid as much for it as for second-rate work. When it is not paid for at all, there is the difficulty of finding leisure for it whilst earning a living at common work. People seldom refuse a higher employment which they feel capable of undertaking. When they do, it is because the higher employment is so much worse paid or so unsuitable to their social position that they cannot afford to take it. A typical case is that of a non-commissioned officer in the army refusing a commission. If the quartermaster-sergeant's earnings and expenses came to no more than those of the officer, and both men were of the same class, no inducement in the way of extra money would be needed to make any soldier accept promotion to the highest rank in which he felt he could do himself credit. When he refuses, as he sometimes does, it is because he would be poorer and less at home in the higher than in the lower rank.

But what about the dirty work? We are so accustomed to see dirty work done by dirty and poorly paid people that we have come to think that it is disgraceful to do it, and that unless a dirty and disgraced class existed it would not be done at all. This is nonsense. Some of the dirtiest work in the world is done by titled surgeons and physicians who are highly educated, highly paid, and move in the best society. The nurses who assist them are often their equals in general education, and sometimes their superiors in rank. Nobody dreams of paying nurses less or respecting them less than typists in city offices, whose work is much cleaner. Laboratory work and anatomical work, which involves dissecting dead bodies, and analysing the secretions and excretions of live ones, is sometimes revoltingly dirty from the point of view of a tidy housekeeper; yet it has to be done by gentlemen and ladies of the professional class. And every tidy housekeeper knows that houses cannot be kept clean without dirty work. The bearing and nursing of children are by no means elegant drawingroom amusements; but nobody dares suggest that they are not in the highest degree honorable, nor do the most fastidiously refined women shirk their turn when it comes.

It must be remembered too that a great deal of work which is now dirty because it is done in a crude way by dirty people can be done in a clean way by clean people. Ladies and gentlemen who attend to their own motor cars, as many of them do, manage to do it with less mess and personal soiling than a slovenly general servant will get herself into when laying a fire. On the whole, the necessary work of the world can be done with no more dirt than healthy people of all classes can stand. The truth of the matter is that it is not really the work that is objected to so much as its association with poverty and degradation. Thus a country gentleman does not object to drive his car; but he would object very strongly to wear the livery of his chauffeur; and a lady will tidy up a room without turning a hair, though she would die rather than be seen in a parlormaid's cap and apron, neat and becoming as they are. These are as honorable as any other uniform, and much more honorable than the finery of an idle woman: the parlormaids are beginning to object to them only because they have been associated in the past with a servile condition and a lack of respect to which parlormaids are no longer disposed to submit. But they have no objection to the work. Both the parlormaid and her employer (I dare not say her mistress), if they are fond of flowers and animals, will grub in a garden all day, or wash dogs or rid them of vermin with the greatest solicitude, without considering the dirt involved in these jobs in the least derogatory to their dignity. If all dustmen were dukes nobody would object to the dust: the dustmen would put little pictures on their notepaper of their hats with flaps down the backs just as now dukes put little pictures of their coronets; and everyone would be proud to have a dustman to dinner if he would condescend to come. We may take it that nobody objects to necessary work of any kind because of the work itself; what everybody objects to is being seen doing something that is usually done only by persons of lower rank or by colored slaves. We sometimes even do things badly on purpose because those who do them well are classed as our inferiors. For example, a foolish young gentleman of property will write badly because clerks write well; and the ambassador of a republic will wear trousers instead of knee-breeches and silk stockings at court, because, though breeches and stockings are handsomer, they are a livery; and republicans consider liveries servile.

Still, when we have put out of our heads a great deal of nonsense about dirty work, the fact remains that though all useful work may be equally honorable, all useful work is most certainly not equally agreeable or equally exhausting. To escape facing this fact we may plead that some people have such very queer tastes that it is almost impossible to mention an occupation that you will not find somebody with a craze for. There is never any difficulty in finding a willing hangman. There are men who are happy keeping lighthouses on rocks in the sea so remote and dangerous that it is often months before they can be relieved. And a lighthouse is at least steady, whereas a lightship may never cease rolling about in a way that would make most of us wish ourselves dead. Yet men are found to man lightships for wages and pensions no better than they could find in good employment on shore. Mining seems a horrible and unnatural occupation; but it is not unpopular. Children left to themselves do the most uncomfortable and unpleasant things to amuse themselves, very much as a blackbeetle, though it has the run of the house, prefers the basement to the drawingroom. The saying that God never made a job but He made a man or woman to do it is true up to a certain point.

But when all possible allowances are made for these idiosyncrasies it remains true that it is much easier to find a boy who wants to be a gardener or an engine driver, and a girl who wants to be a film actress or a telephone operator, than a boy who wants to be a sewerman, or a girl who wants to be a ragpicker. A great deal can be done to make unpopular occupations more agreeable; and some of them can be got rid of altogether, and would have been got rid of long ago if there had been no class of very poor and rough people to put them upon. Smoke and soot can be done away with; sculleries can be made much pleasanter than most solicitors' offices; the unpleasantness of a sewerman's work is already mostly imaginary; coal mining may be put an end to by using the tides to produce electric power; and there are many other ways in which work which is now repulsive can be made no irksomer than the general run of necessary labor. But until this happens all the people who have no particular fancy one way or the other will want to do the pleasanter sorts of work.

Fortunately there is a way of equalizing the attraction of different occupations. And this brings us to that very important part of our lives that we call our leisure. Sailors call it their liberty.

There is one thing that we all desire; and that is freedom. By this we mean freedom from any obligation to do anything except just what we like, without a thought of tomorrow's dinner or any other of the necessities that make slaves of us. We are free only as long as we can say "My time is my own". When workers working ten hours a day agitate for an eight-hour day, what they really want is not eight hours work instead of ten, but sixteen hours off duty instead of fourteen. And out of this sixteen hours must come eight hours sleep and a few hours for eating and drinking, dressing and undressing, washing and resting; so that even with an eight hours working day the real leisure of the workers: that is, the time they have after they are properly rested and fed and cleaned up and ready for any adventures or amusements or hobbies they care for, is no more than a few hours; and these few are reduced in value by the shortness of daylight in winter, and cut down by the time it takes to get into the country or wherever is the best place to enjoy oneself. Married women, whose working place is the man's home, want to get away from home for recreation, just as men want to get away from the places where they work; in fact a good deal of our domestic quarrelling arises because the man wants to spend his leisure at home whilst the woman wants to spend hers abroad. Women love hotels: men hate them.

Take, however, the case of a man and his wife who are agreed in liking to spend their leisure away from home. Suppose the man's working day is eight hours, and that he spends eight hours in bed and four over his breakfast, dinner, washing, dressing, and resting. It does not follow that he can have four hours to spare for amusement with his wife every day. Their spare four hours are more likely to be half wasted in waiting for the theatre or picture show to begin; for they must leave the open air amusements, tennis, golf, cycling, and the seaside, for the week-end or Bank Holiday. Consequently he is always craving for more leisure.

This is why we see people preferring rough and strict employments which leave them some time to themselves to much more gentle situations in which they are never free. In a factory town it is often impossible to get a handy and intelligent domestic servant, or indeed to get a servant at all. That is not because the servant need work harder or put up with worse treatment than the factory girl or the shop assistant, but because she has no time she can call her own. She is always waiting on the doorbell even when you dare not ring the drawingroom bell lest she should rush up and give notice. To induce her to stay, you have to give her an evening out every fortnight; then one every week; then an afternoon a week as well; then two afternoons a week; then leave to entertain her friends in the drawingroom and use the piano occasionally (at which times you must clear out of your own house); and the end is that, long before you have come to the end of the concessions you are expected to make, you discover that it is not worth keeping a servant at all on such terms, and take to doing the housework yourself with modern labor saving appliances. But even if you put up with the evenings out and all the rest of it, the girl has still no satisfying sense of freedom; she may not want to stay out all night even for the most innocent purposes; but she wants to feel that she might if she liked. That is human nature.

We now see how we can make compensatory arrangements as between people who do more or less agreeable and easy sorts of work. Give more leisure, earlier retirement into the superannuated class, more holidays, in the less agreeable employments, and they will be as much sought after as the more agreeable ones with less leisure. In a picture gallery you will find a nicely dressed lady sitting at a table with nothing to do but to tell anyone who asks what is the price of any particular picture, and take an order for it if one is given. She has many pleasant chats with journalists and artists; and if she is bored she can read a novel. Her desk chair is comfortable; and she takes care that it shall be near the stove. But the gallery has to be scrubbed and dusted every day; and its windows have to be kept clean. It is clear that the lady's job is a much softer one than the charwoman's. To balance them you must either let them take their turns at the desk and at the scrubbing on alternate days or weeks; or else, as a first-rate scrubber and duster and cleaner might make a very bad business lady, and a very attractive business lady might make a very bad scrubber, you must let the charwoman go home and have the rest of the day to herself earlier than the lady at the desk.

Public picture galleries, in which the pictures are not sold, require the services of guardians who have nothing to do but wear a respectable uniform and see that people do not smoke nor steal the pictures, nor poke umbrellas through them when pointing out their beauties. Compare this work with that of the steel smelter, who has to exercise great muscular strength among blast furnaces and pools of molten metal; that is to say, in an atmosphere which to an unaccustomed person would seem the nearest thing to hell on earth! It is true that the steel smelter would very soon get bored with the gallery attendant's job, and would go back to the furnaces and the molten metal sooner than stick it; whilst the gallery attendant could not do the steel smelter's job at all, being too old, or too soft, or too lazy, or all three combined. One is a young man's job and the other an old man's job. We balance them at present by paying the steel smelter more wages. But the same effect can be produced by giving him more leisure, either in holidays or shorter hours. The workers do this themselves when they can. When they are paid, not by time, but by the piece; and when through a rise in prices or a great rush of orders they find that they can earn twice as much in a week as they are accustomed to live on, they can choose between double wages and double leisure. They usually choose double leisure, taking home the same money as before, but working from Monday to Wednesday only, and taking a Thursday to Saturday holiday. They do not want more work and more money: they want more leisure for the same work, which proves that money is not the only incentive to work, nor the strongest. Leisure, or freedom, is stronger when the work is not pleasurable in itself.

24

THE TYRANNY OF NATURE

THE very first lesson that should be taught us when we are old enough to understand it is that complete freedom from the obligation to work is unnatural, and ought to be illegal, as we can escape our share of the burden of work only by throwing it on someone else's shoulders. Nature inexorably ordains that the human race shall perish of famine if it stops working. We cannot escape from this tyranny. The question we have to settle is how much leisure we can afford to allow ourselves. Even if we must work like galley slaves whilst we are at it, how soon may we leave off with a good conscience, knowing that we have done our share and may now go free until tomorrow? That question has never been answered, and cannot be answered under our system because so many of the workers are doing work that is not merely useless but harmful. But if by an equal distribution of income and a fair division of work we could find out the answer, then we should think of our share of work as earning us, not so much money, but so much freedom.

And another curious thing would happen. We now revolt against the slavery of work because we feel ourselves to be the slaves, not of Nature and Necessity, but of our employers and those for whom they have to employ us. We therefore hate work and regard it as a curse. But if everyone shared the burden and the reward equally, we should lose this feeling. Nobody would feel put upon; and everybody would know that the more work was done the more everybody would get, since the division of what the work produced would be equal. We should then discover that haymaking is not the only work that is enjoyable. Factory work, when it is not overdriven, is very social and can be very jolly: that is one of the reasons why girls prefer working in weaving sheds in a deafening din to sitting lonely in a kitchen. Navvies have heavy work; but they are in the open air: they talk, fight, gamble, and have plenty of change from place to place; and this is much better fun than the sort of clerking that means only counting another man's money and writing it down in figures in a dingy office. Besides the work that is enjoyable from its circumstances there is the work that is interesting and enjoyable in itself, like the work of the philosophers and of the different kinds of artists who will work for nothing rather than not work at all; but this, under a system of equal division, would probably become a product of leisure rather than of compulsory industry.

Now consider the so-called pleasures that are sold to us as more enjoyable than work. The excursion train, the seaside lodgings, the catchpenny shows, the drink, the childish excitement about football and cricket, the little bands of desperately poor Follies and Pierrots pretending to be funny and cute when they are only vulgar and silly, and all the rest of the attempts to persuade the Intelligent Woman that she is having a glorious treat when she is in fact being plundered and bored and tired out and sent home cross and miserable: do not these shew that people will snatch at anything, however uneasy, for the sake of change when their few whole days of leisure are given to them at long intervals on Bank Holidays and the like? If they had enough real leisure every day as well as work they would learn how to enjoy themselves. At present they are duffers at this important art. All they can do is to buy the alluringly advertized pleasures that are offered to them for money. They seldom have sense enough to notice that these pleasures have no pleasure in them, and are endured only as a relief from the monotony of the daily leisureless drudgery.

When people have leisure enough to learn how to live, and to know the difference between real and sham enjoyment, they will not only begin to enjoy their work, but to understand why Sir George Cornewall Lewis said that life would be tolerable but for its amusements. He was clever enough to see that the amusements, instead of amusing him, wasted his time and his money and spoiled his temper. Now there is nothing so disagreeable to a healthy person as wasting time. See how healthy children pretend to be doing something or making something until they are tired! Well, it would be as natural for grown-up people to build real castles for the fun of it as for children to build sand castles. When they are tired they do not want to work at all, but just to do nothing until they fall asleep. We never want to work at pleasure: what we want is work with some pleasure and interest in it to occupy our time and exercise our muscles and minds. No slave can understand this, because he is overworked and underrespected; and when he can escape from work he rushes into gross and excessive vices that correspond to his gross and excessive labor. Set him free, and he may never be able to shake off his old horror of labor and his old vices; but never mind: he and his generation will die out; and their sons and daughters will be able to enjoy their freedom. And one way in which they will enjoy it will be to put in a great deal of extra work for the sake of making useful things beautiful and good things better, to say nothing of getting rid of bad things. For the world is like a garden: it needs weeding as well as sowing. There is use and pleasure in destruction as well as in construction: the one is as necessary as the other.

To have a really precise understanding of this matter you must distinguish not merely between labor and leisure but between leisure and rest. Labor is doing what we must; leisure is doing what we like; rest is doing nothing whilst our bodies and minds are recovering from their fatigue. Now doing what we like is often as laborious as doing what we must. Suppose it takes the form of running at the top of our speed to kick a ball up and down a field! That is harder than many forms of necessary labor. Looking at other people doing it is a way of resting, like reading a book instead of writing it. If we all had a full share of leisure we could not spend the whole of it in kicking balls, or whacking them about with golf clubs, or in shooting and hunting. Much of it would be given to useful work; and though our compulsory labor, neglect to perform which would be treated as a crime, might possibly be reduced to two or three hours a day, we should add much voluntary work to that in our leisure time, doing for fun a huge mass of nationally beneficial work that we cannot get done at present for love or money. Every woman whose husband is engaged in interesting work knows the difficulty of getting him away from it even to his meals; in fact, jealousy of a man's work sometimes causes serious domestic unhappiness; and the same thing occurs when a woman takes up some absorbing pursuit, and finds it and its associations more interesting than her husband's company and conversation and friends. In the professions where the work is solitary and independent of office and factory hours and steam engines, the number of people who injure their health and even kill themselves prematurely by overwork is so considerable that the philosopher Herbert Spencer never missed an opportunity of warning people against the craze for work. It can get hold of us exactly as the craze for drink can. Its victims go on working long after they are so worn out that their operations are doing more harm than good.

25
THE POPULATION QUESTION

THE second of the two stock objections to equal division of income is that its benefits, if any, would soon be swallowed up by married couples having too many children. The people who say this always declare at the same time that our existing poverty is caused by there being already too many people in the world, or, to put it the other way round, that the world is too small to produce food enough for all the people in it.

Now even if this were true, it would be no objection to an equal division of income; for the less we have, the more important it is that it should be equally divided, so as to make it go as far as possible, and avoid adding the evils of inequality to those of scarcity. But it is not true. What is true is that the more civilized people there are in the world the poorer most of them are relatively; but the plain cause of this is that the wealth they produce and the leisure they provide for are so unequally divided between them that at least half of them are living parasitically on the other half instead of producing maintenance for themselves.

Consider the case of domestic servants. Most people who can afford to keep a servant keep one only; but in Mayfair a young couple moving in the richest society cannot get on without nine servants, even before they have any children to be attended to. Yet everyone knows that the couples who have only one servant, or at most two (to say nothing of those who have none), are better attended to and more comfortable in their homes than the unfortunate young people who have to find room for nine grown-up persons downstairs, and keep the peace between them.

The truth is, of course, that the nine servants are attending mostly to one another and not to their employers. If you must have a butler and footman because it is the fashion, you must have somebody to cook their meals and make their beds. Housekeepers and ladies' maids need domestic service as much as the lady of the house, and are much more particular about not putting their hands to anything that is not strictly their business. It is therefore a mistake to say that nine servants are ridiculous with only two people to be attended. There are eleven people in the house to be attended; and as nine of them have to do all this attendance between them, there is not so much to spare for the odd two as might be imagined. That is why couples with nine servants are continually complaining of the difficulty of getting on with so few, and supplementing them with charwomen and jobbing dressmakers and errand boys. Families of ordinary size and extraordinary income find themselves accumulating thirty servants; and as the thirty are all more or less waiting on oneanother there is no limit except that of sleeping room to the number wanted; the more servants you have, the less time they have to attend to you, and therefore, the more you need, or rather the more they need, which is much jollier for them than for you.

Now it is plain that these hordes of servants are not supporting themselves. They are supported by their employer; and if he is an idle rich man living on rents and dividends: that is, being supported by the labor of his tenants and of the workers in the companies in which he has shares, then the whole establishment, servants, employer and all, is not self-supporting, and would not be even if the world were made ten times as large as it is to accommodate them. Instead of too many people in the world there are too many idlers, and much too many workers wasting their time in attending to idlers. Get rid of the idlers, and set these workers to useful work, and we shall hear no more for a long time yet about the world being overcrowded. Perhaps we shall never hear of it again. Nature has a way with her in these matters.

Some people will find it easier to understand this if I put it to them like a sum in arithmetic. Suppose 20 men are producing by their labor £100 a year each, and they agree, or are forced by law, to give up £50 of it to the owner of the estate on which they work. The owner will receive £1000 a year, not for work, but for owning. The owner can afford to spend £500 a year on himself, which makes him ten times as rich as any of the twenty workers, and use the other £500 to hire six men and a boy at £75 a year each to wait on him as servants and act as an armed force to deal with any of the twenty men who may attempt to rebel and withhold the £50 from him. The six men will not take the part of the men with £50 a year because they themselves get £75; and they are not clever enough to see that if they all joined to get rid of the owner and do useful work, they could have £100 a year apiece.

You have only to multiply the twenty workers and the six or seven retainers by millions to get the ground plan of what exists in every country where there is a class of owners, with a great police force and an army to protect their property, great numbers of servants to wait on them, and masses of workers making luxuries for them, all supported by the labor of the really useful workers who have to support themselves as well. Whether an increase of population will make the country richer or poorer depends, not on the natural fruitfulness of the earth, but on whether the additional people are set to do useful work or not. If they are, then the country will be richer. If, however, the additional people are set to work unproductively for the property owners as servants, or armed guardians of the rights of property, or in any of the other callings and professions to minister only to the owners, then the country will be poorer, though the property owners may become richer, the display of diamonds and fine dresses and cars much more splendid, and the servants and other retainers receiving higher wages and more schooling than their grandfathers.

In the natural course of things the more people there are in a country the richer it ought to be, because of the advantage of division of labor. Division of labor means that instead of every man having to do everything for himself like Robinson Crusoe, the different sorts of work are done by different sets of men, who become very quick and skilful at their job by doing nothing else. Also their work can be directed by others who give their whole minds to directing it. The time saved in this way can be used in making machinery, roads, and all sorts of contrivances for saving more time and labor later on. That is how twenty workers can produce more than twice what ten can produce, and a hundred much more than five times what twenty can produce. If wealth and the labor of producing it were equally shared, a population of a hundred would be much better off than a population of ten, and so on up to modern populations of millions, which ought to be enormously better off than the old communities of thousands. The fact that they are either very little better off or sometimes actually worse off, is due wholly to the idlers and idlers' parasites who are plundering them as we plunder the poor bees.

I must not, however, let you believe that if we all shared equally the increase of wealth per head could go on for ever. Human beings can multiply very fast under favorable conditions. A single pair, if their posterity managed their affairs well enough to avoid war, pestilence, and premature death, might have twenty million descendants alive at the end of four hundred years. If all the couples now alive were to multiply at that rate there would soon not be standing room on the earth, much less fields to grow wheat in. There is a limit to the quantity of food the earth can yield to labor; and if there were no limit to the increase of population we should at last find that instead of increasing our shares of food by breeding more human beings, we should diminish them.

Though we now cultivate the skies by extracting nitrogen from the air, other considerations than that of food will check our multiplication. Man does not live by bread alone; and it is possible for people to be overfed and overcrowded at the same time. After the war there was no exceptional scarcity of food in England; but there was a terrible scarcity of houses. Our cities are monstrously overcrowded: to provide every family they contain with a comfortably spacious house and garden some of our streets would have to be spread over miles of country. Some day we may have to make up our minds how many people we need to keep us all healthy, and stick to that number until we see reason to change it.

In this matter the women who have to bear the children must be considered. It is possible for a woman to bear twenty children. In certain country districts in Europe families of fifteen are not uncommon enough to be regarded as extraordinary. But though a properly cared-for woman of vigorous constitution, with her confinements reasonably spaced out, can apparently stand this strain without permanent disablement or damage, and remain as well and strong as women who have borne no children at all, yet the bearing of each child involves a long period of discomfort and sickness, culminating in temporary disablement, severe pain, and a risk of death. The father escapes this; but at present he has to earn wages to support the children while they are growing; and though there may be plenty of employment for them when they come to working age, that does not provide any bread and butter for them in the meantime. Consequently an increase of population that benefits the country and the world may be an almost unbearable burden to the parents. They therefore restrict their families to the number the father can afford, or the mother cares to bear, except when they do not know how this can be done, or are forbidden by their religion to practise birth control.

This has a very important bearing on the equal distribution of income. To understand this I must go back a little, and seem to change the subject; but the connexion will soon be plain.

If the workers in all occupations are to receive the same income, how are we to deal with the fact that though the cost of living is the same for all workers, whether they are philosophers or farm hands, the cost of their work varies very greatly. A woman in the course of a day's work may use up a reel of cotton costing a few pence whilst her husband, if a scientific worker, may require some radium, which costs £16,000 an ounce. The gunners on the battle-fields in Flanders, working at a dreadful risk of life and limb, needed very little money for themselves; but the cost of the materials they used up in a single day was prodigious. If they had had to pay on the nail, out of their wages, for the cannons they wore out and the shells they fired, there would have been no war.

This inequality of expense cannot be got over by any sort of adjustment of leisure or holidays or privileges of any sort between worker and worker. Still less can it be met by unequal wages. Even the maddest upholder of our wage system will not propose that the man who works a steam hammer costing many thousands of pounds should have wages proportionately higher than the wages of the navvy who swings a sledgehammer or the wood-cutter who wields a beetle costing shillings instead of thousands of pounds. The worker cannot bear the cost of his materials and implements if he is to have only an equal share of the national income: he must either be supplied with them, or repaid for them in the cases in which he has to supply them at his own cost.

Applying this to the labor of child-bearing and the cost of supporting children, it is clear that the expenses of both should not be borne by the parents. At present they are repaid very insufficiently by maternity benefits and by an allowance off income tax for each child in the family. Under a system of equal division of income each child would be entitled to its share from birth; and the parents would be the trustees for the children, subject, no doubt, to the obligation of satisfying the Public Trustee, if any neglect were reported, that the children were getting the full benefit of their incomes. In this way a family of growing children would always be in easy circumstances; and the mother could face the labor and risk of bearing them for the sake of motherhood's natural privileges, dignities, and satisfaction.

But it is conceivable that such pleasant conditions, combined with early marriages and the disappearance of the present terrible infant mortality, would lead to a greater increase of population than might seem desirable, or, what is equally inconvenient, a faster increase; for the pace of the increase is very important: it might be desirable to double the population in a hundred years and very undesirable to double it in fifty. Thus it may become necessary to control our numbers purposely in new ways.

What are the present ways? How is the population kept down to the numbers our system of unequal sharing can support? They are mostly very dreadful and wicked ways. They include war, pestilence, and poverty that causes multitudes of children to die of bad feeding and clothing and housing before they are a year old. Operating side by side with these horrors, we have the practice of artificial birth control by the parents on such an enormous scale that among the educated classes which resort to it, including the skilled artisan class, population is actually decreasing seriously. In France the Government, dreading a dearth of soldiers, urges the people to have more children to make up a deficiency of twenty millions as compared with Germany. To such restrictions on population must be added the criminal practice of abortion, which is terribly prevalent, and, in eastern countries, the more straightforward custom of frank infanticide by literally throwing away the unwanted child, especially the female child, and leaving it to perish of exposure. The humane Mahomet could not convince the Arabs that this was sinful; but he told them that on the Day of Judgment the female child that was exposed would rise up and ask "What fault did I commit?" In spite of Mahomet children are still exposed in Asia; and when exposure is effectually prevented by law as it is in nominally Christian countries, the unwanted children die in such numbers from neglect, starvation, and ill-usage, that they, too, may well ask on the Day of Judgment "Would it not have been kinder to expose us?"

Of all these methods of keeping down the population there can be no doubt that artificial birth control: that is, the prevention of conception, is the most humane and civilized, and by far the least demoralizing. Bishops and cardinals have denounced it as sinful; but their authority in the matter is shaken by their subjection to the tradition of the early Christians, for whom there was no population question. They believed also that marriage is sinful in itself, whether conception be prevented or not. Thus our Churchmen are obliged to start by assuming that sex is a curse imposed on us by the original sin of Eve. But we do not get rid of a fact by calling it a curse and trying to ignore it. We must face it with one eye on the alternatives to birth control, and the other on the realities of our sexual nature. The practical question for the mass of mankind is not whether the population shall be kept down or not, but whether it shall be kept down by preventing the conception of children or by bringing them into the world and then slaughtering them by abortion, exposure, starvation, neglect, ill-usage, plague, pestilence and famine, battle, murder and sudden death. I defy any bishop or cardinal to choose the latter alternatives. St Paul abhorred marriage; but he said "Better marry than burn". Our bishops and cardinals may abhor contraception (so do I, by the way); but which of them would not say, when put to it like St Paul, "Better have no children, by whatever means, than have them and kill them as we are killing them at present".

We have seen how our present unequal sharing of the national income has forced this question of Birth Control prematurely on us whilst there is still plenty of room left in the world. Canada and Australia seem underpopulated; but the Australians say that their waste spaces are uninhabitable, though the overcrowded

Japanese are restrained only by our military prestige from saying "Well, if you will not inhabit them, we will". We have birth control even where the Churches struggle hardest against it. The only thing that can check it is the abolition of the artificial poverty that has produced it prematurely. As equal division of income can do this, those who dislike birth control and would defer it to the latest possible moment, have that reason as well as all the others we have studied, for advocating equal division.

When the last possible moment comes, nobody can foresee how the necessary restriction of the population will be effected. It may be that Nature will interfere and take the matter out of our hands. This possibility is suggested by the fact that the number of children born seems to vary according to the need for them. When they are exposed to such dangers and hard conditions that very few of them can be expected to survive, Nature, without any artificial interference, produces enormous numbers to provide against the complete extinction of the species. We have all heard of the codfish with its million eggs and of the queen bee laying four thousand eggs a day. Human beings are less prolific; but even within human limits Nature apparently distinguishes between poor, undernourished, uncultivated, defective people whose children die early and in great numbers, and people who are fully cultivated mentally and physically. The defectives are appallingly prolific: the others have fewer children even when they do not practise birth control. It is one of the troubles of our present civilization that the inferior stocks are outbreeding the superior ones. But the inferior stocks are really starved stocks, slum stocks, stocks not merely uncultivated but degraded by their wretched circumstances. By getting rid of poverty we should get rid of these circumstances and of the inferior stocks they produce; and it is not at all unlikely that in doing so we should get rid of the exaggerated fertility by which Nature tries to set off the terrible infant mortality among them.

For if Nature can and does increase fertility to prevent the extinction of a species by excessive mortality, need we doubt that she can and will decrease it to prevent its extinction by overcrowding? It is certain that she does, in a mysterious way, respond to our necessities, or rather to her own. But her way is one that we do not understand. The people who say that if we improve the condition of the world it will be overpopulated are only pretending to understand it. If the Socialists were to say positively that Nature will keep the population within bounds under Socialism without artificial birth control, they would be equally pretending to understand it. The sensible course is to improve the condition of the world and see what will happen, or, as some would say, trust in God that evil will not come out of good. All that concerns us at present is that as the overpopulation difficulty has not yet arisen except in the artificial form produced by our unequal distribution of income, and curable by a better distribution, it would be ridiculous to refrain from making ourselves more comfortable on the ground that we may find ourselves getting uncomfortable again later on. We should never do anything at all if we listened to the people who tell us that the sun is cooling, or the end of the world coming next year, or the increase of population going to eat us off the face of the earth, or, generally, that all is vanity and vexation of spirit. It would be quite sensible to say "Let us eat and drink; for tomorrow we die" if only we were certain about tomorrow; but it would be foolish anyhow to say "It is not worth while to live today; for we shall die tomorrow". It is just like saying "It will be all the same a thousand years hence" as lazy people do when they have neglected their duties. The fact is that the earth can accommodate its present population more comfortably than it does or ever did; and whilst we last we may as well make ourselves as comfortable as we can.

Note that as long as two persons can produce more than twice as much as one, and two million very much more than twice as much as one million, the earth is said by the political economists to be under the Law of Increasing Return. And if ever we reach a point when there will be more people than the earth can feed properly, and the next child born will make the whole world poorer, then the earth will be under the Law of Diminishing Return. If any gentleman tries to persuade you that the earth is now under the Law of Diminishing Return you may safely conclude that he has been told to say so at a university for the sons of the rich, who would like you to believe that their riches, and the poverty of the rest, are brought about by an eternal and unchangeable law of Nature instead of by an artificial and disastrous misdistribution of the national income which we can remedy.

All the same, do not overlook the fact that there may be overpopulation in spots whilst the world as a whole is underpopulated. A boat in mid ocean, containing ten castaways, a pint of water, and a pound of biscuits, is terribly overpopulated. The cottage of a laborer with thirty shillings a week and eight children is overpopulated. A tenement house with twelve rooms and fifty people living in them is overpopulated. London is abominably overpopulated. Therefore, though there is no world population question, and the world is under the law of increasing return, there are innumerable spots in the world which are overpopulated and under the law of diminishing return. Equality of income would enable the unfortunate denizens of these plague spots to escape from the slavery of diminishing returns to the prosperity of increasing returns.

26
THE DIAGNOSTIC OF SOCIALISM

WE have now disposed of the only common objections to equal division of income not dealt with in our earlier examination of the various ways in which income is or might be unequally divided. And we have done the whole business without bothering over what the Socialists say, or quoting any of their books. You see how any intelligent woman, sitting down to decide for herself how the national income should be distributed, and without having ever heard the word Socialism or read a line by any Socialist writer, may be driven by her own common sense and knowledge of the world to the conclusion that the equal plan is the only permanent and prosperous one possible in a free community. If you could find a better way out of our present confusion and misery for us, you would be hailed as one of the greatest of discoverers.

"And if I cannot," you will say, "I suppose you will tell me I must join the Socialists!"

Dear lady: have you ever read St Augustine? If you have, you will remember that he had to admit that the early Christians were a very mixed lot, and that some of them were more addicted to blackening their wives' eyes for tempting them, and wrecking the temples of the pagans, than to carrying out the precepts of the Sermon on the Mount. Indeed you must have noticed that we modern Christians are still a very mixed lot, and that it is necessary to hang a certain number of us every year for our country's good. Now I will be as frank as St Augustine, and admit that the professed Socialists are also a very mixed lot, and that if joining them meant inviting them indiscriminately to tea I should strongly advise you not to do it, as they are just like other people, which means that some of them steal spoons when they get the chance. The nice ones are very nice; the general run are no worse than their neighbors; and the undesirable ones include some of the most thoroughpaced rascals you could meet anywhere. But what better can you expect from any political party you could join? You are, I hope, on the side of the angels; but you cannot join them until you die; and in the meantime you must put up with mere Conservatives, Liberals, Socialists, Protestants, Catholics, Dissenters, and other groups of mortal women and men, very mixed lots all of them, so that when you join them you have to pick your company just as carefully as if they had no labels and were entire strangers to you. Carlyle lumped them all as mostly fools; and who can deny that, on the whole, they deserve it?

But, after all, you are an Intelligent Woman, and know this as well as I do. What you may be a little less prepared for is that there are a great many people who call themselves Socialists who do not clearly and thoroughly know what Socialism is, and would be shocked and horrified if you told them that you were in favor of dividing-up the income of the country equally between everybody, making no distinction between lords and laborers, babies in arms and able-bodied adults, drunkards and teetotallers, archbishops and sextons, sinners and saints. They would assure you that all this is a mere ignorant delusion of the man in the street, and that no educated Socialist believes such crazy nonsense. What they want, they will tell you, is equality of opportunity, by which I suppose they mean that Capitalism will not matter if everyone has an equal opportunity of becoming a Capitalist, though how that equality of opportunity can be established without equality of income they cannot explain. Equality of opportunity is impossible. Give your son a fountain pen and a ream of paper, and tell him that he now has an equal opportunity with me of writing plays, and see what he will say to you! Do not let yourself be deceived by such phrases, or by protestations that you need not fear Socialism because it does not really mean Socialism. It does; and Socialism means equality of income and nothing else. The other things are only its conditions or its consequences.

You may, if you have a taste that way, read all the books that have been written to explain Socialism. You can study the Utopian Socialism of Sir Thomas More, the Theocratic Socialism of the Incas, the speculations of Saint Simon, the Communism of Fourier and Robert Owen, the so-called Scientific Socialism of Karl Marx, the Christian Socialism of Canon Kingsley and the Rev. F. D. Maurice, William Morris's News from Nowhere (a masterpiece of literary art which you should read anyhow), the Constitutional Socialism of Sidney and Beatrice Webb and of the highly respectable Fabian Society, and several fancy Socialisms preached by young men who have not yet had time to become celebrated. But clever as they all are, if they do not mean equality of income they mean nothing that will save civilization. The rule that subsistence comes first and virtue afterwards is as old as Aristotle and as new as this book. The Communism of Christ, of Plato, and of the great religious orders, all take equality in material subsistence for granted as the first condition of establishing the Kingdom of Heaven on earth. Whoever has reached this conclusion, by whatever path, is a Socialist; and whoever has not reached it is no Socialist, though he or she may profess Socialism or Communism in passionate harangues from one end of the country to the other, and even suffer martyrdom for it.

So now you know, whether you agree with it or not, exactly what Socialism is, and why it is advocated so widely by thoughtful and experienced people in all classes. Also, you can distinguish between the genuine Socialists, and the curious collection of Anarchists, Syndicalists, Nationalists, Radicals, and malcontents of all sorts who are ignorantly classed as Socialists or Communists or Bolshevists because they are all hostile to the existing state of things, as well as the professional politicians, or Careerists, who are deserting Liberalism for Labor because they think the Liberal ship is sinking. And you are qualified to take at its proper value the nonsense that is talked and written every day by anti-Socialist politicians and journalists who have never given five minutes serious thought to the subject, and who trot round imaginary Bolshies as boys trot round Guys on the fifth of November.

27
PERSONAL RIGHTEOUSNESS

AND now that you know what Socialism is, let me give you a warning, with an apology in advance if the warning is unnecessary. English people, especially English ladies, are so individualistically brought up that the moment they are convinced that anything is right they are apt to announce that they are going to begin practising it at once, and to order their children and servants to do the same. I have known women of exceptional natural intelligence and energy who believed firmly that the world can be made good by independent displays of coercive personal righteousness. When they became convinced of the righteousness of equality, they proceeded to do ridiculous things like commanding their servants to take their meals with the family (forgetting that the servants had not bargained for their intimacy and might strongly object to it), with Heaven knows what other foolishness, until the servants gave notice, and their husbands threatened to run away, and sometimes even did.

It is perhaps natural that ignorant poor women should imagine that inequality is the fault of the rich women. What is more surprising is that many rich women, though they ought to know better than anybody that a woman can no more help being born rich than born poor, feel guilty and ashamed of their wealth, and plunge into almsgiving to relieve their sickly consciences. They often conceive Socialism as a charitable enterprise for the benefit of the poor. Nothing could be further from the truth. Socialism abhors poverty, and would abolish the poor. A hearty dislike and disapproval of poor people as such is the first qualification of a good Equalizer. Under Socialism people would be prosecuted for being poor as they are now for being naked. Socialism loathes almsgiving, not only sentimentally because it fills the paupers with humiliation, the patrons with evil pride, and both with hatred, but because in a country justly and providently managed there could be neither excuse for it on the pauper's part nor occasion for it on the patron's. Those who like playing the good Samaritan should remember that you cannot have good Samaritans without thieves. Saviors and rescuers may be splendid figures in hagiography and romance; but as they could not exist without sinners and victims they are bad symptoms.

The virtues that feed on suffering are very questionable virtues. There are people who positively wallow in hospitals and charitable societies and Relief Funds and the like, yet who, if the need for their charitable exercises were removed, could spend their energy to great advantage in improving their own manners and learning to mind their own business. There will always be plenty of need in the world for kindness; but it should not be wasted on preventible starvation and disease. Keeping such horrors in existence for the sake of exercising our sympathies is like setting our houses on fire to exercise the vigor and daring of our fire brigades. It is the people who hate poverty, not those who sympathize with it, who will put an end to it. Almsgiving, though it cannot be stopped at present, as without it we should have hunger riots, and possibly revolution, is an evil. At present we give the unemployed a dole to support them, not for love of them, but because if we left them to starve they would begin by breaking our windows and end by looting our shops and burning our houses.

It is true that a third of the money has come directly out of their own pockets; but the way in which it is repaid to them is none the less demoralizing. They find out that whether they contribute or not, the rich will pay ransom all the same. In ancient Rome the unemployed demanded not only bread to feed them but gladiator shows to keep them amused (*panem et circenses*); and the result was that Rome became crowded with playboys who would not work at all, and were fed and amused with money taken from the provinces. That was the beginning of the end of ancient Rome. We may come to bread and football (or prize-fights) yet: indeed the dole has brought us to the bread already. There is not even the blessing of kindness on it; for we all grudge the dole (it comes out of all our pockets) and would stop it tomorrow if we dared.

Equalization of Income will be brought about, not by every woman making it her private business, but by every woman making it her public business: that is, by law. And it will not be by a single law, but a long series of laws. These laws will not be commandments saying thou shalt or thou shalt not. The Ten Commandments gave the Israelites a set of precepts which none of their laws were to violate; but the commandments were politically useless until an elaborate set of laws and institutions had been provided to give effect to them. The first and last commandment of Socialism is "Thou shalt not have a greater or less income than thy neighbor"; but before such a commandment can be even approximately obeyed we shall have not only to pass hundreds of new Acts of Parliament and repeal hundreds of old ones, but to invent and organize new Government departments; train and employ no end of women and men as public servants; educate children to look at their country's affairs in a new way; and struggle at every step with the opposition of ignorance, stupidity, custom, prejudice, and the vested interests of the rich.

Imagine a Socialist Government elected by an overwhelming majority of people who have read the preceding chapters of this book and been convinced by them, but not otherwise prepared for any change. Imagine it confronted with a starving woman. The woman says "I want work, not charity". The Government, not having any work for her, replies "Read Shaw; and you will understand all about it". The woman will say "I am too hungry to read Shaw, even if I considered him an edifying author. Will you please give me some food, and a job to enable me to pay for it honestly?" What could the Government do but confess that it had no job to give her, and offer her a dole, just as at present.

Until the Government has acquired all the powers of employment that the private employers now possess, it can give nothing to starving women, but outdoor relief with money taken by taxation from the employers and their landlords and financiers, which is just what any unsocialist government does. To acquire those powers it must itself become the national landlord, the national financier, and the national employer. In other words, it cannot distribute the national income equally until it, instead of the private owners, has the national income to distribute. Until it has done so you cannot practise Socialism even if you want to: you may even be severely punished for trying. You may agitate and vote for all the steps by which equalization of income will be reached; but in your private life you cannot do otherwise than you have to do at present: that is, keep your social rank (know your place, as it is called), paying or receiving the usual wages, investing your money to the best advantage, and so forth.

You see, it is one thing to understand the aim of Socialism, and quite another to carry it into practice, or even to see how it can or ever could be carried into practice. Jesus tells you to take no thought for the morrow's dinner or dress. Matthew Arnold tells you to choose equality. But these are commandments without laws. How can you possibly obey them at present? To take no thought for the morrow as we now are is to become a tramp; and nobody can persuade a really intelligent woman that the problems of civilization can be solved by tramps. As to choosing equality, let us choose it by all means; but how? A woman cannot go into the streets to rifle the pockets of those who have more money than she has, and give money away to those who have less: the police would soon stop that, and pass her on from the prison cell to the lunatic asylum. She knows that there are things that the Government may do by law that no private person could be allowed to do. The Government may say to Mrs Jobson "If you murder Mrs Dobson (or anyone else) you will be hanged". But if Mrs Dobson's husband said to Mrs Jobson "If you murder my wife I will strangle you" he would be threatening to commit a crime, and could be severely punished for it, no matter how odious and dangerous Mrs Jobson might be. In America, crowds sometimes take criminals out of the hands of the law and lynch them. If they attempted to do that in England they would be dispersed by the police, or shot down by the soldiers, no matter how wicked the criminal and how natural their indignation at the crime.

The first thing civilized people have to learn politically is that they must not take the law into their own hands. Socialism is from beginning to end a matter of law. It will have to make idlers work; but it must not allow private persons to take this obligation on themselves. For instance, an Intelligent Woman, having to deal with a lazy slut, might feel strongly tempted to take up the nearest broomstick and say "If you dont get on with your work and do your fair share of it I will lambaste you with this stick until you are black and blue". That occasionally happens at present. But such a threat, and much more its execution, is a worse crime than idleness, however richly the slattern may deserve the thrashing. The remedy must be a legal remedy. If the slattern is to be whacked it must be done by order of a court of law, by an officer of the law, after a fair trial by law. Otherwise life would be unbearable; for if we were all allowed to take the law into our own hands as we pleased, no woman could walk down the street without risk of having her hat torn off and stamped on by some æsthete who happened to think it unbecoming, or her silk stockings tarred by some fanatic who considers women's legs indecent, not to mention mobs of such people.

Besides, the Intelligent Woman might not be stronger than the lazy one; and in that case the lazy one might take the broomstick and whack the intelligent one for working too hard and thereby causing more to be expected from the lazy ones. That, also, has often been done by too zealous Trade Unionists.

I need not labor this point any more. Should you become a convert to Socialism you will not be committed to any change in your private life, nor indeed will you find yourself able to make any change that would be of the smallest use in that direction. The discussions in the papers as to whether a Socialist Prime Minister should keep a motor car, or a Socialist playwright receive fees for allowing his plays to be performed, or Socialist landlords and capitalists charge rent for their land or interest on their capital, or a Socialist of any sort refrain from selling all that she has and giving it to the poor (quite the most mischievous thing she could possibly do with it), are all disgraceful displays of ignorance not only of Socialism, but of common civilization.

28
CAPITALISM

NOBODY who does not understand Capitalism can change it into Socialism, or have clear notions of how Socialism will work. Therefore we shall have to study Capitalism as carefully as Socialism. To begin with, the word Capitalism is misleading. The proper name of our system is Proletarianism. When practically every disinterested person who understands our system wants to put an end to it because it wastes capital so monstrously that most of us are as poor as church mice, it darkens counsel to call it Capitalism. It sets people thinking that Socialists want to destroy capital, and believe that they could do without it: in short, that they are worse fools than their neighbors.

Unfortunately that is exactly what the owners of the newspapers want you to think about Socialists, whilst at the same time they would persuade you that the British people are a free and independent race who would scorn to be proletarians (except a few drunken rascals and Russians and professional agitators): therefore they carefully avoid the obnoxious word Proletarianism and stick to the flattering title of Capitalism, which suggests that the capitalists are defending that necessary thing, Capital.

However, I must take names as I find them; and so must you. Let it be understood between us, then, that when we say Capitalism we mean the system by which the land of the country is in the hands, not of the nation, but of private persons called landlords, who can prevent anyone from living on it or using it except on their own terms. Lawyers tell you that there is no such thing as private property in land because all the land belongs to the King, and can legally be "resumed" by him at any moment. But as the King never resumes it nowadays, and the freeholder can keep you off it, private property in land is a fact in spite of the law.

The main advantage claimed for this arrangement is that it makes the landholders rich enough to accumulate a fund of spare money called capital. This fund is also private property. Consequently the entire industry of the country, which could not exist without land and capital, is private property. But as industry cannot exist without labor, the owners must for their own sakes give employment to those who are not owners (called proletarians), and must pay them enough wages to keep them alive and enable them to marry and reproduce themselves, though not enough to enable them ever to stop working regularly.

In this way, provided the owners make it their duty to be selfish, and always hire labor at the lowest possible wage, the industry of the country will be kept going, and the people provided with a continuous livelihood, yet kept under a continuous necessity to go on working until they are worn out and fit only for the workhouse. It is fully admitted, by those who understand this system, that it produces enormous inequality of income, and that the cheapening of labor which comes from increase of population must end in an appalling spread of discontent, misery, crime, and disease, culminating in violent rebellion, unless the population is checked at the point up to which the owners can find employment for it; but the argument is that this must be faced because human nature is so essentially selfish, and so inaccessible to any motive except pecuniary gain, that no other practicable way of building up a great modern civilization stands open to us.

This doctrine used to be called the doctrine of The Manchester School. But as the name became unpopular, it is now described generally as Capitalism. Capitalism therefore means that the only duty of the Government is to maintain private property in land and capital, and to keep on foot an efficient police force and magistracy to enforce all private contracts made by individuals in pursuance of their own interests, besides, of course, keeping civil order and providing for naval and military defence or adventure.

In opposition to Capitalism, Socialism insists that the first duty of the Government is to maintain equality of income, and absolutely denies any private right of property whatever. It would treat every contract as one to which the nation is a party, with the nation's welfare as the predominant consideration, and would not for a moment tolerate any contract the effect of which would be that one woman should work herself to death prematurely in degrading poverty in order that another should live idly and extravagantly on her labor. Thus it is quite true that Socialism will abolish private property and freedom of contract: indeed it has done so already to a much greater extent than people realize; for the political struggle between Capitalism and Socialism has been going on for a century past, during which Capitalism has been yielding bit by bit to the public indignation roused by its worst results, and accepting instalments of Socialism to palliate them.

Do not, by the way, let yourself be confused by the common use of the term private property to denote personal possession. The law distinguished between Real Property (lordship) and Personal Property until the effort to make a distinction between property in land and property in capital produced such a muddle that it was dropped in 1926. Socialism, far from absurdly objecting to personal possessions, knows them to be indispensable, and looks forward to a great increase of them. But it is incompatible with real property.

To make the distinction clear let me illustrate. You call your umbrella your private property, and your dinner your private property. But they are not so: you hold them on public conditions. You may not do as you please with them. You may not hit me on the head with your umbrella; and you may not put rat poison into your dinner and kill me with it, or even kill yourself; for suicide is a crime in British law. Your right to the use and enjoyment of your umbrella and dinner is a personal right, rigidly limited by public considerations. But if you own an English or Scottish county you may drive the inhabitants off it into the sea if they have nowhere else to go. You may drag a sick woman with a newly born baby in her arms out of her house and dump her in the snow on the public road for no better reason than that you can make more money out of sheep and deer than out of women and men. You may prevent a waterside village from building a steamboat pier for the convenience of its trade because you think the pier would spoil the view from your bedroom window, even though you never spend more than a fortnight a year in that bedroom, and often do not come there for years together. These are not fancy examples: they are things that have been done again and again. They are much worse crimes than hitting me over the head with your umbrella. And if you ask why landowners are allowed to do with their land what you are not allowed to do with your umbrella, the reply is that the land is private property, or, as the lawyers used to say, real property, whilst the umbrella is only personal property. So you will not be surprised to hear Socialists say that the sooner private property is done away with the better.

Both Capitalism and Socialism claim that their object is the attainment of the utmost possible welfare for mankind. It is in their practical postulates for good government, their commandments if you like to call them so, that they differ. These are, for Capitalism, the upholding of private property in land and capital, the enforcement of private contracts, and no other State interference with industry or business except to keep civil order; and, for Socialism, the equalization of income, which involves the complete substitution of personal for private property and of publicly regulated contract for private contract, with police interference whenever equality is threatened, and complete regulation and control of industry and its products by the State.

As far as political theory is concerned you could hardly have a flatter contradiction and opposition than this; and when you look at our Parliament you do in fact see two opposed parties, the Conservative and the Labor, representing roughly Capitalism and Socialism. But as members of Parliament are not required to have had any political education, or indeed any education at all, only a very few of them, who happen to have made a special study, such as you are making, of social and political questions, understand the principles their parties represent. Many of the Labor members are not Socialists. Many of the Conservatives are feudal aristocrats, called Tories, who are as keen on State interference with everything and everybody as the Socialists. All of them are muddling along from one difficulty to another, settling as best they can when they can put it off no longer, rather than on any principle or system. The most you can say is that, as far as the Conservative Party has a policy at all, it is a Capitalistic policy, and as far as the Labor Party has a policy at all it is a Socialist policy; so that if you wish to vote against Socialism you should vote Conservative; and if you wish to vote against Capitalism you should vote Labor. I put it in this way because it is not easy to induce people to take the trouble to vote. We go to the polling station mostly to vote against something instead of for anything.

We can now settle down to our examination of Capitalism as it comes to our own doors. And, as we proceed, you must excuse the disadvantage I am at in not knowing your private affairs. You may be a capitalist. You may be a proletarian. You may be betwixt-and-between in the sense of having an independent income sufficient to keep you, but not sufficient to enable you to save any more capital. I shall have to treat you sometimes as if you were so poor that the difference of a few shillings a ton in the price of coal is a matter of serious importance in your housekeeping, and sometimes as if you were so rich that your chief anxiety is how to invest the thousands you have not been able to spend.

There is no need for you to remain equally in the dark about me; and you had better know whom you are dealing with. I am a landlord and capitalist, rich enough to be supertaxed; and in addition I have a special sort of property called literary property, for the use of which I charge people exactly as a landlord charges rent for his land. I object to inequality of income not as a man with a small income, but as one with a middling big one. But I know what it is to be a proletarian, and a poor one at that. I have worked in an office; and I have pulled through years of professional unemployment, some of the hardest of them at the expense of my mother. I have known the extremes of failure and of success. The class in which I was born was that most unlucky of all classes: the class that claims gentility and is expected to keep up its appearances without more than the barest scrap and remnant of property to do it on. I intrude these confidences on you because it is as well that you be able to allow for my personal bias. The rich often write about the poor, and the poor about the rich, without really knowing what they are writing about. I know the whole gamut from personal experience, short of actual hunger and homelessness, which should never be experienced by anybody. If I cry sour grapes, you need not suspect that they are only out of my reach: they are all in my hand at their ripest and best.

So now let us come down to tin tacks.

29

YOUR SHOPPING

ASK yourself this question: "Where does unequal distribution of the national income hit me in my everyday life?"

The answer is equally plain and practical. When you go out to do your marketing it hits you in every purchase you make. For every head of cabbage you buy, every loaf of bread, every shoulder of mutton, every bottle of beer, every ton of coals, every bus or tram fare, every theatre ticket, every visit from your doctor or charwoman, every word of advice from your lawyer, you have to pay not only what they cost, but an additional charge which is handed over finally to people who have done nothing whatever for you.

Now though every intelligent woman knows that she cannot expect to have goods or services for less than they cost in education, materials, labor, management, distribution, and so on, no intelligent woman will consent, if she knows about it and can help it, to pay over and above this inevitable cost for the luxuries and extravagances of idlers, especially if she finds great difficulty in making both ends meet by working pretty hard herself.

To rid her of this overcharge, Socialists propose to secure goods for everyone at cost price by nationalizing the industries which produce them. This terrifies the idlers and their dependents so much that they do their best to persuade the Intelligent Woman in their newspapers and speeches and sermons that nationalization is an unnatural crime which must utterly ruin the country. That is all nonsense. We have plenty of nationalization at present; and nobody is any the worse for it. The army and navy, the civil service, the posts and telegraphs and telephones, the roads and bridges, the lighthouses and royal dockyards and arsenals, are all nationalized services; and anyone declaring that they were unnatural crimes and were ruining the country would be transferred to the county lunatic asylum, also a national institution.

And we have much more nationalization than this in the form called municipalization, the only difference being that instead of the central Westminster Parliament owning and conducting the industry for the nation, as it does the Post Office, the industry is owned and conducted by City Corporations or County Councils for the local ratepayers. Thus we get publicly owned electric light works, gas works, water works, trams, baths and washhouses, public health services, libraries, picture galleries, museums, lavatories, parks and piers with pavilions and bands and stages, besides many other public services which concern the maintenance of the Empire, and of which the public knows nothing.

Most of these things could be done by private companies and shops; indeed many of them are done at present partly by private enterprise and partly by public: for instance, in London private electric lighting companies supply light in one district whilst the Borough Councils provide a municipal supply in others. But the municipal supply is cheaper, and with honest and capable management always must be cheaper than the private company's supply.

You will ask, why must it? Well, shortly, because it pays less for its capital, less for its management, and nothing at all for profits, this triple advantage going to the consumer in cheapness. But to take in the whole scope of public enterprise as compared with private, let us begin with the nationalized services. Why is it that the nationalized Post Office is so much cheaper and more extensive than a private letter-carrying company could make it, that private letter-carrying is actually forbidden by law?

The reason is that the cost of carrying letters differs greatly as between one letter and another. The cost of carrying a letter from house to house in the same terrace is so small that it cannot be expressed in money: it is as near nothing as does not matter: to get a figure at all you would have to take the cost per thousand letters instead of per letter. But the cost of carrying the same letter from the Isle of Wight to San Francisco is considerable. It has to be taken from the train to the ship to cross the Solent; changed into another ship at Southampton or perhaps at Liverpool after another train journey; carried across the Atlantic Ocean; then across the continent of North America; and finally delivered at the opposite side of the world to the Isle of Wight. You would naturally expect the Postmaster-General to deliver a dozen letters for you in the same terrace for a penny, and charge you a pound or so for sending one letter to San Francisco. What he actually does for you is to deliver the thirteen letters for threehalfpence apiece. By the time these lines are in print he may be charging you only a penny apiece, as he used to before the war. He charges you less than the cost of sending the long-distance letter, and more than the cost of sending the short-distance letters; but as he has thousands of short-distance letters to send and only dozens of long-distance ones he can make up for the undercharge on the long by an overcharge on the short. This charging the same for all letters is called by economists averaging. Others call it gaining on the swings what we lose on the roundabouts.

Our reason for forbidding private persons or companies to carry letters is that if they were allowed to meddle, there would soon be companies selling stamps at threepence a dozen to deliver letters within a few miles. The Postmaster-General would get nothing but long-distance letters: that is, the ones with a high cost of carriage. He would have to put up the price of his stamps; and when we found that the advantage of sending a letter a mile or two for a farthing was accompanied by the disadvantage of paying sixpence or a shilling when we wanted to write to someone ten miles off, we should feel that we had made a very bad bargain. The only gainers would be the private companies who had upset our system. And when they had upset it they would raise their short-distance prices to the traditional penny, if not higher.

Now let us turn from this well-established nationalized service to one that might be nationalized, and that concerns every housekeeper in the country very intimately. I mean the coal supply. Coals have become a necessary of life in our climate; and they are dreadfully dear. As I write these lines it is midsummer, when coals are cheapest; and a circular dated the 16th June offers me drawingroom coal for thirty-six and threepence a ton, and anthracite for seventy shillings. That is much more than the average cost. Why must I pay it? Why must you pay it? Simply because the coal industry is not yet nationalized. It is private property.

The cost price of coal varies from nothing to a pound a ton or more, without counting what it costs to carry and distribute the coal throughout the country. Perhaps you do not believe that coals can be had for nothing; but I assure you that on the Sunderland coast when the tide is out coals can be picked up on the shore by all comers as freely as shells or seaweed. I have seen them with my own eyes doing it. A sack and a back to carry it on is all that anybody needs there to set up as a hawker of coals in a small way, or to fill the cellar at home. Elsewhere on our coasts coal is so hard to reach that shafts have been sunk and mines dug for miles under the sea, the coal not having been reached until after twenty years work and a heavy expenditure of money. Between these two extremes there are all sorts of mines, some yielding so little coal at such high cost that they are worked only when the price of coal rises to exceptional heights, and others in which coal is so plentiful and easily got at that it is always profitable to work them even when coal is unusually cheap. The money they cost to open up varies from £350 to over a million. But the price you have to pay never falls below the cost from the very dearest mines.

The reason is this. What makes prices high is scarcity: what brings them down is plenty. Coals rise and fall in price just like strawberries. They are dear when scarce, cheap when plenty.

Now an article can become scarce in several ways. One is by reducing the quantity in the market by slackening or ceasing to manufacture. Another is to increase the number of people who want to buy the article and have money enough to pay for it. Yet another is to find out new uses for it. A scarcity of coal can be produced not only by the increase of the population, but by the people who formerly wanted only a scuttle of coals for the kitchen fire wanting thousands of tons for blast furnaces and ocean steamers. It is the scarcity produced in these ways that has raised the price of coal to such a point that it is now worth while to tunnel out mines under the sea. The cost of such mines is heavy; but it is not incurred until the price of coal has gone up sufficiently to cover it with a profit. If the price falls enough to cut off that profit the mine stops working and is abandoned. And what is the consequence of that? The stopping of the mine cuts off the supply of coals it used to send to the market; and the scarcity produced by the stoppage sends the price up again until it is high enough to restart the mine without losing money by it.

In this way the Intelligent Woman (and also the unintelligent one) finds herself condemned always to pay for her coals the full cost of getting them from the very dearest mines in use, though she may know that only the fag end of the supply comes from these mines, the rest coming from mines where the cost is much lower. She will be assured, if she remonstrates, that the price is barely sufficient to enable some of the collieries to continue working; and this will be quite true. What she will not be told, though it also is quite true, is that the better mines are making excessive profits at her expense, to say nothing of landlord's royalties.

And here comes in another complication. The miners who hew out the coal for wages in the better mines are paid no more than those in the worse ones which can barely afford to keep going, because the men, unlike the coal, can go from one mine to another, and what the poorest miner must accept all must accept. Thus the wages of all the miners are kept down to the poverty of the worst mines, just as the coal bills of all the housekeepers are kept up to their high cost. The dissatisfied miners strike, making coals scarcer and dearer than ever. The housekeepers grumble, but cannot bring down prices, and blame "the middleman". Nobody is satisfied except the owners of the better mines.

The remedy here is, of course, the Postmaster-General's plan of averaging. If all the coal mines belonged to a Coalmaster-General he could set off the good mines against the bad, and sell coal for the average cost of getting the whole supply instead of having to sell it for the cost of getting it in the very worst mines. To take fancy figures, if half the supply cost a pound a ton to raise and the other half cost half a crown a ton, he could sell at eleven and threepence a ton instead of at a pound. A Commercial Coal Trust, though it might come to own all the mines, would not do this, because its object would be to make as much profit as possible for its shareholders instead of to make coal as cheap for you as possible. There is only one owner who would work in your interest, and not want to make any profit at all. That owner would be a Government Coalmaster-General, acting for the nation: that is, acting for you and all the other housekeepers and users of coal.

Now you understand why you have the miners and the intelligent users and buyers of coal demanding the nationalization of the coal mines, and all the owners of the mines and the sellers of coal shrieking that nationalization would mean waste, corruption, ruinously high prices, the destruction of our commerce and industry, the end of our empire, and anything else they can think of in their dismay at the prospect of losing the profits they make by compelling us to pay a great deal more for our coal than it costs. But however recklessly they shriek, they are careful never to mention the real point of the whole business: that is, the procuring of coal for everybody at cost price. To keep the attention of the public off that, they will declare that nationalization is a wicked invention of the Bolshevists, and that the British Government is so corrupt and incompetent that it could not manage a baked potato stand honestly and capably, much less a coal mine. You may read ten debates in the House of Commons on coal nationalization, and a hundred newspaper articles on those debates, without ever learning what I have just told you about the difference between the mines, and how by averaging the cost of working them the price of your coals could be greatly reduced. Once these facts are known and understood there is no room for further argument: every purchaser of coal becomes a nationalizer at once; though every coal proprietor is ready to spend the last penny he can spare to discredit and prevent nationalization.

You see then how separate private property in coal mines hits a woman every time she buys coals. Well, it hits her in precisely the same way every time she buys a pair of scissors or a set of knives and forks or a flat-iron, because iron mines and silver mines differ like coal mines. It hits her every time she buys a loaf of bread, because wheat farms differ in fertility just like mines: a bushel of wheat will cost much more to raise on one farm than on another. It hits her every time she buys anything that is made in a factory, because factories differ according to their distance from railways or canals or seaports or big market towns or places where their raw materials are plentiful, or where there is natural water power to drive their works. In every case the shop price represents the cost of the article in the few mines and factories where the cost of production is greatest. It never represents the average cost taking one factory and one mine with another, which is the real national cost. Thus she is kept poor in a rich country because all the difference between the worst and the best in it is skimmed off for the private owners of the mines and factories by simply charging her more for everything she uses than the things cost. And it is to save her from this monstrous imposition that the Socialists, and many people who never dream of calling themselves Socialists, propose that the mines and factories shall be made national property instead of private property. The difference between the Socialist and non-Socialist nationalizers is that the non-Socialists aim only at cheap coal, whereas the Socialists have the ulterior object of bringing the mines into national ownership and control so as to prevent their remaining an instrument of inequality of income. On the immediate practical question of nationalization they are agreed. That is how Socialism can advance without a majority of professed Socialists in Parliament, or even without any.

Note that the difference between the highest cost of production under the worst circumstances and the lower costs under more favorable circumstances is called by economists rent. Mining rents and rents of copyrights and patent rights are called royalties; and most people call nothing rent except what they pay for house and land. But rent is part of the price of everything that has a price at all, except things that are communized, and things that are produced under the most unfavorable conditions.

30
YOUR TAXES

BESIDES buying things in the shops you have to pay rates, taxes, telephone rent (if you have a telephone), and rent of house and land. Let us examine this part of your expenditure, and see whether you get hit here again and again.

People grumble a great deal about the rates, because they get nothing across the counter for them; and what they do get they share with everyone else, so that they have no sense of individual property in it, as they have in their clothes and houses and furniture. But they would not possess their clothes or their furniture or their houses very long in peace but for the paved and lighted and policed streets, the water supply and drainage, and all the other services the rates pay for. The Intelligent Woman, when she begins to study these matters, soon realizes that she gets better value for her rates than for any other part of her expenditure, and that the municipal candidates who ask for her vote on the ground that they are going to abolish or reduce the rates (which they fortunately cannot do) are mostly either fools or humbugs, if not both. And she has the satisfaction of knowing that she gets these services as nearly as possible at their cost to the local authority, which not only does not profiteer at her expense, but does for nothing a great deal of directorial work that in any private business would have to be paid for, and under present circumstances ought to be paid for, in public business as well.

The same advantage can be claimed for taxes. Of all the public services which you pay for in taxes to the Government it can be said that there is no direct profiteering in them: you get them for what they cost the Government: that is, for much less than you would have to pay if they were private business concerns.

So far it would seem that when you pay your rates and taxes you escape the exactions which pursue you whenever you spend money in any other way. You are perhaps beginning to feel that the next time the collector calls you will hear his knock with joy, and welcome him with the beaming face of the willing giver.

I am sorry to spoil it all; but the truth is that Capitalism plunders you through the Government and the municipalities and County Councils as effectually as it does through the shopkeeper. It is not only that the Government and the local authorities, in order to carry on their public services, have to buy vast quantities of goods from private profiteers who charge them more than cost price, and that this overcharge is passed on to you as a ratepayer and taxpayer. Nor is it that the Government of the country, acting for the people of the country, cannot use the land of the country without paying some private person heavily for leave to do so. There are ways of getting round these overcharges, as, for instance, when the Government buys a piece of land for its operations, but raises the money to pay for it by a tax on rent which only the landlords pay, or when it raises capital by a tax on unearned incomes. By this expedient it can, and sometimes does, give you a complete and genuine cost price service. It can even give it to you for nothing and make richer people pay for it.

But you are rated and taxed not only to pay for public services which are equally useful to all, but for other things as well; and when you come to these you may, if you are a rich woman, complain that you are being plundered by Socialists for the benefit of the poor, or, if you are a poor woman, that you are being plundered by Capitalists who throw on the rents and taxes certain expenses which they should pay out of their own pockets.

Let us see what foundation there is for such complaints. Let us begin with the rich. By taxation rich people have a quarter or a third of their incomes, and very rich people more than half, taken from them by the Government, not for any specified public service, but as pure nationalization (communization) of their income to that extent without any compensation, and by simple coercion. This is now taken so completely as a matter of course that the rich never dream of asking for compensation, or refusing to pay until their goods are forcibly seized, or even of calling it Bolshevik confiscation; and so we are apt to talk as if such things never happened except in the imaginations of wicked Communists; but they happen in Great Britain regularly every January; and the Act authorizing them is brought in every April by the Chancellor of the Exchequer. Though reassuringly called the Appropriation Act it is really an Expropriation Act.

There is nothing in the law or the Constitution, or in any custom or tradition or parliamentary usage or any other part of our established morality, to prevent this confiscated third or half being raised to three-quarters, nine-tenths, or the whole. Besides this, when a very rich person dies, the Government confiscates the entire income of the property for the next eight years. The smallest taxable properties have to give up their incomes to the Government for ten months, and the rest for different periods between these extremes, in proportion to their amount.

In addition, there are certain taxes paid by rich and poor alike, called indirect taxes. Some of them are taxes on certain articles of food, and on tobacco and spirits, which you pay in the shop when you buy them, as part of the price. Others are stamp duties: twopence if you give a receipt for £2 or more, sixpence if you make a simple written agreement, hundreds of pounds on certain other documents which propertyless people never use. None of these taxes are levied for a named service like the police rate or the water rate: they are simple transfers of income from private pockets to the national pocket, and, as such, acts of pure Communism. It may surprise you to learn that even without counting the taxes on food, which fall on all classes, the private property thus communized already amounts to nearly a million a day.

The rich may well gasp at the figure, and ask what does the Government do with it all? What value do they get for this contribution which appears so prodigious to most of us who have to count our incomes in hundreds a year and not in millions a day? Well, the Government provides an army and navy, a civil service, courts of law and so forth; and, as we have seen, it provides them either at cost price or more nearly at cost price than any commercial concern would. But over a hundred million solid pounds of it are handed over every year in hard cash in pensions and doles to the unfortunate people who have small incomes or none.

This is pure redistribution of income: that is, pure Socialism. The officers of the Government take the money from the rich and give it to the poor because the poor have not enough and the rich have too much, without regard to their personal merits. And here again there is no constitutional limit to the process. I can remember a time when there was no supertax, and the income tax was twopence in the pound instead of four-and-sixpence or five shillings, and when Gladstone hoped to abolish it altogether. Nobody dreamt then of using taxation as an instrument for effecting a more equal distribution of income. Nowadays it is one of the chief uses of taxation; and it could be carried to complete equality without any change in our annual exchequer routine.

So far the poor have the better of the bargain. But some of the rich do very well out of the taxes. By far the heaviest single item of Government expenditure is the annual payment for the hire of the money we borrowed for the war. It is all spent and gone; but we must go on paying for the hire until we replace and repay it. Most of it was borrowed from the rich, because they alone had any spare money to lend. Consequently the Government takes a vast sum of money every year from the whole body of rich, and immediately hands it back to those who lent it money for the war. The effect of this transaction is simply to redistribute income between the rich themselves. Those who lose by it make a fuss about what they call the burden of the National Debt; but the nation is not a penny the poorer for taking money from one bold Briton and giving it to another. Whether the transfer is for better or worse depends on whether it increases or diminishes the existing inequality. Unfortunately, it is bound, on the whole, to increase it, because the Government, instead of taking money from some capitalists and dividing it among them all, is taking money from all capitalists and dividing it among some of them. This is the real mischief of the National Debt, which, in so far as it is owed to our own people, is not a debt at all. To illustrate, one may say that an elephant does not complain of being burdened because its legs have to carry its own weight; but if all the weight were on one side instead of being equally distributed between the legs, the elephant would hardly be able to carry it, and would roll over on its back when it met the slightest obstacle, which is very much what our trade does under our unequal system.

It is sometimes said that the capitalists who lent the Government the money for the war deserve the hire of it because they made sacrifices. As I was one of them myself I can tell you without malice that this is sentimental nonsense. They were the only people who were not called on to make any sacrifice: on the contrary, they were offered a gilt-edged investment at five per cent when they would have taken four. The people who were blinded, maimed, or killed by the war were those really sacrificed; and those who worked and fought were the real saviors of the country; whilst the people who did nothing but seize the national loaf that others had made, and take a big bite out of it (they and their servants) before passing on what they left of it to the soldiers, did no personal service at all: they only made the food shortage still shorter. The reason for pampering them in this absurd fashion was not for any service or merit on their part: it was the special consideration we have to shew to spare money as such because we are afraid there would not be any available if we did not pamper a class by giving it more than it can spend. We shall have to go further into this when we examine the nature of capital later on. Meanwhile, if you had the misfortune to lose an eye during one of the air raids, or if you lost your husband or son, or if you "did your bit" strenuously throughout the war, and are now a taxpayer, it must seem to you, to say the least, funny to have money taken from you by the Government and handed over to some lady who did nothing but live as indulgently as she could all the time. You will not easily be convinced that it would have been a more dreadful thing for the Government to commandeer her money than your husband's limbs, or your son's life. The utmost that can be said is that it may have been more expedient.

One more example of how your taxes may be used to enrich profiteers instead of to do you any service. At the beginning of the war, the influence of the profiteers was so strong that they persuaded the Government to allow them to make all the shells instead of having them made in national factories. The result was that you were paying taxes to keep workmen standing idle in Woolwich Arsenal at full wages in order that the profiteering firms should have all the work at a profit. You had to pay their workmen too, and the profit into the bargain. It soon turned out that they could not make nearly enough shells. Those they did make were unnecessarily expensive and not always explosive. The result was an appalling slaughter of our young men in Flanders, who were left almost defenceless in the trenches through the shortage of munitions; and we were on the verge of being defeated by simple extermination when the Government, taking the matter in hand itself, opened national factories (you may have worked in some of them) in which munitions were produced on such a scale that we have hardly yet got rid of what was left of them when the war ended, besides controlling the profiteers, teaching them their business (they did not know even how to keep proper accounts, and were wasting money like water), and limiting their profits drastically. And yet, in the face of this experience (which was of course a tremendous triumph for the advocates of nationalized industries), the war was no sooner at an end than the capitalist papers began again with their foolish and corrupt declarations that Governments are such incompetent and dishonest and extravagant jobbers, and private firms so splendidly capable and straightforward, that Governments must never do anything that private firms can make profits by doing; and very soon all the national factories were sold for an old song to the profiteers, and the national workers were in the streets with the demobilized soldiers, living on the dole, two millions strong.

This is only a sensational instance of something that is always going on: namely, the wasting of your money by employing profiteering contractors to do the work that could be done better by the authorities themselves without charging you any profit.

You see therefore that when you pay rates and taxes you are not safe from being charged not only the cost price of public services, but huge sums which go to private employers as unnecessary or excessive profits, to the landlords and capitalists whose land and capital these employers use, and to those property owners who hold the War Loan and the other stocks which represent the National Debt. But as you may also get back some of it as a pensioner or a recipient of public relief in some form or other, or as you may yourself be a holder of War Loan or Consols, or a shareholder in one of the commercial concerns which get contracts from the Government and the municipalities, it is impossible for me to say whether, on the whole, you gain or lose. I can only say that the chances are ten to one that you lose on balance; that is, that the rich get more out of you through the Government than you get out of them. So much for the taxes. Now for the rates.

31
YOUR RATES

THE rates are not paid equally by everybody. The local authorities, like the Government, have to recognize the fact that some people are better able to pay than others, and make them pay accordingly. They do this by calculating the rates on the value of the house occupied by the ratepayer, and of his place of business, guessing that a person with a house or shop worth a hundred a year will be richer than one with a house or shop worth twenty, and rating him on the valuation.

Thus every rate is really a graduated income tax as well as a payment for public services. Then there are the municipal debts as well as the national debt; and as municipalities are as lazy and wasteful as central governments in the way of giving public jobs out to profiteering contractors, everything that happens with the taxes happens with the rates as well on a smaller scale.

But there are other anomalies which rating brings out.

Just consider what happens when even the quite genuine part of our national and municipal Communism, paying its way honestly by taxing and rating, is applied, as we apply it, to people of whom some are very poor and some are very rich. If a woman cannot afford to feed herself well enough to nurse her baby properly she clearly cannot afford to contribute to the maintenance of a stud of cream-colored ponies in the stables of Buckingham Palace. If she lives with her husband and children in a single room in a back-to-back dwelling in a slum, hopelessly out of reach of the public parks of the great cities, with their flowers and bands and rides and lakes and boats, it is rather hard on her to have to pay a share of the cost of these places of recreation, used largely by rich people whose horses and motor cars shew that they could easily pay a charge for admission sufficient to maintain the place without coming to her for a contribution.

In short, since communistic expenditure is compulsory expenditure, enforced on everybody alike, it cannot be kept within everybody's means unless everybody has the same income. But the remedy is, not to abolish the parks and the cream-colored ponies, and to tell the Prince of Wales that he cannot have more than one suit of clothes until every poor woman's son has two, all of which is not only impossible but envious and curmudgeonish, but to equalize incomes. In the meantime we must pay our rates and taxes with the best grace we can, knowing that if we tried to drag down public expenditure to the level of the worst private poverty our lives would be unendurable even by savages.

This, however, does not apply to certain ways in which the ratepayer is "exploited". To exploit a person is to make money out of her without giving her an equivalent return. Now practically all private employers exploit the ratepayer more or less in a way that she never notices unless she has studied the subject as we are studying it at present. And the way they do it is this.

A woman who employs domestic servants gives regular employment to most of them; but to some she gives only casual employment. The housemaid and cook are in regular employment; the nurse is in temporary employment; and the charwoman is in casual employment: that is, she is taken on for a few hours or for a day, and then cast off to shift for herself as best she can until she gets another equally short job. If she is ill, none of her occasional employers need concern herself; and when rich people die and make provision for their servants in their wills, they never think of including a legacy for the charwoman.

Now no doubt it is very convenient to be able to pick up a woman like a taxi for an hour or so, and then get rid of her without any further responsibility by paying her a few shillings and turning her into the street. But it means that when the charwoman is ill or out of employment or getting so old that younger and stronger women are preferred to her, somebody has to provide for her. And that somebody is the ratepayer, who provides the outdoor relief and the workhouse, besides, as taxpayer, the old age pension and part of the dole. If the ratepayer did not do this the householder would have either to do without the charwoman or pay her more. Even regular servants could not, as at present, be discharged without pensions when they are worn out, if the ratepayers made no provision for them. Thus the householder is making the other ratepayers, many of whom do not employ charwomen, pay part of the cost of her domestic service.

But this is perhaps not the most impressive case, because you, as an experienced woman, can tell me that charwomen do not do so badly for themselves; that they are hard to get; and that steady ones often have their pick of several jobs, and make a compliment of taking one. But think of the great industrial concerns which employ huge armies of casuals. Take the dock companies for example. The men who load and unload the ships are taken on by the hour in hundreds at a time; and they never know whether there will be an hour's work for them or eight hours, or whether they will get two days in the week or six. I can remember when they were paid twopence an hour, and how great a victory they were supposed to have gained when they struck for sixpence an hour and got it. The dock companies profit; but the men and their families are nearly always living more or less on the rates.

Take the extreme case of this. The ratepayers have to maintain a workhouse. If any man presents himself at that workhouse as a destitute person, he must be taken in and lodged and fed and clothed. It is an established practice with some men to live at the workhouse as ablebodied paupers until they feel disposed for a night of drinking and debauchery. Then they demand their discharge, and must be let out to go about their business. They unload a ship; spend all the money they earn in a reckless spree; and return to the workhouse next morning as destitute persons to resume their residence there at the ratepayers' expense. A woman can do the same when there are casual jobs within her reach. This, I repeat, is the extreme case only: the decent respectable laborers do not do it; but casual labor does not tend to make people decent and respectable. If they were not careless, and did not keep up their spirits and keep down their prudence by drinking more than is good for them, they could not endure such worrying uncertainty.

Now, as it happens, dock labor is dangerous labor. In busy times in big docks an accident happens about every twenty minutes. But the dock company does not keep a hospital to mend its broken casuals. Why should it? There is the Poor Law Infirmary, supported by the ratepayers, near at hand, or a hospital supported by their charitable subscriptions; and nothing is simpler than to carry the victim of the accident there to be cured at the public expense without troubling the dock company. No wonder the dock company chairmen and directors are often among our most ardent advocates of public charity. With them it begins at home.

Another public institution kept by the ratepayers and taxpayers is the prison, with its police force, its courts of law, its judges, and all the rest of its very expensive retinue. An enormous proportion of the offences they deal with are caused by drink. Now the trade in drink is extremely profitable: so much so that in England it is called *The* Trade, which is short for The Trade of Trades. But why is it profitable? Because the trader in drink takes all the money the drunkard pays for his liquor, and when he is drunk throws him into the street, leaving the ratepayer to pay for all the mischief he may do, all the crimes he may commit, all the illness he may bring on himself and his family, and all the poverty to which he may be reduced. If the cost of these were charged against the drink trade instead of against the police rates and poor rates, the profits of the trade would vanish at once.

As it is, the trader gets all the takings; and the ratepayer stands all the losses. That is why they made the trade unlawful in America. They shut up the saloons (public houses), and found immediately that they could shut up a good many of the prisons as well. But if they had municipalized the drink traffic: that is, if the ratepayer had kept the public house as well as the prison, the greatest care would have been taken to discourage drunkenness, because drunkenness would have produced a loss in the municipal accounts instead of a profit. As it is, the ratepayer is being exploited outrageously by the drink trade, and the whole nation weakened and demoralized in order that a handful of people may become unnaturally rich. It is true that they rebuild our tumble-down cathedrals for us occasionally; but then they expect to be made peers for it. The bargain is an insanely bad one anyhow.

There is one more trick that can be played on you both by the municipality and the Government. In spite of their obligation not to profiteer, but to give you every service at cost price, they often do profiteer quite openly, and actually boast of their profits as a proof of their business efficiency. This takes place when you pay for the service, not by a tax or a rate, but by the ordinary process of paying for what you consume. Thus when you want a letter sent, you pay the Government three halfpence across the counter for the job. When you live where electric light is made and supplied by the municipality, you do not pay for it in your rates: you pay so much for every unit you consume.

I am sorry to have to add that the Postmaster-General takes advantage of this to charge you more for carrying your letter than the average cost of it to the Post Office. In this way he makes a profit which he hands over to the Chancellor of the Exchequer, who uses it to keep down the income tax and supertax. You pay more that the income tax payers may pay less. A fraction of your three halfpence goes into the pockets of the millionaires. True, if you are an income tax payer you get a scrap of it back yourself; but as most people do not pay income tax and everybody buys at least a few postage stamps, the income tax payers in effect exploit the purchasers of stamps. The principle is wrong, and the practice a dangerous abuse, which is nevertheless applauded and carried to greater and greater lengths as the Government adds telegraphs to posts, telephones to telegraphs, and wireless to both.

In the case of a municipal electric lighting supply, I must tell you that in spite of the fact that the municipality, unlike a private company, has to begin paying off the cost of setting up its works from the moment it borrows it, and must clear it all off within a certain period, yet even when it does this and yet supplies electricity at a lower price than the private companies, it makes a profit in spite of itself. It applies the profit to a reduction of the rates; and the ratepayers are so pleased by this, and so accustomed to think that a business which makes profits must be a sound one, that the municipality is tempted to make a profit on purpose, and even a big one, by charging the consumer more than the supply costs. When this happens, it is clear that the overcharged people who use electric light are paying part of the rates of those who do not. Even if everybody used electric light there would still be inequalities in the consumption of current. A struggling shopkeeper, who must make his shop blaze with light to attract custom, must have a heavier bill for electric light than much richer people who have only their private houses to illuminate.

We must not spend any more time on your rates and taxes. If they were entirely abolished (how popular that would be!) and their places taken by profiteering charges for State and municipal services, the result would be, not State and municipal Socialism but State and municipal Capitalism. As it is, you can see how even in your rates, which ought to be quite free from the idler's toll, you can be and to some extent are "exploited" just as you are in your ordinary shopping.

32
YOUR RENT

WHEN we come from your rates and taxes to your rent, your grievance is far clearer, because when you pay your rent you have to hand your money directly to your exploiter to do what she or he likes with instead of to a public treasurer who gives you value for part of it in public service to yourself, and tells you nothing about the remainder which goes to septuagenarians, paupers, ground landlords, profiteering contractors, and so forth, some of whom are poorer than you, which makes for equality of income and is therefore a move in the right direction, and others richer, which aggravates inequality and is therefore a move in the wrong direction.

Rent paying is simpler. If you rent a piece of land and work on it, it is quite clear that the landlord is living on your earnings; and you cannot prevent him, because the law gives him the power to turn you off the land unless you pay him for leave to use it. You are so used to this that it may never have struck you as extraordinary that any private person should have the power to treat the earth as if it belonged to him, though you would certainly think him mad if he claimed to own the air or the sunlight or the sea. Besides, you may be paying rent for a house; and it seems reasonable that the man who built the house should be paid for it. But you can easily find out how much of what you are paying is the value of the house. If you have insured the house against fire (very likely the landlord makes you do this), you know what it would cost to build the house, as that is the sum you have insured it for. If you have not insured it, ask a builder what it would cost to build a similar house. The interest you would have to pay every year if you borrowed that sum on the security of the house is the value of the house apart from the value of the land.

You will find that what you are paying exceeds this house value, unless you are in the landlord's employment or the house has become useless for its original purpose: for instance, a medieval castle. In big cities like London, it exceeds it so enormously that the value of the building is hardly worth mentioning in comparison. In out-of-the-way places the excess may be so small that it hardly goes beyond a reasonable profit on the speculation of building the house. But in the lump over the whole country it amounts to hundreds of millions of pounds a year; and this is the price, not of the houses, but of the landlords' permission to live on the native earth on which the houses have been built.

That any person should have the power to give or refuse an Englishwoman permission to live in England, or indeed—for this is what it comes to—to live at all, is so absurdly opposed to every possible conception of natural justice that any lawyer will tell you that there is no such thing as absolute private property in land, and that the King, in whom the land is vested, may take it all back from its present holders if he thinks fit. But as the landlords were for many centuries also both the lawmakers and the kingmakers, they took care that, king or no king, land should become in practice as much private property as anything else, except that it cannot be bought and sold without paying fees to lawyers and signing conveyances and other special legal documents. And this private power over land has been bought and sold so often that you never know whether your landlord will be a bold baron whose ancestors have lived as petty kings on their tenants since the days of William the Conqueror, or a poor widow who has invested all her hardearned savings in a freehold.

Howbeit the fact remains that the case of landlord and tenant is one in which an idle and possibly infamous person can with the police at his back come quite openly to an industrious and respectable woman, and say, "Hand me over a quarter of your earnings or get off the earth". The landlord can even refuse to accept a rent, and order her off the earth unconditionally; and he sometimes does so; for you may remember that in Scotland whole populations of fishermen and husbandmen with their families have been driven from their country to the backwoods of America because their landlords wanted the land on which they lived for deer forests. In England people have been driven from the countryside in multitudes to make room for sheep, because the sheep brought more money to the landlord than the people. When the great London railway stations, with their many acres of sidings, were first made, the houses of great numbers of people were knocked down, and the inhabitants driven into the streets; with the result that the whole neighbourhood became so overcrowded that it was for many years a centre of disease infecting all London. These things are still happening, and may happen to you at any moment, in spite of a few laws which have been made to protect tenants in towns in times of great scarcity of houses such as that which followed the war, or in Ireland, where the Government bought the agricultural land and resold it to the farmers, which eased matters for a time, but in the long run can come to nothing but exchanging one set of landlords for another.

It is in large towns and their neighbourhood that the Intelligent Woman will find not only how much the landlord can make her give up to him, but, oddly enough, how devoutly he believes in equality of income for his tenants, if not for himself. In the middle of the town she will find rents very high. If she or her husband has work to do there it will occur to her that if she were to take a house in the suburbs, where rents are lower, and use the tram to come to and fro, she might save a little. But she will find that the landlord knows all about that, and that though the further she moves out into the country the lower the rents, yet the railway fare or tram fare will bring up the yearly cost to what she would have to pay if she lived close enough in to walk to her market or for her husband to walk to his work. Whatever advantage she may try to gain, the landlord will snatch its full money value from her sooner or later in rent, provided it is an advantage open to everyone. It ought to be plain even to a fairly stupid woman that if the land belongs to a few people they can make their own terms with the rest, who must have land to live and work on or else starve on the highway or be drowned in the sea. They can strip them of everything except what is barely enough to keep them alive to earn money for the landowner, and bring up families to do the same in the next generation.

It is easy to see how this foolish state of things comes about. As long as there is plenty of land for everybody private property in land works very well. The landholders are not preventing anyone else from owning land like themselves; and they are quite justified in making the strongest laws to protect themselves against having their lands intruded on and their crops taken by rascals who want to reap where they have not sown. But this state of things never lasts long with a growing population, because at last all the land gets taken up, and there is none left for the later comers. Even long before this happens the best land is all taken up, and later comers find that they can do as well by paying rent for the use of the best land as by owning poorer land themselves, the amount of the rent being the difference between the yield of the poorer land and the better. At this point the owners of the best land can let their land; stop working; and live on the rent: that is, on the labor of others, or, as they call it, by owning.

When big towns and great industries arise, the value of the land goes up to enormous heights: in London bits of land with frontages on the important streets sell at the rate of a million pounds an acre; and men of business will pay the huge rents that make the land worth such a figure, although there is land forty miles away to be had for next to nothing. The land that was first let gets sublet, and yet again and again sublet until there may be half a dozen leaseholders and subleaseholders drawing more rent from it than the original ground landlord; and the tenant who is in working occupation of it has to make the money for all of them. Within the last hundred and fifty years villages in Europe and pioneer encampments in the other continents have grown into towns and cities making money by hundreds of millions; yet most of the inhabitants whose work makes all this wealth are no better off, and many of them decidedly worse off, than the villagers or pioneer campers-out who occupied the place when it was not worth a pound an acre. Meanwhile the landlords have become fabulously rich, some of them taking every day, for doing nothing, more than many a woman for sixty years drudgery.

And all this could have been avoided if we had only had the sense and foresight to insist that the land should remain national property in fact as well as in legal theory, and that all rents should be paid into a common stock and used for public purposes. If that had been done there need have been no slums, no ugly mean streets and buildings, nor indeed any rates or taxes: everybody would benefit by the rent; everybody would have to contribute to it by work; and no idler would be able to live on the labor of others. The prosperity of our great towns would be a real prosperity, shared by everyone, and not what it is now, the enslavement and impoverishment of nine persons out of every ten in order that the tenth should be idle and rich and extravagant and useless. This evil is so glaring, so inexcusable by any sophistry that the cleverest landlord can devise, that, long before Socialism was heard of, a demand arose for the abolition of all taxation except the taxation of landowners; and we still have among us people called Single Taxers, who preach the same doctrine.

33
CAPITAL

NOW the Single Taxers are not wrong in principle; but they are behind the times. Out of landowning there has grown a lazier way of living on other people's labor without doing anything for them in return. Land is not the only property that returns a rent to the owner. Spare money will do the same if it is properly used. Spare money is called Capital; its owner is called a capitalist; and our system of leaving all the spare money in the country in private hands like the land is called Capitalism. Until you understand Capitalism you do not understand human society as it exists at present. You do not know the world, as the saying is. You are living in a fool's paradise; and Capitalism is doing its best to keep you there. You may be happier in a fool's paradise; and as I must now proceed to explain Capitalism, you will read the rest of this book at the risk of being made unhappy and rebellious, and even of rushing into the streets with a red flag and making a greater fool of yourself than Capitalism has ever made of you. On the other hand, if you do not understand Capitalism you may easily be cheated out of all your money, if you have any, or, if you have none, duped into sacrificing yourself in all sorts of ways for the profit of mercenary adventurers and philanthropic humbugs under the impression that you are exercising the noblest virtues. Therefore I will risk letting you know where you are and what is happening to you.

Nothing but a very narrow mind can save you from despair if you look at all the poverty and misery around you and can see no way out of it all. And if you had a narrow mind you would never have dreamt of buying this book and reading it. Fortunately, you need not be afraid to face the truth about our Capitalism. Once you understand it, you will see that it is neither eternal nor even very old-established, neither incurable nor even very hard to cure when you have diagnosed it scientifically. I use the word cure because the civilization produced by Capitalism is a disease due to shortsightedness and bad morals; and we should all have died of it long ago if it were not that happily our society has been built up on the ten commandments and the gospels and the reasonings of jurists and philosophers, all of which are flatly opposed to the principles of Capitalism. Capitalism, though it has destroyed many ancient civilizations, and may destroy ours if we are not careful, is with us quite a recent heresy, hardly two hundred years old at its worst, though the sins it has let loose and glorified are the seven deadly ones, which are as old as human nature.

And now I hear you say "My gracious goodness me, what on the face of the earth has all this to do with the possession of spare money by ordinary ladies and gentlemen, which you say is all that Capitalism is?" And I reply, farfetched as it may seem, that it is out of that innocent looking beginning that our huge burden of poverty and misery and drink and crime and vice and premature death has grown. When we have examined the possibilities of this apparently simple matter of spare money, *alias* Capital, you will find that spare money is the root of all evil, though it ought to be, and can be made, the means of all betterment.

What is spare money? It is the money you have left when you have bought everything you need to keep you becomingly in your station in life. If you can live on ten pounds a week in the way you are accustomed and content to live, and your income is fifteen pounds a week, you have five pounds spare money at the end of the week, and are a capitalist to that amount. To be a capitalist, therefore, you must have more than enough to live on.

Consequently a poor person cannot become a capitalist. A poor person is one who has less than enough to live on. I can remember a bishop, who ought to have known better, exhorting the poor in the east end of London, at a time when poverty there was even more dreadful than it is at present, to become capitalists by saving. He really should have had his apron publicly and officially torn off him, and his shovel hat publicly and officially jumped on, for such a monstrously wicked precept. Imagine a woman, without enough money to feed her children properly and clothe them decently and healthily, letting them starve still more, and go still more ragged and naked, to buy Savings Certificates, or to put her money in the Post Office Savings Bank and keep it there until there is enough of it to buy stocks and shares! She would be prosecuted for neglecting her children; and serve her right! If she pleaded that the bishop incited her to commit this unnatural crime, she would be told that the bishop could not possibly have meant that she should save out of her children's necessary food and clothing, or even out of her own. And if she asked why the bishop did not say so, she would be told to hold her tongue; and the gaoler would be ordered to remove her to the cells.

Poor people cannot save, and ought not to try. Spending is not only a first necessity but a first duty. Nine people out of ten have not enough money to spend on themselves and their families; and to preach saving to them is not only foolish but wicked. Schoolmistresses are already complaining that the encouragement held out by Building Societies to poor parents to buy their own houses has led to the underfeeding of their children. Fortunately most of the poor neither save nor try to. All the spare money invested in the Savings Banks and Building Societies and Co-operative Societies and Savings Certificates, though it sounds very imposing when it is totalled up into hundreds of millions, and all credited to the working classes, is such a mere fleabite compared to the total sums invested that its poor owners would gain greatly by throwing it into the common stock if the capital owned by the rich were thrown in at the same time. The great bulk of British capital, the capital that matters, is the spare money of those who have more than enough to live on. It saves itself without any privation to the owner. The only question is, what is to be done with it? The answer is, keep it for a rainy day: you may want it yet. This is simple; but suppose it will not keep! Of course Treasury notes will keep; and Bank notes will keep; and metal coins will keep; and cheque books will keep; and entries of sums of money in the ledgers in the bank will keep safely enough. But these things are only legal claims to the goods we need, chiefly food. Food, we know, will not keep. And what good will spare money be to us when the food it represents has gone rotten?

The Intelligent Woman, when she realizes that money really means the things that money can buy, and that the most important of these things are perishable, will see that spare money cannot be saved: it must be spent at once. It is only the Very Simple Woman who puts her spare money into an old stocking and hides it under a loose board in the floor. She thinks that money is always money. But she is quite wrong in this. It is true that gold coins will always be worth the metal they are made of; but in Europe at present gold coins are not to be had: there is nothing but paper money; and within the last few years we have seen English paper money fall in value until a shilling would buy no more than could be bought for sixpence before the war, whilst on the Continent a thousand pounds would not buy a postage stamp, and notes for fifty thousand pounds would hardly pay a tram fare. People who thought themselves and their children provided for for life were reduced to destitution all over Europe; and even in England women left comfortably-off by insurances made by their fathers found themselves barely able to get along by the hardest pinching. That was what came of putting their trust in money.

Whilst people were being cheated in this fashion out of their savings by Governments printing heaps of Treasury notes and Bank notes with no goods at their back, several rich men of business became enormously richer because, having obtained goods on credit, they were able to pay for them in money that had become worthless. Naturally these rich men of business used all their power and influence to make their Governments go from bad to worse with their printing of bogus notes, whilst other rich men of business who, instead of owing money were owed it, used their influence in the opposite direction; so that the Governments never knew where they were: one set of business men telling them to print more notes, and another set to print less, and none of them seeming to realize that they were playing with the food of the people. The bad advice always won, because the Governments themselves owed money, and were glad enough to pay it in cheap paper, following the example of Henry VIII, who cheated his creditors by giving short weight in his silver coins.

The Intelligent Woman will conclude, and conclude rightly, that hoarding money is not a safe way of saving. If her money is not spent at once she can never be sure what it will be worth ten years hence, or ten weeks or even ten days or minutes in war time.

But you, prudent lady, will remind me that you do not want to spend your spare money: you want to keep it. If you wanted anything that it could buy it would not be spare money. If a woman has just finished a good dinner it is no use advising her to order another and eat it immediately so as to make sure of getting something for her money: she had better throw it out of the window. What she wants to know is how she can spend it and save it too. That is impossible; but she can spend it and increase her income by spending it. If you would like to know how, read the next chapter.

34
INVESTMENT AND ENTERPRISE

IF, having finished your dinner, you can find a hungry person who can be depended on to give you a dinner, say after a year's time, for nothing, you can spend your spare money in giving him a dinner for nothing; and in this way you will in a sense both spend your money on the spot and save it for next year, or, to put it the other way, you will have your spare food eaten while it is fresh and yet have fresh food to eat a year hence.

You will at once reply that you can find a million hungry persons only too easily, but that none of them can be depended on to provide a dinner for themselves, much less for you, next year: if they could, they would not be hungry. You are quite right; but there is a way round the difficulty. You will not be able to find dependable men who are hungry; but your banker or stockbroker or solicitor will find you plenty of more or less dependable persons, some of them enormously rich, who, though overfed, are nevertheless always in want of huge quantities of spare food.

What do they want it for? Why, to feed the hungry men who cannot be depended on, not on the chance of their returning the compliment next year, but for doing some work immediately that will bring in money later on. There is nothing to prevent any Intelligent Woman with spare money enough from doing this herself if she has enough invention and business ability.

Suppose, for instance, she has a big country house in a big park. Suppose her park blocks up the shortest way from one important town to another, and that the public roads that go round her park are hilly and twisty and dangerous for motor cars. She can then use her spare food to feed the hungry men while they make a road for motors through her park. When this is done she can send the hungry men away to find another job as best they can, leaving herself with a new road for the use of which she can charge a shilling to every motorist who uses it, as they all will to save time and risk and difficulty. She can keep one of the hungry men to collect the shillings for her. In this way she will have changed her spare food into a steady income. In city language, she will have gone into business as a roadmaker with her own capital.

Now if the traffic on the road be so great that the shillings, and the spare food they represent, pile themselves up on her hands faster than she can spend them (or eat them), she will have to find some new means of spending them to prevent the new spare food going bad. She will have to call the hungry men back and find something new for them to do. She might set them to build houses all along the road. Then she could present the road to the local authorities to be maintained by the ratepayers as a public street, and yet greatly increase her income by letting the houses. Having in this way obtained more spare money than ever, she could establish a service of motor buses to the nearest town to enable her tenants to work there and her workmen to live there. She could set up an electric lighting plant and gasworks to supply their houses. She could turn her big house into a hotel, or knock it down and cover its site and the park with new houses and streets. The hungry would do all the executive work for her: what she would have to do would be to give them the necessary orders and allow them to live on her spare food meanwhile.

But, you will say, only an exceptionally able and hardworking woman of business could plan all this and superintend its carrying-out. Suppose she were too stupid or too lazy to think of these things, or a genius occupied with art or science or religion or politics! Well, if only she had the spare money, hungry women and men with the requisite ability would come to her and offer to develop her estate and to pay her so much a year for the use of her land and of her spare money, arranging it all with her solicitor so that she would not have to lift her little finger in the matter except to sign her name sometimes. In business language, she could invest her capital in the development of her estate.

Now consider how much further these operations can be carried than the mere investment of one lady's savings, and the development of one lady's estate in the country. Big companies, by collecting millions of spare subsistence in small or large sums from people all over the country who are willing to take shares according to their means, can set the hungry to dig those mines that run out under the sea and need twenty years work before the coal is reached. They can make railways and monster steamships; they can build factories employing thousands of men, and equip them with machinery; they can lay cables across the ocean: there is no end or limit to what they can do as long as they can borrow spare food enough for the hungry men until the preparations are finished and the businesses begin to pay their own way.

Sometimes the schemes fail, and the owners of the spare food lose it; but they have to risk this because, as the food will not keep, they would lose it all the same if they did not invest it. So there is always spare money being offered to the big men of business and their companies; and thus our queer civilization, with its many poor and its few rich, grows as we see it with all its shops, factories, railways, mines, ocean liners, aeroplanes, telephones, palaces, mansions, flats, and cottages, on top of the fundamental sowing and reaping of the food that it all depends on.

Such is the magic of spare subsistence, called capital. That is how idle people who have land and spare subsistence become enormously rich without knowing how, and make their babies enormously rich in their cradles, whilst the landless penniless persons who do it all by slaving from dawn to dusk are left as poor at the end of the job as they were at the beginning.

35
LIMITATIONS OF CAPITALISM

MANY people are so impressed with the achievements of Capitalism that they believe that if you overthrow it you overthrow civilization. It seems to them indispensable. We must therefore consider, first, what are the disadvantages of this way of doing it? and, second, is there any other way?

Now in one sense there is no other way. All the businesses that need to have many weeks or months or years of work done on them by large bodies of men before they can pay their way, require great quantities of spare subsistence. If it takes ten years to make a harbor or twenty years to make a coal mine, the men who are making it will be eating their heads off all that time. Other people must be providing them with food, clothes, lodging, and so forth without immediate return, just as parents have to provide for growing children. In this respect it makes no difference whether we vote for Capitalism or Socialism. The process is one of natural necessity which cannot be changed by any political revolution nor evaded by any possible method of social organization.

But it does not follow that the collection and employment of spare subsistence for these purposes must be done by private companies touting for the money that very rich people are too gorged with luxuries to be able to spend, and that people of more moderate means are prudent enough to put by for a rainy day.

To begin with, there are many most necessary things that the private companies and employers will not do because they cannot make people pay for them when they are done. Take for instance a lighthouse. Without lighthouses we should hardly dare to go to sea; and the trading ships would have to go so slowly and cautiously, and so many of them would be wrecked, that the cost of the goods they carry would be much higher than it is. Therefore we all benefit greatly by lighthouses, even those of us who have never seen the sea and never expect to. But the capitalists will not build lighthouses. If the lighthouse keeper could collect a payment from every ship that passed, they would build them fast enough until the cost was lighted all round like the sea front in Brighton; but as this is impossible, and the lighthouses must shine on every ship impartially without making the captain put his hand in his pocket for it, the capitalists leave the coast in the dark. Therefore the Government steps in and collects spare subsistence in the shape of taxes from everybody (which is quite fair, as everybody shares the benefit), and builds the lighthouses. Here we see Capitalism failing completely to supply what to a seafaring nation like ours is one of the first necessaries of life (for we should starve without our shipping) and thereby forcing us to resort to Communism.

But Capitalism often refuses necessary work even when some money can be made out of it directly.

For example, a lighthouse reminds us of a harbor, which is equally necessary. Every ship coming into a harbor has to pay harbor dues; therefore anyone making a harbor can make money by it. But great harbors, with their breakwaters and piers built up in the sea, take so many years to construct, and the work is so liable to damage and even destruction in storms, and the impossibility of raising harbor dues beyond a certain point without sending the ships round to cheaper harbors so certain, that private capital turns away from it to enterprises in which there is more certainty as to what the cost will be, less delay, and more money to be made. For instance, distilleries make large profits. There is no uncertainty about the cost of building them and fitting them up; and a ready sale for whiskey can always be depended on. You can tell to within a few hundred pounds what a big distillery will cost, whereas you cannot tell to within a million what a big harbor will cost. All this would not influence the Government, which has to consider only whether another distillery or another harbor is more wanted for the good of the nation. But the private capitalists have not the good of the nation in their charge: all they have to consider is their duty to themselves and their families, which is to choose the safest and most profitable way of investing their spare money. Accordingly they choose the distillery; and if we depended on private capitalists alone the country would have as many distilleries as the whiskey market could support, and no harbors. And when they have established their distillery they will spend enormous sums of money in advertisements to persuade the public that their whiskey is better and healthier and older and more famous than the whiskey made in other distilleries, and that everybody ought to drink whiskey every day as a matter of course. As none of these statements is true, the printing of them is, from the point of view of the nation, a waste of wealth, a perversion of labor, and a propaganda of pernicious humbug.

The private capitalists not only choose what will make most money for them, but what will make it with least trouble: that is, they will do as little for it as possible. If they sell an article or a service, they will make it as dear as possible instead of as cheap as possible. This would not matter if, as thoughtless people imagine, the lower the price the bigger the sale, and the bigger the sale the greater the profit. It is true in many cases that the lower the price the bigger the sale; but it is not true that the bigger the sale the greater the profit. There may be half a dozen prices (and consequently sales) at which the profit will be exactly the same.

Take the case of a cable laid across the ocean to send messages to foreign countries. How much a word is the company to charge for the messages? If the charge is a pound a word very few people can afford to send them. If the charge is a penny a word the cable will be crowded with messages all day and all night. Yet the profit may be the same; and, if it is, it will be far less trouble to send one word at a pound than two hundred and forty words at a penny.

The same is true of the ordinary telegraph service. When it was in the hands of private companies, the service was restricted and expensive. When the Government took it over, it not only extended lines of all sorts to out-of-the-way places; cheapened the service; and did without a profit: it actually ran it at what the private capitalist calls a loss. It did this because the cheap service was such a benefit to the whole community, including the people who never send telegrams as well as those who send a dozen every day, that it paid the nation and was much fairer as well to reduce the price charged to the actual senders below the cost of the service, the difference being made up by everybody in taxes.

This very desirable arrangement is quite beyond the power of private Capitalism, which not only keeps the price as high as possible above the cost of production and service for the sake of making the utmost profit, but has no power to distribute that cost over all the people who benefit, and must levy it entirely on those who actually buy the goods or pay for the service. It is true that business people can pass the cost of their telegrams and telephone messages on to their customers in the price of the things they sell; but a great deal of our telegraphing and telephoning is not business telegraphing and telephoning; and its cost cannot be passed on by the senders to anyone. The only objection to throwing the cost entirely on public taxation is that if we could all send telegrams of unlimited length without having to pay across the counter enough ready money to prevent us using the telegraph service when the post would do as well, or sticking in "kind regards from all to dear Aunt Jane and a kiss from Baby" at the end of every message, the lines would be so choked that we should not be able to send telegrams at all. As to the telephone, some women would hang on to it all day if it made no difference to their pockets. Even as it is, a good deal of unnecessary work is put upon the telegraph service by people spinning out their messages to twelve words because they are not allowed to pay for less, and they think they are not getting full value for their money if they say what they have to say in six. It does not occur to them that they are wasting their own time and that of the officials, besides increasing their taxes. It seems a trifle; but public affairs consist of trifles multiplied by as many millions as there are people in the country; and trifles cease to be trifles when they are multiplied on that scale. Snowball letters, which seem a kindly joke to the idiots who start them, would wreck our postal system if sensible people did not conscientiously throw them into the waste paper basket.

It is necessary to understand these things very clearly, because most people are so simple and ignorant of big business matters that the private capitalists are actually able to persuade them that Capitalism is a success because it makes profits, and public service (or Communism) a failure because it makes none. The simpletons forget that the profits come out of their own pockets, and that what is the better for the private capitalists in this respect is the worse for their customers, the disappearance of profit being simply the disappearance of overcharge.

36
THE INDUSTRIAL REVOLUTION

YOU now see how it is that the nation cannot depend on private capital because there are so many vitally necessary things, from town drainage to lighthouses, which it will not provide at all, and how what it does provide it provides in the wrong order, refusing to make a harbor until it has made as many distilleries as the trade will hold, and building five luxurious houses for one rich person whilst a shocking proportion of the nation's children is dying of overcrowding in slums.

In short, the private capitalists, instead of doing the most desirable work first, begin at the wrong end. All that can be said for this policy is that if you begin at the wrong end you may be driven towards the right end when you have done your worst and can get no further in the wrong direction; and this is in fact the position into which our most respectable capitalists have been forced by circumstances. When the poor have bought all the strong drink they can afford to pay for, and the rich their racing stables and all the pearls they can find room for on their wives' necks, the capitalists are forced to apply their next year's accumulations of capital to the production of more necessary things.

Before the hungry can be set to work building mills and making machinery to equip them, somebody, possibly a woman, must invent the machinery. The capitalists buy her invention. If she is good at business, which very few inventors are, she makes them pay her enough to become a capitalist herself; but in most cases she makes a very poor bargain, because she has to sell the lion's share in her invention for a few pounds to enable her to pay for the necessary models and trials. It is only in modern Big Business that inventiveness in method and organization superadded to mechanical ingenuity has a chance against capital. If you have that talent the Big Business people will not trouble to buy your patents: they will buy *you* at a handsome price, and take you into the concern. But the simpleminded mechanical inventor has no such luck. In any case, the capitalists have made a communist law nationalizing all inventions after fourteen years, when the capitalists can use them without paying the inventor anything. They soon persuade themselves, or at least try to persuade others, that they invented the machines themselves, and deserve their riches for their ingenuity. Quite a number of people believe them.

Thus equipped with mechanical devices which are quite beyond the means of small producers, the big capitalists begin to wipe the small producers off the face of the earth. They seize on the work done by the handloom weaver in his cottage, and do it much more cheaply in great mills full of expensive machine looms driven by steam. They take the work of the oldtime miller with his windmill or waterwheel, and do it in vast buildings with steel rollers and powerful engines. They set up against the blacksmith a Nasmyth hammer that a thousand Vulcans could not handle, and scissors that snip sheet steel and bite off heavy bars more easily than he could open a tin of condensed milk. They launch huge steel ships, driven by machinery which the shipwrights who built for Columbus would have called devil's work. They raise houses in skyscraping piles of a hundred dwellings one on top of another, in steel and concrete, so that in place of one horizontal street you have bunches of perpendicular ones. They make lace by machinery, more of it in a day than ten thousand women could make by hand. They make boots by machinery, clocks by machinery, pins and needles by machinery. They sell you machines to use yourself in your own house, such as vacuum cleaners, to replace your old sweeping brush and tea leaves. They lay on the electric power and hydraulic power that they use in their factories to your house like water or gas; so that you can light and heat your house with it, and have yourself carried in a lift from the basement to the attic and back again without the trouble of climbing the stairs. You can boil your kettle and cook your dinner with it. You could even make toast with it (they sell you a little oven for the purpose) if it were not that you always forget to take the toast out before it is burnt to a cinder.

Bad as the machine-made goods are at first compared to handmade goods, they end by being sometimes better, sometimes as good, sometimes as well worth buying at the lower price, and always in the long run the only goods you can get. For at last we forget how to make things by hand, and become dependent on the bigger machine industries in spite of the little groups of artists who try to keep the old handicrafts alive. When William Morris, a great artist and craftsman, invented a story about the handle coming off a rake in a village, and nobody knowing how to put it on again, so that they had to get a big machine and eight engineers down from London to do it, his tale was not at all so improbable as it would have been in the days of Queen Anne. Our consolation is that if machinery makes rakes so cheap that it is not worth while mending them instead of throwing them away and going on with new ones, the loss is greater than the gain. And if the people who work the machines have a better life of it than the old handy people, then the change is for the better.

Mind: I do not say that these advantages are always gained at present. Most of us are using cheap and nasty articles, and living a cheap and nasty life; but this is not the fault of the machines and the great factories, nor of the application of spare money to construct them: it is the fault of the unequal distribution of the product and of the leisure gained by their saving of labor.

Now this misdistribution need not have occurred if the spare money had not been in private hands. If it had been in the hands of national and municipal banks controlling its use in the interest of all of us the capitalization of industry on a large scale would have been an unmixed blessing, instead of being, as it is at present, a blessing so mixed with curses of one kind or another that in Samuel Butler's famous Utopia, called Erewhon, the making and even the possession of machinery is punished as a crime.

Some of our cleverest anti-Socialists advocate a return to the life of the early eighteenth century, before the machines and factories came in. But that would mean going back to the small population of that time, as the old methods would not produce enough for our fortytwo millions. High capitalization of industry, in which a million of spare money is spent to provide us with fourpenny reels of cotton, has come to stay; but if Socialism prevails, the million will be public and not private property, and the reels will cost considerably less than twopence. To put it shortly, capitalization is one thing, and Capitalism quite another. Capitalization does not hurt us as long as capital is our servant and not our master. Capitalism inevitably makes it our master instead of our servant. Instead of public servants we are private slaves.

Note that the great change from cottage handicraft to factories and machine industries in the eighteenth and nineteenth centuries is called by economists and historians The Industrial Revolution.

37
SENDING CAPITAL OUT OF THE COUNTRY

SO far we have considered the growth of Capitalism as it occurs at home. But capital has no home, or rather it is at home everywhere. It is a quaint fact that though professed Socialists and Communists call themselves Internationalists, and carry a red flag which is the flag of the workers of all nations, and though most capitalists are boastfully national, and wave the Union Jack on every possible occasion, yet when you come down from the cries and catchwords to the facts, you find that every practical measure advocated by British Socialists would have the effect of keeping British capital in Britain to be spent on improving the condition of their native country, whilst the British Capitalists are sending British capital out of Britain to the ends of the earth by hundreds of millions every year. If, with all our British spare money in their hands, they were compelled to spend it in the British Isles, or were patriotic or public spirited or insular enough to do so without being compelled, they could at least call themselves patriots with some show of plausibility. Unfortunately we allow them to spend it where they please; and their only preference, as we have seen, is for the country in which it will yield them the largest income. Consequently, when they have begun at the wrong end at home, and have exhausted its possibilities, they do not move towards the right end until they have exhausted the possibilities of the wrong end abroad as well.

Take the drink trade again as the most obvious example of the wrong end being the most profitable end commercially.

It soon became so certain that free Capitalism in drink in England would destroy England, that the Government was forced to interfere. Spirits can be distilled so cheaply that it is quite possible to make a woman "drunk for a penny: dead drunk for twopence", and make a handsome profit by doing it. When the capitalists were allowed to do this they did it without remorse, having nothing to consider commercially but their profits. The Government found that masses of people were poisoning, ruining, maddening themselves with cheap gin. Accordingly a law was made by which every distiller had to pay the Government so much money for every gallon of strong drink he manufactured that he could make no profit unless he added this tax to the price of the drink; and this made the drink so dear that though there was still a great deal too much drunkenness, and working women suffered because much more had to come out of the housekeeping money for the men's beer and spirits, yet the working people could not afford to drink as recklessly and ruinously as they did in the days when Hogarth's picture of Gin Lane was painted.

In the United States of America the resistance of the Government to the demoralization of the people by private traffic in drink has gone much further. These States, after trying the plan of taxing strong drink, and finding it impossible to stop excessive drinking in this way, were driven one by one to a resolution to exterminate the trade altogether, until at last it was prohibited in so many States that it became possible to make a Federal law (that is, a law for all the States) prohibiting the sale or even the possession of intoxicating liquor anywhere within the United States. The benefits of this step were so immediate and so enormous that even the Americans who buy drink from smugglers (bootleggers) whenever they can, vote steadily for Prohibition; and so, of course, do the bootleggers, whose profits are prodigious. Prohibition will sooner or later be forced on every Capitalist country as a necessary defence against the ruinous effect of private profiteering in drink. The only practicable alternative is the municipalization of the drink trade: that is, socialism.

When our drink profiteers and their customers fill the newspapers with stories about Prohibition being a failure in America, about all Americans taking to drugs because they cannot get whiskey, about their drinking more whiskey than ever, and when they quote a foolish saying of a former bishop of Peterborough, that he would rather see England free than England sober (as if a drunken man could be free in any sense, even if he escaped arrest by the police), you must bear in mind the fact, never mentioned by them, that millions of Americans who have never been drunk in their lives, and who do not believe that their moderate use of the intoxicants they have found pleasant has ever done them the slightest harm, have yet voted away this indulgence for the general good of their country and in the interests of human dignity and civilization. Remember also that our profiteers have engaged in the smuggling trade, and actually tried to represent the measures taken against it by the American Government as attacks on British liberties. If America were as weak militarily as China was in 1840 they would drive us into a war to force whiskey on America.

Do not, however, rush to the conclusion that Prohibition, because it is a violently effective method of combating unscrupulous profiteering in drink, is an ideal method of dealing with the drink question. It is not certain that there would be any drink question if we got rid of capitalism. We shall consider that later on: our present point is simply that capital has no conscience and no country. Capitalism, beaten in a civilized country by Prohibition, can send its capital abroad to an uncivilized one where it can do what it likes. Our capitalists wiped multitudes of black men out of existence with gin when they were forcibly prevented by law from doing the same to their own countrymen. They would have made Africa a desert white with the bones of drunkards had they not discovered that more profit could be made by selling men and women than by poisoning them. The drink trade was rich; but the slave trade was richer. Huge profits were made by kidnapping shiploads of negroes and selling them as slaves. Cities like Bristol have been built upon that black foundation. White queens put money into it. The slave trade would still be a British trade if it had not been forbidden by law through the efforts of British philanthropists who, with their eyes in the ends of the earth, did not know that British children were being overworked and beaten in British factories as cruelly as the negro children in the plantations.

If you are a softhearted person, be careful not to lose your head as you read of these horrors. Virtuous indignation is a powerful stimulant, but a dangerous diet. Keep in mind the old proverb: anger is a bad counsellor. Our capitalists did not begin in this way as perversely wicked people. They did not soil their own hands with the work. Their hands were often the white hands of refined, benevolent, cultivated ladies of the highest rank. All they did or could do was to invest their spare money in the way that brought them the largest income. If milk had paid better than gin, or converting negroes to Christianity better than converting them into slaves, they would have traded in milk and Bibles just as willingly, or rather just as helplessly, as in gin and slaves.

When the gin trade was overdone and exhausted, and the slave trade suppressed, they went on into ordinary industrial work, and found that profits could be made by employing slaves as well as by kidnapping and selling them. They used their political power to induce the British Government to annex great tracts of Africa, and to impose on the natives taxes which they could not possibly pay except by working for the capitalists like English working men, only at lower wages and without the protection of English Factory Acts and English public opinion. Great fortunes were made in this way. The Empire was enlarged: "trade followed the flag" they said, meaning that the flag followed trade and then more trade followed the flag; British capital developed the world everywhere (except at home); the newspapers declared that it was all very splendid; and generals like Lord Roberts expressed their belief that God meant that three-quarters of the earth should be ruled by young gentlemen from our public schools, in which schools, by the way, nothing whatever was done to explain to them what this outrageous pillage of their own country for the development of the rest of the earth really meant over and above the temporary enrichment of their own small class.

Nothing in our political history is more appalling than the improvidence with which we have allowed British spare money, desperately needed at home for the full realization of our own powers of production, and for the clearing away of our disgraceful slum centres of social corruption, to be driven abroad at the rate of two hundred millions every year, loading us with unemployed, draining us by emigration, imposing huge military and naval forces upon us, strengthening the foreign armies of which we are afraid, and providing all sorts of facilities for the foreign industries which destroy our powers of self-support by doing for us what we could and should do just as well for ourselves. If a fraction of the British spare money our capitalists have spent in providing South America with railways and mines and factories had been spent in making roads to our natural harbors and turning to account the gigantic wasted water power of the tideways and torrents of barren savage coasts in Scotland and Ireland, or even in putting an end to such capitalistic absurdities as the sending of farm produce from one English county to another by way of America, we should not now be complaining that the countries our spare money has developed can undersell our merchants and throw our workers on public charity for want of employment

38

DOLES, DEPOPULATION, AND PARASITIC PARADISES

I BECAME a little rhetorical at the end of the last chapter, as Socialists will when they have, like myself, acquired the habit of public speaking. I hope I have not carried you away so far as to make you overlook in your indignation the fact that, whilst all these dreadful things have been going on, the profits of the capital which has gone abroad are coming into the country gratuitously (imports without equivalent exports) and being spent here by the capitalists, and that their expenditure gives employment. The capital went out; but the income comes in; and the question arises, are we any the worse for being pampered paupers, living on the labor of other nations? If the money that is coming in in income is more than went out as capital, are we not better off?

One's impulse is to say certainly not, because the same money spent as capital at home would have brought us in just as large an income, and perhaps larger, than it fetches from abroad, though the capitalists might not have got so much of it. Indeed they might have got none of it if it had been spent in great public works like clearing slums, embanking rivers, roadmaking, smoke abatement, free schools and universities, and other good things that cannot be charged for except communistically through rates and taxes. But the question is more complicated than that.

Suppose yourself a mill hand in a factory, accustomed to tend a machine there, and to live with your people in a poor quarter of a manufacturing town. Suddenly you find yourself discharged, and the factory shut up, because the trade has mysteriously gone abroad. You find that mill hands are not wanted, but that there is a scarcity of lady's maids, of assistants in fashionable shops, of waitresses in week-end motoring hotels, of stewardesses in palatial steamships, of dressmakers, of laundresses, of fine cooks (hidden in the kitchen and spoken of as "the *chef*"), of all sorts of women whose services are required by idle rich people. But you cannot get one of these jobs because you do not know the work, and are not the sort of person, and have not the speech, dress, and manners which are considered indispensable. After a spell of starvation and despair you find a job in a chocolate cream factory or a jam and pickles works, or you become a charwoman. And if you have a daughter you bring her up to the chocolate cream or lady's maid business, and not to weaving and spinning.

It is possible that in the end your daughter may be better paid, better dressed, more gently spoken, more ladylike than you were in the old mill. You may come to thank God that some Indian, or Chinaman, or negro, or simply some foreigner is doing the work you used to do, and setting your daughter free to do something that is considered much more genteel and is better paid and more respected. Your son may be doing better as a trainer of racehorses than his father did as a steel smelter, and be ever so much more the gentleman. You might, if you lived long enough, see the ugly factory towns of the Manchester and Sheffield and Birmingham districts, and of the Potteries, disappear and be replaced by nice residential towns and pleasure resorts like Bournemouth, Cheltenham, and the Malverns. You might see the valleys of Wales recover the beauty they had before the mines spoiled them. And it would be quite natural for you to call these changes prosperity, and vote for them, and sincerely loathe anyone who warned you that all it meant was that the nation, having become a parasite on foreign labor, was going to the devil as fast as it could.

Yet the warning would be much needed. If a nation turns its rough mill hands into well-educated, well-dressed, well-spoken, ladylike mill officials, properly respected, and given a fair share of the wealth they help to produce, the nation is the stronger, the richer, the happier, and the holier for the change. If it turns them into lady's maids and sellers of twenty-guinea hats, it breaks its own backbone and exchanges its page in honorable history for a chapter in The Ruins of Empires. It becomes too idle and luxurious to be able to compel the foreign countries to pay the tribute on which it lives; and when they cease to feed it, it has lost the art of feeding itself and collapses in the midst of its genteel splendor.

But this dismal sketch of the future of countries that let themselves become dependent on the labor of other countries and settle down into a comfortable and ladylike parasitism is really much too favorable. If all our factory foremen could be turned into headwaiters with a touch of Cinderella's godmother's wand, neither they nor their wives might object. But this is not what happens. The factory foreman may bring up his son to be a waiter; but he himself becomes an unemployed man. If he is not fit for any of the new jobs, and too old to learn, and his trade is not merely going through one of the usual periods of depression but has left the country for good, he becomes a permanently unemployed man, and consequently a starving man. Now a starving man is a dangerous man, no matter how respectable his political opinions may be. A man who has had his dinner is never a revolutionist: his politics are all talk. But hungry men, rather than die of starvation, will, when there are enough of them to overpower the police, begin by rioting, and end by plundering and burning rich men's houses, upsetting the government, and destroying civilization. And the women, sooner than see their children starve, will make the men do it, small blame to them.

Consequently the capitalists, when they have sent their capital abroad instead of giving continuous employment with it at home, and are confronted at home with masses of desperate men for whom they can find no suitable jobs, must either feed them for nothing or face a revolution. And so you get what we call the dole. Now small as the dole may be it must be sufficient to live on; and if two or three in one household put their doles together, they grow less keen on finding employment, and develop a taste for living like ladies and gentlemen: that is, amusing themselves at the expense of others instead of earning anything. We used to moralize over this sort of thing as part of the decline and fall of ancient Rome; but we have been heading straight for it ourselves for a long while past, and the war has plunged us into it head over ears. For it was after the war that the capitalists failed to find employment for no less than two million demobilized soldiers who had for four years been not only well fed and clothed, but trained in the handling of weapons whilst occupied in slaughtering, burning, destroying, and facing terrible risks of being themselves destroyed. If these men had not been given money to live on they would have taken it by violence. Accordingly the Government had to take millions of spare money from the capitalists and give it to the demobilized men; and they are still doing so, with the grudged consent of the capitalists themselves, who complain bitterly, but fear that if they refuse they will lose everything.

At this point Capitalism becomes desperate, and quite openly engages in attempts to get rid of the unemployed: that is, to empty the country of part of its population, which it calls over-population. How is it to be done? As the unemployed will not let themselves be starved, still less will they let themselves be gassed or poisoned or shot, which would be the logical Capitalist way out of the mess. But they can perhaps be induced to leave the country and try their luck elsewhere if the Government will pay the fare, or as much of it as they cannot scrape up themselves. As I write these lines the Government announces that if any Englishwoman or Englishman will be so kind as to clear out of England to the other side of the world it will cost them only three pounds apiece instead of five times that sum, as the Government will provide the odd twelve pounds. And if sufficient numbers do not jump at this offer before these lines are printed, the Government may be driven to offer to send them away for nothing and give them ten pounds apiece to start with in their new country. That would be cheaper than keeping them at home on the dole.

Thus we see Capitalism producing the amazing and fantastic result that the people of the country become a drawback to it, and have to be got rid of like vermin (polite people call the process Assisted Emigration), leaving nobody in it but capitalists and landlords and their attendants, living on imported food and manufactures in an elegant manner, and realizing the lady's and gentleman's dream of a country in which there is lavish consumption and no production, stately parks and palatial residences without factories or mines or smoke or slums or any unpleasantness that heaps of gratuitous money can prevent, and contraception in full swing to avoid any further increase in the population.

Surely, you will say, if Capitalism leads to this, it leads to an earthly paradise. Leaving out of account the question whether the paradise, if realized, would not be a fool's paradise (for, I am sorry to say, we have all been brought up to regard such a state of things as the perfection of human society), and admitting that something like it has been half realized in spots in many places from Monte Carlo to Gleneagles, and from Gleneagles to Palm Beach, it is never realized for a whole country. It has often been carried far enough to reduce powerful empires like Rome and

Spain to a state of demoralized impotence in which they were broken up and plundered by the foreigners on whom they had allowed themselves to become dependent; but it never has, and never can, build up a stable Parasitic State in which all the workers are happy and contented because they share the riches of the capitalists, and are kept healthy and pleasant and nice because the capitalists are cultivated enough to dislike seeing slums and shabby ugly people and running the risk of catching infectious diseases from them. When capitalists are intelligent enough to care whether the whole community is healthy and pleasant and happy or not, even when the unpleasantnesses do not come under their own noses, they become Socialists, for the excellent reason that there is no fun in being a capitalist if you have to take care of your servants and tradesmen (which means sharing your income with them) as affectionately as if they were your own family. If your taste and conscience were cultivated to that extent you would find such a responsibility unbearable, because you would have to be continually thinking of others, not only to the necessary and possible extent of taking care that your own activities and conveniences did not clash unreasonably and unkindly with theirs, but to the unnecessary and impossible extent of doing all the thinking for them that they ought to do, and in freedom could do, for themselves. It is easy to say that servants should be treated well not only because humanity requires it but because they will otherwise be unpleasant and dishonest and inefficient servants. But if you treat your servants as well as you treat yourself, which really amounts to spending as much money on them as on yourself, what is the use of having servants? They become a positive burden, expecting you to be a sort of Earthly Providence to them, which means that you spend half your time thinking for them and the other half talking about them. Being able to call your servants your own is a very poor compensation for not being able to call your soul your own. That is why, even as it is, you run away from your comfortable house to live in hotels (if you can afford it), because, when you have paid your bill and tipped the waiter and the chambermaid, you are finished with them, and have not to be a sort of matriarch to them as well.

Anyhow, most of those who are ministering to your wants are

not in personal contact with you. They are the employees of your tradesmen; and as your tradesmen trade capitalistically, you have inequality of income, unemployment, sweating, division of society into classes, with the resultant dysgenic restrictions on marriage, and all the other evils which prevent a capitalist society from achieving peace or permanence. A self-contained, self-supporting Capitalism would at least be safe from being starved out as Germany was in the war in spite of her military successes; but a completely parasitic Capitalism, however fashionable, would be simply Capitalism with that peril intensified to the utmost.

39

FOREIGN TRADE AND THE FLAG

NOW let us turn back to inquire whether sending our capital abroad, and consenting to be taxed to pay emigration fares to get rid of the women and men who are left without employment in consequence, is all that Capitalism can do when our employers, who act for our capitalists in industrial affairs, and are more or less capitalists themselves in the earlier stages of capitalistic development, find that they can sell no more of their goods at a profit, or indeed at all, in their own country.

Clearly they cannot send abroad the capital they have already invested, because it has all been eaten up by the workers, leaving in its place factories and railways and mines and the like; and these cannot be packed into a ship's hold and sent to Africa. It is only the freshly saved capital that can be sent out of the country. This, as we have seen, does go abroad in heaps. But the British employer who is working with capital in the shape of works fixed to British land held by him on long lease, must, when once he has sold all the goods at home that his British customers can afford to buy, either shut up his works until the customers have worn out their stock of what they have bought, which would bankrupt him (for the landlord will not wait), or else sell his superfluous goods somewhere else: that is, he must send them abroad.

Now it is not so easy to send them to civilized countries, because they practise Protection, which means that they impose heavy taxes (customs duties) on foreign goods. Uncivilized countries, without Protection, and inhabited by natives to whom gaudy calicoes and cheap showy brass ware are dazzling and delightful novelties, are the best places to make for at first.

But trade requires a settled government to put down the habit of plundering strangers. This is not a habit of simple tribes, who are often friendly and honest. It is what civilized men do where there is no law to restrain them. Until quite recent times it was extremely dangerous to be wrecked on our own coasts, as wrecking, which meant plundering wrecked ships and refraining from any officious efforts to save the lives of their crews, was a well-established business in many places on our shores. The Chinese still remember some astonishing outbursts of looting perpetrated by English ladies of high position, at moments when law was suspended and priceless works of art were to be had for the grabbing. When trading with aborigines begins with the visit of a single ship, the cannons and cutlasses it carries may be quite sufficient to overawe the natives if they are troublesome. The real difficulty begins when so many ships come that a little trading station of white men grows up and attracts the white ne'er-do-wells and violent roughs who are always being squeezed out of civilization by the pressure of law and order. It is these riffraff who turn the place into a sort of hell in which sooner or later missionaries are murdered and traders plundered. Their home Governments are appealed to to put a stop to this. A gunboat is sent out and an inquiry made. The report after the inquiry is that there is nothing to be done but set up a civilized government, with a post office, police, troops, and a navy in the offing. In short, the place is added to some civilized Empire. And the civilized taxpayer pays the bill without getting a farthing of the profits.

Of course the business does not stop there. The riffraff who have created the emergency move out just beyond the boundary of the annexed territory, and are as great a nuisance as ever to the traders when they have exhausted the purchasing power of the included natives and push on after fresh customers. Again they call on their home Government to civilize a further area; and so bit by bit the civilized Empire grows at the expense of the home taxpayers, without any intention or approval on their part, until at last, though all their real patriotism is centred on their own people and confined to their own country, their own rulers, and their own religious faith, they find that the centre of their beloved realm has shifted to the other hemisphere. That is how we in the British Islands have found our centre moved from London to the Suez Canal, and are now in the position that out of every hundred of our fellow-subjects, in whose defence we are expected to shed the last drop of our blood, only eleven are whites or even Christians. In our bwilderment some of us declare that the Empire is a burden and a blunder, whilst others glory in it as a triumph. You and I need not argue with them just now, our point for the moment being that, whether blunder or glory, the British Empire was quite unintentional. What should have been undertaken only as a most carefully considered political development has been a series of commercial adventures thrust on us by capitalists forced by their own system to cater for foreign customers before their own country's needs were one-tenth satisfied.

40
EMPIRES IN COLLISION

IF the British Empire were the only State on earth, the process might go on peacefully (except for ordinary police coercion) until the whole earth was civilized under the British flag. This is the dream of British Imperialism. But it is not what the world is like. There are all the other States, large and small, with their Imperialist dreamers and their very practical traders pushing for foreign markets, and their navies and armies to back the traders and annex these markets. Sooner or later, as they push their boundaries into Africa and Asia, they come up against oneanother. A collision of that kind (called the Fashoda incident) very nearly involved us in a war with France. Fortunately France gave way, not being prepared to fight us just then; but France and Britain were left with the whole Sudan divided between them. France had before this pushed into and annexed Algeria and (virtually) Tunisia; and Spain was pushing into Morocco. Italy, alarmed lest there should be nothing left for her, made a dash at Tripoli and annexed it. England was in Egypt as well as in India.

Now imagine yourself for a moment a German trader, with

more goods than you can sell in Germany, having either to shut up your factory and be ruined, or find a foreign market in Africa. Imagine yourself looking at the map of Africa. The entire Mediterranean coast, the pick of the basket, is English, Italian, French, and Spanish. The Hinterland, as you call it, is English and French. You cannot get in anywhere without going through the English Suez Canal or round the Cape to some remote place down south. Do you now understand what the German Kaiser meant when he complained that Germany had not been left "a place in the sun"? That hideous war of 1914-18 was at bottom a fight between the capitalists of England, France, and Italy on the one side, and those of Germany on the other, for command of the African markets. On top, of course, it was about other things: about Austria making the murder of the Archduke a pretext for subjugating Serbia; about Russia mobilizing against Austria to prevent this; about Germany being dragged into the Austro-Russian quarrel by her alliance with Austria; about France being dragged in on the other side by her alliance with Russia; about the German army having to make a desperate attempt to conquer the French army before the Russian troops could reach her; about England having to attack Germany because she was allied to France and Russia; and about the German army having taken the shortest cut through Belgium, not knowing that Belgium had a secret arrangement with England to have a British expedition sent to defend her if Germany invaded her. Of course the moment the first shot was fired all the Britons and Belgians and Germans and French and Austrians and Russians became enraged sheep, and imagined all sorts of romantic reasons for fighting, in addition to the solid reason that if Tommy and the Poilu and Ivan did not kill Hans and Fritz, Hans and Fritz would kill Tommy and the Poilu and Ivan. Before the killing had gone on very long, the Turks, the Bulgarians, the Japanese, the Americans, and other States that had no more to do with the first quarrel than you had, were in it and at it hammer and tongs. The whole world went mad, and never alluded to markets except when they ridiculed the Kaiser for his demand for a place in the sun.

Yet there would have been no war without the alliances; and the alliances could not have fought if they had not set up great armaments, especially the new German navy, to protect their foreign markets and frontiers. These armaments, created to produce a sense of security, had produced a sense of terror in which no nation dared go unarmed unless it was too small to have any chance against the great Powers, and could depend on their jealousy of oneanother to stave off a conquest by any one of them. Soon the nations that dared not go unarmed became more terrified still, and dared not go alone: they had to form alliances and go in twos and threes, like policemen in thieves' quarters, Germany and Austria in one group and England, France, and Russia in another, both trying to induce Italy and Turkey and America to join them. Their differences were not about their own countries: the German navy was not built to bombard Portsmouth nor the British navy to bombard Bremerhaven. But when the German navy interfered in the north of Africa, which was just what it was built for, and the French and British navies frightened it off from that market in the sun, the capitalist diplomatists of these nations saw that the first thing to concentrate on was not the markets but the sinking of the German navy by the combined French and British navies (or vice versa) on any available pretext. And as you cannot have fleets fighting on the sea without armies fighting on the land to help them, the armies grew like the fleets; the Race of Armaments became as familiar as the Derby; all the natural and kindly sentiments of white civilized nations towards oneanother were changed into blustering terror, the parent of hatred, malice, and all uncharitableness; and after all, when the explosive mixture blew up at last, and blew millions of us with it, it was not about the African markets, but about a comparatively trumpery quarrel between Austria and Serbia which the other Powers could have settled with the greatest ease, without the shedding of one drop of blood, if they had been on decent human terms with oneanother instead of on competitive capitalistic terms.

And please do not fail to note that whereas in the early days of Capitalism our capitalists did not compel us to fight for their markets with our own hands, but hired German serfs and British voluntary professional soldiers for the job, their wars have now become so colossal that every woman's husband, father, son, brother, or sweetheart, if young and strong enough to carry a rifle, must go to the trenches as helplessly as cattle go to the slaughterhouse, abandoning wife and children, home and business, and renouncing normal morality and humanity, pretending all the time that such conduct is splendid and heroic and that his name will live for ever, though he may have the greatest horror of war, and be perfectly aware that the enemy's soldiers, against whom he is defending his hearth, are in exactly the same predicament as himself, and would never dream of injuring him or his if the pressure of the drive for markets were removed from both.

I have purposely brought you to the question of war because your conscience must be sorely troubled about it. You have seen the men of Europe rise up and slaughter oneanother in the most horrible manner in millions. Your son, perhaps, has received a military cross for venturing into the air in a flying machine and dropping a bomb on a sleeping village, blowing several children into fragments, and mutilating or killing their parents. From a militarist, nationalist, or selfishly patriotic point of view such deeds may appear glorious exploits; but from the point of view of any universally valid morality: say from the point of view of a God who is the father of Englishmen and Germans, Frenchmen and Turks alike, they must seem outbursts of the most infernal wickedness. As such they have caused many of us to despair of human nature. A bitter cynicism has succeeded to transports of pugnacious hatred of which all but the incorrigibly thoughtless, and a few incurables who have been mentally disabled for life by the war fever, are now heartily ashamed. I can hardly believe that you have escaped your share of this crushing disillusion. If you are human as well as intelligent you must feel about your species very much as the King of Brobdingnag did when he took Gulliver in his hand as a child takes a tin soldier, and heard his boastful patriotic discourse about the glories of military history.

Perhaps I can console you a little. If you will look at the business in the light of what we have just been studying I think you will see that the fault lay not so much in our characters as in the capitalist system which we had allowed to dominate our lives until it became a sort of blind monster which neither we nor the capitalists could control. It is absurd to pretend that the young men of Europe ever wanted to hunt each other into holes in the ground and throw bombs into the holes to disembowel oneanother, or to have to hide in those holes themselves, eaten with lice and sickened by the decay of the unburied, in unutterable discomfort, boredom, and occasionally acute terror, or that any woman ever wanted to put on her best Sunday clothes and be gratified at the honor done to her son for killing some other woman's babies. The capitalists and their papers try to persuade themselves and us that we are like that and always will be, in spite of all the Christmas cards and Leagues of Nations. It is not a bit true. The staggering fact about all these horrors was that we found ourselves compelled to do them in spite of the fact that they were so unintended by us, and so repugnant and dreadful to us that, when at last the war suddenly stopped, our heroic pretences dropped from us like blown-off hats, and we danced in the streets for weeks, mad with joy, until the police had to stop us to restore the necessary traffic. We still celebrate, by two minutes' national silence, not the day on which the glorious war broke out, but the day on which the horrible thing came to an end. Not the victory, which we have thrown away by abusing it as helplessly as we fought for it, but the Armistice, the Cessation, the stoppage of the Red Cross vans from the terminuses of the Channel railways with their heartbreaking loads of mutilated men, was what we danced for so wildly and pitifully. If ever there was anything made clear in the world it was that we were no more directly guilty of the war than we were guilty of the earthquake of Tokio. We and the French and the Germans and the Turks and the rest found ourselves conscripted for an appalling slaughtering match, ruinous to ourselves, ruinous to civilization, and so dreaded by the capitalists themselves that it was only by an extraordinary legal suspension of all financial obligations (called the Moratorium) that the City was induced to face it. The attempt to fight out the war with volunteers failed: there were not enough. The rest went because they were forced to go, and fought because they were forced to fight. The women let them go partly because they could not help themselves, partly because they were just as pugnacious as the men, partly because they read the papers (which were not allowed to tell them the truth), and partly because most of them were so poor that they grasped at the allowances which left most of them better off with their husbands in the trenches than they had ever been with their husbands at home.

How had they got into this position? Simply by the original sin of allowing their countries to be moved and governed and fed and clothed by the pursuit of profit for capitalists instead of by the pursuit of righteous prosperity for "all people that on earth do dwell". The first ship that went to Africa to sell things to the natives at more than cost price because there was no sale for them at home began not only this war, but the other and worse wars that will follow it if we persist in depending on Capitalism for our livelihood and our morals. All these monstrous evils begin in a small and apparently harmless way. It is not too much to say that when a nation, having five shillings to divide-up, gives four to Fanny and one to Sarah instead of giving half a crown to each and seeing that she earns it, it sows the seed of all the evils that now make thoughtful and farseeing men speak of our capitalistic civilization as a disease instead of a blessing.

41
THE SORCERER'S APPRENTICE

DO not, however, disparage foreign trade. There is nothing wrong with foreign trade as such. We could have no gold without foreign trade; and gold has all sorts of uses and all sorts of beauties. I will not add that we could have no tea, because I happen to think that we should be better without this insidious Chinese stimulant. It is safer and probably healthier for a nation to live on the food and drink it can itself produce, as the Esquimaux manage to do under much harder conditions. But there are many necessaries of a high civilization that nations cannot find within their own boundaries, and must buy from oneanother. We must trade and travel and come to know oneanother all over the habitable globe. We have to make international institutions as well as national ones, beginning with Trading Treaties and Postal Conventions and Copyright Conventions, and going on to the Leagues of Nations. The necessities of travelling and trade, and the common interest of all nations in the works and discoveries of art, literature, and science, have forced them to make international agreements and treaties with one-another which are making an end of "keeping ourselves to ourselves", and throwing half bricks at foreigners and strangers. Honest foreign trade would never have got us into trouble.

Neither is the combination of little States in great Federations and Commonwealths undesirable: on the contrary, the fewer frontiers the better. The establishment of law and order in uncivilized places should not have made us hated there: it should have made us popular; and it often did—at first. The annexation of other countries under our flag, when it was really needed, should have been a welcome privilege and a strengthening partnership for the inhabitants of the annexed regions. Indeed we have always pretended that this was actually the case, and that we were in foreign countries for the good of the inhabitants and not for our own sake. Unfortunately we never could make these pretensions good in the long run. However noble the aspirations of our Imperialist idealists might be, our capitalist traders were there to make as much profit out of the inhabitants as they could, and for no other purpose. They had abandoned their own country because there was no more profit to be made there, or not so much; and it is not to be expected that they would become idealistically disinterested the moment they landed on foreign shores. They stigmatized the Stay-at-homes, the anti-Expansionists, the Little-Englanders, as friends of every country but their own; but they themselves were the enemies of every country, including their own, where there was a sweatable laborer to make dividends for them. They pretended that the civilization of the annexed country was "the white man's burden", and posed as weary Titans reluctantly shouldering the public work of other nations as a duty imposed on them by Providence; but when the natives, having been duly civilized, declared that they were now quite ready to govern themselves, the capitalists held on to their markets as an eagle holds on to its prey, and, throwing off their apostolic mask, defended their annexations with fire and sword. They said they would fight to the last drop of their blood for "the integrity of the Empire"; and they did in fact pay many thousands of hungry men to fight to that extremity. In spite of them half of North America broke loose, after a war which left a volcano of hatred that is still smouldering and winning Chicago elections after a century of American independence. Roman Catholic Ireland, South Africa, and Egypt have extorted self-government from us. India is doing the same. But they do not thank us for it, knowing how loth our Capitalism was to let them go.

On the other hand look at Australia, New Zealand, and Canada. We did not dare coerce them after our failure in North America. We provide a costly fleet gratuitously to protect their shores from invasion. We give them preferences in trade whilst allowing them to set up heavy protective duties against us. We allow them to be represented at international congresses as if they were independent nations. We even allow them access to the King independently of the London Cabinet. The result is that they hang on to us with tyrannical devotion, waving the Union Jack as enthusiastically as the Americans wave the Stars and Stripes. And this is not because they are of our own race. The Americans were that; yet they broke away; so were the Irish and their leaders. The French Canadians, who are of the same race with us only in the sense that we all belong to the human race, cling to us just as hard. They all follow us to war so boldly that we begin to have misgivings as to whether someday they may not make us follow them to war. The last land to strike for independence of the British Empire may be Protestant England herself, with Ulster and Scotland for allies, and the Irish Free State heading her Imperialist opponents.

But Capitalism can be depended on to spoil all these reconciliations and loyalties. True, we no longer exploit colonies capitalistically: we allow them to do it for themselves, and to call the process self-government. Whilst we persisted in governing them they blamed us for all the evils Capitalism brought upon them; and they finally refused to endure our government. When we left them to govern themselves they became less and less hostile to us. But the change always impoverishes them, and leaves them in comparative disorder. The capitalistic evils for which they blamed us still oppress them. Their self-government is more tyrannical than our alien government ever dared to be. Their new relation to the Imperial State becomes more dangerously strained than the old relation, precisely as the relation of England to Germany was more dangerously strained in 1913 than the relation of England to Ireland. The most liberal allowance of self-government cannot reconcile people as long as their capitalists are competing for markets. Nationalism may make Frenchmen and Englishmen, Englishmen and Irishmen, savage enemies when it is infringed. Frenchmen and Irishmen laid their own countries waste to get rid of English rule. But Capitalism makes all men enemies all the time without distinction of race, color, or creed. When all the nations have freed themselves Capitalism will make them fight more furiously than ever, if we are fools enough to let it.

Have you ever seen the curiosity called a Prince Rupert's Drop? It is a bead of glass in such a state of internal strain that if you break off the tiniest corner the whole bead flies violently to bits. Europe was like that in 1914. A handful of people in Serbia committed a murder, and the next moment half Europe was murdering the other half. This frightful condition of internal strain and instability was not set up by human nature: it was, I repeat, intensely repugnant to human nature, being a condition of chronic terror that at last became unbearable, like that of a woman who commits suicide because she can no longer endure the dread of death. It was set up by Capitalism. Capitalism, you will say, is at bottom nothing but covetousness; and covetousness is human nature. That is true; but covetousness is not the whole of human nature; it is only a part, and one that vanishes when it is satisfied, like hunger after a meal, up to which point it is wholesome and necessary. Under Capitalism it becomes a dread of poverty and slavery, which are neither wholesome nor necessary. And, as we have just seen, capital is carried by its own nature beyond the control of both human covetousness and human conscience, marching on blindly and automatically, until we find on the one hand the masses of mankind condemned to poverty relieved only by horrible paroxysms of bloodshed, and on the other a handful of hypertrophied capitalists gasping under the load of their growing millions, and giving it away in heaps in a desperate attempt, partly to get rid of it without being locked up as madmen for throwing it into the sea, and partly to undo, by founding Rockefeller institutes and Carnegie libraries, and hospitals and universities and schools and churches, the effects of the welter of ignorance and poverty produced by the system under which it has accumulated on their hands. To call these unfortunate billionaires monsters of covetousness in the face of their wild disgorgings (to say nothing of their very ordinary portraits) is silly. They are rather to be compared to the sorcerer's apprentice who called up a demon to fetch a drink for him, and, not knowing the spell for stopping him when he had brought enough, was drowned in an ocean of wine.

42
HOW WEALTH ACCUMULATES AND MEN DECAY

I WANT to stress this personal helplessness we are all stricken with in the face of a system that has passed beyond our knowledge and control. To bring it nearer home, I propose that we switch off from the big things like empires and their wars to little familiar things. Take pins for example! I do not know why it is that I so seldom use a pin when my wife cannot get on without boxes of them at hand; but it is so; and I will therefore take pins as being for some reason specially important to women.

There was a time when pinmakers could buy the material; shape it; make the head and the point; ornament it; and take it to market or to your door and sell it to you. They had to know three trades: buying, making, and selling; and the making required skill in several operations. They not only knew how the thing was done from beginning to end, but could do it. But they could not afford to sell you a paper of pins for a farthing. Pins cost so much that a woman's dress allowance was called pin money.

By the end of the eighteenth century Adam Smith boasted that it took eighteen men to make a pin, each man doing a little bit of the job and passing the pin on to the next, and none of them being able to make a whole pin or to buy the materials or to sell it when it was made. The most you could say for them was that at least they had some idea of how it was made, though they could not make it. Now as this meant that they were clearly less capable and knowledgeable men than the old pinmakers, you may ask why Adam Smith boasted of it as a triumph of civilization when its effect was so clearly a degrading effect. The reason was that by setting each man to do just one little bit of the work and nothing but that, over and over again, he became very quick at it. The men, it is said, could turn out nearly five thousand pins a day each; and thus pins became plentiful and cheap. The country was supposed to be richer because it had more pins, though it had turned capable men into mere machines doing their work without intelligence, and being fed by the spare food of the capitalist as an engine is fed with coals and oil. That was why the poet Goldsmith, who was a farsighted economist as well as a poet, complained that "wealth accumulates, and men decay".

Nowadays Adam Smith's eighteen men are as extinct as the diplodocus. The eighteen flesh-and-blood machines are replaced by machines of steel which spout out pins by the hundred million. Even sticking them into pink papers is done by machinery. The result is that with the exception of a few people who design the machines, nobody knows how to make a pin or how a pin is made: that is to say, the modern worker in pin manufacture need not be one-tenth so intelligent and skilful and accomplished as the old pinmaker; and the only compensation we have for this deterioration is that pins are so cheap that a single pin has no expressible value at all. Even with a big profit stuck on to the cost-price you can buy dozens for a farthing; and pins are so recklessly thrown away and wasted that verses have to be written to persuade children (without success) that it is a sin to steal a pin.

Many serious thinkers, like John Ruskin and William Morris, have been greatly troubled by this, just as Goldsmith was, and have asked whether we really believe that it is an advance in wealth to lose our skill and degrade our workers for the sake of being able to waste pins by the ton. We shall see later on, when we come to consider the Distribution of Leisure, that the cure for this is not to go back to the old ways; for if the saving of time by modern machinery were equally divided among us, it would set us all free for higher work than pinmaking or the like. But in the meantime the fact remains that pins are now made by men and women who cannot make anything by themselves, and could not arrange between themselves to make anything even in little bits. They are ignorant and helpless, and cannot lift their finger to begin their day's work until it has all been arranged for them by their employers, who themselves do not understand the machines they buy, and simply pay other people to set them going by carrying out the machine maker's directions.

The same is true of clothes. Formerly the whole work of making clothes, from the shearing of the sheep to the turning out of the finished and washed garment ready to put on, had to be done in the country by the men and women of the household, especially the women; so that to this day an unmarried woman is called a spinster. Nowadays nothing is left of all this but the sheep-shearing; and even that, like the milking of cows, is being done by machinery, as the sewing is. Give a woman a sheep today and ask her to produce a woollen dress for you; and not only will she be quite unable to do it, but you are as likely as not to find that she is not even aware of any connection between sheep and clothes. When she gets her clothes, which she does by buying them at a shop, she knows that there is a difference between wool and cotton and silk, between flannel and merino, perhaps even between stockinet and other wefts; but as to how they are made, or what they are made of, or how they came to be in the shop ready for her to buy, she knows hardly anything. And the shop assistant from whom she buys is no wiser. The people engaged in the making of them know even less; for many of them are too poor to have much choice of materials when they buy their own clothes.

Thus the capitalist system has produced an almost universal ignorance of how things are made and done, whilst at the same time it has caused them to be made and done on a gigantic scale. We have to buy books and encyclopedias to find out what it is we are doing all day; and as the books are written by people who are not doing it, and who get their information from other books, what they tell us is from twenty to fifty years out of date, and unpractical at that. And of course most of us are too tired of our work when we come home to want to read about it: what we need is a cinema to take our minds off it and feed our imagination.

It is a funny place, this world of Capitalism, with its astonishing spread of ignorance and helplessness, boasting all the time of its spread of education and enlightenment. There stand the thousands of property owners and the millions of wage workers, none of them able to make anything, none of them knowing what to do until somebody tells them, none of them having the least notion of how it is that they find people paying them money, and things in the shops to buy with it. And when they travel they are surprised to find that savages and Esquimaux and villagers who have to make everything for themselves are more intelligent and resourceful! The wonder would be if they were anything else. We should die of idiocy through disuse of our mental faculties if we did not fill our heads with romantic nonsense out of illustrated newspapers and novels and plays and films. Such stuff keeps us alive; but it falsifies everything for us so absurdly that it leaves us more or less dangerous lunatics in the real world.

Excuse my going on like this; but as I am a writer of books and plays myself, I know the folly and peril of it better than you do. And when I see that this moment of our utmost ignorance and helplessness, delusion and folly, has been stumbled on by the blind forces of Capitalism as the moment for giving votes to everybody, so that the few wise women are hopelessly overruled by the thousands whose political minds, as far as they can be said to have any political minds at all, have been formed in the cinema, I realize that I had better stop writing plays for a while to discuss political and social realities in this book with those who are intelligent enough to listen to me.

43
DISABLEMENT ABOVE AND BELOW

YOU must not conclude from what I have just said that I grudge the people their amusements. I have made most of my money by amusing them. I recognize more clearly than most people that not only does all work and no play make Jill a dull girl, but that she works so that she may be able to enjoy life as well as to keep herself from dying of hunger and exposure. She wants, and needs, leisure as well as wages. But breadwinning must come before charabancs and cinemas. I have the strongest sympathy, as I daresay you have, with the French gentleman who said that if he could have the luxuries of life he could do without the necessities; but unfortunately Nature does not share our sympathy, and ruthlessly puts breadwinning first on pain of death. The French gentleman is less important than the women who are asking for an eight-hour working day, because, though what they are really asking for is for a few hours more leisure when they have rested and slept, cooked and fed and washed up, yet they know that leisure must be worked for, and that no woman can shirk her share of the work except by putting it on some other woman and cutting short *her* leisure.

Therefore when I say that Capitalism has reduced our people to a condition of abject helplessness and ignorance in their productive capacity as workers, you cannot reassure me by pointing out that factory girls are no fools when it comes to gossiping and amusing themselves; that they are resourceful enough to learn lip reading in the weaving-sheds, where the banging of the looms makes it impossible to hear each other speak; that their dances and charabanc excursions and whist drives and dressing and wireless concerts stimulate and cultivate them to an extent unknown to their grandmothers; that they consume frightful quantities of confectionery; and that they limit their families to avoid too much mothering. But all this is consumption, not production. When they are engaged in producing these amusements: when they take the money for the tickets at the pay-boxes, or do some scrap of the work of making a charabanc, or wind the wire on a coil for broadcasting, they are mere machines, taking part in a routine without knowing what came before or what is to follow.

In giving all the work to one class and all the leisure to another as far as the law will let it, the Capitalist system disables the rich as completely as the poor. By letting their land and hiring out their spare money (capital) to others, they can have plenty of food and fun without lifting their little fingers. Their agents collect the rent for the land, and lodge it in the bank for them. The companies which have hired their spare money lodge the half-yearly hire (dividends) in the same way. Bismarck said of them that they had only to take a pair of scissors and cut off a coupon; but he was wrong: the bank does even that for them; so that all they have to do is to sign the cheques with which they pay for everything. They need do nothing but amuse themselves; and they would get their incomes just the same if they did not do even that. They can only plead that their ancestors worked productively, as if everybody's ancestors had not worked productively, or as if this were any excuse for their not following their ancestors' excellent example. We cannot live on the virtues of our grandmothers. They may have farmed their own land, and invented the ways in which their spare money was applied to the land to make them richer; but when their successors found that all this trouble would be taken for them by others, they simply let the land and put out their spare money for hire (invested it).

Some of our great landholders inherit their land from feudal times, when there were no factories nor railways, and when towns were so small that they were walled in as gardens are now. In those days the landholders, with the king at their head, had to raise armies and defend the country at their own cost. They had to make the laws and administer them, doing military work, police work, and government work of all sorts. Henry IV, who died of overwork, found to his cost how true it was in those days that the greatest among us must be servant to all the rest. Nowadays it is the other way about: the greatest is she to whom all the rest are servants. All the chores and duties of the feudal barons are done by paid officials. In country places they may still sit on the Bench as unpaid magistrates; and there remains the tradition that military service as officers is proper for their sons. A few of them, with the help of solicitors and agents, manage the estates on which they actually live, or allow their wives to do it. But these are only vestiges of a bygone order, maintained mostly by rich purchasers of estates who are willing to take a little trouble to be ranked as country gentlemen and county ladies. There are always newly enriched folk who have this vanity for a while, and will buy the estate of a real country gentleman to take on his position in the country. But at any moment our landed gentry, whether they are so by descent or purchase, can sell their country houses and parks, and live anywhere they please in the civilized world without any public duties or responsibilities. Sooner or later they all do so, thus breaking the only link that binds them to the old feudal aristocracy save their names and titles. For all the purposes of the real world of today there is no longer a feudal aristocracy: it is merged in the industrial capitalist class, with which it associates and intermarries without distinction, money making up for everything. If it be still necessary to call the rich an ocracy of any kind, they must be called a plutocracy, in which the oldest ducal estate and the newest fortune made in business are only forms of capital, imposing no public duties on the owner.

Now this state of things may seem extremely jolly for the plutocracy from the point of view of those who are so overworked and underamused that they can imagine nothing better than a life that is one long holiday; but it has the disadvantage of making the plutocrats as helpless as babies when they are left to earn their own living. You know that there is nothing more pitiable on earth within the limits of good health than born ladies and gentlemen suddenly losing their property. But have you considered that they would be equally pitiable if their property were thrown on their own hands to make what they could of it? They would not know how to farm their lands or to work their mines and railways or to sail their ships. They would perish surrounded by what Dr Johnson called "the potentiality of growing rich beyond the dreams of avarice". Without the hungry they would have to say "I cannot dig: to beg (even if I knew how) I am ashamed". The hungry could do without them, and be very much the better for it; but they could not do without the hungry.

Yet most of the hungry, left to themselves, would be quite as helpless as the plutocrats. Take the case of a housemaid, familiar to the intelligent lady who can afford to keep one. A woman may be a very good housemaid; but you have to provide the house for her and manage the house before she can set to work. Many excellent housemaids, when they marry, make a poor enough job of their own housekeeping. Ask them to manage a big hotel, which employs dozens of housemaids, and they will think you are laughing at them: you might as well ask the porter at the Bank of England to manage the bank. A bricklayer may be a very good bricklayer; but he cannot build a house nor even make the bricks he lays. Any laborer can lay a plank across a stream, or place a row of stepping-stones in it; but just ask him to build a bridge, whether it be the simplest sort of canal bridge or a gigantic construction like the Forth Bridge! You might as well ask your baby to make its cot and knit its jumper, or your cook to design and construct a kitchen range and water supply.

This helplessness gets more and more complete as civilization advances. In villages you may still find carpenters and blacksmiths who can make things. They can even choose and buy their materials, and then sell the finished article. But in the cities on which our existence now depends you find multitudes of workers and plutocrats who cannot make anything; do not know how anything is made; and are so inept at buying and selling that without fixed-price-shops they would perish.

44
THE MIDDLE STATION IN LIFE

AND now, if the landlords and capitalists can neither make anything nor even tell others how to make it; and if the workers can do nothing until they are told what to do, how does the world get on? There must be some third class standing between the propertied class on the one hand and the propertyless class on the other, to lease the land and hire the capital and tell the workers what to do with them.

There is. You can see for yourself that there is a middle class which does all the managing and directing and deciding work of the nation, besides carrying on the learned and literary and artistic professions. Let us consider how this class arose, and how it is continually recruited from the capitalist families.

The capitalists do something more than merely own. They marry and have children. Now an income which is comfortable for two people may not be enough for three or four children in addition, to say nothing of possibly twice or thrice that number. And when the three or four children grow up and marry and have three or four children each, what meant riches for the grandparents may mean poverty for the grandchildren.

To avoid this, propertied families may arrange that only the eldest son shall inherit the property, leaving the younger sons to shift for themselves, and the daughters to marry men of property if they can. This is called primogeniture. Until 1926 it was the law of the land in England when the owner of a landed estate died without leaving a will to the contrary. Where there is no such law, and all the children inherit equal shares of the parents' property, as they do among the peasant proprietors in France, the family must come to an arrangement of the same kind between themselves, or else sell the property and leave its owners with a few pounds each that will not last them very long. Therefore they almost always do agree that the younger children shall live by working like the hungry, whilst the eldest keeps the farm and cultivates it. This cannot be done when the property is not land but capital, and all the members of the family are living on the interest of hired out spare money. Parents may make wills leaving all of it or most of it to one son; but they do not do this as a rule; and sooner or later the property gets divided and divided among children and other next-of-kin until the inheritors cannot live on their shares.

But please remark that the younger sons who are thus thrown on the world to earn their living have the tastes and habits and speech and appearance and education of rich men. They are well connected, as we say. Their near relations may be peers. Some of them have been schooled at Eton and Harrow, and have taken degrees at Oxford and Cambridge. Others have less distinguished connections. Their parents or grandparents may have made money in business; and they may have gone to the big city schools, or to day schools, instead of to Eton, and either to one of the new democratic universities or to no university at all. Their most important relative may be a mayor or alderman. But they are educated at secondary as distinguished from elementary schools; and though not what they themselves call great swells, they have the manners and appearance and speech and habits of the capitalist class, are described as gentlemen, and politely addressed by letter as Esquires instead of plain Misters.

All these propertyless people who have the ways and the culture of propertied ones have to live by their wits. They go into the army and navy as officers, or into the upper grades of the civil service. They become clergymen, doctors, lawyers, authors, actors, painters, sculptors, architects, schoolmasters, university professors, astronomers and the like, forming what we call the professional class. They are treated with special respect socially; but they see successful men of business, inferior to themselves in knowledge, talent, character, and public spirit, making much larger incomes. The highest sorts of mental work are often so unremunerative that it is impossible to make a living by practising them commercially. Spinoza lived by grinding lenses, and

Rousseau by copying music. Einstein lives by professorships. Newton lived, not by discovering gravitation and measuring fluxions, but by acting as Master of the Mint, which other men could have done as well. Even when a profession is comparatively lucrative and popular, its gains are restricted by the fact that the work must all be done by the practitioner's own hand; for a surgeon cannot employ a thousand subordinates to deal with a million patients as a soap king deals with a million customers, nor the President of the Royal Academy hand over a two thousand guinea portrait sitter to his secretary. The years of professional success are usually preceded by a long struggle with scanty means. I myself am held to be a conspicuous example of success in the most lucrative branch of the literary profession; but until I was thirty I could not make even a bare living by my pen. At thirty-eight I thought myself passing rich on six or seven pounds a week; and even now, when I am seventy, and have achieved all that can be achieved commercially at my job, I see in the paper every day, under the heading Wills and Bequests, that the widow of some successful man of business, wholly unknown to fame, has died leaving a fortune which reduces my gains to insignificance.

The consequence is that professional men and civil servants, when they are not incurable old-fashioned snobs who regard trade as beneath the dignity of their family, and when their sons have no overwhelming aptitude for one or other of the professions, advise them strongly to go in for business. The man of business may not have much chance of a public statue unless he pays for it and presents it to his native town with a spacious public park attached; and his occupation may be a dry one in itself, however exciting the prospect of pocketing more and more money may make it. But he can make profits not only out of his work, like the surgeon or painter, but out of the work of thousands of others as well. And his work is not necessarily dry: modern businesses tend to become more interesting and important, and even more scientific, than average professional work. Their activities are much more varied: in fact modern commercial magnates, when they control a dozen different businesses, become better informed and better developed mentally than the rank and file of the professions. What is more, they are learning to snap up the ablest university scholars and civil servants, and take them into partnership not as office managers but as thinkers, diplomatists, and commercial scientists. It is in industrially undeveloped countries that professional men rank as an aristocracy of learning and intellect: in European centres today commercial society is a more effective reserve of culture than professional society. When the professional man or the public servant tells his son that a berth in the civil service is a blind alley, or doctoring at the call of the night bell a dog's life, contrasting them with the unlimited prospects and the infinite scope for personal initiative in business, he is recommending the young man to improve on his father's condition instead of starting him on the downward path socially.

And what is business in the lump? It is hiring land from landlords and spare money from capitalists, and employing the hungry to make enough money out of them day by day to pay the wages for their keep and bring in a profit as well. Astonishing fortunes can be made in this way by men and women with the necessary ability and decision who have the particular sort of pecuniary keenness and pertinacity that business requires. Even more staggering profits are made sometimes by accident, the business man hitting by chance on something new that the public happens to fancy. Millions are made by medicines which injure people's health instead of improving it (read Tono-Bungay), and hair restorers that leave the buyer as bald as before. Articles that nobody needs, and sham pleasures that give only fatigue and boredom at extravagant prices, are advertized and advertized until people are beglamored into thinking they cannot do without them.

But the main scope in business is for honorable and useful activity, from growing food and building houses and making clothes, or manufacturing spades and sewing-machines, to laying cables round the world, and building giant ships to turn the ocean or the air into a highway. The planning and management and ordering of this gives employment to able and energetic men who have no property, but have the education and social address of the propertied class. The educated who are neither able nor energetic, and who have no professions, find employment as agents or clerks carrying out the routine and keeping the accounts of businesses which the able ones have established and are directing.

And the women of their class are forced to live by marrying them.

In this way we get, between the propertied class and the hungry mass, a middle class which acts as a sort of Providence to both of them. It cultivates the land and employs the capital of the property holders, paying them the rent of their lands and the hire of their spare money without asking them to lift a finger, and giving the hungry wages to live on without asking them to think or decide or know or do anything except their own little bit of the job in hand. The hungry have neither to buy the material nor to sell the product, neither to organize the service nor find the customer. Like children they are told what to do, and fed and lodged and clothed whilst they are doing it, not always very handsomely perhaps; but at worst they are kept alive long enough to produce a fresh set of hungry ones to replace them when they are worn out.

There are always a few cases in which this management is done, not by descendants of propertied folk, but by men and women sprung from the hungriest of the hungry. These are the geniuses who know most of the things that other people have to be taught, and who educate themselves as far as they need any education. But there are so few of them that they need not be taken into account. In great social questions we are dealing with the abilities of ordinary citizens: that is, the abilities we can depend on everyone except invalids and idiots possessing, and not with what one man or woman in ten thousand can do. In spite of several cases in which persons born in poverty and ignorance have risen to make vast fortunes, to become famous as philosophers, discoverers, authors, and even rulers of kingdoms, to say nothing of saints and martyrs, we may take it that business and the professions are closed to those who cannot read and write, travel and keep accounts, besides dressing, speaking, behaving, and handling and spending money more or less in the manner of the propertied classes.

This is another way of saying that until about fifty years ago the great mass of our people working for weekly wages were as completely shut out from the professions and from business as if there had been a law forbidding them on pain of death to attempt to enter them. I remember wondering when I was a lad at a man who was in my father's employment as a miller. He could neither read nor write nor cipher (that is, do sums on paper); but his natural faculty for calculation was so great that he could solve instantly all the arithmetical problems that arose in the course of his work: for instance, if it were a question of so many sacks of flour at so much a sack, he could tell you the answer straight off without thinking, which was more than my father or his clerks could do. But because he did not know his alphabet, and could not put pen to paper, and had not the speech and manners and habits and dress without which he would not have been admitted into the company of merchants and manufacturers, or of lawyers, doctors, and clergymen, he lived and died a poor employee, without the slightest chance of rising into the middle class, or the faintest pretension to social equality with my father. And my father, though he was propertyless, and worked as a middle class civil servant and subsequently as a merchant, was not at all proud of being a member of the middle class: on the contrary, he resented that description, holding on to his connexion with the propertied class as a younger son of many former younger sons, and therefore, though unfortunately reduced to living not very successfully by his wits, a man of family and a gentleman.

But this was sixty years ago. Since then we have established Communism in education. If my father's miller were a boy now, he would go to school for nine years, whether his parents liked it or not, at the expense of the whole community; and his mathematical gift would enable him to win a scholarship that would take him on to a secondary school, and another scholarship there that would take him to the university and qualify him for a profession. At the very least he would become an accountant, even were it only as a bookkeeper or clerk. In any case he would be qualified for middle class employment and pass into that class.

Now the social significance of this is that the middle class, which the younger sons and their descendants formerly had all to themselves as far as the most desirable positions in it were concerned, is now recruited from the working class as well. These recruits, with no gentlemanly nonsense about them, are not only better taught than the boys who go to cheapish middle class schools, but better trained to face the realities of life. Also the old differences in speech and dress and manners are much less than they were, partly because the working class is picking up middle class manners, but much more because they are forcing their own manners and speech on the middle class as standards. A man like my father, half a merchant, but ashamed of it and unable to make up his mind to it, and half a gentleman without any property to uphold his pretension, would, if he were a boy nowadays, be beaten hollow in the competition for land, for capital, and for position in the civil service by the sons of men whose grandfathers would never have dreamed of presuming to sit down in his presence. The futile propertyless gentlemen, the unserviceable and grossly insolent civil servants whom Dickens described, have to be content nowadays with the refuse of middle class employment. They are discontented, unhappy, impecunious, struggling with a false position, borrowing (really begging) from their relatives, and unable to realize, or unwilling to admit, that they have fallen out of the propertied class, not into an intermediate position where they have a monopoly of all the occupations and employments that require a little education and manners, but right down into the ranks of the hungry, without the hardening that makes the hungry life bearable.

And what of the daughters? Their business is to get married; and I can remember the time when there was no other hopeful opening in life for them. When they failed to find husbands, and no special provision had been made for them, they became governesses or school teachers or "companions" or genteel beggars under the general heading of poor relations. They had been carefully trained to feel that it was unladylike to work, and still more unladylike to propose marriage to men. The professions were closed to them. The universities were closed to them. The business offices were closed to them. Their poverty cut them off from propertied society. Their ladylikeness cut them off from the society of working people as poor as themselves, and from intermarriage with them. Life was a ghastly business for them.

Nowadays, there are far more careers open to women. We have women barristers and women doctors in practice. True, the Church is closed against them, to its own great detriment, as it could easily find picked women, eloquent in the pulpit and capable in parish management, to replace the male refuse it has too often to fall back on; but women can do without ecclesiastical careers now that the secular and civil services are open. The closing of the fighting services is socially necessary, as women are far too valuable to have their lives risked in battle as well as in child-bearing. If ninety out of every hundred young men were killed we could recover from the loss, but if ninety out of every hundred young women were killed there would be an end of the nation. That is why modern war, which is not confined to battle fields, and rains high explosives and poison gas on male and female civilians indiscriminately in their peaceful homes, is so much more dangerous than war has ever been before.

Besides, women are now educated as men are: they go to the universities and to the technical colleges if they can afford it; and, as Domestic Service is now an educational subject with special colleges, a woman can get trained for such an occupation as that of manageress of a hotel as well as for the practice of law or medicine, or for accountancy and actuarial work. In short, nothing now blocks a woman's way into business or professional life except prejudice, superstition, old-fashioned parents, shyness, snobbery, ignorance of the contemporary world, and all the other imbecilities for which there is no remedy but modern ideas and force of character. Therefore it is no use facing the world today with the ideas of a hundred years ago, when it was practically against the law for a lady who was not a genius to be self-supporting; for if she kept a shop, or even visited at the house of a woman who kept a shop, she was no lady. I know better than you (because I am probably much older) that the tradition of those bad old times still wastes the lives of single gentlewomen to a deplorable extent; but, for all that, every year sees an increase in the activities of gentlewomen outside the home in business and the professions, and even in perilous professional exploration and adventure with a cinematographic camera in attendance.

This increase is hastened by the gigantic scale of capitalist production, which, as we have seen, reduces the old household labor of baking and brewing, spinning and weaving, first to shopping at separate shops, and then to telephoning the day's orders to one big multiple shop. We have seen also how it leads prematurely to Birth Control, which has reduced the number of children in the middle class households very notably. Many middle-class women who could formerly say with truth that there was no end to a woman's work in the house are now underworked, in spite of the difficulty of finding servants. It is conceivable that women may drive men out of many middle class occupations as they have already driven them out of many city offices. We are losing the habit of regarding business and the professions as male employments.

Nevertheless males are in a vast majority in these departments, and must remain so as long as our family arrangements last, because the bearing and rearing of children, including domestic housekeeping, is woman's natural monopoly. As such, being as it is the most vital of all the functions of mankind, it gives women a power and importance that they can attain to in no other profession, and that man cannot attain to at all. In so far as it is a slavery, it is a slavery to Nature and not to Man: indeed it is the means by which women enslave men, and thus create a Man Question which is called, very inappropriately, the Woman Question. Woman as Wife and Mother stands apart from the development we are dealing with in this chapter, which is, the rise of a business and professional middle class out of the propertied class. This is a sexless development, because when the unmarried daughters, like the younger sons, become doctors, barristers, ministers in the Free Churches, managers, accountants, shopkeepers, and clerks under the term typist (in America stenographer), they virtually leave their sex behind them, as men do. In business and the professions there are neither men nor women: economically they are all neuters, as far as that is humanly possible. The only disadvantage the woman is at in competition with the man is that the man must either succeed in his business or fail completely in life, whilst the woman has a second string to her bow in the possibility of getting married. A young woman who regards business employment as only a temporary support until she can find an eligible husband will never master her work as a man must.

45
DECLINE OF THE EMPLOYER

AT first sight it would seem that the employers must be the most powerful class in the community, because the others can do nothing without them. So they were, a hundred years ago. The dominant man then was not the capitalist nor the landlord nor the laborer, but the employer who could set capital and land and labor to work. These employers began as office employees; for business in those days was mostly on so small a scale that any middle class employee who had learnt the routine of business as a clerk or apprentice, in his father's office or elsewhere, and who could scrape together a few hundred pounds, could enter into partnership with another thrifty employee, and set up in almost any sort of business as an employer.

But as spare money accumulated in larger and larger quantity, and enterprise expanded accordingly, business came to be done on a larger and larger scale until these old-fashioned little firms found their customers being taken away from them by big concerns and joint stock companies who could, with their huge capitals and costly machinery, not only undersell them, but make a greater profit out of their lower prices. Women see this in their shopping. They used to buy their umbrellas at an umbrella shop, their boots at a boot shop, their books at a book shop, and their lunches-out at a restaurant. Nowadays they buy them all at the same shop, lunch and all. Huge bazaars like Selfridge's and Whiteley's in London, and the great multiple shops in the provincial cities, are becoming the only shops where you can buy anything, because they are taking away the trade of the small separate shops and ruining the shopkeepers who kept them. These ruined shopkeepers may think themselves lucky if they get jobs in the multiple shops as shop assistants, managers of departments, and the like, when they are not too old for the change.

Sometimes the change is invisible. Certain retail trades have to be carried on in small shops scattered all over the place. For example, oil shops, public houses, and tobacconists. These look like separate small businesses. But they are not. The public houses are tied houses practically owned in dozens by the brewers. A hundred oil shops or tobacco shops may belong to a single big company, called a Trust. Just as the little businesses conducted by a couple of gentlemen partners, starting with a capital which they counted in hundreds, had to give way to companies counting their capital in thousands, so these companies are being forced to combine into Trusts which count their capital in millions.

These changes involve another which is politically very important. When the employers had it all their own way, and were in business for themselves separately and independently, they worked with what we should call small capitals, and had no difficulty in getting them. Capital was positively thrown down their throats by the bankers, who, as we shall see later, have most of the spare money to keep. Those were the days of arrogant cotton lords and merchant princes. The man who could manage a business took every penny that was left in the till when the landlord had had his rent, the capitalist (who was often himself) his interest, and the employees their wages. If he were a capable man, what remained for him as profit was enough to make him rich enough to go into Parliament if he cared to. Sometimes it was enough to enable him to buy his way into the peerage. Capital being useless and Labor helpless without him, he was, as an American economist put it, master of the situation.

When joint stock companies, which were formerly supposed to be suitable for banking and insurance only, came into business generally, the situation of the employers began to change. In a joint stock concern you have, instead of one or two capitalists, hundreds of capitalists, called shareholders, each contributing what spare money she or he can afford. It began with £100 shares, and has gone on to £10 and £1 shares; so that a single business today may belong to a host of capitalist proprietors, many of them much poorer people than could ever have acquired property in pre-company days. This had two results. One was that a woman with a £5 note to spare could allow a company to spend it, and thereby become entitled to, say, five shillings a year out of the gains of that company as long as it lasted. In this way Capitalism was strengthened by the extension of property in industry from rich people with large sums of spare money to poor people with small ones. But the employers were weakened, and finally lost their supremacy and became employees.

It happened in this way. The joint stock company system made it possible to collect much larger capitals to start business with than the old separate firms could command. It was already known that the employer with a thousand pounds worth of machinery and other aids to production (called plant) could be undersold and driven out of the market by the employer with twenty thousand pounds worth. Still, employers could get twenty thousand pounds lent to them easily enough if it was believed that they could handle it profitably. But when companies came into the field equipped with hundreds of thousands of pounds, and these companies began to combine into Trusts equipped with millions, the employers were outdone. They could not raise such sums among their acquaintances. No bank would allow them to overdraw their accounts on such a gigantic scale. To get more capital, they had to turn their businesses into joint stock companies.

This sounds simple; but the employers did not find it so. You, I hope, would not buy shares in a new company unless you saw what are called good names on the prospectus, shewing that half a dozen persons whom you believe to be wealthy, trustworthy, good judges of business, and in responsible social stations were setting you the example. If ever you do you will regret it, possibly in the workhouse. Now the art of getting at the people with the good names, and interesting them, is one at which practical employers are for the most part incurably unskilled. Therefore when they want to raise capital on the modern scale they are forced to go to persons who, having made a special profession of it, know where to go and how to proceed. These persons are called Promoters, though they usually call themselves financiers. They naturally charge a very high commission for their services; and the accountants and solicitors whose reputations inspire confidence put a high price on their names also. They all find that they can make so much by raising large capitals that it is not worth their while to trouble themselves with small ones; and the quaint result of this is that an employer finds it easier to raise large sums than small ones. If he wants only £20,000, the promoters and financiers shew him the door contemptuously: the pickings on so small a sum are beneath their notice. If, however, he wants

£100,000, they will listen superciliously, and perhaps get it for him. Only, though he has to pay interest on £100,000, and stand indebted in that amount, he is very lucky if he receives £70,000 in cash. The promoters and financiers divide the odd £30,000 among themselves for their names and their trouble in raising the money. The employers are helpless in their hands: it is a case of take it or leave it: if they refuse the terms they get no capital. Thus the financiers and their go-betweens are now masters of the situation; and the men who actually conduct and order the industry of the country, who would have been great commercial magnates in Queen Victoria's reign, are now under the thumbs of men who never employed an industrial workman nor entered a factory or mine in their lives, and never intend to.

And that is not all. When an employer turns his business into a joint stock company he becomes an employee. He may be the head employee who orders all the other employees about, engaging and dismissing them as he thinks fit; but still he is an employee, and can be dismissed by the shareholders and replaced by another manager if they think he is taking too much for his services. Against this possibility he usually protects himself by selling his establishment to the company at first for a number of shares sufficient to enable him to outvote all the discontented shareholders (each share carries a vote); and in any case his position as the established head who has made a success of the business, or at least persuaded the shareholders that he has, is a strong one. But he does not live for ever. When he dies or retires, a new manager must be found; and this successor is not his heir, but a stranger entering as a removable employee, managing the concern for a salary and perhaps a percentage of the profits.

Now an able employee-manager can command a high salary, and have a good deal of power, because he is felt to be indispensable until he is worn out. But he can never be as indispensable as the old employers who invented their own methods, and clung to their "trade secrets" jealously. Their methods necessarily resolved themselves into an office routine which could be picked up, however unintelligently, by those employed in it. The only trade secret that really counted was the new machinery, which was not secret at all; for all the great mechanical inventions are soon communized by law: that is, instead of the inventor of a machine being allowed to keep it as his private property for ever and make all the employers who use it pay him a royalty, he is allowed to monopolize it in this way under a patent for fourteen years only, after which it is at everybody's disposal.

You can guess the inevitable result. It may take a genius to invent, say a steam-engine, but once it is invented a couple of ordinary workmen can keep it going; and when it is worn out any ordinary engineering firm can replace it by copying it. Also, though it may need exceptional talent, initiative, energy, and concentration to set up a new business, yet when it is once set up, and the routine of working it established, it can be kept going by ordinary persons who have learnt the routine, and whose rule is "When in doubt as to what to do, see what was done the last time, and do it over again". Thus a very clever man may build up a great business, and leave it to his quite ordinary son to carry on when he is dead; and the son may get on very well without ever really understanding the business as his father did. Or the father may leave it to his daughter with the certainty that if she cannot or will not do the directing work herself, she can easily hire employee-employers who can and will, for a salary plus a percentage. The famous Krupp factory in Germany belongs to a lady. I will not go so far as to say that managerial ability has become a drug in the market, though, in the little businesses which are still conducted in the old way in the poorer middle class, the employer often has to pay his more highly skilled employees more than he gets out of the business for himself. But the monopoly of business technique which made the capitalist-employer supreme in the nineteenth century has gone for ever. Employers today are neither capitalists nor monopolists of managerial ability. The political and social power which their predecessors enjoyed has passed to the financiers and bankers, who monopolize the art of collecting millions of spare money. That monopoly will be broken in its turn by the communization of banking, to which we shall come presently.

Meanwhile you, putting all these developments together in your mind, can now contemplate the Middle Class understandingly. You know now how it sprang from the propertied class as an educated younger-son class without property, and supported itself by practising the professions, and by doing the business of the propertied class. You know how it rose to supreme power and riches when the development of modern machinery (called the Industrial Revolution) made business so big and complicated that neither the propertied class nor the working class could understand it, and the middle class men who did (called generally employers), became masters of the situation. You know how, when the first generations of employers had found out how to do this work, and established a routine of doing it which any literate man could learn and practise, and when all that remained was to find more and more capital to feed it as its concerns grew bigger and bigger, the supremacy passed from the employers to the financiers who hold it at present. You know also that this last change has been accompanied by a change in the status of the employer, who instead of hiring the land and capital of the propertied classes for a fixed payment of rent and interest, and taking as his profit all that remains, is now simply employed to manage for companies and trusts, the shareholders taking everything that is left after they have paid rent and wages (including his salary). You see that in applying for such posts he has to meet the competition not only of other middle class men as of old, but of clever sons of the working class, raised into the middle class by education at the public expense by our system of scholarships, which act as ladders from the elementary school to the University or the Polytechnic. You see that this applies not only to employers, but much more to their clerks. Clerking was formerly a monopoly of the less energetic sons of the middle class. Now that everybody has to go to school the middle class monopoly of reading, writing, and ciphering is gone; and skilled manual workers are better paid than clerks, being scarcer. As to parlormaids, what ordinary typist does not envy their creature comforts?

The Middle Station in Life no longer justifies the pæan in its praise which Daniel Defoe raised in Robinson Crusoe. For those who possess no special talent of a lucrative kind, it is now the least eligible class in the community.

46

THE PROLETARIAT

WE have disposed of the Middle Classes: let us turn to the Lower Classes, the Hungry Ones, the Working Classes, the Masses, the Mob, or whatever else you call them. Classical culture has invented a general name for all people, of whatever nation, color, sex, sect, or social pretension, who, having no land nor capital (no property), have to hire themselves out for a living. It calls them proletarians, or, in the lump, The Proletariat. Karl Marx, who was born in Rhenish Germany in 1818, and died in London in 1883, after spending the last thirtyfour years of his life in England making a special study of the development of Capitalism among us, was, and still is, the most famous champion of the Proletariat as the really organic part of civilized society to which all the old governing and propertied classes must finally succumb. When Marx raised his famous slogan, "Proletarians of all lands: unite", he meant that all who live by the sale or hire of their labor should combine to do away with private property in land and capital, and to make everyone do her or his bit of the labor of the world, and share the product without paying toll to any idler.

The difficulty at that time was that the employers, without whom the proletarians could do nothing, were, as we have seen, strong, rich, independent, and masterful. They not only owned a good deal of land and capital themselves, but fully intended to become propertied country gentlemen when they retired. It was not until they began to slip down into a salaried, or proletarian class, that they also began to listen to Karl Marx. You see, they were losing their personal interest in private property with its rents and dividends, and were becoming interested solely in the price that could be got out of the landlords and capitalists for active services: that is, for labor of hand and brain. Instead of wanting to give Labor as little as possible and get as much out of it as possible, they wanted property to get as little as possible, and the sort of labor they themselves did to get as much as possible. They found that skilled manual work, and even unskilled manual strength, was coming more and more to be better paid than book-keeping work and routine managing and professional work.

Now it is no use pretending to be better than other people when you are poorer. It only leads to keeping up more expensive appearances on less money, and forbidding your children to associate with most people's children whilst they forbid their children to speak to yours. If the parents do not realize the vanity of such pretension the children do. I remember thinking when I was a boy how silly it was that my father, whose business was wholesale business, should consider himself socially superior to his tailor, who had the best means of knowing how much poorer than himself my father was, and who had a handsome residence, with ornamental grounds and sailing-boats, at the seaside place where we spent the summer in a six-roomed cottage-villa with a small garden. The great Grafton Street shopkeepers of Dublin outshone the tailor with their palaces and yachts; and their children had luxuries that I never dreamt of as possible for me, besides being far more expensively educated. My father's conviction that they were too lowly to associate with me, when it was so clear that I was too poor to associate with them, may have had some sort of imaginary validity for him; but for me it was snobbish nonsense. I lived to see those children entertaining the Irish peerage and the Viceroy without a thought of the old social barriers; and very glad the Irish peers were to be entertained by them. I lived to see those shops become multiple shops managed by salaried employees who have less chance of entertaining the peerage than a baked-potato man of entertaining the King.

My father was an employer whose whole capital added to that of his partner would not have kept a big modern company in postage stamps for a fortnight. But at my start in life I found it impossible to become an employer like him: I had to become a clerk at fifteen. I was a proletarian undisguised. Therefore, when I began to take an interest in politics, I did not join the Conservative Party. It was the party of the landlords; and I was not a landlord. I did not join the Liberal Party. It was the party of the employers; and I was an employee. My father voted Conservative or Liberal just as the humor took him, and never imagined that any other party could exist. But I wanted a proletarian party; and when the Karl Marx slogan began to take effect in all the countries in Europe by producing proletarian political societies, which came to be called Socialist societies because they aimed at the welfare of society as a whole as against class prejudices and property interests, I naturally joined one of these societies, and so came to be called, and was proud to call myself, a Socialist.

Now the significant thing about the particular Socialist society which I joined was that the members all belonged to the middle class. Indeed its leaders and directors belonged to what is sometimes called the upper middle class: that is, they were either professional men like myself (I had escaped from clerkdom into literature) or members of the upper division of the civil service. Several of them have since had distinguished careers without changing their opinions or leaving the Society. To their Conservative and Liberal parents and aunts and uncles fifty years ago it seemed an amazing, shocking, unheard-of thing that they should become Socialists, and also a step bound to make an end of all their chances of success in life. Really it was quite natural and inevitable. Karl Marx was not a poor laborer: he was the highly educated son of a rich Jewish lawyer. His almost equally famous colleague, Friedrich Engels, was a well-to-do employer. It was precisely because they were liberally educated, and brought up to think about how things are done instead of merely drudging at the manual labor of doing them, that these two men, like my colleagues in The Fabian Society (note, please, that we gave our society a name that could have occurred only to classically educated men), were the first to see that Capitalism was reducing their own class to the condition of a proletariat, and that the only chance of securing anything more than a slave's share in the national income for anyone but the biggest capitalists or the cleverest professional or business men lay in a combination of all the proletarians without distinction of class or country to put an end to Capitalism by developing the communistic side of our civilization until Communism became the dominant principle in society, and mere owning, profiteering, and genteel idling were disabled and discredited. Or, as our numerous clergymen members put it, to worship God instead of Mammon. Communism, being the lay form of Catholicism, and indeed meaning the same thing, has never had any lack of chaplains.

I may mention, as illustrating the same point, that The Fabian Society, when I joined it immediately after its foundation in 1884, had only two rival Socialist Societies in London, both professing, unlike the Fabian, to be working-class societies. But one of them was dominated by the son of a very rich man who bequeathed large sums to religious institutions in addition to providing for his sons, to whom he had given a first-rate education. The other was entirely dependent on one of the most famous men of the nineteenth century, who was not only a successful employer and manufacturer in the business of furnishing and decorating palaces and churches, but an eminent artistic designer, a rediscoverer of lost arts, and one of the greatest of English poets and writers. These two men, Henry Mayers Hyndman and William Morris, left their mark on the working-class proletariat as preachers of Socialism, but failed in their attempts to organize a new working-class Socialist Party in their own upper middle class way under their own leadership and in their own dialect (for the language of ladies and gentlemen is only a dialect), because the working classes had already organized themselves in their own way, under their own leaders, and in their own dialect. The Fabian Society succeeded because it addressed itself to its own class in order that it might set about doing the necessary brain work of planning Socialist organization for all classes, meanwhile accepting, instead of trying to supersede, the existing political organizations which it intended to permeate with the Socialist conception of human society.

The existing form of working-class organization was Trade Unionism. Trade Unionism is not Socialism: it is the Capitalism of the Proletariat. This requires another chapter of explanation, and a very important one; for Trade Unionism is now very powerful, and occasionally leaves the Intelligent Woman without coals or regular trains for weeks together. Before we can understand it, however, we must study the Labor Market out of which it grew; and this will take several preliminary chapters, including a somewhat grim one on the special position of women as sellers in that market.

47
THE LABOR MARKET AND THE FACTORY ACTS

THE workwoman working for weekly wages is like her employer in one respect. She has something to sell; and she has to live on the price of it. That something is her labor. The more she gets for it the better-off she is: the less she gets for it the worse-off she is: if she can get nothing for it she starves or becomes a pauper. When she marries, she finds her husband in the same position; and he has to pay for the upkeep of her domestic labor out of the price of his industrial labor. Under these circumstances they are both naturally keen on getting as much for his industrial labor as possible, and giving as little for its price as the purchaser (the employer) will put up with. This means that they want the highest wages and the shortest hours of work they can get. Unless they are exceptionally thoughtful and public spirited persons, their ideas are limited to that.

The employer is in the same predicament. He does not sell labor: he has to buy it: what he sells are the goods or services produced under his direction; and if he, as mostly happens, is neither thoughtful nor public spirited, his ideas are limited to getting as much for what he sells as possible and giving as little for the money as the purchaser will put up with. In buying labor his interest and policy are to pay as little and get as much as he can, being thus precisely the opposites of the workers' interest and policy.

This not only produces that unhappy and dangerous conflict of feeling and interest between employers and employed called Class War, but leads to extremities of social wickedness that are hardly credible of civilized people. The Government has been forced again and again to interfere between the buyers and sellers of labor to compel them to keep their bargains within the barest limits of common humanity. To begin with, all the employers want is labor, and whether the labor is done by a child or a woman or a man is nothing to them: they buy whatever labor is cheapest. Also the effect of the work on the health and morals of the employed is nothing to the employer except in so far as they may make a difference in his profit; and when he takes them into consideration with this in view he may conclude that an inhuman disregard of all natural kindness will pay him better than any attempt to reconcile his interest with the welfare of his employees.

To illustrate this I may cite the case of the London tramways when the cars were drawn by horses, and of certain plantations in America before negro slavery was abolished there. The question to be decided by the tramway managers was, what is the most moneymaking way of treating tramway horses? A well-cared-for horse, if not overworked, may live twenty years, or even, like the Duke of Wellington's horse, forty. On the other hand, reckless ill-usage will kill a horse in less than a year, as it will kill anyone else. If horses cost nothing, and a new horse could be picked up in the street when the old one died, it would be more profitable commercially to work horses to death in six months, say, than to treat them humanely and let them retire to the salt marshes of Norfolk at the age of eighteen or so. But horses cost money; and the tramway managers knew that if they wore out a horse too quickly he would not pay for his cost. After figuring it out they decided that the most profitable way of treating tram horses was to wear them out in four years. The same calculation was made on the plantations. The slave, like the horse, cost a substantial sum of money; and if he were worked to death too soon his death would result in a loss. The most businesslike planters settled that the most paying plan was to wear out their slaves in seven years; and this was the result they instructed their overseers to aim at.

The Intelligent Woman will naturally exclaim "What a dreadful thing to be a company's horse or a slave!" But wait a moment. Horses and slaves are worth something: if you kill them you have to pay for new ones. But if instead of employing horses and slave you employ "free" children and women and men, you may work them to death as hard and as soon as you like: there are plenty more to be had for nothing where they came from. What is more, you need not support them, as you have to support slaves, during the weeks when you have no work for them. You take them on by the week; and when trade is slack, and you have no work for them, you just discharge them, leaving them to starve or shift for themselves as best they can. In the heyday of Capitalism, when this system was in full swing, and no laws had been made to limit its abuse, small children were worked to death under the whip until it was commonly said that the northern factory employers were using up nine generations in one generation. Women were employed at the mines under conditions of degradation which would have horrified any negress in South Carolina. Men were reduced to lives which savages would have despised. The places these unhappy people lived in were beyond description. Epidemics of cholera and smallpox swept the country from time to time; typhus was commoner than measles today; drunkenness and brutal violence were considered as natural to the working classes as fustian coats and horny hands. The respectability and prosperity of the propertied and middle classes who grew rich on sweated labor covered an abyss of horror; and it was by raising the lid from that abyss that Karl Marx, in his terrible and epoch-making book called Capital, became the prophet of that great revolt of outraged humanity against Capitalism which is the emotional force of the Socialist movement. However, your subject and mine just now is not Emotional Socialism but Intelligent Socialism; so let us keep calm. Anger is a bad counsellor.

Long before Marx published his book the Government had been forced to interfere. A succession of laws called the Factory Acts, which include regulation of mines and other industries, were passed to forbid the employment of children below a certain age; to regulate the employment of women and young persons; to limit the hours during which a factory employing such persons could be kept open; to force employers to fence in machines which crushed and tore to pieces the employees who brushed against them in moments of haste or carelessness; to pay wages in money instead of in credit at employers' shops where bad food and bad clothes were sold at exorbitant prices; to provide sanitary conveniences; to limewash factory walls at frequent intervals; to forbid the practice of taking meals at work in the factory instead of during an interval and in another place; to frustrate the dodges by which these laws were at first evaded by the employers; and to appoint factory inspectors to see that the laws were carried out. These laws were the fruit of an agitation headed, not by Socialists, but by a pious Conservative nobleman, Lord Shaftesbury, who did not find in his Bible any authority for the Capitalist theory that you could and should produce universal well-being by breaking all the laws of God and Man whenever you could make a commercial profit by doing so. This amazing theory was not only put into practice by greedy people, but openly laid down and explicitly advocated in books by quite sincere and serious professors of political economy and jurisprudence (calling themselves The Manchester School) and in speeches made in opposition to the Factory Acts by moral and highminded orator-manufacturers like John Bright. It is still taught as authentic political science at our universities. It has broken the moral authority of university bred Churchmen, and reduced university bred Statesmen to intellectually self-satisfied impotence. It is perhaps the worst of the many rationalist dogmas that have in the course of human history led naturally amiable logicians to countenance and commit villainies that would revolt professed criminals.

Now one would suppose on first thoughts that the Factory Acts would have been opposed by all the employers and supported by all their employees. But there are good employers as well as bad ones; and there are ignorant and shortsighted laborers as well as wise ones. The employers who had tender consciences, or who, like some of the Quakers, had a form of religion which compelled them to think sometimes of what they were doing by throwing all the responsibility for it on themselves and not on any outside authority like the professors of Capitalist political economy, were greatly troubled by the condition of their employees. You may ask why, in that case, they did not treat them better. The answer is that if they had done so they would have been driven out of business and ruined by the bad employers.

It would have occurred in this way. Cheap sweated labor meant not only bigger profits: it also meant cheaper goods. If the good employer paid a decent living wage to his workpeople, and worked them for eight hours a day instead of from twelve to sixteen, he had to charge high enough prices for his goods to enable him to pay such wages. But in that case the bad employer could and would at once offer the same goods at a lower price and thus take all the good employer's customers away from him. The good employer was therefore obliged to join Lord Shaftesbury in telling the Government that unless laws were passed to force all employers, good and bad alike, to behave better, there could never be any improvement, because the good employers would have either to sweat the workers like the bad ones, or else be driven out of business, leaving matters worse than ever. They found that social problems cannot be solved by personal righteousness, and that under Capitalism not only must men be made moral by Act of Parliament, but cannot be made moral in any other way, no matter how benevolent their dispositions may be.

The opposition to the Factory Acts by the workers themselves was actually harder to overcome in some ways than that of the employers, because the employers, when they were forced by law to try the experiment, found that extreme sweating, like killing the goose that laid the golden eggs, was not the best way to make business pay, and that they could more than make up for the cost of complying with the very moderate requirements of the Acts by putting a little more brains into their work. Even the stupid ones found that by speeding up their machinery, and thus making their employees pull themselves together and work harder, they could get more out of them in ten hours than in twelve. The Intelligent Woman, if she has travelled, may have noticed that in countries where there is no Shop Hours Act, and shops remain open until everyone has gone to bed, the shopkeepers and their assistants are far less tired and strained at nine in the evening than the assistants in a big shop in a big English city are at five in the afternoon, though the shop closes at six. Impossible as it may sound, in the ginning mills of Bombay, before any factory legislation was introduced, the children employed went into the factory, not for so many hours a day, but for months at a time; and there are such things in the world as Italian cafés that are open day and night without regular night and day waiters, the employees taking a nap when and where they can. And this lazy happy-go-lucky way of doing business may do no great harm, whilst an eight hour day at high wages under modern scientific management may mean work so intense that it takes the last inch out of the workers, and cannot be done except by persons in the prime of life, nor even by them for many consecutive months.

The employers had another resource in the introduction of machinery. When employers can get plenty of cheap labor they will not introduce machinery: it is too much trouble, and though the machine may do the work of several persons it may cost more. At this moment (1925) in Lisbon the very rough and dirty business of coaling steamships can be done by machinery. The machinery is actually there ready for use. But the work is done by women, because they are cheaper and there is no law against it. If a Portuguese Factory Act were passed, forbidding the employment of women, or imposing restrictions and regulations on it (possibly not really for the sake of the women, but only to keep them out of the job and thus reserve it for men), the machinery would be turned on at once; and it would soon be improved and added to until it became indispensable. But as the women would lose their employment, they would object to any such Factory Act much more vociferously than the employers.

All the protestations of the employers that they would be ruined by the Factory Acts were contradicted by experience. By better management, more and better machinery, and speeding up the work, they made bigger profits than ever. If they had been half as clever as they claimed to be, they would have imposed on themselves all the regulations the Factory Acts imposed on them, without waiting to be forced by law. But profiteering does not cultivate men's minds as public service does. The greatest advances in industrial organization have been forced on employers in spite of their piteous protests that they would be unable to carry on under them, and that British industry must consequently perish. It may shock you to learn that the employees themselves resisted the Factory Acts at first because the Acts began by putting a stop to the ill treatment and overworking of children too young to be decently put to commercial work at all. At first these victims of unregulated Capitalism were little Oliver Twists, sold into slavery by the Guardians of the Poor to get rid of them. But the later generations were the children of the employees; and the wage on which the employee kept his family in squalid poverty was added to by the children's earnings. When people are very poor the loss of a shilling a week is much worse than the loss of £500 a week to a millionaire: it means, for the woman who has a desperate struggle to keep the house and make both ends meet every Saturday, that her task becomes impossible. It is easy for comparatively rich people to say "You should not send your young children out to work under such inhuman conditions", or, "You should rejoice in a new Factory Act which makes such infamies impossible". But if the immediate result of listening to them is that the children who were only half starved before are now to be three-quarters starved, such pious remonstrances produce nothing but exasperation. The melancholy truth is that, as the Factory Acts were passed one after another, gradually raising the age at which children might be employed in factories from infancy to fourteen and sixteen, and half the children's time below a certain age had to be spent in school, the parents were the fiercest opponents of the Acts; and when they got the vote, and became able to influence Parliament directly, they made it impossible for anybody to get elected as a member for a factory town where children's labor was employed unless he pledged himself to oppose any extension of the laws restricting child labor. The common saying that the parents are the best people to take care of the interests of the children depends not only on the sort of people the parents are, but on whether they are well enough off to be able to afford to indulge their natural parental instinct. Only a small proportion of parents, and these not the poorest, will deliberately bring up their children to be thieves and prostitutes; but practically all parents will, and indeed must, sweat their children if they are themselves sweated so mercilessly that they cannot get on without the few pence their children can earn.

Now that I have explained the seeming heartlessness of the parents, you have still to ask me why these parents accepted wages so low that they were forced to sacrifice their children to the employers' greed for profits. The answer is that the increase of population which produced the younger son class in the propertied class, and finally built up the middle class, went on also among the employees who lived from hand to mouth on the wages of manual labor. Now manual labor is like fish or asparagus, dear when it is scarce, cheap when it is plentiful. As the numbers of propertyless manual workers grew from thousands to millions the price of their labor fell and fell. In the nineteenth century everybody knew that wages were higher in America and Australia than in Great Britain and Ireland, because labor was scarcer there; and those who could afford it emigrated to these countries. Half the population of Ireland went to America, where labor was so scarce that immigrants were welcomed from all countries. But today the labor market in America is so choked with them that immigration is sternly restricted to a fixed number from each European country every year. Australia restricts its births artificially, and refuses to admit Chinamen or Japanese on any terms. America also excludes Japanese. But in the days when the Factory Acts were made really effective (the first ones were evaded by all sorts of employers' tricks) emigration from our islands was unrestricted, and went on at a great rate among those who could afford the passage money.

This shewed that our labor market was overstocked. When the fish market is overstocked the fish are thrown back into the sea. Emigration was, in effect, throwing men and women into the sea with a ship to cling to and a chance of reaching another country in it. The value of men and women in England, unless they could do some sort of work that was still scarce, had fallen to nothing. Doctors and dentists and lawyers and parsons were still worth something (parsons shamefully little: £70 a year for a curate with a family); and exceptionally skilled or physically powerful workmen could earn more than the poorer clergy; but the mass of manual employees, those who could do nothing except under direction, and even under direction could do nothing that any ablebodied person could not learn to do in a very short time, were literally worth nothing: you could get them for what it cost to keep them alive, and to enable them to bring up children enough to replace them when they were worn out. It was just as if steam-engines had been made in such excessive quantities that the manufacturers would give them for nothing to anyone who would take them away. Whoever took them away would still have to feed them with coal and oil before they could work; but this would not mean that they had any value, or that they would be taken proper care of, or that the coal and oil would be of decent quality.

You see, people without property have no other way of living than selling themselves for their market value, or, when their value falls to nothing, offering to work for anyone who will feed them. They have no land, and cannot afford to buy any; and even if land were given to them few of them would know how to cultivate it. They cannot become capitalists, because capital is spare money, and they have no money to spare. They cannot set up in business for themselves with borrowed money, because nobody will lend them money: if anyone did, they would lose it all and become bankrupt for want of the requisite education and training. They must find an employer or starve; and if they attempt to bargain for anything more than a bare subsistence wage they are told curtly but only too truthfully that if they do not choose to take it there are plenty of others who will.

Even at this they cannot all get employment. Although the plea made for Capitalism by the professors of The Manchester School was that at least it would always provide the workers with employment at a living wage, it has never either kept that promise or justified that plea. The employers have had to confess that they need what is called "a reserve army of unemployed", so that they can always pick up "hands" when trade is good and throw them back into the street when it is bad. Throwing them back into the street means forcing them to spend the few shillings they may have been able to put by while employed, selling or pawning their clothes and furniture, and finally going on the rates as paupers. The ratepayers naturally object very strongly to having to support the employer's workmen whenever he does not happen to want them; consequently, when the Capitalist system developed on a large scale, the ratepayers made Poor Law relief such a disgraceful, cruel, and degrading business that decent working class families would suffer any extremity rather than resort to it. We said to the unemployed father of a starving family, "We must feed you and your children if you are destitute, because the Statute of Elizabeth obliges us to; but you must bring your daughters and sons into the workhouse with you to live with drunkards, prostitutes, tramps, idiots, epileptics, old criminals, the very dregs and refuse of human society at its worst, and having done that you will never be able to hold up your head again among your fellows". The man naturally said "Thank you: I had rather see my children dead", and starved it out as best he could until trade revived, and the employers had another job for him. And to get that job he would accept the barest wages the family could support life on. If his children could earn a little in a factory he would snatch at wages that were just enough, when the children's earnings were thrown in, to support them all; and in this way he did not benefit in the long run by letting his children go out to work, as it ended in their earnings being used to beat down his own wages; so that, though he at first sent his children into the factories to get a little extra money, he was at last forced to do it to make up his own wages to subsistence point; and when the law stepped in to rescue the children from their slavery, he opposed the law because he did not see how he could live unless his children earned something instead of going to school.

48

WOMEN IN THE LABOR MARKET

THE effect of the system on women was worse in some respects than on men. As no industrial employer would employ a woman if he could get a man for the same money, women who wished to get any industrial employment could do so only by offering to do it for less than men. This was possible, because even when the man's wage was a starvation wage it was the starvation wage of a family, not of a single person. Out of it the man had to pay for the subsistence of his wife and children, without whom the Capitalist system would soon have come to an end for want of any young workers to replace the old ones. Therefore even when the men's wages were down to the lowest point at which their wives and children could be kept alive, a single woman could take less without being any worse off than her married neighbors and their children. In this way it became a matter of course that women should be paid less than men; and when any female rebel claimed to be paid as much as a man for the same work ("Equal wages for equal work"), the employer shut her up with two arguments: first, "If you dont take the lower wage there are plenty of others who will", and, second, "If I have to pay a man's wages I will get a man to do the work".

The most important and indispensable work of women, that of bearing and rearing children, and keeping house for them, was never paid for directly to the woman but always through the man; and so many foolish people came to forget that it was work at all, and spoke of Man as The Breadwinner. This was nonsense. From first to last the woman's work in the home was vitally necessary to the existence of society, whilst millions of men were engaged in wasteful or positively michievous work, the only excuse for which was that it enabled them to support their useful and necessary wives. But the men, partly through conceit, partly through thoughtlessness, and very largely because they were afraid that their wives might, if their value were recognized, become unruly and claim to be the heads of the household, set up a convention that women earned nothing and men everything, and refused to give their wives any legal claim on the housekeeping money. By law everything a woman possessed became the property of her husband when she married: a state of things that led to such monstrous abuses that the propertied class set up an elaborate legal system of marriage settlements, the effect of which was to hand over the woman's property to some person or persons yet unborn before her marriage; so that though she could have an income from the property during her life, it was no longer her property, and therefore her husband could not make ducks and drakes of it. Later on the middle classes made Parliament protect their women by The Married Women's Property Acts under which we still live; and these Acts, owing to the confusion of people's minds on the subject, overshot the mark and produced a good deal of injustice to men. That, however, is another part of the story: the point to be grasped here is that under the Capitalist system women found themselves worse off than men because, as Capitalism made a slave of the man, and then, by paying the woman through him, made her his slave, she became the slave of a slave, which is the worst sort of slavery.

This suits certain employers very well, because it enables them to sweat other employers without being found out. And this is how it is done. A laborer finds himself bringing up a family of daughters on a wage of twenty-nine shillings a week in the country (it was thirteen in the nineteenth century) or, in or near a city, of from thirty (formerly eighteen) to seventy, subject to deductions for spells of unemployment. Now in a household scraping along on thirty shillings a week another five shillings a week makes an enormous difference: far more, I repeat, than another five hundred pounds makes to a millionaire. An addition of fifteen shillings or a pound a week raises the family of a laborer to the money level of that of a skilled workman. How were such tempting additions possible? Simply by the big girls going out to work at five shillings a week each, and continuing to live at home with their fathers. One girl meant another five shillings, two meant another ten shillings, three another fifteen shillings. Under such circumstances huge factories sprang up employing hundreds of girls at wages of from four-and-sixpence to seven-and-sixpence a week, the great majority getting five. These were called starvation wages; but the girls were much better fed and jollier and healthier than women who had to support themselves altogether. Some of the largest fortunes made in business: for example in the match industry, were made out of the five shilling girl living with, and of course partly on, her father, or as a lodger on somebody else's father, a girl lodger being as good as a daughter in this respect. Thus the match manufacturer was getting three-quarters of his labor at the father's expense. If the father worked in, say, a brewery, the match manufacturer was getting three-quarters of his labor at the expense of the brewer. In this way one trade lives by sweating another trade; and factory girls getting wages that would hardly support a prize cat are plump and jolly and willing and vigorous and rowdy, whilst older women, many of them widows with young children, are told that if they are not satisfied with the same wages there are plenty of strong girls who will be glad to get them.

It was not merely the daughters but the wives of working men who brought down women's wages in this way. In the cities young women, married to young men, and not yet burdened with many children or with more than a room or two to keep tidy at home (and they were often not too particular about tidiness), or having no children, used to be quite willing to go out as charwomen for an hour a day for five shillings a week, plus such little perquisites and jobs of washing as might be incidental to this employment. As such a charwoman had nothing to do at home, and was not at all disposed to go on to a second job when she had secured the five shillings that made all the difference between pinching and prodigality to her and her husband, the hour easily stretched to half a day. The five shillings have now become ten or so; but as they buy no more, the situation is not altered.

In this way the labor market is infested with subsidized wives and daughters willing to work for pocket money on which no independent solitary woman or widow can possibly subsist. The effect is to make marriage compulsory as a woman's profession: she has to take anything she can get in the way of a husband rather than face penury as a single woman. Some women get married easily; but others, less attractive or amiable, are driven to every possible trick and stratagem to entrap some man into marriage; and that sort of trickery is not good for a woman's self-respect, and does not lead to happy marriages when the men realize that they have been "made a convenience of".

This is bad enough; but there are lower depths still. It may not be respectable to live on a man's wages without marrying him; but it is possible. If a man says to a destitute woman "I will not take you until death do us part, for better for worse, in sickness and in health and so forth; nor will I give you my name and the status of my legal wife; but if you would like to be my wife illegally until tomorrow morning, here is sixpence and a drink for you, or, as the case may be, a shilling, or a pound, or ten pounds, or a hundred pounds, or a villa with a pearl necklace and a sable mantle and a motor car", he will not always meet with a refusal. It is easy to ask a woman to be virtuous; but it is not reasonable if the penalty of virtue be starvation, and the reward of vice immediate relief. If you offer a pretty girl twopence halfpenny an hour in a match factory, with a chance of contracting necrosis of the jawbone from phosphorus poisoning on the one hand, and on the other a jolly and pampered time under the protection of a wealthy bachelor, which was what the Victorian employers did and what employers still do all over the world when they are not stopped by resolutely socialistic laws, you are loading the dice in favor of the devil so monstrously as not only to make it certain that he will win, but raising the question whether the girl does not owe it to her own self-respect and desire for wider knowledge and experience, more cultivated society, and greater grace and elegance of life, to sell herself to a gentleman for pleasure rather than to an employer for profit. To warn her that her beauty will not last for ever only reminds her that if she takes reasonable care of her beauty it will last long past the age at which women, "too old at twenty-four", find the factory closed to them, and their places filled by younger girls. She has actually less security of respectable employment than of illicit employment; for the women who sell labor are often out of work through periods of bad trade and consequent unemployment; but the women who sell pleasure, if they are in other respects well conducted and not positively repulsive, are seldom at a loss for a customer. The cases which are held up as terrible warnings of how a woman may fall to the lowest depths of degradation by listening to such arguments are pious inventions, supported by examples of women who through drink, drugs, and general depravity or weakness of character would have fallen equally if they had been respectably married or had lived in the strictest celibacy. The incidental risks of venereal diseases are unfortunately not avoidable by respectable matrimony: more women are infected by their husbands than by their lovers. If a woman accepts Capitalist morality, and does what pays her best, she will take what district visitors call (when poor women are concerned) the wages of sin rather than the wages of sweated labor.

There are cases, too, where the wedding ring may be a drawback instead of a makeweight. Illicit unions are so common under the Capitalist system that the Government has had to deal with them; and the law at present is that if an unmarried woman bears a child she can compel its father to pay her seven-and-sixpence a week for its support until it is sixteen, at which age it can begin to help to support her. Meanwhile the child belongs to her instead of to the father (it would belong to him if they were married); and she is free from any obligation to keep his house or do any ordinary drudgery for him. Rather than be brought into court he will pay without demur; and when he is goodnatured and not too poor he will often pay her more than he is legally obliged to. The effect of this is that a careful, discreet, sensible, pleasant sort of woman who has not scrupled to bear five illegitimate children may find herself with a legally guaranteed steady income of thirty-seven-and-sixpence a week in addition to what she can earn by respectable work. Compared to a widow with five legitimate children she was on velvet until the Government, after centuries of blind neglect, began to pension widows.

In short, Capitalism acts on women as a continual bribe to enter into sex relations for money, whether in or out of marriage; and against this bribe there stands nothing beyond the traditional respectability which Capitalism ruthlessly destroys by poverty, except religion and the inborn sense of honor which has its citadel in the soul and can hold out (sometimes) against all circumstances.

It is useless to pretend that religion and tradition and honor always win the day. It is now a century and a half since the poet Oliver Goldsmith warned us that "Honor sinks where commerce long prevails"; and the economic pressure by which Capitalism tempts women grew fiercer after his time. We have just seen how in the case of the parents sending their children out to work in their infancy to add a little to the family income, they found that their wages fell until what they and the children between them could earn was no more than they had been able to earn by themselves before, so that in order to live they now had to send their children to work whether they liked it or not. In the same way the women who occasionally picked up a little extra money illicitly, presently found themselves driven to snatch at employment by offering to take lower wages and depending on the other resource to make them up to subsistence point. Then the women who stood on their honor were offered those reduced wages, and, when they said they could not live on them, were told as usual that others could, and that they could do what the others did.

In certain occupations prostitution thus became practically compulsory, the alternative being starvation. Hood's woman clad in unwomanly rags, who sang the Song of the Shirt, represents either the woman who would starve rather than sell her person or the woman neither young enough nor agreeable enough to earn even the few pence she could hope for from the men within her reach. The occupations in which prostitution is almost a matter of course are by no means the sensationally abject and miserable ones. It is rather in the employments in which well-dressed and goodlooking but unskilled women are employed to attract the public, that wages are paid on which they cannot possibly keep up the appearance expected from them. Girls with thirty shillings a week come to their work in expensive motor cars, and wear strings of pearls which, if not genuine, are at least the best imitations. If one of them asks how she can dress as she is expected to on thirty shillings a week she is either met with the old retort, "If you wont take it there are plenty who will", or else told quite frankly that she is very lucky to get thirty shillings in addition to such a splendid advertisement and show-case for her attractions as the stage or the restaurant, the counter or the show-room, afford her. You must not, however, infer from this that all theatres, restaurants, showrooms and so forth exploit prostitution in this way. Most of them have permanent staffs of efficient respectable women, and could not be conducted in any other way. Neither must it be inferred that the young gentlemen who provide the motor cars and furs and jewels are always allowed to succeed in their expensive courtship. Sir Arthur Pinero's play Mind the Paint is instructively true to life on this point. But such relations are not made edifying by the plea that the gentlemen are bilked. It is safe to assume that when women are employed, not to do any specially skilled work, but to attract custom to the place by their sex, their youth, their good looks and their smart dressing, employers of a certain type will underpay them, and by their competition finally compel more scrupulous employers to do the same or be undersold and driven out of the business. Now these are extremities to which men cannot be reduced. It is true that smart ladies can and do hire dancing partners at fifty francs an evening on the Riviera; but this quite innocent transaction does not mean that Capitalism can as yet say to a man, "If your wages are not enough to live on, go out into the streets and sell pleasures as others do". When the man deals in that commodity he does so as a buyer, not as a seller. Thus it is the woman, not the man, who suffers the last extremity of the Capitalist system; and this is why so many conscientious women are devoting their lives to the replacement of Capitalism by Socialism.

But let not anyone imagine that men escape prostitution under Capitalism. If they do not sell their bodies they sell their souls. The barrister who in court strives "to make the worse appear the better cause" has been held up as a stock example of the dishonesty of misrepresenting for money. Nothing could be more unjust. It is agreed, and necessarily agreed, that the best way of learning the truth about anything is not to listen to a vain attempt at an impartial and disinterested statement, but to hear everything that can possibly be said for it, and then everything that can possibly be said against it, by skilled pleaders on behalf of the interested parties on both sides. A barrister is bound to do his utmost to obtain a verdict for a client whom he privately believes to be in the wrong, just as a doctor is bound to do his utmost to save the life of a patient whose death would, in his private opinion, be a good riddance. The barrister is an innocent figure who is used to distract our attention from the writer and publisher of lying advertisements which pretend to prove the worse the better article, the shopman who sells it by assuring the customer that it is the best, the agents of drugging and drink, the clerk making out dishonest accounts, the adulterator and giver of short weight, the journalist writing for Socialist papers when he is a convinced Liberal, or for Tory papers when he is an Anarchist, the professional politician working for his party right or wrong, the doctor paying useless visits and prescribing bogus medicines to hypochondriacs who need only Abernethy's advice, "Live on sixpence a day, and earn it", the solicitor using the law as an instrument for the oppression of the poor by the rich, the mercenary soldier fighting for a country which he regards as the worst enemy of his own, and the citizens of all classes who have to be obsequious to the rich and insolent to the poor. These are only a few examples of the male prostitutions, so repeatedly and vehemently denounced by the prophets in the Bible as whoredoms and idolatries, which are daily imposed on men by Capitalism.

We see, then, that when the reproach of prostitution is raised neither woman nor man dares cast the first stone; for both have been equally stained with it under Capitalism. It may even be urged by special pleaders on behalf of women that the prostitution of the mind is more mischievous, and is a deeper betrayal of the divine purpose of our powers, than the prostitution of the body, the sale of which does not necessarily involve its misuse. As a matter of fact nobody has ever blamed Nell Gwynne for selling her body as Judas Iscariot for selling his soul. But whatever satisfaction the pot may have in calling the kettle blacker than itself the two blacks do not make a white. And the abstract identity of male and female prostitution only brings out more strongly the physical difference, which no abstract argument can balance. The violation of one's person is a quite peculiar sort of outrage. Anyone who does not draw a line between it and offences to the mind ignores the plain facts of human sensitiveness. For instance, landlords have had the power to force Dissenters to send their children to Church schools, and have used it. They have also had a special power over women to anticipate a husband's privilege, and have either used it or forced the woman to buy them off. Can a woman feel about the one case as about the other? A man cannot. The quality of the two wrongs is quite different. The remedy for the one could wait until after the next general election. The other does not bear thinking of for a moment. Yet there it is.

49
TRADE UNION CAPITALISM

NOW we must go into the history of the resistance offered by the proletariat to the capitalists. It was evident, to begin with, that no woman or man could do anything against the employers single-handed. The stock retort, "If you will not take the wage offered, and do the work put upon you, there are plenty who will", checkmated the destitute solitary bargainer for a decent living wage and a reasonable day's work. The first necessity for effective resistance was that the employees should form some sort of union and stand together. In many cases this was impossible, because the employees did not know oneanother, and had no opportunities of coming together and agreeing on a joint course of action. For instance, domestic servants could not form unions. They were in private kitchens all over the country, more or less imprisoned in them, and working singly, or at most in groups of two or three, except in the houses of the very rich, where the groups might be as large as thirty or forty. Or take agricultural laborers. It is very difficult to organize them into unions, and still more difficult to keep their unions together for any length of time. They live too far apart. The same thing is true more or less of almost every kind of labor except labor in factories and mines or on railways.

In some callings there are such differences of pay and social position that even if all their members could be brought together they would not mix. Thus on the stage an actor may be a highly accomplished gentleman with a title, who plays Hamlet, or a lady who is an aristocrat and a Dame of the British Empire, and plays Portia: both of them receiving weekly salaries counted in hundreds of pounds. With them are working every night actors and actresses who never utter a word, because, if they did, their speech would betray the fact that, far from being the court lords and ladies they are dressed up to look like, they are not earning as much as the carpenters who shift the scenes. It is even possible for an acrobat or clown to be more highly paid than Hamlet, and yet in private life be so illiterate, and have such shocking table manners, that the titled Hamlet could endure neither his conversation nor his company at dinner. For this reason a union of actors is difficult: a class split is inevitable. Union is possible only in trades where the members work together in large bodies; live in the same neighborhoods; belong all to the same social class; and earn about the same money. The miners in the coalfields, the cotton spinners in the factory towns of Lancashire, the metal smelters and fitters in the Midlands, were the first to form enduring and powerful unions. The bricklayers, masons, carpenters, and joiners who come together in the building trades were also early in the field with attempts at unionism. Under the stress of some intolerable oppression they would combine to make the employers see their situation in some particular point; and when they had carried that point, or were defeated, the union would dissolve until another emergency arose. Then they began to subscribe to form little insurance funds against unemployment, which obliged them to keep the union together; and in this way the unions grew from momentary rebellions into permanent Trade Unions of the kind we know.

We now have to consider what a union of proletarians can do to defend their livelihood from the continual encroachments of Capitalism. First, when the union is sufficiently complete, it enables them to face the employer without any risk of being told that if they will not submit to his terms others will. If nearly all the bricklayers in a town form a union, and each pays into it week by week a small contribution until they have a little fund to fall back on, then, if their employers attempt to reduce their wages, they can, by refusing to work and living on their fund, bring the employers' business to a dead stop for weeks or months, according to the size of the fund. This is called a strike. They can strike not only against a reduction of wages but for an increase, or for a reduction of their working hours, or for anything that may be in dispute between them and the employers. Their success will depend on the state of the employers' business. The employers can practically always wait if they choose until the strike fund is exhausted, and thus starve the strikers into submission. But if trade is so flourishing at the moment, and the employers consequently in such a hurry to get on with their profit making, that they would lose more by an interruption to their business than by giving the strikers what they demand, then the employers will give in.

But the employers will bide their time for a counterstrike. When trade gets slack again, and they have little or nothing to lose by shutting up their works for a while, they reduce the wage, and lock out all the workers who will not submit to the reduction. This is why an employers' strike is called a lock-out. The newspapers use the word strike for strikes and lock-outs indiscriminately, because their readers blame the workers instead of the employers for a strike; but some of the greatest so-called strikes should have been called lock-outs. A boom in trade always produces a series of strikes which are generally successful. A falling-off in trade produces a series of lock-outs; and they, too, are generally successful, the one series undoing the work of the other in a dreary see-saw. After the war we went through a gigantic boom followed by a disastrous slump, with strikes and lock-outs all complete. Your own experience of these civil wars of strike and lock-out must have left you convinced that they are public disasters which would have no sort of sense in a well ordered community. But let that pass for the moment. We have not yet finished our study of primitive Trade Unionism, nor seen what it led to besides saving up for a strike and then "downing tools".

The first necessity of the situation was that everybody in the trade should join the union, as outsiders could be used by employers to break the strike by taking on the work that the strikers refused. Consequently a fierce hatred of the men who would not join the unions grew up. They were called scabs and blacklegs, and boycotted in every possible way by the unionists. But vituperation and boycotting were not sufficient to deter the scabs. The unions, when they declared a strike, stationed bodies of strikers at the gates of the works to persuade the scabs not to enter. No Intelligent Woman will need to be told that unless there was a strong force of police on the spot the persuasion was so vigorous that the scabs felt lucky when they survived it without broken bones. At last there came a time in Sheffield and Manchester when scabs working at furnaces found bombs there that blew them to pieces; when machinery and tools were tampered with so as to make them dangerous to those who used them (this was called rattening); and when factory chimneys were shattered by explosives like fulminate of mercury, so risky to handle that only very ignorant and desperate men would venture on their use. This was stopped less by punishing the perpetrators than by forcing the employers to relax the provocation. For instance, the Sheffield sawgrinders died prematurely, and suffered miserably during their lifetimes, because the air they breathed was half steel dust. It was quite easy to prevent this by using vacuum cleaners (as we call them) to suck away the deadly dust; but the employers would not fit them, because, as they cost extra capital on which there was no extra profit, an employer who fitted them could be undersold by those who did not. At that time a Sheffield steel worker of fifty (when he was lucky enough to reach that age) looked like a weedy and very unhealthy lad of seventeen. In the face of such murderous conditions, persisted in for a hundred years, the burst of outrage on the part of the victims seems trifling enough. At last the Government had to come to the rescue and force all the employers to fit suction fans. Sheffielders' lungs are now no worse than most people's, and better than those of many who are not so carefully protected by the law.

But accepting a lower wage than that demanded by the union was not the only way in which an employee could drag down his fellows. In many trades it was not much use fixing the wage the worker was to receive unless the quantity of work he gave for it was also fixed. You must be tired by this time of the silly joking of the Capitalist newspapers about bricklayers who are not allowed by their unions to lay more than three bricks a day. A bricklayer has clearly as much right to charge a day's wages for laying three bricks as his employer has to sell the house when it is built for the biggest price he can get for it. Those who condemn either of them are condemning the Capitalist system, like good Bolshevists. The three-brick joke is only a comic exaggeration of what actually occurs. The employers, to find out how much work can be got out of a man, pick out an exceptionally quick and indefatigable man called a slogger, and try to impose what he can do in a day on all the rest. The unions naturally retort by forbidding any of their members to lay a brick more than he must do if he is to be worth employing at all. This practice of deliberately doing the least they dare instead of the most they can is the ca'canny of which the employers complain so much, though they all do the same thing themselves under the more respectable name of "restricting output" and selling in the dearest market. It is the principle on which the Capitalist system is avowedly founded.

Thus Capitalism drives the employers to do their worst to the employed, and the employed to do the least for them. And it boasts all the time of the incentive it provides to both to do their best! You may ask why this does not end in a deadlock. The answer is it is producing deadlocks twice a day or thereabouts. The King's speeches in opening Parliament now contain regularly an appeal to the workers and employers to be good boys and not paralyze the industry of the nation by the clash of their quite irreconcilable interests. The reason the Capitalist system has worked so far without jamming for more than a few months at a time, and then only in places, is that it has not yet succeeded in making a conquest of human nature so complete that everybody acts on strictly business principles. The mass of the nation has been humbly and ignorantly taking what the employers offer and working as well as it can, either believing that it is doing its duty in that station of life to which it has pleased God to call it, or not thinking about the matter at all, but suffering its lot as something that cannot be helped, like the weather. Even late in the nineteenth century, when there were fourteen million wage workers, only a million and a half of them were in trade unions, which meant that only a million and a half of them were selling their labor on systematic Capitalist business principles. Today nearly four and a half millions of them are converts to Capitalism, and duly enrolled in militant unions. Between six and seven hundred battles a year, called trade disputes, are fought; and the number of days of work lost to the nation by them sometimes totals up to ten millions and more. If the matter were not so serious for all of us one could laugh at the silly way in which people talk of the spread of Socialism when what is really threatening them is the spread of Capitalism. The moment the propertyless workers refuse to see the finger of God in their poverty, and begin organizing themselves in unions to make the most money they can out of their labor exactly as they find the landlord doing with his land, the capitalist with his capital, the employer with his knowledge of business, and the financier with his art of promotion, the industry of the country, on which we all depend for our existence, begins rolling faster and faster down two opposite slopes, at the bottom of which there will be a disastrous collision which will bring it to a standstill until either Property drives Labor by main force into undisguised and unwilling slavery, or Labor gains the upper hand, and the long series of changes by which the mastery of the situation has already passed from the landlord-capitalist to the individual employer, from the individual employer to the joint stock company, from the joint stock company to the Trust, and finally from the industrialists in general to the financiers, will culminate in its passing to capitalized Labor. The battle for this supremacy is joined; and here we are in the thick of it, our country ravaged by strikes and lockouts, a huge army of unemployed billeted upon us, the ladies and gentlemen declaring that it is all the fault of the workers, and the workers either declaring that it is all the fault of the ladies and gentlemen, or else, more sensibly, concluding that it is the fault of the Capitalist system, and taking to Socialism not so much because they understand it as because it promises a way out.

When this open war was first declared, the employers used their command of Parliament to have it punished as a crime. The unions were classed as conspiracies; and anybody who joined one was held to be a conspirator and punished accordingly. This did not prevent the unions: it only "drove them underground": that is, made secret societies of them, and thereby put them into the hands of more determined and less law-abiding leaders. The Government at last found it impossible to go on with such coercion; for the few cases in which the law could be carried out had the effect of martyrdoms, producing noisy popular agitations, and stimulating Trade Unionism instead of suppressing it.

Then the employers tried what they could do for themselves. They refused to employ unionists. This was no use: they could not get enough non-unionist labor to go on with; and the unionists whom they had to employ refused to work with non-unionists. Then the employers refused to "recognize" the unions, which meant that they refused to negotiate questions of wages with the secretaries of the unions, and insisted on dealing with their employees directly and individually, one at a time. This also failed. Making a separate bargain with each employee is easy enough in the case of a woman engaging a domestic servant or an oldfashioned merchant engaging a clerk or warehouseman; but when men have to be taken on by the hundred, and sometimes by the thousand, separate bargaining is impossible. The big employers who talked about it at first really meant that there was to be no bargaining at all. The men were to come in and just take what they were told were the wages of the firm, and not presume to argue. The moment the formation of the unions enabled the men to bargain, the big employers, to save their own time, had to insist on its being done with a single representative of the men who was experienced in bargaining and qualified to discuss business: that is, with the secretary of the Trade Union; so that all the fuss ended in the unions being not only recognized by the big employers, but looked on as a necessary part of their industry. Finally the unions were legalized; and here, as in the case of the Married Women's Property Acts, the change from outlawry to legal protection went a little beyond the mark, in its reaction against previous injustice, and gave the Trade Unions privileges and immunities which are not enjoyed by ordinary societies. The employers then found that they also must act together in dealing with the Trade Unions. Accordingly, they formed unions of their own, called Employers' Federations. The war of Capital with Labor is now a war of Trade Unions with Employers' Federations. Their battles, or rather blockades, are lock-outs and strikes, lasting, like modern military battles, for months.

Though some of the battles are about victimization (that is, discharging an employee for actively advocating Trade Unionism, or refusing to reinstate a prominent striker when the strike is over), all the disputes in which ground is won or lost are about wages or hours of work. You must understand that there are two sorts of wages: time wages and piecework wages. Time wages are paid for the employee's time by the month, week, day, or hour, no matter how much or how little work may be done during those periods. Piecework wages are paid according to the work done: so much for each piece of work turned out.

Now you would suppose that the employees would be unanimously in favor of time wages, and the employers of piecework wages: indeed this was roughly so in early days. But the introduction of machinery altered the case. Piecework wages are really only time wages paid in such a way as to prevent the employee from slacking. He has to keep hard at it to earn the wage; but the amount of the wage is arrived at by considering whether what he can make in an hour or a day or a week at piecework will enable him to live in the way he is accustomed to live, or, as it is called, to maintain his standard of subsistence. Now suppose a machine is invented by which he can turn out twice as many pieces in a day as before. He will then find that he has earned as much in the week by Wednesday evening as he had previously earned by Saturday. What will he do? You may think, if you are a very energetic lady, that he will put in the whole week as usual, and rejoice his wife by bringing home twice as much money. But that is not what a man is like. He prefers a shillingsworth of leisure to another shillingsworth of bread and cheese or a new hat for his wife. What he actually does is to bring her just what he brought her before, and have a holiday on Thursday, Friday, and Saturday, leaving his employer with no labor to go on with, and perhaps with the most pressing contracts to be finished by a certain date. To force him to remain at work the whole week the employer has to "cut the rate": that is, to reduce the piecework wage by half. Then the fat is in the fire: the Trade Union resists the reduction fiercely, and threatens that if the employees are to have no benefit from the new machine they will refuse to work it. There was a time when the introduction of machines led to riots and the wrecking of newly equipped factories by furious mobs of handworkers. When the mobs were replaced by Trade Unions the introduction of new machines was often followed by strikes and lock-outs. But when the heated personal disputes of hot-headed employers with resentful employees gave way to cool negotiations between experienced secretaries of Employers' Federations and equally experienced secretaries of Trade Unions, who had settled similar difficulties many times before, it became an established practice to readjust the piecework wage so as to allow the employee to share the benefit of the machine with the employer. The only question was how much each could claim.

On time wages the employee gets no benefit from the introduction of a machine. The product of his labor may be multiplied a hundred times; but he remains as poor as before. That is why in many industries the employees insist on piecework wages, and the employers would be only too glad to pay time wages: all the more because, when machinery comes into play, the machine works the man instead of the man working the machine, and slacking becomes either impossible or easy to detect.

But it often happens that neither the time wage worker nor the piece wage worker has any say in the matter at all, for the very simple reason that the introduction of the machine enables the employer to "slack the lot" and replace them by girls who are only machine minders. And we have already seen what the effect of women's and girls' labor has on wages. Besides, Trade Unionism is weaker among women than among men, because, as most women regard industrial employment as merely a temporary expedient to keep them going until they get married, they will not take the duty of combination as seriously as the men, who know that they will be industrial employees all their lives. In the Lancashire weaving industry, where women do not retire from the factory when they marry, the women's unions are as strong as the men's.

In the long run the reserves of the employer are so much greater than those of the employees that though John Stuart Mill's statement in the middle of last century that the wage workers had not benefited by the introduction of machinery is no longer quite true, yet they have gained so little in comparison with the prodigiously greater national output from the machines, that it is putting it very mildly to say that they have not only not gained but lost ground heavily relatively to the capitalists.

50
DIVIDE AND GOVERN

THE weakness of Trade Unionism was that the concessions wrung from the employers when trade was good were taken back again when trade was bad, because, as the employers commanded the main national store of spare money, they could always stop working without starving for longer than their employees. The Trade Unions soon had to face the fact that unless they could get the concessions fixed and enforced by law, they were certain to lose by the lock-outs all they gained by the strikes. At the same time they saw that Parliament had put a permanent stop to the sweating of very young children in factories; and though, as I have explained, their members had been driven by poverty to object to this reform, nevertheless it convinced them that Parliament, if it liked, could fix any reform so firmly that the employers could not go back on it. They wanted a permanent reduction in the then monstrous length of the factory working day. The cry for a reduction to eight hours was set up. At first it seemed an unattainable ideal; and it is still very far from being completely attained. But a ten hours day for women and children and young persons seemed reasonable and possible. As to the men, they were told they were grown-up independent Britons, and that it would be an outrage on British liberty to prevent an Englishman from working as long as he liked. But when the women and young children go home the factory engine is stopped, because its work cannot go on without them. When the engine stops the men may as well go home too, as their work cannot go on without the engine. So the men got the factory hours shortened by law "behind the petticoats of the women".

And how did the employees, who had no votes at that time,

induce Parliament, in which there were only landlords, capitalists, and employers, to pass these benevolent Acts of Parliament for the protection of the employees against the employers?

If I were to reply that they were acts of pure conscience, nobody nowadays would believe me, because Capitalism has destroyed our belief in any effective power but that of self-interest backed by force. But even Capitalist cynicism will admit that however unconscionable we may be when our own interests are affected, we can be most indignantly virtuous at the expense of others. The Intelligent Woman must guard herself against imagining that the property owners and employers in Parliament a hundred years ago had read this book, and therefore understood that their interests were the same, though their occupations and habits and social positions were so very different. The country gentlemen despised the employers as vulgar tradesmen, and made them feel it. The employers, knowing that any fool might be a peer or a country gentleman if he had the luck to be born in a country house, whilst success in business needed business ability, were determined to destroy the privileges of the landed aristocracy. This had been done in France in 1789 by a revolution; and it was by threatening a similar revolution that the English employers, in 1832, forced the King and the peerage, after a long popular agitation, to pass into law the famous Reform Bill which practically transferred the command of Parliament in England from the hereditary landed aristocracy to the industrial employers.

You know what a popular agitation means. It means a little reasoning and a great deal of abuse of the other side. Before 1832 the employers did not confine themselves to pointing out the absurdity of allowing a couple of cottages owned by a county aristocrat to send a member to Parliament when the city of Birmingham was not represented there. Most people thought it quite natural that great folk should have great privileges, and cared nothing about Birmingham, which they had heard of only as a dirty place where most of the bad pennies (Brummagem buttons) came from. The employers therefore stirred up public feeling against the landed gentry by exposing all their misdeeds: their driving of whole populations out of the country to make room for sheep or deer; their ruthless enforcement of the Game Laws, under which men were transported with the worst felons for poaching a few hares or pheasants; the horrible condition of the laborers' cottages on their estates; the miserable wages they paid; their bigoted persecution of Nonconformists not only by refusing to allow any places of worship except those of the Church of England to be built on their estates, but by nominating to the Church livings such clergymen as could be depended on to teach the children in the village schools that all Dissenters were disgraced in this world and damned in the next; their equally bigoted boycotting of any shopkeeper who dared to vote against their candidates at elections; with all the other tyrannies which in those days made it a common saying, even among men of business, that "the displeasure of a lord is a sentence of death". By harping on these grievances the employers at last embittered public opinion against the squires to such a pitch that the fear of a repetition in England of the French Revolution broke down the opposition to the Reform Bill. The employers, after propitiating King William IV by paying his debts, were able to force Parliament to pass the Bill; and that event inaugurated the purseproud reign of the English middle class under Queen Victoria.

Naturally the squires were not disposed to take this defeat lying down. They revenged themselves by taking up Lord Shaftesbury's agitation for the Factory Acts, and shewing that the employer's little finger was thicker than the country gentleman's loins; that the condition of the factory employees was worse than that of the slaves on the American and West Indian plantations; that the worst cottages of the worst landlords had at least fresher air than the overcrowded slums of the manufacturing towns; that if the employers did not care whether their "hands" were Church of England or Methodist, neither did they care whether they were Methodists or Atheists, because they had no God but Mammon; that if they did not persecute politically it was only because the hands had no votes; that they persecuted industrially as hard as they could by imprisoning Trade Unionists; and that the personal and often kindly relations between the peasantry and the landlords, the training in good manners and decent housekeeping traditions learnt by the women in domestic service in the country houses, the kindnesses shewn to the old and sick on the great estates, were all lost in the squalor and misery, the brutality and blasphemy, the incestuous overcrowding, and the terrible dirt epidemics in the mining and factory populations where English life was what the employer's greed had made it.

All this, though quite true, was merely the pot again calling the kettle black; for the country gentlemen did not refuse the dividends made for them by the employers in the mines and factories, nor refuse to let factories and slums be built all over their estates in Lancashire; nor did the employers, when they had made fortunes, hesitate to buy country estates and "found families" to be brought up in the strictest county traditions, nor to disparage trade as vulgar when the generation that remembered what their grandfathers were had died out. But the quarrel between them explains how it was that when Parliament consisted exclusively of landlords and capitalist employers or their nominees, and the proletariat had no votes, yet the Factory Acts got passed. The Acts were the revenge of the squires for the Reform Act.

Also, the poor were not wholly voteless. The owner of a freehold worth forty shillings a year had a vote; and a number of odd old franchises existed which gave quite poor people a certain weight at elections. They could not return a Labor member (such a thing was then unheard of); but they could sometimes turn the scale as between the Conservative landlord and the Liberal employer. If the Conservatives and Liberals had understood that their political interests were the same, and that they must present a united front to Labor, the employees would have had no hope except in revolution. But the Conservatives and Liberals did not understand their commercial interests. The Conservative clung blindly to his old privileges: the Liberal followed the slot of his new profits as thoughtlessly as a hound follows the slot of a fox. Both of them wanted to be in Parliament because it gave them personal importance, opening the way to the front bench, where the Cabinet Ministers sit, and to knighthoods, baronetcies, and peerages. The Liberals considered themselves the party of reform because they had carried the Reform Bill, and, as the employees wanted all sorts of reform very badly, took it for granted that they would always vote gratefully for the Liberals.

Under this delusion a Liberal Government made a bid for

popular support by offering votes to the working class. The Conservatives at first opposed this so fiercely that they turned the Liberals out at the next election; but a very clever Conservative leader named Benjamin Disraeli, afterwards Earl of Beaconsfield, a Jew who had begun his political career, like Karl Marx, as a champion of the proletariat, persuaded the Conservatives that they were really more popular in the country than the Liberals, and induced them to make the very extension of the franchise they had just been opposing. Naturally the employees, when they got some votes in this way, used them to get more votes; and the end of it was that everybody got a vote, including at long last the women, though the women had to make a special and furious fight for their inclusion, and did not win it until the national work they did when they took the place of the absent men during the war of 1914-18 shamed the country into enfranchising them.

The proletarian voters who could formerly only turn the scale between Conservative and Liberal can now turn out both Conservative and Liberal, and elect candidates of their own. They did not at first realize this, and have not fully realized it yet. They began by timidly sending into Parliament about a dozen men who were not called Labor members, but working class members of the Liberal Party. It became the custom for Liberal Governments to give a minor ministerial post to some mild middle class professor who was vaguely supposed to be interested in factory legislation and popular education, and who was openly treated as a negligible nobody by the rest of the Cabinet.

Meanwhile Socialist societies were growing up among students of Karl Marx's famous exposure of the sins of Capitalism, and of a very widely circulated book called Progress and Poverty, written by an American named Henry George, who had seen within his own lifetime American villages, where people were neither poor enough to be degraded and miserable nor rich enough to be idle and extravagant, changed by the simple operation of private property in land and capital into cities of fabulous wealth, so badly divided that the mass of the people were weltering in shocking poverty whilst a handful of owners wallowed in millions. These Societies broke the tradition of proletarian attachment to the Liberal Party by making the workers what Marx called class-conscious, a phrase which the Intelligent Woman has probably met several times in the papers without knowing any more clearly than the newspaper writers exactly what it means. The voters who had believed that there were only two parties in politics, the Conservatives and the Liberals (or Tories and Whigs), representing the two great religious parties of the Churchmen and the Dissenters, and the two great economic interests of the country farmers with their landlords and the town men of business with their capitalists, were now taught that from the point of view of the employee there is not a penny to choose between Conservatives and Liberals, as the gain of either means the employee's loss, and that the only two parties who really have opposed interests are the party of the propertied class on the one hand and the party of the propertyless proletariat on the other: in other words, the party of Capital and the party of Labor. What mattered was not the Parliamentary struggle between the Liberal Mr Gladstone and the Conservative Mr Disraeli as to which should be Prime Minister, or between their successors Mr Balfour, Mr Bonar Law, and Mr Baldwin of the one party, and Sir Henry Campbell-Bannerman, Mr Asquith, and Mr Lloyd George of the other. To the class-conscious proletarian all that is mere Tweedledum and Tweedledee: what is really moving the world is the Class Struggle, the Class War (both terms are in use) between the proprietors and the proletariat for the possession of the land and capital of the country (the Means of Production). When a man realized that, he was said to be class-conscious. These terms are misleading because they imply that all the proletarians are in one camp and all the bourgeoisie in the other, which is untrue; but as the Intelligent Woman who has read thus far now knows what they mean, let them pass for the moment.

The Socialist Societies had begun badly by treating Parliament as the enemy's camp; boycotting the Churches as mere contrivances for doping the workers into submission to Capitalism; and denouncing Trade Unionism and Co-operation as mistaken remedies. Under Marx and Engels, Morris and Hyndman, Socialism was a middle class movement caused by the revolt of the consciences of educated and humane men and women against the injustice and cruelty of Capitalism, and also (this was a very important factor with Morris) against its brutal disregard of beauty and the daily human happiness of doing fine work for its own sake. Now the strongest and noblest feelings of this kind were quite compatible with the most complete detachment from and ignorance of proletarian life and history in the class that worked for weekly wages. The most devoted middle class champions of the wage workers knew what housemaids and gardeners and railway porters and errand boys and postmen were like; but factory hands, miners, and dockers might as well have been fairies for all their lady and gentleman sympathizers knew about them.

Whenever your sympathies are strongly stirred on behalf of some cruelly ill used person or persons of whom you know nothing except that they are ill used, your generous indignation attributes all sorts of virtues to them, and all sorts of vices to those who oppress them. But the blunt truth is that ill used people are worse than well used people: indeed this is at bottom the only good reason why we should not allow anyone to be ill used. If I thought you would be made a better woman by ill treatment I should do my best to have you ill treated. We should refuse to tolerate poverty as a social institution not because the poor are the salt of the earth, but because "the poor in a lump are bad". And the poor know this better than anyone else. When the Socialist movement in London took its tone from lovers of art and literature who had read George Borrow until they had come to regard tramps as saints, and passionate High Church clergymen (Anglo-Catholics) who adored supertramps like St Francis, it was apt to assume that all that was needed was to teach Socialism to the masses (vaguely imagined as a huge crowd of tramplike saints) and leave the rest to the natural effect of sowing the good seed in kindly virgin soil. But the proletarian soil was neither virgin nor exceptionally kindly. The masses are not in the least like tramps; and they have no romantic illusions about oneanother, whatever illusions each of them may cherish about herself. When John Stuart Mill was a Parliamentary candidate in Westminster, his opponents tried to defeat him by recalling an occasion on which he had said flatly that the British workman was neither entirely truthful, entirely sober, entirely honest, nor imbued with a proper sense of the wickedness of gambling: in short, that he was by no means the paragon he was always assumed to be by parliamentary candidates when they addressed his class as "Gentlemen", and begged for his vote. Mill probably owed his success on that occasion to the fact that instead of denying his opinion he uncompromisingly reaffirmed it. The wage workers are as fond of flattery as other people, and will swallow any quantity of it from candidates provided it be thoroughly understood that it is only flattery, and that the candidates know better; but they have no use for gushingly idealistic ladies and gentlemen who are fools enough to think that the poor are cruelly misunderstood angels.

In the eighteen-eighties the Socialists found out their mistake. The Fabian Society got rid of its Anarchists and Borrovians, and presented Socialism in the form of a series of parliamentary measures, thus making it possible for an ordinary respectable religious citizen to profess Socialism and belong to a Socialist Society without any suspicion of lawlessness, exactly as he might profess himself a Conservative and belong to an ordinary constitutional club. A leader of the society, Mr Sidney Webb, married Miss Beatrice Potter, who had made a study at first hand of working-class life and organization, and had published a book on Co-operation. They wrote the first really scientific history of Trade Unionism, and thereby not only made the wage-workers conscious of the dignity of their own political history (a very important step in the Marxian class-consciousness) but shewed the middle-class Socialists what the public work of the wage-working world was really like, and convinced them of the absurdity of supposing that Socialists could loftily ignore the organization the people had already accomplished spontaneously in their own way. Only by grafting Socialism on this existing organization could it be made a really powerful proletarian movement.

The Liberals, still believing themselves to be the party of progress, assumed that all progressive movements would be grafted on the Liberal Party as a matter of course, to be patronized and adopted by the Liberal leaders in Parliament as far as they approved. They were disagreeably surprised when the first effect of the adoption of constitutional parliamentarism by the Fabian Society was an attack on the Liberal Government of that day, published in one of the leading reviews, for being more reactionary and hostile to the wage-workers than the Conservatives. The Liberals were so astonished and scandalized that they could only suggest that the Fabian Society had been bribed by the Conservatives to commit what seemed to all Liberals to be an act of barefaced political treachery. They soon had their eyes opened much more widely. The Fabian Society followed up its attack by a proposal for the establishment of a Labor Party in Parliament to oppose both Conservatives and Liberals impartially. A working-class leader, Keir Hardie, formerly a miner, founded a Society called the Independent Labor Party to put this proposal into practice. Among the members of the Fabian Society who became a leader in this new Society was Mr Ramsay MacDonald, who, by his education and knowledge of the world outside the wage-working class, was better qualified than Keir Hardie for successful leadership in Parliament. From the Independent Labor Party sprang The Labor Party, a political federation, much more powerful, of Trade Unions and of Socialist Societies, whose delegates sat on its executive committee. As all the persons who were members of Trade Unions at that time could, by subscribing a penny a week each, have provided a political fund of over £325,000 (there are three times as many now), this combination with the Trade Unionists was decisive. At the election of 1906 enough Labor members were elected to form an independent party in Parliament. By 1923 they had encroached so much that neither the Liberals nor the Conservatives had a majority in the House; and Mr Ramsay MacDonald was challenged to form a Government and shew whether Labor could govern or not. He accepted the challenge, and became British Prime Minister with a Cabinet of Socialists and Trade Unionists. It was a more competent government than the Conservative Government that preceded it, partly because its members, having risen from poverty or obscurity to eminence by their personal ability, were unhampered by nonentities, and partly because it knew what the world is like today, and was not dreaming, as even the cleverest of the Conservative leaders still were, of the Victorian mixture of growing cotton lordship and decaying feudal lordship in the capitalist class, with starved helpless ignorance and submissive servitude in the proletariat, which had not even lasted out Queen Victoria's lifetime. In fact, the Labor leaders were to an extraordinary degree better educated and more experienced than their opponents, who infatuatedly took it for granted that rich men must be superior in education because they graduate in the two aristocratic universities instead of in the school of economically organic life.

The Liberals and Conservatives, disgusted with this result, and ruefully sorry that by derisively giving Labor a chance to prove its relative incompetence it had proved the opposite, combined to throw Mr MacDonald out of office in 1924. Although he had as yet no real chance of a majority in the country, he had so scared the plutocrats in Parliament by his comparative success as Secretary of State for Foreign Affairs, which they had regarded as the department in which Labor was certain to break down ridiculously, that they overdid their attack by persuading the country that he was connected with the Communist Government of Russia. The panic which followed, lasting until the election was over, wiped out at the polls, not the Labor Party, which just managed to hold its own, but the innocent Liberal Party.

The danger of stampeding a general election is that all sorts of political lunatics, whom no one would dream of taking seriously in quiet times, get elected by screaming that the country is in danger, whilst sober candidates are defeated ignominiously. In 1906, when a general election was stampeded by an alarm of Chinese labor, third rate Liberal candidates ousted first rate Conservative ones by the score. In 1924 the Red Russian scare enabled third rate Conservatives to oust first rate Liberals. In both cases the result was a grave falling-off in the quality of the victorious party. When the Sirdar, our representative in Egypt, was unluckily assassinated just after the election, the Conservatives, drunk with their victory, could not be restrained by the Prime Minister, Mr Baldwin, from hurling at the assassins an insane threat to cut off the water supply of Egypt. This extravagance, which startled all Europe, was felt to be just the sort of thing that Mr MacDonald would not have done. The Government had to climb down rather abjectly when it discovered that it could neither carry out its threat nor expect anything but reprobation from all sides, both at home and abroad, for having been so absurd as to make it; for though a forceful wickedness is, I am sorry to say, rather popular than otherwise when our Governments indulge in it at the expense of foreigners, we expect it to be successful. A climb-down is unpopular in proportion to the arrogance of the climb-up. Consequently the Government lost on the Egyptian fiasco the support won by the Russian scare; but it lost its head again at a crazy threat of a general strike by the Trade Unions. The Russians sent us a very handsome subscription to the strike funds; and the Government, frightened and infuriated, and quite incapable of measuring the danger (which need not have alarmed a mouse) brought in a futile but provocative Bill to make Trade Unionism illegal, and broke off diplomatic relations with Russia after raiding the offices of the Russian Government in London. Meanwhile, Labor in Parliament, having recovered from the shock of the election, settled into its place as the official Opposition.

To sum up the story to the point it has now reached (1927), the Proletariat, having begun its defensive operations in the Class War by organizing its battalions into Trade Unions, only to discover that it could not retain its winnings without passing them into law, organized itself politically as a Labor Party, and returned enough members to Parliament to change the House of Commons from a chamber in which two capitalist parties, calling themselves Conservative and Liberal, contended for the spoils of office and the honor and glory of governing, to an arena in which the Proletariat and the Proprietariat face each other on a series of questions which are all parts of two main questions: first, whether the national land and capital and industry shall be held and controlled by the nation for the nation, or left in the hands of a small body of private men to do as they please with; second, whilst the capitalist system lasts, which shall be top dog, the provider of capital or the provider of labor. The first is a Socialist question, because until land and capital and the control of industry are in the hands of the Government it cannot equalize the distribution either of the product or of the labor of producing it.

The second is a Trade Unionist question. The Labor Party consists not only of Socialists aiming at equality of income, but of Trade Unionists who have no objection to the continuance of the capitalist method in industry provided that Labor gets the lion's share. It should be easier to maintain the capitalist system with the proletarians taking the lion's share, and the landlords, capitalists, and employers reduced to comparative penury, than to maintain it as at present; for the laborers and mechanics and their wives and daughters form about nine-tenths of the nation; and on all accounts it should be safer and steadier to have only one discontented person to every nine contented ones than nine discontented persons to every one contented one. To put it another way, it should be easier for a government supported by nine-tenths of the voters to collect income tax and supertax from landlords and capitalists until they had to sell their country houses and motor cars to their tenants and employees, and live in the gardener's cottage themselves, than it is for a landlord to collect his rents or a capitalist to find investments on which he can live in luxury. An engineer designing a Forth Bridge, or an architect a cathedral or a palace, can quite easily be reduced to accept less money for his work than the riveters and fitters and masons and bricklayers and painters who carry out the designs. It is true that labor could no more do without them than they could do without labor; but labor would have the advantage in bargaining, because the talented worker, sooner than waste his talent, would rather exercise it for a low wage than fix rivets or pile bricks for a high one. At his own job he will work on any terms for the pleasure of working, and loathe any other job; whilst the reluctant laborer will do nothing for nothing and very little for a halfpenny.

Thus a Trade Unionist Government, with the mass of the people at its back, could, by ruthless taxation of unearned incomes, by Factory Acts, by Wages Boards fixing wages, by Commissions fixing prices, by using the income tax to subsidize trades in which wages were low (all of these devices are already established in parliamentary practice) could redistribute the national income in such a way that the present rich would become the poor, and the laborer would be cock of the walk. What is more, that arrangement would be much more stable than the present state of affairs in which the many are poor and the few rich. The only threat to its permanence would come from the owners of property refusing to go on collecting rent and interest merely to have it nearly all seized by the tax collector. If you have a thousand a year and a turn for business, you must sometimes feel that you are really only collecting money for the Government at a commission of seventy per cent or thereabouts. Suppose the commission were reduced to twenty-five per cent, what could you do but pay £750 out of your thousand as helplessly as you now pay £250? Just as the owners of property, when they controlled Parliament, used their power to extort the utmost farthing from Labor, Labor can and probably will use its power to extort the utmost farthing from Property unless equal distribution for all is made a fundamental constitutional dogma. At present the propertied classes are looking to capitalist Trade Unions to save them from Socialism. The time is coming when they will clamor for Socialism to save them from capitalist Trade Unionism: that is, from Capitalized Labor. Already in America Trade Unionism is combining with Big Business to squeeze the sleeping partner. More of that later on.

51
DOMESTIC CAPITAL

AFTER talking so long about Capitalism in the lump, let us take a few chapters off to examine it as it affects you personally if you happen to be a lady with a little capital of your own: one who, after living in the style customary in her class, still has some money to spare to use as capital so as to increase her income. I will begin by the simple case of a woman earning money, not as an employer, but by her own work.

Let us assume that her work involves doing sums (she is an accountant), or writing (she is an author or scrivener), or visiting clients instead of waiting in an office to receive them (she is a doctor). It is evident that if she can spare money enough to buy an adding-machine which will enable her to do the work of three ordinary bookkeepers, or a sewing-machine, or a typewriter, or a bicycle, or a motor car, as the case may be, the machine will enable her to get through so much more work every day that she will be able to earn more money with them than without them. The machine will be carelessly called her capital (most people muddle themselves with that mistake when they discuss economics); but the capital was the money saved to pay for the machine, and as it was eaten up by the workers who made the machine, it no longer exists. What does exist is the machine, which is continually wearing out, and can never be sold second-hand for its price when new. Its value falls from year to year until it falls to nothing but the value of the old iron of which it is made.

Now suppose she marries, thus changing her profession for that of wife, mother, housekeeper, and so forth! Or suppose that the introduction of an electric tram service, and the appearance of plenty of taxis in the streets, enable her to do all the travelling she wants as well and more cheaply than her private car! What is she to do with her adding-machine or sewing-machine, her typewriter or her car? She cannot eat them or wear them on her back. The adding-machine will not iron shirt fronts: the sewing-machine will not fry eggs: the typewriter will not dust the furniture: the motor car, for all its marvels, will not wash the baby.

If you shew what I have just written to the sort of male who calls himself a practical business man, he will at once say that I am childishly wrong: that you *can* eat an adding- or sewing-machine; dust the furniture with a typewriter; and wash a hundred babies with a motor car. All you have to do is to sell the sewing-machine and buy food with the price you get for it; sell the typewriter and buy a vacuum cleaner; sell the motor car and hire a few nurses after buying a bath and soap and towels. And he will be so far right that you certainly can do all these things *provided too many other people are not trying to do them at the same time.* It is because the practical business man always forgets this proviso that he is such a hopeless idiot politically. When you have sold the sewing-machine and bought food with the price, you have not really turned the sewing-machine into food. The sewing-machine remains as uneatable as ever: not even an ostrich could get a tooth into it or digest it afterwards. What has happened is that you, finding yourself with a sewing-machine which you no longer want, and being in want of food, find some other woman who has some spare food which she does not want, but who wants a sewing-machine. You have a sewing-machine for which you have no use, and an unsatisfied appetite. She has food for which she has no appetite, and wants a sewing-machine. So you two make an exchange; and there you are! Nothing could be simpler.

But please remark that it takes two to make the bargain, and that the two must want opposite things. If they both want the same thing, or want to get rid of the same thing, there will be no deal. Now suppose the Chancellor of the Exchequer took it into his head as a practical business man to raise money by a tax on capital instead of on income. Suppose he were to say that as thousands of women have capital in the form of sewing-machines which they can sell for, say, £5 apiece, they can each afford to pay a tax of £3. Suppose he actually induced the House of Commons to impose such a tax under the title of a Capital Levy or some such practical business nonsense, and that every woman had to sell her sewing-machine to pay the tax! What would be the result? Each woman trying to sell her machine would find all the other women trying to sell their machines too, and nobody wanting to buy them. She could sell it as old iron for a shilling perhaps, but that would not enable her to pay the tax. The tax collector, not being paid, would distrain on her goods: that is, he would seize the sewing-machine. But as he also could not sell it, he would have to hand it over unsold to the Chancellor of the Exchequer, who would find himself heaped up with thousands of unsellable sewing-machines instead of the thousands of pounds he was looking forward to. He would have no money; and the women would have no sewing-machines: all because the practical business men told him that sewing-machines could be turned into bread.

If you consider this a little you will see that the difference between private affairs and State affairs is that private affairs are what people can do by themselves, one at a time and once in a way, whereas State affairs are what we are all made to do by law at the same moment. At home you are a private woman dealing with your own private affairs; but if you go into Parliament and perhaps into the Cabinet, you become a stateswoman. As a private woman all you have to consider is, "Suppose I were to do this or that". But as a stateswoman you must consider "Suppose everybody had to do this or that". This is called the Kantian test.

For instance, if you become Chancellor of the Exchequer, your common sense as a private woman will save you from such a folly as supposing that a sewing-machine in the house is the same as £5 in the house. But that very same private common sense of yours may persuade you that an income of £5 a year is the same as £100 ready money, because you know that if you want £100 your stockbroker can get it for you in exchange for £5 a year of your income. You might therefore be tempted to lay a tax of £30 on everyone with £5 a year, and imagine that you would not only get the £30, but that the taxpayer would have £70 left to go on with. Let me therefore explain the nature of this business of £5 a year being worth £100 cash to you privately, and worth just £5 a year to the Chancellor publicly and not a rap more.

When we were dealing with the impossibility of saving I pointed out that there are certain everyday transactions that are like saving and that are called saving, very much as selling a sewing-machine and buying food with the price may be called eating the sewing-machine. Do not bother to try to remember this now: it is easier to go over it again. Suppose you have £100 and you wish to save it: that is, to consume it at some future time instead of immediately! The objection is that as the things the money represents will rot unless they are used at once, what you want to do is impossible. But suppose there is in the next street a woman who has been left by the death of her parents with nothing but an income of £5 a year. Evidently she cannot live on that. But if she had £100 in ready money she could emigrate, or set up a typewriting office, or stock a little shop, or take lessons in some moneymaking art, or buy some smart clothes to improve her chances of getting respectable employment, or any of the things that poor women imagine they could do if only they had a little ready money. Now nothing is easier than for you to make an exchange with this woman. She gives you her right to take £5 every year fresh-and-fresh out of each year's harvest as it comes; and you give her your hundred pounds to spend at once. Your stockbroker or banker will bring you together. You go to him and say that you want him to invest your £100 for you at five per cent; and she goes to him and says that she wants to sell her £5 a year for ready money. He effects the change for a small commission. But the transaction is disguised under such fantastic names (like the water and breadcrumb in doctors' prescriptions) that neither you nor the other woman understands what has really happened. You are said to have invested £100, and to be "worth" £100, and to have added £100 to the capital of the country; and she is said to have "realized her capital". But all that has actually occurred is that your £100 has been handed over to be spent and done for by the other woman, and that you are left with the right to take £5 out of the income of the country without working for it year after year for ever, or until you in your turn sell that right for £100 down if you should unhappily find yourself in the same predicament as the other lady was in when you bought it.

Now suppose you brought in your tax of £30 on every £5 a year in the country! Or suppose a Conservative Government, led by the nose by practical business men who know by experience that people who have £5 a year can sell it for £100 whenever they want to, were to do it! Or suppose a Labor Government, misled by the desire to take capital out of private hands and vest it in the State, were to do it! They would call it a levy of thirty per cent on capital; and most of them would vote for it without understanding what it really meant. Its opponents would vote against it in equal ignorance of its nature; so that their arguments would convince nobody. What would happen? Evidently no woman could pay £30 out of £5 a year. She would have to sell the £5 a year for £100, and then reinvest the odd £70. But she would not get the £100 because, as the tax would not fall on her alone, but on all the other capitalists as well, her stockbroker would find everybody asking him to sell future incomes for ready money and nobody offering ready money for future incomes. It would be the story of the sewing-machines over again. She would have to tell the tax collector that she could not pay the tax, and that he might sell her furniture and be damned (intelligent women use recklessly strong language under such circumstances). But the tax collector would reply that her furniture was no good to him; for as he was selling up all the other capitalists' furniture at the same time, and as only those who were too poor to have any capital to be taxed were buying it, Chippendale chairs were down to a shilling a dozen and dining room tables to five shillings; so that it would cost him more to take her furniture away and sell it or store it than it would fetch. He would have to go away empty handed; and all the Government could do would be to take her £5 a year from her for six years and four months, the odd months being for the interest to pay for waiting. In other words it would find that her income was real, and her capital imaginary.

But even this would not work if the tax were imposed every year, like the income tax, because at the end of the six years she would owe £180, incurring a debt of £30 every year and getting only £5 to pay it with; so that it would be much better for her to give up her £5 a year for ever and support herself entirely by work. And the Government would have to admit that a tax on capital is an impossibility, for the unanswerable reason that the capital has no existence, having been eaten up long ago.

There is a tax on capital actually in existence which is often referred to as proving that such taxes are possible. When we die, taxes called Death Duties (officially Estate Duties) are levied on the fictitious capital value of our estates, if we leave any. The reason people manage to pay them is that we do not all die simultaneously every year on the 5th April and thus incur death duties payable on the following 31st December. We die seldom and slowly, less than twenty out of every thousand of us in one year, and out of that twenty not more than two at the outside have any capital. Their heirs, one would think, would find it easy to sell part of their income for enough ready money to pay the duties, the purchasers being capitalists whose fathers or uncles have not died lately. And yet the Government has to wait for its money often and long. The tax is a stupid one, not because it confiscates property by making the State inherit part of it (why not?) but because it operates cruelly and unfairly. One estate, passing by death from heir to heir three times in a century, will hardly feel the duties. Another, passing three times in one year (as happens easily during a war), is wiped out by them, and the heirs reduced from affluence to destitution. When you make your will, be careful how you leave valuable objects to poor people. If they keep them they may have to pay more for them in death duties than they can afford. Probably they will have to sell them to pay the duty.

This is so little understood, that men not otherwise mad are found estimating the capital of the country at sums varying from ten thousand millions before the war to thirty thousand millions after it (as if the war had made the country richer instead of poorer), and actually proposing in the House of Commons to tax that thirty thousand millions as available existing wealth and to pay off the cost of the war with it. They all know that you cannot eat your cake and have it too; yet, because we have spent seven thousand millions on a frightful war, and, as they calculate, twenty thousand millions more on mines and railways and factory plant and so on, and because these sums are written down in the books of the Bank of England and the balance sheets of the Companies and Trusts, they think they still exist, and that we are an enormously rich nation instead of being, as anyone can see by the condition of nine-tenths of the population, a disgracefully poor one.

52
THE MONEY MARKET

AND now, still assuming that you are a lady of some means, perhaps I can be a little useful to you in your private affairs if I explain that mysterious institution where your investments are made for you, called the Money Market, with its chronic ailment of Fluctuations that may at any moment increase your income pleasantly without any trouble to you, or swallow it up and ruin you in ways that a man can never make a woman understand because he does not understand them himself.

A market for the purchase and sale of money is nonsense on the face of it. You can say reasonably "I want five shillingsworth of salmon"; but it is ridiculous to say "I want five shillingsworth of money". Five shillingsworth of money is just five shillings; and who wants to exchange five shillings for five shillings? Nobody buys money for money except money changers, who buy foreign coins and notes to sell to you when you are going abroad.

But though nobody in England wants to buy English money, we often want to hire it, or, as we say, to borrow it. Borrow and hire, however, do not always mean the same thing. You may borrow your neighbor's frying-pan, and return it to her later on with a thank you kindly. But in the money market there is no kindness: you pay for what you get, and charge for what you give, as a matter of business. And it is quite understood that what you hire you do not give back: you consume it at once. If you ask your neighbor to lend you, not a frying-pan, but a loaf of bread and a candle, it is understood that you eat the bread and burn the candle, and repay her later on by giving her a fresh loaf and a new candle. Now when you borrow money you are really borrowing what it will buy: that is, bread and candles and material things of all sorts for immediate consumption. If you borrow a shilling you borrow it because you want to buy a shillingsworth of something to use at once. You cannot pay that something back: all you can do is to make something new or do some service that you can get paid a shilling for, and pay with that shilling. (You can, of course, borrow another shilling from someone else, or beg it or steal it; but that would not be a ladylike transaction.) At all events, not until you pay can the lender consume the things that the shilling represents. If you pay her anything additional for waiting you are really hiring the use of the money from her.

In that case you are under no obligation to her whatever, because you are doing her as great a service as she is doing you. You may not see this at first; but just consider. All money that is lent is necessarily spare money, because people cannot afford to lend money until they have spent enough of it to support themselves. Now this spare money is only a sort of handy title deed to spare things, mostly food, which will rot and perish unless they are consumed immediately. If your neighbor has a loaf left over from her week's household supply you are doing her a service in eating it for her and promising to give her a fresh loaf next week. In fact a woman who found herself with a tenpenny loaf on her hands over and above what her family needed to eat, might, sooner than throw the loaf into the dustbin, say to her neighbor, "You can have this loaf if you will give me half a fresh loaf for it next week": that is to say, she might offer half the loaf for the service of saving her from the total loss of it by natural decay.

The economists call this paying negative interest. What it means is that you pay people to keep your spare money for you until you want it instead of making them pay you for allowing them to keep it, which the economists call paying positive interest. One is just as natural as the other; and the sole reason why nobody at present will pay you to borrow from them, whereas everyone will pay you to lend to them, is that under our system of unequal division of income there are so very few of us with spare money to lend, and so very many with less than they need for immediate consumption, that there are always plenty of people offering not only to spend the spare money at once, but to replace it later on in full with fresh goods and pay the lenders for waiting into the bargain. The economists used to call this payment the reward of abstinence, which was silly, as people do not need to be rewarded for abstaining from eating a second dinner, or from wearing six suits of clothes at a time, or living in a dozen houses: on the contrary, they ought to be extremely obliged to anyone who will use these superfluities for them and pay them something as well. If instead of having a few rich amid a great many poor, we had a great many rich, the bankers would charge you a high price for keeping your money; and the epitaph of the dead knight in Watts's picture, "What I saved I lost", would be true materially as well as spiritually. If you then had £100 to spare, and wanted to save it until next year, and took it to the manager of your bank to keep it for you, he would say "I am sorry, madam; but your hundred pounds will not keep. The best I can do for you is to promise you seventy pounds next year (or fifty, or twenty, or five, as the case might be); and you are very fortunate to be able to get that with so much spare money lying about. You had really much better not save. Increase your expenditure; and enjoy your money before what it represents goes rotten. Banking is not what it was."

This cannot happen under Capitalism, because Capitalism distributes the national income in such a way that the many are poor and the few enormously rich. Therefore for the present you may count on being able to lend (invest) all your spare money, and on being paid so much a year for waiting until the borrower replaces what you have lent. The payment for waiting is called interest, or, in the Bible, usury. Interest is the polite word. The borrower, in short, hires the use of your spare money from you; and there is nothing dishonest nor dishonorable in the transaction. You hand over your spare ready money (your capital) to the borrower; and the borrower binds herself to pay you a certain yearly or monthly or weekly income until she repays it to you in full.

The money market is the place in the city where yearly incomes are bought for lump sums of spare ready money. The income you can buy for £100 (which is the measuring figure) varies from day to day, according to the plenty or scarcity of spare money offered for hire and of incomes offered for sale. It varies also according to the security of the income and the chances of its fluctuating from year to year. When you take your spare £100 to your stockbroker to invest for you (that is, to hire out for an income in the money market) he can, at the moment when I write these lines (1926) get you £4 : 10s. a year certain, £6 a year with the chance of its rising or falling, or £10 a year and upwards if you will take a sporting chance of never receiving anything at all.

The poor do not meddle with this official money market, because the only security they can give when borrowing ready money from anyone but the pawnbroker is their promise to pay so much a week out of their earnings. This being much more uncertain than a share certificate or a lease of land, they have to pay comparatively prodigious prices. For instance, a poor working woman can hire a shilling for a penny a week. This is the usual rate; and it seems quite reasonable to very poor people; but it is more than eighty-six times as much as the Government pays for the hire of money. It means paying at the rate of £433 : 10s. a year for the use of £100, or, as we say, interest at 433½ per cent: a rate no rich man would dream of paying. The poorer you are the more you pay, because the risk of your failing to pay is greater. Therefore when you see in the paper that the price of hiring money has been fixed by the Bank of England (that is why it is called the Bank Rate) at five per cent, or reduced to four-and-a-half per cent, or raised to six per cent, or what not, you must not suppose that you or anyone else can hire money at that rate: it means only that those who are practically certain to be able to pay, like the Government or the great financiers and business houses, can borrow from the banks at that rate. In their case the rate changes not according to any risk of their being unable to pay, but according to the quantity of spare money available for lending. And no matter how low the rate falls, the charwoman still has to pay 433½ per cent, partly because the risk of her being unable to pay is great, partly because the expense of lending money by shillings and collecting the interest every week is much greater than the expense of lending it by millions and collecting the interest every six months, and partly because the charwoman is ignorant and helpless and does not know that the slum usurer, whom she regards as her best friend in need, is charging her anything more than a millionaire is charged.

The price of money varies also according to the purpose for which it is borrowed. You are, I hope, concerned with the money market as a lender rather than as a borrower. Do not be startled at the notion of being a moneylender (not, I repeat, that there is anything dishonorable in it) : nobody will call your investments loans. But they are loans for all that. Only, they are loans made, not to individuals, but to joint stock companies on special conditions. The business people in the city are always forming these companies and asking you to lend them money to start some big business undertaking, which may be a shop in the next street, or a motor bus service along it, or a tunnel through the Andes, or a harbor in the Pacific, or a gold mine in Peru, or a rubber plantation in Malaya, or any mortal enterprise out of which they think they can make money. But they do not borrow on the simple condition that they pay you for the hire of the money until they pay it back. Their offer is that when the business is set up it shall belong to you and to all your fellow lenders (called shareholders) ; so that when it begins to make money the profits will be distributed among you all in proportion to the amount each of you has lent. On the other hand, if it makes no profits you lose your money. Your only consolation is that you can lose no more. You cannot be called on to pay the Company's debts if it has spent more than you lent it. Your liability is limited, as they say.

This is a chancy business; and to encourage you if you are timid (or shall we say cautious?) these companies may ask you to lend your spare money to them at the fixed rate of, say, six or seven per cent, on the understanding that this is to be paid before any of the ordinary lenders get anything, but that you will get nothing more no matter how big the profits may be. If you accept this offer you are said to have debentures or preference shares in the company; and the others are said to have ordinary shares. There are a few varieties both of preference and ordinary shares; but they are all ways of hiring spare money: the only difference is in the conditions on which you are invited to provide it.

When you have taken a share, and it is bringing you in an income, you can at any time, if you are pressed for ready money, sell your share for what it may be worth in the money market to somebody who has spare money and wants to "save" it by exchanging it for an income. The department of the money market in which shares are bought and sold in this way is called the Stock Exchange. To sell a share you have to employ an agent (called a stockbroker), who takes your share to the Exchange and asks another agent (called a stockjobber) to "make him a price". It is the jobber's business to know what the share is worth, according to the prospects of the company, the quantity of spare money being offered for incomes, and the number of income producing shares being offered for sale. Never speak disrespectfully of stockjobbers: they are very important people, and consider themselves greater masters of the money business than the stockbrokers.

The legitimate business of the Stock Exchange is this selling and buying of shares in companies already established. It is largely occupied also with a curious game called speculation, in which phantom prices are offered for imaginary shares; but for the moment let us keep to the point that the shares dealt in are practically all in established companies, because what is nationally important is the application of spare money, not to the purchase of shares in old companies, but to the foundation of new ones, or at least to the extension of the plant and operations of the old ones. Now the business done on the Stock Exchange is no index to this, and indeed may have nothing to do with it. Suppose, for example, that you have £50,000 to spare, and you invest it all in railway shares! You will not by doing so create a single yard of railway, nor cause a single additional train to be run, nor even supply an existing train with an extra footwarmer. Your money will have no effect whatever on the railways. All that will happen is that your name will be substituted for some other name or names in the list of shareholders, and that for the future you will get the income the owners of those names would get if they had not sold their shares to you. Also, of course, that they will get your £50,000 to do what they like with. They may spend it on the gambling tables at Monte Carlo, or on the British turf; or they may present it to the funds of the Labor Party. You may disapprove strongly of gambling; and you may have a horror of the

Labor Party. You may say "If I had thought this was going to happen to my money, I would have bought shares privately from some persons whose principles were well known to me and whom I could trust not to spend it foolishly instead of from that wicked stockjobber who has no more conscience than a cash register, and does not care what becomes of my money". But your protest will be vain. In practice you will find that you must buy your shares in established companies on the Stock Exchange; that your money will never go into the company whose shares you buy; and that its real destination will be entirely beyond your control. A day's work on the Stock Exchange, nominally a most gratifying addition of hundreds of thousands of pounds of spare money to the industrial capital of the country, may be really a waste of them in extravagant luxury, or ruinous vice, to say nothing of the possibility of their being sent abroad to establish some foreign business which will capture the business of the company whose shares you have bought, and thus reduce you to indigence.

And now you will say that if this is so, you will take particular care to buy nothing but new shares in new companies, sending the money directly to their bankers according to the form enclosed with the prospectus, without allowing any stockbroker or stockjobber to know anything about it, thus making sure that your money will be used to create a new business and add it to the productive resources of your country's industry. My dear lady, you will lose it all unless you are very careful, very well informed as to the risks involved, and very intelligent in money matters. Company promotion, I am sorry to say, is a most rascally business in its shadier corners. Act after Act of Parliament has been passed, without much effect, to prevent swindlers from forming companies for some excellent object, and, when they have collected as much money as they can by selling shares in it, making no serious attempt to carry out that object, but simply taking offices, ordering goods, appointing themselves directors and managers and secretaries and anything else that carries a salary, taking commissions on all their orders, and, when they have divided all the plunder in this way (which is perfectly legal), winding up the company as a failure. All you can do in that case is to go to the shareholders' meeting and make a row, being very careful not to tell the swindlers that they are swindlers, because if you do they will immediately take an action against you for slander and get damages out of you. But making a row will not save your money. The amount that is stolen from innocent women every year in this way is appalling; and it has been done as much by sham motor bus companies, which if genuine would have been very sensible and publicly useful investments, as by companies to work bogus gold mines, which are suspect on the face of them.

Even if you escape this swindling by blackguards who know what they are doing, and would be as much disconcerted by the success of their companies as a burglar if he found himself politely received and invited to dinner in a house he had broken into, you may be tempted by the companies founded by genuine enthusiasts who believe in their scheme, who are quite right in believing in it, who are finally justified by its success, and who put all their own spare money and a great deal of hard work into it. But they almost always underestimate its cost. Because it is new, they have no experience to guide them; and they have their own enthusiasm to mislead them. When they are half way to success the share money is all used up; and they are forced to sell out all they have done for an old song to a new company formed expressly to take advantage of them. Sometimes this second company shares the fate of the first, and is bought out by a third. The company which finally succeeds may be built on the money and work of three or four successive sets of pioneers who have run short of the cash needed for completion of the plant. The experienced men of the city know this, and lie in wait until the moment has come for the final success. As one of them has put it "the money is made by coming in on the third reconstruction". For them it may be a splendid investment; but the original shareholders, who had the intelligence to foresee the successful future of the business, and the enterprise to start it, are cleaned out. They see their hopes fulfilled and their judgment justified; but as they have to look through the workhouse windows, they are a warning rather than an example to later investors.

You can avoid these risks by never meddling with a new company, but calling in your stockbroker to buy shares in a well established old one. You will not do it any good; but at all events you will know that it is neither a bogus company nor one which has started with too little capital and will presently have to sell out at a heavy or total loss. Beware of enterprise: beware of public spirit: beware of conscience and visions of the future. Play for safety. Lend to the Government or the Municipalities if you can, though the income may be less; for there is no investment so safe and useful as a communal investment. And when you find journalists glorifying the Capitalist system as a splendid stimulus to all these qualities against which I have just warned you, restrain the unladylike impulse to imitate the sacristan in the Ingoldsby Legends, who said no word to indicate a doubt, but put his thumb unto his nose, and spread his fingers out.

53
SPECULATION

IN the preceding chapter I have been assuming that you are a capitalist. I am now going to assume that you are perhaps a bit of a gambler. Even if you abhor gambling it is a necessary part of your education in modern social conditions to know how most of it is done. Without such knowledge you might, for instance, marry a gambler after having taken the greatest pains to assure yourself that he had never touched a playing card, sat at a roulette table, or backed a horse in his life, and was engaged solely in financial operations on the Stock Exchange. You might find him encouraging you to spend money like water in one week, and in the next protesting that he could not possibly afford you a new hat. In short, you might find yourself that tragic figure, the gambler's wife who is not by temperament a gambler.

A page or two ago I dropped a remark about a game played on the Stock Exchange and called Speculation, at which phantom prices are offered for imaginary shares. I will explain this game to you, leaving it to your taste and conscience to decide whether you will shun it or plunge into it. It is by far the most widely practised and exciting form of gambling produced by Capitalism.

To understand it you must know that on the London Stock Exchange you can buy a share and not have to pay for it, or sell a share and not have to hand over the share certificate, until next settling day, which may be a fortnight off. You may not see at first what difference that makes. But a great deal may happen in a fortnight. Just recollect what you have learnt about the continual fluctuations in the prices of incomes and of spare subsistence in the Money Market! Think of the hopes and fears raised by the flourishing and decaying of the joint stock companies as their business and prospects grow or shrink according as the harvests are good or bad: rubber harvests, oil harvests, coal harvests, copper harvests, as well as the agricultural harvests: all meaning that there will be more or less money to divide among the shareholders as yearly income, and more or less spare money available to buy shares with. The prices of shares change not only from year to year but from day to day, from hour to hour, and, in moments of excitement on the Stock Exchange, from minute to minute. The share that was obtained years ago or centuries ago by giving £100 spare money to start a new company may bring its owner £5000 a year, or it may bring her thirty shillings, or it may bring her nothing, or it may bring her all three in succession. Consequently that share, which cost somebody £100 spare money when it was new, she may be able to sell for £100,000 at one moment, for £30 at another, whilst at yet another she may be unable to sell it at all, for love or money. As she opens her newspaper in the morning she looks at the city page, with its list of yesterday's prices of stocks and shares, to see how rich she is today; and she seldom finds that her shares are worth the same price for a week at a time unless she has been prudent enough to lend it to the Government or to a municipality (in which case she has communal security) instead of to private companies.

Now put these two things together: the continual change in the prices of shares, and the London Stock Exchange rule that they need not be paid for nor delivered until next settling day. Suppose you have not a penny of spare cash in your possession, nor a share (carrying an income) to sell! Suppose you believe for some reason or other that the price of shares in a certain company (call it company A) is going to rise in value within the next few days! And suppose you believe that the price of shares in a certain other company (company B) is going to fall. If you are right, all you have to do to make some money by your good guessing is to buy shares in company A and sell shares in company B. You may say "How am I to buy shares without money or sell them without the share certificates?" It is very simple: you need not produce either the money or the certificates until settling day. Before settling day you sell the A shares for more than you bought them for on credit; and you buy the B certificates for less than you pretended to sell them for. On settling day you will get the money from the people you sold to, and the certificates from the people you bought from; and when you have paid for the A shares and handed over the B certificates, you will be in pocket by the difference between their values on the day you bought and sold them and their values on settling day. Simple enough, is it not?

This is the game of speculation. Nobody will blame you for engaging in it; but on the Stock Exchange they will call you a bull for pretending to buy the A shares, and a bear for pretending to sell the B shares. If you pay a small sum to get shares allotted to you in a new company on the chance of selling them at a profit before you have to pay up, they will call you a stag. If you ask why not a cow or a hind, the reply is that as the Stock Exchange was founded by men for men its slang is exclusively masculine.

But, you may say, suppose my guess was wrong! Suppose the price of the A shares goes down instead of up, and the price of the B shares up instead of down! Well, that often happens, either through some unforeseen event affecting the companies, or simply because you guessed badly. But do not be too terrified by this possibility; for all you can lose is the difference between the prices; and as this may be only a matter of five or ten pounds for every hundred you have been dealing in you can pawn your clothes and furniture and try again. You can even have your account "carried over" to next settling day by paying "contango" if you are a bull, or "backwardation" if you are a bear, on the chance of your luck changing in the extra fortnight.

I must warn you, however, that if a great many other bears have guessed just as you have, and sold imaginary shares in great numbers, you may be "cornered". This means that the bears have sold either more shares than actually exist, or more than the holders will sell except at a great advance in price. Bulls who are cunning enough to foresee this and to buy up the shares which are being beared may make all the money the bears lose. Cornering the bears is a recognized part of the game of speculation.

As the game is one of knowledge and skill and character (or no character) as well as of chance, a good guesser, or one with private (inside) information as to facts likely to affect share prices, can make a living at it; and some speculators have made and lost princely fortunes. Some women play at it just as others back horses. Sometimes they do it intelligently through regular stockbrokers, with a clear understanding of the game. Sometimes they are blindly tempted by circulars sent out from Bucket Shops; so I had better enlighten you as to what a bucket shop is.

You will remember that a speculator does not stand to lose the whole price she offers for a share, or the whole value of the share she pretends to buy. If she loses she loses only the difference between the prices she expected and the prices she has to pay. If she has a sufficient sum in hand to meet this she escapes bankruptcy. This sufficient sum is called "cover". A bucket shop keeper is one who undertakes to speculate for anyone who will send him cover. His circulars say, in effect, "Send me ten pounds, and the worst that can happen to you is to lose it; but I may be able to double it for you or even double it many times over. I can refer you to clients who have sent me £10 and got back £50 or £100." A lady, not understanding the business in the least, is tempted to send him £10, and very likely loses it, in which case she usually tries to get it back by risking another £10 note if she has one left. But she may be lucky and pocket some winnings; for bucket shops must let their clients win sometimes or they could hardly exist. But they can generally prevent your winning, if they choose, by taking advantage of some specially low price of shares to shew that your cover has disappeared, or even by selling two or three shares themselves at a low price and quoting it against you. Besides, if you sue them for your winnings they can escape by pleading the Gaming Act. They cannot be mulcted or expelled by the Stock Exchange Committee; for they are not members of the Stock Exchange, and have given no securities. A bucket shop keeper is not necessarily a swindler any more than a bookmaker is necessarily a welsher; but if he fleeces you you have no remedy, whereas if a stockbroker cheats you it may cost him his livelihood.

If you speculate through a regular stockbroker you must bear in mind that he is supposed to deal in genuine investments only: that is, in the buying of shares by clients who have the money to pay for them, and the sale of shares by those who really possess them and wish to exchange them for a lump sum of spare money. The difference is that if you go into a bucket shop and say frankly "Here is a five pound note, which is all I have in the world. Will you take it as cover, and speculate with it for me in stocks of ten times its value", the bucket shop will oblige you; but if you say this to a stockbroker he must have you shewn out. You must allow him to believe, or pretend to believe, that you really have the spare money or the shares in which you want to deal.

You will now understand what gambling on the London Stock Exchange means. The game can be played with certain variations, called options and double options and so on, which are as easily picked up as the different hazards of the roulette table; and the foreign stock exchanges have rules which are not so convenient for the bears as our rules; but these differences do not change the nature of the game. Every day speculative business is done in Capel Court in London, on Wall Street in New York, in the Bourses on the Continent, to the tune of millions of pounds; and it is literally only a tune: the buyers have no money and the sellers no goods; and their countries are no richer for it all than they are for the gaming tables at Monte Carlo or the bookmakers' settlements at the end of a horse race. Yet the human energy, audacity, and cunning wasted on it would, if rightly directed, make an end of our slums and epidemics and most of our prisons in fewer hours than it has taken days of Capitalism to produce them.

54
BANKING

THE Stock Exchange is only a department of the money market. The commonest way of hiring money for business purposes is to keep an account at a bank, and hire spare money there when you want it. The bank manager will lend it to you if he feels reasonably sure that you will be able to repay him: in fact that is his real business, as we shall see presently. He may do it by letting you overdraw your account. Or if somebody with whom you are doing business has given you a written promise to pay you a sum of money at some future time (this written promise is called a bill of exchange) and the bank manager thinks the promise will be kept, he will give you the money at once, only deducting enough to pay him for its hire until your customer pays it. This is called discounting the bill. All such transactions are forms of hiring spare money; and when you read in the city articles in the papers that money is cheap or money is dear, it means that the price you have to pay your banker for the hire of spare money is low or high as the case may be.

Sometimes you will see a fuss made because the Bank of England has raised or lowered the Bank Rate. This means that the Bank of England is going to charge more or less, as the case may be, for discounting bills of exchange, because spare money has become dearer or cheaper: that is to say, because spare subsistence has become scarcer or more plentiful. If you are overdrawn at your bank, the announcement that the Bank Rate is raised may bring you a letter from the manager to say that you must not overdraw any more, and that he will be obliged to you if you will pay off your overdraft as soon as possible. What he means is that as spare subsistence has become scarce and dear he cannot go on supplying you with it, and would like you to replace what he has already supplied. This may be very inconvenient to you, and may prevent you from extending your business. That is why there is great consternation and lamentation among business people when the Bank Rate goes up, and jubilation when it goes down. For when the terms on which spare money can be hired at the Bank of England go up, they go up everywhere; so that the Bank Rate is an index to the cost of hiring spare money generally.

And now comes the question, where on earth do the banks get all the spare money they deal in? To the Intelligent Woman who is not engaged in business, or who, if she has a bank account, never overdraws it or brings a bill to be discounted, a bank seems only a place where they very kindly pay her cheques and keep her money safe for her for nothing, as if she were paying them a compliment by allowing them to do it. They will even hire money from her when she has more than enough to go on with, provided she will agree not to draw it out without giving them some days' notice (they call this placing it on deposit). She must ask herself sometimes how they can possibly afford to keep up a big handsomely fitted building and a staff of respectably dressed clerks with a most polite and sympathetic manager to do a lot of her private business for her and charge her nothing for it.

The explanation is that people hardly ever draw as much money from the bank as they put in; and even when they do, it remains in the bank for some time. Suppose you lodge a hundred pounds in the bank on Monday to keep it safe because you will have to draw a cheque for it on Saturday! That cheque will not be presented for payment until the following Monday. Consequently the bank has your hundred pounds in its hands for a week, and can therefore hire it out for a week for a couple of shillings.

But very few bank transactions are as unprofitable as this. Most people keep their bank accounts open all the year round; and instead of paying in every week exactly what they want to spend and drawing it out again by their cheques as they spend it, they keep a round sum always at their call so as to be ready when they may happen to want it. The poorest woman who ever dreams of keeping a bank account at all is not often driven to draw the last half crown out: when her balance falls as low as that, she knows it is time to put in another pound or two. Indeed it is not every bank that will do business on so small a scale as this: the Governor of the Bank of England would turn blue and order the porters to remove you if you offered him an account of that sort. Bank customers are people some of whom keep £20 continually at call, some £100, some £1000, and some many thousands, according to the extent of their business or the rate at which they are living. This means that no matter how much money they may put into the bank or take out, there always remains in the bank a balance that they never draw out; and when all these balances are added up they come to a huge amount of spare money in the hands of the bank. It is by hiring out this money that the banks make their enormous profits. They can well afford to be polite to you.

And now the Intelligent Woman who keeps a bank account, and most conscientiously never lets her balance fall below a certain figure, may ask in some alarm whether her bank, instead of keeping her balance always in the bank ready for her to draw out if she should need it, actually lends it to other people. The reply is, Yes: that is not only what the bank does, but what it was founded to do. But, the Intelligent Woman will exclaim, that means that if I were to draw a cheque for my balance there would be no money in the bank to pay it with. And certainly that would happen if all the other customers of the bank drew cheques for their balances on the same day. But they never do. "Still", you urge, "they might." Never mind: the bank does not trouble about what might happen. It is concerned only with what does happen; and what does happen is that if out of every pound lodged with them the bankers keep about three shillings in the till to pay their customers' cheques it will be quite sufficient.

Only, please remember that the woman who has a bank account should never frighten the others by letting them know this. They would all rush to the bank and draw out their balances; and when the bankers had paid to the first comers all the three shillingses they had kept, they would stop payment and put up the shutters. This sometimes actually happens when a report is spread that some particular bank is not to be trusted. Something or somebody starts a panic; there is "a run on the bank"; the bank is broken; and its customers are very angry with the directors, clamoring to have them prosecuted and sent to prison, which is unreasonable; for they ought to have known that banks, with all the services they give for nothing, can exist only on condition that their customers do not draw out their balances all on the same day.

Perhaps, by the way, you know some woman who not only always draws her full balance, but overdraws it; so that she is always in debt to the bank. Her case is very simple. The bank lends her the other customers' money to go on with, and charges her for the hire of it. That sort of business pays them very well.

And now that you know what banking is from the inside, and how the bankers get all the spare money they let on hire, may I remind you again, if I am not too tiresome, that this spare money is really spare subsistence, mainly perishable stuff that must be used at once. One of the greatest public dangers of our day is that the bankers do not know this, because they never handle or store the stuff themselves; and the right to take it away and use it which they sell on the hire system is disguised under the name of Credit. Consequently they come to think that credit is something that can be eaten and drunk and worn and made into houses and railways and factories and so on, whereas real credit is only the lender's opinion that the borrower will be able to pay him.

Now you cannot feed workmen or build houses or butter parsnips with opinions. When you hear of a woman living on credit or building a house on credit or having a car on credit you may rest assured that she is not doing anything of the kind: she is living on real victuals; having her house built of bricks and mortar by men who are eating substantial meals; and driving about in a steel car full of highly explosive petrol. If she has not made them nor paid for them somebody else has; and all that her having them on credit means is that the bank manager believes that at some future time she will replace them with equally substantial equivalent goods of the same value after paying the bank for waiting meanwhile. But when she goes to the bank manager she does not ask for food and bricks and cars: she says she wants credit. And when the bank manager allows her to draw the money that is really an order for so much food and so many bricks and a car, he says nothing about these things. He says, and thinks, that he is giving her credit. And so at last all the bankers and the practical business men come to believe that credit is something eatable, drinkable, and substantial, and that bank managers can increase or diminish the harvest by becoming more credulous or more sceptical as to whether the people to whom they lend money will pay them or not (issuing or restricting credit, as they call it). The city articles in the papers, the addresses of bank chairmen at the annual shareholders' meetings, the financial debates in Parliament, are full of nonsensical phrases about issuing credit, destroying credit, restricting credit, as if somebody were shovelling credit about with a spade. Clever men put forward wonderful schemes based on the calculation that when a banker lends five thousand pounds worth of spare subsistence he also gives the borrower credit for five thousand pounds, the five thousand credit added to the five thousand spare subsistence making ten thousand altogether! Instead of being immediately rushed into the nearest lunatic asylum, these clever ones find disciples both in

Parliament and in the city. They propose to extend our industries (that is, build ships and factories and railway engines and the like) with credit. They believe that you can double the quantity of goods in the country by changing the cipher 2 into the cipher 4. Whenever a scarcity of spare subsistence forces the Bank of England to raise the Bank Rate they accuse the directors of playing them a dirty trick and preventing them from extending their business, as if the Governor and Company of the Bank of England could keep the rate down any more than the barometer can keep the mercury down in fair weather. They think they know, because they are "practical business men". But for national purposes they are maniacs with dangerous delusions; and the Governments who take their advice soon find themselves on the rocks.

What is it, then, that really fixes the price you have to pay if you hire ready money from your bank, or that you receive for lending it to the bank (on deposit), or to trading companies by buying shares, or to the Government or the Municipalities? In other words, what fixes the so-called price of money, meaning the cost of hiring it? And what fixes the price of incomes when their owners sell them for ready money in the Stock Exchange?

Well, it depends on the proportion between the quantity of spare subsistence ("saved" money) there may be in the market to be hired, and how much the people who want to use it up are able and willing to pay for the hire of it. On the one hand you have the property owners who are living on less than their incomes and therefore want to dispose of their spare stuff before it goes rotten. On the other are the business men who want what the property owners have not consumed to feed the proletarians whose labor they need to start new businesses or extend old ones. Beside these, you have the spendthrift property owners who have lived beyond their incomes, and must therefore sell the incomes (or part of them) for ready money to pay their debts. Between them all, you get a Supply and Demand according to which spare money and incomes are cheap or dear. The price runs up when the supply runs short or the demand becomes more pressing. It runs down when the supply increases or the demand slackens.

By the way, now that we are picking up the terms Supply and Demand, remember that Demand in the money market sense does not mean want alone: it means only the want that the wanter can afford to satisfy. The demand of a hungry child for food is very strong and very loud; but it does not count in business unless the mother has money to buy food for the child. But with this rather inhuman qualification supply and demand (called "effective demand") settle the price of everything that has a price.

Banks are safe when they lend their money (or rather yours) judiciously. If they make bad investments, or trust the wrong people, or speculate, they may ruin themselves and their customers. This happened occasionally when there were many banks. But now that the big ones have swallowed up the little ones they are so few and so big that they could not afford to let oneanother break, nor indeed could the Government. So you are fairly safe in keeping your money at a big bank, and need have no scruple about availing yourself of its readiness to oblige you in many ways, including acting as your stockbroker, borrowing from you at interest (on deposit account), and lending you, though at a considerably higher rate, any ready money for the repayment of which you can offer reasonably satisfactory security.

As we now see why the hiring terms for money vary from time to time, sometimes from hour to hour, let us amuse ourselves by working out what would happen at the banks if the Government, misled by the practical business men, or by the millennial amateurs, were to attempt to raise say £30,000 millions by a tax on capital, and another £30,000 millions by a tax on credit.

The announcement of the tax on credit would make an end of that part of the business at once by destroying all credit. The financial magnate who the day before could raise a million at six or seven per cent by raising his finger would not be able to borrow five shillings from his butler unless the butler let him have it for the sake of old times without the least hope of ever seeing it again.

To pay the tax the capitalists would have to draw out every farthing they had in the bank, and instruct their stockbrokers to sell out all their shares and debentures and Government and municipal stock. There would be such a prodigious demand for ready money that the Governor and Company of the Bank of England would meet at eleven o'clock and resolve, after some hesitation, to raise the Bank Rate boldly to ten per cent. After lunch they would be summoned hurriedly to raise it to a hundred per cent; and before they could send out this staggering announcement they would learn that they might save themselves the trouble, as all the banks, after paying out three shillings in the pound, had stopped payment and stuck up a notice on their closed doors that they hoped to be able to pay their customers the rest when they had realized their investments: that is, called in their loans and sold their stocks and shares. But the stockbrokers would report only one price for all stocks, that price being no pounds, no shillings, and no pence, not even farthings. For that is the price in a market where there are all sellers and no buyers.

When the tax collector called for his money, the taxpayer would have to say "I can get no money for you; so instead of paying the tax on my capital, here is the capital itself for you. Here is a bundle of share certificates which you can sell to the waste paper dealer for a halfpenny. Here is a bundle of bonds payable to bearer which you can try your luck with, and a sheet of coupons which in a few years' time will be as valuable as rare and obsolete postage stamps. Here is a transfer which will authorize the Bank of England to run its pen through my name in the War Loan register and substitute your own. And much good may they all do you! I must shew you out myself, as my servants are in the streets starving because I have no money to pay their wages: in fact, I should not have had anything to eat myself today if I had not pawned my evening clothes; and precious little the pawnbroker would give me on them, as he is short of money and piled up to the ceiling with evening suits. Good morning."

You may ask what, after all, would that matter? As nine out of every ten people have no capital and no credit in the financial sense (that is to say, though a shopkeeper might trust them until the end of the week, no banker would dream of lending them a sixpence), they could look on and laugh, crying "Let the rich take their turn at being penniless, as we so often are". But what about the great numbers of poor who live on the rich, the servants, the employers and employed in the luxury trades, the fashionable doctors and solicitors? Even in the productive trades what would happen with the banks all shut up and bankrupt, the money for wages all taken by the Government, no cheque payable and no bill of exchange discountable? Unless the Government were ready instantly to take over and manage every business in the country: that is, to establish complete nationalization of industry in a thunderclap without ever having foreseen or intended such a thing, ruin and starvation would be followed by riot and looting: riot and looting would only make bad worse; and finally the survivors, if there were any, would be only too glad to fall on their knees before any Napoleon or Mussolini who would organize the violence of the mob and re-establish the old state of things, or as much of it as could be rescued from the chaos, by main force applied by a ruthless dictator.

55
MONEY

YOU now know more than most people about the money market. But it is not enough to know what settles the value of stocks and shares in spare money from day to day. All money is not spare money. Few of us spend as much on shares as on food and clothes and lodging. Most of us, having no spare money, would as soon dream of buying shooting lodges in Scotland as of investing or speculating on the Stock Exchange; yet we use money. Suppose there were no spare money on earth, what would fix the value of money? What is money?

Take a gold coin for instance. You are probably old enough to remember such things before the war swept them away and substituted bits of paper called Treasury notes; and you may be young enough to live until they come back again. What is a gold coin? It is a tool for buying things in exactly the same sense as a silver spoon is a tool for eating an egg. Buying and selling would be impossible without such tools. Suppose they did not exist, and you wanted to go somewhere in a bus! Suppose the only movable property you had was twenty ducks and a donkey! When the bus conductor came round for the fare you would offer him the donkey and ask for the change in potatoes, or offer him a duck and ask for the change in eggs. This would be so troublesome, and the bargaining so prolonged, that next time you would find it cheaper to ride the donkey instead of taking the bus: indeed there would be no buses because there would be nobody willing to take them, unless buses were communized and fares abolished.

Now it is troublesome to take a donkey about, even when it takes you, but quite easy to carry as much gold as a donkey is worth. Accordingly, the Government cuts up gold into conveniently shaped bits weighing a little over 123 grains of standard gold (22 carat) apiece, to be used for buying and selling. For transactions that are too small to be settled by a metal so costly as gold it provides bronze and silver coins, and makes a law that so many of these coins shall pass as worth one of the gold coins. Then buying and selling become quite easy. Instead of offering your donkey to the bus conductor you exchange it for its worth in coins; and with these in your pocket you can pay your bus fare in two seconds without having any words about it.

Thus you see that money is not only a necessary tool for buying and selling, but also a measure of value; for when it is introduced we stop saying that a donkey is worth so many ducks or half a horse, and say instead that it is worth so many pounds or shillings. This enables accounts to be kept, and makes commerce possible.

All this is as easy as A B C. What is not so easy is the question why the donkey should be worth, say, three-quarters of a sovereign (fifteen bob, it would be called at this price), or, to put it the other way, why fifteen bob should be worth a donkey. All you can say is that a buyer at this price is a person with fifteen shillings who wants a donkey more than she wants the fifteen shillings, and a seller at this price a person with a donkey who would rather have fifteen shillings than keep the donkey. The buyer, though she wants a donkey, does not want it badly enough to give more than fifteen shillings for it; and the seller, though she wants money, will not let the donkey go for less than fifteen; and so they exchange. Their respective needs just balance at that figure.

Now a donkey represents just a donkey and nothing else; but fifteen shillings represents fifteen shillingsworth of anything you like, from food and drink to a cheap umbrella. Any fund of money represents subsistence; but do not forget that though you can eat and drink and wear subsistence, you cannot eat or drink or wear Treasury notes and metal coins. Granted that if you have two shillings the dairyman will give you a pound of butter for it; still, a pound of butter is no more a round piece of metal than a cat is a flat iron; and if there were no butter you would have to eat dry bread, even if you had millions and millions of shillings.

Besides, butter is not always two shillings: it is sometimes two and twopence or even two and sixpence. There are people now living who have bought good fresh butter for fourpence a pound, and complained of its being dear at that. It is easy to say that butter is cheap when it is plentiful, and dear when it is scarce; but this is only one side of the bargain. If ten pounds of butter cost a sovereign on Monday and a sovereign and a quarter on Saturday, is that because there is less butter or more gold?

Well, it may be one or the other or both combined. If the Government were to strike off enough new sovereigns at the Mint to double the number in circulation we should have to pay two sovereigns for ten pounds of butter, not because butter would be scarcer but because gold would be more plentiful. But there is no danger of this happening, because gold is so scarce and hard to get that if the Government turned more of it into sovereigns than were needed to conduct our buying and selling, the superfluous ones would be melted down, and the gold used for other purposes, in spite of the law against it; and this would go on until sovereigns were so scarce that you could get more for gold in the form of sovereigns than in the form of watch chains or bracelets. For this reason people feel safe with gold money: the gold in the sovereign keeps its value for other purposes than buying and selling; and if the worst came to the worst, and the British Empire were annexed by the planet Mars, and only Martian money were current, the sovereigns would still be taken in exchange for as much butter or anything else as before, not as money, but as so much gold; so that the British sovereign would buy as much as a Martian gold sovereign of equal weight.

Suppose, however, you had a dishonest Government! Suppose the country and its Mint were ruled by a king who was a thief. Suppose he owed large sums of money, and wished to cheat his creditors. He could do it by paying in sovereigns which were made of lead, with just gold enough in them to make them look genuine. Henry the Eighth did it less crudely by giving short weight in silver coins; and he was not the only ruler who played the same trick when pressed for money. When such frauds are discovered prices go up and wages follow them. The only gainers were those who, like the king, had borrowed heavy money and were paying it in light; and what they gained the creditors lost. But it was a low trick, damaging English as well as royal credit, as all English debtors were inextricably and involuntarily engaged in the swindle as deeply as the king.

The moral is that a dishonest ruler is one of the greatest dangers a nation has to dread. People who do not understand these things make a great fuss because Henry married six wives and had very bad luck with most of them, and because he allowed the nobles to plunder the Church. But we are far more concerned today with his debasement of the coinage; for that is a danger that is hanging over our own heads. Henry's trick is now played not only by kings, but by republican governments with Socialist majorities and by the Soviets of proletarian States, with the result that innocent women, provided comfortably for by years of self-denial on the part of their parents in paying insurance premiums, find themselves starving; pensions earned by lifetimes of honorable and arduous service lose their value, leaving the pensioners to survive their privations as castaways survive in a boat at sea; and enormous fortunes are made without the least merit by A, B, and C, whilst X, Y, and Z, without the least fault, go bankrupt. The matter is so serious and so menacing that you must summon all your patience while I explain it more particularly.

At present (1927) we do not use sovereigns. We use bits of paper, mostly dirty and smelly, with the words *One Pound* printed in large letters on them, and a picture of the Houses of Parliament on the back. There is also a printed notice that the bit of paper is a currency note, and that by Act of Parliament IV and V Geo. V, ch. XIV, if you owe anyone a pound you can pay him by handing him the bit of paper, which he must accept as a full discharge of your debt to him whether he likes or not.

Now there is no use pretending that this bit of paper which you can pass as a pound is worth anything at all as paper. It is too small and too crowded with print and pictures to be usable for any of the uses to which paper can be put, except that of a short title deed to a poundsworth of goods. Yet there is no law to prevent the Government, which owes 7700 million pounds to its creditors, from printing off 7700 millions of these one pound Treasury notes, and paying off all its home creditors with them, even though a thousand of them would not buy a cigarette.

You may say that this is too monstrous to be possible. But it has been done, and that quite recently, as I know to my cost. The German Government did it after the war when the conquerors, with insane spite, persisted in demanding sums of money that the Germans had not got. The Austrian Government did it. The Russian Government did it. I was owed by these countries sums sufficient to support me for the rest of my days; and they paid me in paper money, four thousand million pounds of which was worth exactly twopence halfpenny in English money. The British Government thought it was making Germany pay for the war; but it was really making me and all the other creditors of Germany pay for it. Now as I was a foreigner and an alien enemy, the Germans probably do not feel very sorry for me. But the same occurred to the Germans who were owed German money, whether by foreigners or by other Germans. Merchants who had obtained goods for bills payable in six months paid those bills with paper Marks and thus got the goods for nothing. Mortgages on land and houses, and debentures and loan stocks of every redeemable sort, were cleared off in the same way. And one very unexpected result of this was that German employers, relieved of the burden of mortgages and loans such as the English employers were bearing, were able to undersell the English even in the English market. All sorts of extraordinary things happened. Nobody saved money, because its value fell from hour to hour: people went into a restaurant for a five million lunch, and when they came to pay found that the price had gone up to seven millions whilst they were eating. The moment a woman got a scrap of money she rushed to the shops to buy something with it; for the thing she bought would keep its usefulness, but the money that bought it, if she kept it until tomorrow, might not purchase half so much, or a tenth so much, or indeed anything at all. It was better to pay ten million marks for a frying-pan, even if you had two frying-pans already, than to buy nothing; for the frying-pan would remain a frying-pan and fry things (if you had anything to fry) whatever happened; but the ten million marks might not pay a tram fare by five o'clock the same evening.

A still better plan in Germany then was to buy shares if you could get them; for factories and railways will keep as well as frying-pans. Thus, though people were in a frantic hurry to spend their money, they were also in a frantic hurry to invest it: that is, use it as capital; so that there was not only a delusive appearance of an increase in the national capital produced by the simple expedient of calling a spare loaf of bread fifty thousand pounds, but a real increase in the proportion of their subsistence which people were willing to invest instead of spending. But however the money was spent, the object of everyone was to get rid of it instantly by exchanging it for something that would not change in value. They soon began to use foreign money (American dollars mostly); and this expedient, eked out with every possible device for doing without money altogether by bartering, tided them over until the Government was forced to introduce a new gold currency and leave the old notes to be thrown into the waste paper basket or kept to be sold fifty years hence as curiosities, like the famous assignats of the French Revolution.

This process of debasement of the currency by a Government in order that it may cheat its creditors is called by the polite name, which few understand, of Inflation; and the reversal of the process by going back to a currency of precious metal is called Deflation. The worst of it is that the remedy is as painful as the disease, because if Inflation, by raising prices, enables the debtor to cheat the creditor, Deflation, by lowering them, enables the creditor to cheat the debtor. Therefore the most sacred economic duty of a Government is to keep the value of money steady; and it is because Governments can play tricks with the value of money that it is of such vital importance that they should consist of men who are honest, and who understand money thoroughly.

At present there is not a Government in the world that answers fully to this description. Between our own Government, which took advantage of the war to substitute Treasury notes for our gold currency, and the German and Russian Governments, which issued so many notes that a vanload of them would hardly buy a postage stamp, the difference is only one of degree. And this degree was not in the relative honesty of Englishmen, Russians, and Germans, but in the pressure of circumstances on them, and consequently of temptation. Had we been defeated and forced to pay impossible sums to our conquerors, or momentarily wrecked as Russia was by the collapse of the Tsardom, we should not have been any honester; for though the doubling of prices that occurred here seems to have been caused by scarcity of goods and labor rather than by an excessive issue of paper money, we still treat with great respect as high financial authorities gentlemen who recommend Inflation as a means of providing industry with additional capital. Whether these gentlemen really believe that we could double our wealth by simply printing twice as many Treasury notes, or whether they owe so much money that they would be greatly relieved if only they could be let pay it in paper pounds worth only ten shillings, is not always easy to guess. But if you catch your Parliamentary representative advocating Inflation, and ask him, at the risk of being told that you are no lady, whether he is a fool or a rogue, you will give him a salutary shock, and force him to think for a moment instead of merely grabbing at the illusion of enriching the nation by calling a penny twopence.

And now, if you agree with me that it is the duty of a Government to keep the value of its money always as nearly as possible at the same level, we are both up against the question, "What level?" Well, you may take it as a rule of thumb that the answer always is the existing level, unless it has been tampered with and has wobbled badly, in which case the easiest answer is "Whatever level it had before it began to wobble". But if you want a real explanation and not a mere rule of thumb, you must think of coins and notes as useful articles which you carry about because without them you cannot take a bus or a taxi or a train, or buy a bun. There must be enough of them to supply you and all the other people who have purchases to make. In short, coins and notes are like needles or shovels; and their value is settled in the same way. If the manufacturers make ten times as many needles as anyone wants, then their needles will fetch nothing as needles, because no woman will pay anything for the one needle she wants if there are nine lying about to be had for nothing. So all that can be done is to take the nine worthless needles and use the steel in them to make something else (say steel pens), after which there will be no longer any useless needles, and the remaining useful ones will be worth at least what it cost to make them, because sempstresses will want them badly enough to be willing to pay that price. An intelligent community will try to regulate the supply of needles so as to keep their value at that level as nearly as possible. A Capitalist community, on the contrary, will regulate it so as to make needles yield the utmost profit to the capitalist. But anyhow the value will depend on the quantity available.

Now just as a needle is for sewing, and is of no legitimate use for anything else, so coins and notes are for enabling people to buy and sell, and no use for anything else. And one coin will do for many sales as it passes from hand to hand, just as one needle will do to hem many handkerchiefs. This makes it very difficult to find out how many needles and coins are wanted. You cannot say "There are so many handkerchiefs in the country which must be hemmed; so we will make a needle for every one of them", or "There are so many loaves of bread to be sold every morning; so we will make coins or issue notes for the price of every one of them". No person or Government on earth can say beforehand how many needles or coins will be enough. You can count the mouths you have to feed, and say how many loaves will be required to fill them, because a slice of bread can be eaten only once, and is destroyed by being eaten; but a needle or a sovereign or a Treasury note can be used over and over again. One pound may be lying in an old stocking until the landlord calls for it, whilst another may be changing hands fifty times a day and effecting a sale every time. How then is a Government to settle how many coins and notes it shall issue? And how is a needle manufacturer to decide how many needles he shall make?

There is only one way of doing it. The needle makers just keep on making needles at a fancy price until they find they cannot sell them all without charging less for them; and then they go on charging less and less, but selling more and more (because of the cheapness), until the price is so low that they would make less profit if it went any lower, after which they make no more needles than are necessary to keep the supply, and consequently the price, just at that point. The Government has to do the same with gold coins. At first, because gold is more useful for coins than for anything else, an ounce of gold coined into sovereigns will be worth more than an ounce of uncoined gold (called bar or bullion). But if the Government issues more sovereigns than are needed for our buying and selling there will be more sovereigns than are wanted; and their value per ounce of gold will fall below that of gold bullion. This will be shewn by all prices going up, including that of gold in bars and ingots. The result will be that gold merchants will find it profitable to melt down sovereigns into bars of gold to be made into watches and bracelets and other things than coins. But this melting down reduces the number of sovereigns, which immediately begin to rise in value as they become scarcer until gold in the form of sovereigns is worth as much as gold in any other form. In this way, as long as money consists of gold, and melting down cannot be prevented as soon as it becomes profitable, the value of the coinage fixes and maintains itself automatically. It is against the British law to melt down a British sovereign in the British Empire; but as this silly law cannot restrain, say, a Dutch goldsmith in Amsterdam from melting down as many British sovereigns as he pleases, it does not count.

Though this settles the value of gold money, and all prices can be fixed in terms of gold, a penny being the two hundred and fortieth part of a sovereign, half a crown the eighth part of a sovereign, and so on, yet you cannot have gold pennies or even sixpences: they would be too small to handle. Also, if you want to make or receive a payment of five thousand pounds, you would find five thousand sovereigns more than you would care to carry. We get out of the penny and sixpenny difficulty by using coins of bronze and silver, making a law that bronze pennies shall be accepted, provided not more than twelve are offered at a time, as worth the two hundred and fortieth part of a sovereign, and that silver coins shall pass up to £2. We get over the five thousand pound difficulty by allowing the Bank of England to issue promissory notes, payable at sight in gold at the Bank, for sums of five pounds, ten pounds, a hundred pounds, and so on. People hand these notes from one to another in buying and selling, knowing them to be "as good as gold". Certain Scottish and Irish banks have the same privilege on condition that they hold sufficient gold in their cellars to redeem the notes when presented, and, of course, that they do not pay their debts in their own notes.

In this way we all get used to paper money as well as to bronze and silver coins: that is, we get used to pretending that a scrap of paper with a water mark is worth 615 grains of gold or thereabouts; that a bit of metal that is only half silver is worth a much larger piece of pure silver; that 240 bits of bronze are worth a sovereign, and so on. We find these cheap substitutes do just as well as gold coins; and we naturally begin to ask what is the use of having any gold money at all, seeing that we get on quite well without it. Paper is just as effective as an instrument of exchange, and much less heavy to handle. We measure prices in quantities of gold; but imaginary gold does for that as well as real gold, just as you can measure fluids by pints and quarts without having a drop of beer in the house. If only the honesty of Governments could be depended on, the use of gold for money would be a pure luxury, like using gold safety pins and diamond shirt studs instead of common ones, which fasten quite as well.

But that is a very large If. When there is a genuine gold currency, the purchasing power of the coins does not depend on the honesty of the Government: they are valuable as precious metal, and can be turned to other purposes if the Government issues more of them than are needed for buying and selling. But the Government can go on printing and issuing paper money until it is worthless. Where should it stop when the check of gold is removed? As we have seen, it should stop the moment there is any sign of a general rise of prices, because the only thing that can cause a general rise of prices is a fall in the value of money. This or that article may become cheaper by the discovery of new ways of making it, or dearer by a failure in the crops, or worthless by a change of fashion; but all the articles do not move together from these causes: some rise and others fall. When they all rise or fall simultaneously, then it is not the articles that are changing in value but the money. In a paper money country the Government should watch carefully for such movements; and when prices all rise together they should withdraw notes from circulation until prices all fall again. When all prices fall simultaneously the Government should issue fresh notes until they rise again. What is needed is just enough money to do all the ready money selling and buying in the country. When less is issued money gets a scarcity value; so that when you go into a grocer's shop he will give you more for your money (falling prices); and when more is issued there is a glut of it and the grocer will give less for it (rising prices). The business of an honest and understanding Government is to keep it steady by adjusting the supply to the demand. When Governments are either dishonest or ignorant, or both, there is no safety save in a currency of precious metal.

Remember, by the way, that modern banking makes it possible to do an enormous quantity of business without coinage or notes or money of any sort. Suppose Mrs John Doe and Mrs Richard Roe are both in business. Suppose Mrs Doe sells Mrs Roe five hundred pounds' worth of goods, and at the same time buys goods from her to the value of five hundred pounds and one penny. They do business to the amount of a thousand pounds and one penny; yet all the money they need to settle their accounts is the odd penny. If they keep their accounts at the same bank even the penny is not necessary. The banker transfers a penny from Mrs Doe's account to Mrs Roe's; and the thing is done. When you have to pay a business debt you do not give your creditor the money: you give him an order on your banker for it (a cheque); and he does not go to your bank and cash the cheque: he gives it to his own banker to collect. Thus every bank finds every day that it has to pay a heap of money to other banks which hold cheques on it for collection, and at the same time to receive a heap of money for the cheques it has received for collection from the other banks. These cheques taken together may amount to hundreds of thousands of pounds, yet the difference between the ones to be paid and the ones to be collected may be only a few pounds or less. So the banks began by setting up a Clearing House, as they call it, to add up all the cheques and find out what each bank ought to pay or receive on balance. This saved a great deal of money handling, as the transfer of a single pound from one bank to another would settle transactions involving huge sums. But it presently occurred to the banks that even this pound might be saved if they all kept an account at the same bank. So the banks themselves opened accounts at the Bank of England;

and now their accounts with oneanother are settled by a couple of entries in the Bank of England's books; and trade to the amount of millions and millions is done by pure figures without the use of coinage or notes. If we were all well enough off to have banking accounts money might disappear altogether, except for small transactions between strangers whose names and addresses were unknown to oneanother: for instance, you give an order and pay by a cheque in a shop because you can count on finding the shopkeeper in the same place if there is anything wrong with the goods; and he can count on finding you similarly if there is anything wrong with your cheque; but if you take a taxi on the way home, you can hardly expect the driver to open an account for you; so you settle with him by handing him his fare in coin.

This need for pocket money (change) is greatly reduced by Communism. In the days of turnpike roads and toll bridges every traveller had to keep a supply of money to pay tolls at every turnpike gate and bridge head. Now that the roads and bridges are communized he can travel by road from London to Aberdeen in his car without having to put his hand in his pocket once to pay for the roads, because he has already paid when taking out the communal license for his car. If he pays his hotel bills by cheque he needs no money for his journey except for tips; and when these fall into disuse, as the old custom of making presents to judges has done, it is easy to conceive motoring trips, in the Communist future, being carried out in the greatest luxury by highly prosperous but literally penniless persons.

In this way actual money is coming to be replaced more and more by money of account: that is, we still count our earnings and our debts in terms of money, and value our position in the same way, earning hundreds of pounds, paying hundreds of pounds, owning hundreds of poundsworth of furniture and clothes and motor cars, and yet never having more than a few pounds and a handful of silver in our pockets from one end of our lives to the other. The cost of providing coins and notes for the nation to buy and sell with is dwindling continuously to a smaller and smaller percentage of the value of the goods bought and sold.

It may amuse you to realize that when coinage disappears altogether it does not matter whether we call our debts sovereigns and pennies and shillings or millions and billions and trillions. When the Germans were paying millions for tram fares and postage stamps, no harm was done by the apparent magnitude of the price: poor men could still ride in trams and send letters. If only those prices could have been depended on to stay put, so that the poor man (or the rich one for that matter) could have felt sure that his million mark note would buy as much tomorrow as today, and as much next year as this year, it would not have inconvenienced him in the least that the million mark note used to be a bronze coin. Germany has now stabilized her currency at the old rate of twenty marks to the English pound. Austria stabilized hers at first at the startling rate of 300,000 tenpences to the English pound but had to alter this to 34½ sevenpenny schillings later on. Except for the look of the thing the change made no great difference to the marketing housekeeper. When prices are in millions she soon gets into the habit of dropping the six noughts in conversation across the counter. Such prices seem silly to us because we are not accustomed to millionaire scavengers and beef at billions a pound. We are accustomed to pounds worth 160 ounces of butter; but pounds worth half a grain of butter or ten tons of butter will do as long as they are stabilized at that, and as long as the money is either money of account, existing only as ink marks in ledgers, or paper notes of no intrinsic value. If a tram ticket costs a million pounds it can be paid more cheaply than by a penny, provided the million pounds be only a scrap of paper costing less than a disk of bronze.

To sum up, the most important thing about money is to maintain its stability, so that a pound will buy as much a year hence or ten years hence or fifty years hence as today, and no more. With paper money this stability has to be maintained by the Government. With a gold currency it tends to maintain itself even when the natural supply of gold is increased by discoveries of new deposits, because of the curious fact that the demand for gold in the world is practically infinite. You have to choose (as a voter) between trusting to the natural stability of gold and the natural stability of the honesty and intelligence of the members of the Government. And, with due respect for these gentlemen, I advise you, as long as the Capitalist system lasts, to vote for gold.

56

NATIONALIZATION OF BANKING

YOU now know enough about banking and the manufacture of money to understand that they are necessities of civilization. They are in some respects quite peculiar businesses. Banking heaps up huge masses of capital in the banker's hands for absolutely nothing but the provision of a till to put it in, and clerks to keep an account of it. Coinage is useless without a Government guarantee of the genuineness of the coins, and a code of laws making it a serious crime for any private person to make counterfeit coins, besides settling the limits within which coins that are stamped with more than their value as metal (called token coinage) can be used for paying debts.

As it is impossible for any private person or company to fulfil these coinage conditions satisfactorily, the manufacture of money is a nationalized business, unlike the manufacture of boots. You do not see a mint in every street as you see a bootmaker's. All the money is made in THE Mint, which is a Government factory of coins. If, in your disgust at the disagreeable white metal shillings which have been substituted since the war for the old silver ones, you were to set up a private mint of your own, you would be sent to prison for coining, even though you could prove that your nice shillings were worth more than the nasty ones of the Government. Formerly, if you had a quantity of gold, you could take it to the Mint, and have it made into sovereigns for you at a small charge for the King's image and guarantee called seignorage; but you were not allowed to make the coins for yourself out of your own gold. Today the Mint will not do that for you because it is easier for you to give your gold to your banker, who will give you credit for its worth in money. Thus the whole business is as strictly nationalized as that of the Post Office. Perhaps you do not know that you can be prosecuted for carrying a letter for hire instead of giving it to the Postmaster-General to carry. But you can, just as you can be prosecuted for making a coin, or for melting one down. And nobody objects. The people who, when it is proposed to nationalize the coal mines and the railways, shriek into your ears that nationalization is robbery and ruin, are so perfectly satisfied with the nationalization of the Mint that they never even notice that it is nationalized, poor dears!

However, private persons can issue a currency of their own, provided it is not an imitation of the Government currency. You may write a cheque, or a bill of exchange, and use it as paper money as often as you please; and no policeman can lay a finger on you for it provided (*a*) that you have enough Government money at your bank to meet the cheque when it is presented for payment, and (*b*) that the piece of paper on which your cheque is printed, or your bill of exchange drawn, bears no resemblance to a Treasury note or a bank note. An enormous volume of business is done today by these private currencies of cheques and bills of exchange. But they are not money: they are only title deeds to money, just as money itself is only a title deed to goods. If you owe money to your grocer he may refuse to take a cheque in payment; but if you offer him Treasury notes or sovereigns, he must take them whether he likes them or not. If you are trading with a manufacturer, and offer him a bill of exchange pledging you to pay for his goods in six months, he may refuse it and insist on Government money down on the nail. But he may not refuse Government money. Your offer of it is "legal tender".

Besides, money, as we have seen, is a measure of value; and cheques and bills are not. The cheques and bills would have no meaning and no use unless they were expressed in terms of money. They are all for so many pounds, shillings, and pence; and if there were no pounds, shillings, and pence in the background, a cheque would have to run "Pay to Emma Wilkins or Order two pairs of secondhand stockings, slightly laddered, my share of the family Pekingese dog, and half an egg". No banker would undertake to pay cheques of that sort. Both cheques and banking depend on the existence of nationalized money.

Banking is not yet nationalized; but it will be, because the public gain from nationalization will lead people to vote for it when they understand it just as they will vote for nationalization of the coal mines. Business people need capital to start and extend their businesses just as they need coal to warm themselves. As we have seen, when they want hundreds of thousands they get them by paying enormous commissions to financiers, who are so spoiled by huge profits that they will not deign to look at what they regard as small business. Those who want tens of thousands are not catered for; and those who want modest hundreds are often driven to borrow from money lenders at high rates of interest because the bank manager does not think it worth the bank's while to let them overdraw. If you could shew these traders a bank working not to make profits at the expense of its customers but to distribute capital as cheaply as possible for the good of the country to all the businesses, large or small, which needed it, they would rush to it and snap their fingers at the profiteering financiers. A national or municipal bank would be just that. It would bring down the price of capital just as nationalization of the coal mines would bring down the price of coal, by eliminating the profiteer; and all the profiteers except the money profiteers (financiers and bankers) will be finally converted to it by this prospect, because, though they aim at making as much profit as possible out of you when you go shopping, they are determined that other people shall make as little profit as possible out of them.

Nationalization of Banking therefore needs no Socialist advocacy to recommend it to the middle class. It is just as likely to be finally achieved by a Conservative Government as by a Labor one. The proof is that the first municipal bank has been established in Birmingham, which returns twelve members to Parliament of whom eleven are Conservatives, and strong ones at that. Only one is Labor. The Birmingham municipal bank has been so easily and brilliantly successful that unless it be deliberately sabotaged in the interests of the financiers by a press campaign against it, which is practically impossible in a city of manufacturers, it will lead to a development of municipal banking all over the manufacturing districts. Already there are several others.

Meanwhile the bankers and financiers continue to assure us that their business is such a mysteriously difficult one that no Government or municipal department could deal with it successfully. They are right about the mystery, which is due to the fact that they only half understand their own business, and their customers do not understand it at all. By this time I hope you understand it much better than an average banker. But the difficulty is all nonsense. Let us see again what a bank has to do.

By simply offering to keep people's money safe for them, and to make payments out of it for them to anyone they choose to name (by cheque), and to keep a simple cash account of these payments for them, it gets into its hands a mass of spare money which it professes to keep at its customers' call, but which it finds by experience it can hire out to the extent of about sixteen shillings in the pound because each customer keeps a balance to his credit all the time. There is no mystery or difficulty about this. It can be done by government or municipal banks as easily as petty banking, with its currency of postal notes and stamps, is done by our national post offices and savings banks. The only part of it that is not automatically successful is the hiring out of the money when it is paid in. A bank manager whose judgment was bad would very soon get his bank into difficulties by hiring out the spare money to traders who are in a bad way, either because their businesses were being superseded by new businesses, or because they were too honest, or not honest enough, or extravagant, or drunken, or lazy, or not good men of business, or poetically unfitted to succeed. But a manager who was too cautious to lend any money at all would be still more disastrous; for we must continually remember that the things represented by the spare money in the bank will not keep, and that if fifty billions' worth of food were saved out of the year's harvest and lodged in a State bank (or any other bank) it would be a dead loss and waste if it were not eaten pretty promptly by workers building up facilities for producing future harvests. The bank manager can choose the person to whom he lends the bank's spare money; but he cannot choose not to lend it at all; just as a baker, when he has sold all the bread he can for ready money, must either give credit for the rest to somebody or else throw the loaves into the dustbin.

Only, there is this difference between the baker and the banker. The baker can refrain from baking more loaves than he can reasonably expect to sell; but the banker may find himself heaped up with far more spare money than he can find safe hirers for; and then he has not only to take chances himself, but to tempt tradesmen by low rates of hire to take them ("the banks are granting credit freely" the city articles in the papers will say), whereas at other times his spare money will be so short that he will pick and choose and charge high interest ("the bankers are restricting credit"); and this is why it takes more knowledge and critical judgment to manage a bank than to run a baker's shop.

No wonder the bankers, who make enormous profits, and consequently have the greatest dread of having these cut off by the nationalization of banking, declare that no Government could possibly do this difficult work of hiring out money, and that it must be left to them, as they alone understand it! Now, to begin with, they neither understand it nor do it themselves. Their bad advice produced widespread ruin in Europe after the war, simply because they did not understand the rudiments of their business, and persisted in reasoning on the assumption that spent capital still exists, and that credit is something solid that can be eaten and drunk and worn and lived in. The people who do the really successful work of hiring out the heaps of spare money in the bank for use in business are not the bankers but the bank managers, who are only employees. Their position as such is not more eligible either in money or social standing than that of an upper division civil servant, and is in many respects much less eligible. They would be only too glad to be civil servants instead of private employees. As to the superior direction which deals with what may be called the wholesale investment of the banked spare money as distinguished from its retail hirings to ordinary tradesmen and men of business, the pretence that this could not be done by the Treasury or any modern public finance department is a tale for the marines. The Bank of England is as glad to have a former Treasury official on its staff as the London Midland and Scottish Railway to have a former civil servant for its Chairman.

57
COMPENSATION FOR NATIONALIZATION

BY the way, when demonstrating the need for the nationalization of banking to you I did not forget that you may be a bank shareholder, and that your attention may have been distracted by your wonder as to what will become of your shares when the banks are nationalized. I have had to consider this question rather closely myself, because, as it happens, my wife is a bank shareholder. We might have to cut down our household expenses if everyone went to a national or municipal bank instead of to her bank. In fact, when banking is nationalized, private banking will probably be made a crime, like private coining or letter carrying. So we shall certainly insist on the Government buying her shares when it nationalizes banking.

The Government will buy them willingly enough, for the excellent reason that it will get the money by taxing all capitalists' incomes; so that if my wife were the only capitalist in the country the transaction would be as broad as it was long: the Government would take from her with one hand what it gave her with the other. Fortunately for her there are plenty of other capitalists to be taxed along with her; so that instead of having to provide all the money to buy herself out, she will have to provide only a little bit of it; and all the little bits that the other capitalists will have to provide will go into her pocket. This transaction is called Compensation.

It is very important that you should grasp this quaint process which seems so perfectly fair and ordinary. It explains how Governments compensate without really compensating, and how such compensation costs the nation nothing, being really a method of expropriation. Just consider. If the Government purchases a piece of land or a railway or a bank or a coal mine, and pays for it out of the taxes, it is evident that the Government gets it for nothing: it is the taxpayers who pay. And if the tax is a tax like the income tax, from which the bulk of the nation is wholly or partially exempt, or the supertax and estate duties, which fall on the capitalist classes only, then the Government has compelled the capitalist class to buy out one of themselves and present her property to the nation without any compensation whatever. The so-called compensation is only an adjustment by which the loss is shared by the whole capitalist class instead of being borne wholly by the particular member of it whose piece of land or bank shares or other property the Government happens to want. Even that member pays her share of the tax without compensation.

Some ladies may find this clearer if an imaginary case is put before them in figures. Suppose the Government wants a piece of land of the market value of £1000! Suppose it raises that sum, not by taxing the nation, but by taxing the incomes of a hundred rich landlords, including the owner of the piece of land, making each of them contribute £10! The Government then takes the piece of land, and solemnly hands £1000 to its former owner, telling him that he has nothing to complain of, as he has been paid the full market value of his land instead of having had it wrested from him violently in a revolutionary manner, as the Bolshevists took the land from the Russian landlords in 1917. Nothing can be more reasonable and constitutional and customary; the most Conservative Government might do it; in fact (except for the substitution of all the landlords for a hundred selected ones) Conservative Governments have done it over and over again. None the less, at the end of the transaction a piece of land has passed from private property into national property; and a hundred landlords have had their incomes reduced by ten shillings a year each (the interest on £10 at 5 per cent). It is quite clear that if such a transaction is repeated often enough the nation will have all the land, and the incomes of the landlords will be reduced to nothing, although every acre has been bought from its owner at full market price. The process can be applied to bank shares or any other shares as easily as to acres.

Let me repeat that this is not something that may be done: it is something that has been done and is being done. It has gone so far already that a huge quantity of property formerly owned by private persons is now owned by the Government and the municipalities: that is, by the nation; whilst taxation has risen to such a point that the rich have to remind themselves continually that their pounds are only thirteen-and-fourpences or less, because the Government will take the other six and eightpence or more as income tax and supertax, and that even out of the thirteen and fourpence the municipalities of the places where their houses are (rich men keep from two to five houses) will take a considerable dollop in rates for pure Communism. At present they are selling their houses in all directions to speculators and contractors who have made large fortunes out of inflation and War; but these New Rich will in their turn be forced to buy oneanother out just as the Old Rich, now called the New Poor, were.

In this way you get the constitutional rule for nationalization of private property, which is, always to pay the full market price or more to the proprietors for every scrap of property nationalized. Pay for it by taxing incomes derived from property (there is, of course, no compensation for taxation). Your own rule as a voter should be never to vote for a candidate who advocates expropriation without compensation, whether he calls himself a Socialist or Communist, in which case he does not understand his own political business, or a Liberal. The Liberal impulse is almost always to give a dog a bad name and hang him: that is, to denounce the menaced proprietors as enemies of mankind, and ruin them in a transport of virtuous indignation. But Liberals are not, as such, hostile to capitalists, nor indeed to anybody but publicans and imaginary feudal landlords. Conservatives are practically always for compensation to property owners; and they are right; but they do not see through the trick of it as you now do.

Anyhow, always vote against the no-compensation candidate unless you are opposed to nationalization, and are subtle enough to see that the surest way to defeat it is to advocate its being carried out vindictively without a farthing of compensation.

There is, however, an alternative to compensated nationalization of private industries. Why should not the Government set up for itself in the industry it desires to nationalize, and extinguish its private competitors just as the big multiple shops extinguish the small shops, by underselling them, and by all the other methods of competitive trade? The Birmingham municipality has begun the nationalization of banking without troubling itself about the private banks: it has simply opened its bank in the street and gone ahead. The parcel post was established without any compensation to private carriers; and the Cash on Delivery development of it was effected without any consideration for the middlemen whom it superseded. Private employers have always proceeded in this manner on competitive principles; why should not the State, as public employer, do just the same?

The reason is that the competitive method is an extremely wasteful one. When two bakeries are set up in a district that could be quite well served by one, or two milk carts ply in the same street, each trying to snatch the other's custom, it means that the difference between the cost of running two and one is sheer waste. When a woman wears out her hat, or rather when the hatmakers change the fashion so as to compel her to buy a new hat before the one she is wearing is half worn out, and fifty shops make new hats on the chance of selling that one to her, there is overproduction, with its sequel of unemployment.

Now apply this to, for example, the nationalization of railways. The Government could, no doubt, construct a network of State railways parallel with the existing railways; so that you could go from London to Penzance either by the Great Western or by a new State line running side by side with it. The State could then, by introducing the system of Penny Transport proposed by Mr Whately Arnold on the lines of Penny Postage, undersell the separate private companies and take all their traffic from them. That would be the competitive method. Then there would be two railways to Penzance and Thurso and Bristol and Cromer and everywhere else, one of them carrying nearly all the traffic, and the other carrying only its leavings and holiday overflows until it fell into hopeless and dangerous decay and ruin.

But can you imagine anything more idiotically wasteful? The cost of making the competing State railway would be enormous, and quite unnecessary. The ruin of the private railway would be sheer destruction of a useful and sufficient means of communication which had itself cost a huge sum. The land occupied by one of the railways would be wasted. What Government in its senses would propose such a thing when it could take over the existing railways by compensating the shareholders in the manner I have described: that is, distributing their loss over the propertied class without a farthing of expense to the nation as a whole?

The same considerations must lead the State to take over the existing banks. Municipal banks on the Birmingham model may be competing banks; but when a national banking service comes, it will come by way of nationalizing the existing private banks.

There is another objection to the competitive method. If the State is to compete with private enterprise, it must allow private enterprise to compete with it. Now this is not practicable if the full advantage of nationalization is to be obtained. The Post Office is able to establish a letter service and C.O.D. parcel post in every village in the country, and a telephone and telegraph service in most of them, with charges reckoned in pence and halfpence, on condition that profiteers are not allowed to come in and pick out the easy bits of the business to exploit for themselves. The Postmaster-General does things for the nation that no profiteer would or could do; but his rule is All or Nothing.

A Banker-General would have to insist on the same rule. He would establish banks, if not literally everywhere, at least in hundreds of places where the private banks would no more dream of opening a branch, even on the open-once-a-week scale, than of building a Grand Opera House. But he, too, would say "All or Nothing: I will not have any intelligent Jewish gentleman, or rapacious Christian person trained in the intelligent Jewish gentleman's office, picking the plums out of my pudding".

Yet do not conclude that all State activities will be State monopolies. Indeed the nationalization of banking will certainly enlarge the possibilities of private activity in all sorts of ways. But as the big public services will have to be made practically ubiquitous, charging more than they cost in one place and less in another, they must be protected against sectional private competition. Otherwise we should have what prevails at present in municipal building, where all the lucrative contracts for the houses of the rich and the offices of the capitalists and the churches and institutions and so forth go to the private employer, whilst the municipality may build only dwellings for the poor at a loss, which they conceal from the ratepayers by fictitious figures as to the value of the land. Municipal building is always insolvent. If it had a monopoly it could afford to make every town in the land a ratepayers' and tenants' paradise.

This reminds me to remind you that every nationalization of an industry or service involves the occupation of land by the State. This land should always be nationalized by purchase and compensation. For if it is merely rented, as I am sorry to say it sometimes is, the charges made to the public must be raised by the amount of the rent, thus giving the ground landlord the money value of all the advantages of the nationalization.

I have said nothing about one of the cruelest effects of superseding an industry by competition instead of buying it up. The process consists fundamentally of the gradual impoverishment and ruin of those who are carrying on the superseded business.

Capitalism is ruthless on this point: its principle is "Each for himself; and devil take the hindmost!" But the State has to consider the loser as well as the winner. It must not impoverish anybody. It must let the loser down easily; and there is no other way of doing this except the way of purchase and compensation.

58
PRELIMINARIES TO NATIONALIZATION

YOU now see that nationalization and municipalization are so desirable as a means of cheapening the things we all need that the most violently anti-Socialist Parliaments and municipal corporations have established nationalized and municipalized industries in the past, and are quite likely to do so in future under electoral pressure from Conservative voters. You see also that the alleged enormous expense of buying out private owners, which has been alleged by a Coal Commission as an insuperable objection to the nationalization of our coal mines, is a bogey, because, though the coalowners (of whom, by the way, I am one) will be fully compensated, the proprietary class as a whole will pay the bill out of their unearned incomes, leaving the nation richer instead of poorer by the transaction. So far so good. Theoretically, nationalization is perfectly sound.

Practically, it takes, as the people very accurately put it, a lot of doing. A mere proclamation that such and such an industry is nationalized can do nothing but just put a stop to it. Before any industry or service can be effectively nationalized a new department of the Civil Service must be created to carry it on. Unless we had a War Office we could not have an army, because no soldier could get his pay, or his uniform, or his weapons. Without an Admiralty, no navy. Without a General Post Office and a Postmaster-General, no letters in the morning. Without a Royal Mint and a Master of the Mint, no money. Without Scotland Yard in London, and Watch Committees in the country, no police. And as in the present so in the future. Without a great extension of the Treasury, banking cannot be nationalized, nor coal without the creation of a Department of Mines much bigger than our existing Department of Woods and Forests, nor railways without a Railway Board and a Railroadmaster-General as important as the Post Office and the Postmaster-General.

Such institutions can be set up by stable and highly organized States only, which means—and here is the political moral of it—that they cannot be done by revolutions, or by improvised dictatorships, or even by permanent States in which, as in America, where in some cases the civil services are still regarded as the spoils of office, a new set of officials oust the old ones whenever the Opposition ousts the Government. What a revolution can do towards nationalization is to destroy the political power of the class which opposes nationalization. But such a revolution by itself cannot nationalize; and the new Government it sets up may be unable even to carry on the nationalized services it finds in existence, and be obliged to abandon them to private enterprise.

A nationalizing Government must also be financially honest, and determined to make the nationalization a success, and neither plunder it to eke out the general revenue, nor discredit and wreck it so to have an excuse for giving the nationalized service back to the private profiteers. State railways have sometimes been standing examples of what State management can be at its worst. The Governments, instead of keeping the railways in proper repair, grabbed all the money paid by the public in fares and freightage; applied it to the relief of general taxation; and let the stations and rolling stock decay until their railways were the worst in the world, and there was a general clamor for their denationalization. Private profiteering enterprises have gone to pieces in the same way and worse; but, as they have been responsible to themselves only, their failures and frauds have passed unnoted, whilst the failures and frauds of Governments have raised great popular agitations and even provoked revolutions. The misdeeds of Governments are public and conspicuous: the misdeeds of private traders are practically invisible; and thus an illusion is created that Governments are less honest and efficient than private traders. It is only an illusion; but all the same, honesty and good faith are as necessary in nationalized businesses as in private ones. Our British nationalized services are held up as models of integrity; yet the Postmaster-General overcharges us a little for our letters, and puts the profit into the pockets of the propertied class in the form of reduced income tax; and the Admiralty is continually fighting against the tendency to keep down taxation by starving the navy. These depredations do not amount to much; but they illustrate what may be done when voters are not vigilant and well instructed.

59
CONFISCATION WITHOUT COMPENSATION

OUR study of nationalization by compensated or distributed confiscation has no doubt relieved you from all anxiety as to the need for nationalization without compensation. But there is always a loud-mouthed, virtuously indignant political group, still saturated with the revolutionary traditions of Liberalism, which opposes compensation. If the property owner is, in effect, a thief, they say, why should he be compensated for being compelled to cease to do evil and learn to do well? If by taxation we can make the whole capitalist class find the money to buy out the coalowners, and thus transfer their property to the nation to that extent, why not take the rest of their property simply for the sake of transferring it also to the nation? Our joint stock companies work as well with one set of shareholders as with another: in fact their shares change hands so continually in the Money Market that they never have the same set of shareholders from one working day to the next. If all the railway shares in the country were held on Monday by the inhabitants of Park Lane, and on Tuesday by the British Government, the railways would go on just the same. In like case so would any other of the great industrial services now in joint stock ownership. If a landlord had to hand over the title-deeds of half a dozen farms and an urban street to the Exchequer, the farmers would go on farming, and the tenants go on living in the street, unaffected by the obligation to pay their rents in future to an agent of the Government instead of to the agent of a duke or any other plutocrat. The business of a bank would proceed just as smoothly after as before the owners had handed over their claims on its profits to the Chancellor of the Exchequer. Then why not at once push taxation of capital to the point at which the capitalist taxpayer, unable to find the money, will be forced to surrender to the Government his share certificates, his War Loan interest, and his title-deeds? The share certificates would not be worth a farthing on the Stock Exchange, because there would be all sellers and no buyers there; but none the less each certificate would, like the title-deeds to the land, carry the right to an income out of the future harvests of the country; and if the Government could immediately use that income for the benefit of the nation, it would be extremely well worth its while to get hold of it by accepting the certificates at their face value.

It could even do so with a show of generosity; for it could say to the capitalist, "You owe the tax collector a thousand pounds (say); but instead of selling you up we are authorizing him to give you a clean receipt, not for the money, but for ten paper certificates marked a hundred pounds each, for which the cleverest stockbroker in London could not get you twopence". "But", exclaims the cornered capitalist, "what becomes of my income? What am I to do for a living?" "Work for it, as others have to do", is the reply. In short, from the point of view of its Socialist advocates, taxation of capital, though absurd as a means of raising ready money for the expenses of Government, is a way of confiscating without compensation the title-deeds of, and thereby nationalizing, the land and the mines and the railways and all the other industries which the capitalists now hold as their private property.

The scheme is plausible enough.

60

REVOLT OF THE PARASITIC PROLETARIAT

BUT there is an objection to it; and that objection may be learnt from the stupidest woman you ask in the street. She will tell you that you must not take away the property of the rich, because "they give employment". Now, as we have seen, it is quite true that fundamentally it is nonsense to say that an unproductive rich person can give employment in any other sense than as a lunatic gives employment to her keeper. An idle rich woman can give no productive employment: the employment she gives is wasteful. But wasteful or not, she gives it and pays for it. She may not have earned the money she pays with; but it will buy as good bread and clothes for her employee as the most honestly earned money in the kingdom. The idler is a parasite: and the idler's employee, however industrious, is therefore a parasite on a parasite; but if you leave the parasite destitute you leave the parasite's parasites destitute; and unless you have productive employment ready for them they will have to starve or steal or rebel; and as they will certainly not choose to starve, their choice of the remaining two alternatives (which they will probably combine) may upset the Government if they are numerous enough. And they are, as a matter of fact, very numerous, as you may see by counting the Conservative votes that are given at every General Election by people who work for weekly wages in wholly or partly parasitic occupations. The plunder of the proletariat is shared handsomely by the plunderers with the proletarians. If our capitalists could not plunder our proletarians, our proletarians and their middle class organizers, from the Bond Street art dealers and jewellers to the errand boys of Bournemouth, could not live on the custom of our capitalists. That is why neither Bond Street nor Bournemouth can be persuaded to vote for uncompensated expropriation, and why, if it came to fighting instead of voting, they would fight against it.

The trouble would begin, not with the nationalized industries, but with the others. As we have seen, the mines and banks and railways, being already organized as going concerns, and managed by directors elected by the votes of the shareholders, could be confiscated by taxing the shareholders heavily enough to oblige them to transfer their shares to the Government in payment of the tax. But the income derived from these shares would therefore go into the pocket of the Government instead of into the pockets of the shareholders. Thus the purchasing power of the shareholders would pass to the Government; and every shop or factory that depended on their custom would have to shut up and discharge all its employees. The saving power of the shareholders, which means, as we now understand, the power of supplying the spare money needed for starting new industrial enterprises or extending old ones to keep pace with civilization, would also pass to the Government. These powers, which must be kept in action without a moment's interruption, operate by continual expenditure (mainly household expenditure) and continual investment of the enormous total of all our private incomes.

What could the Government do with that total? If it simply dropped it into the national till, and sat on it, most of it would perish by natural decay; and meanwhile a great many of the people would perish too. There would be a monster epidemic of bankruptcy and unemployment. The tide of calamity would sweep away any Government unless it proclaimed itself a Dictatorship, and employed, say, a third of the population to shoot down another third, whilst the remaining third footed the bill with its labor. What could the Government do to avert this, short of handing back the confiscated property to the owners with apologies for having made a fool of itself?

61

SAFETY VALVES

IT could distribute the money in doles; but that would only spread the very evil the confiscation was intended to destroy: that is to say, the evil of unearned income. A much sounder plan (and do not forget this when next you are tempted to give a spare £5 note to a beggar instead of putting it on deposit at your bank) would be to throw all the money into the confiscated banks, and lend it to employers at unprecedentedly cheap rates. Another expedient would be to raise wages handsomely in the confiscated industries. Another, the most desperate of all, but by no means the least probable, would be to go to war, and waste on the soldier the incomes formerly wasted on the plutocrat.

These expedients do not exclude oneanother. Doles, cheap capital available in Government-owned banks, and high wages, could be resorted to simultaneously to redistribute purchasing power and employing power. The doles and pensions would tide over the remaining years of those discharged servants of the ruined rich who were incapable of changing their occupations, and of the ruined rich themselves. The cheap capital at the banks would enable employers to start new businesses, or modify old ones, and to cater for the increased purchasing power of the workers whose wages had been raised, thereby giving employment to the workers who had lost their jobs in Bournemouth or Bond Street. The art dealers could sell pictures to the National Gallery and the provincial municipal galleries. There would be a crisis; but what of that? Capitalism has often enough produced displacements of purchasing power and loss of livelihood to large bodies of citizens, and fallen back on doles in the shape of Mansion House Funds and the like as safety valves to ease the pressure when the unemployed began to riot and break windows. Why should we not muddle through as we have always done?

Well, we might. But serious as the biggest crises of Capitalism have been, they have never been as big as the crash that would follow confiscation by the Government of the entire property of the whole propertied class without any preparation for the immediate productive employment not only of the expropriated owners (who are too few to give much trouble) but of the vast parasitic proletariat who produce their luxuries. Would the safety valves act quickly enough and open widely enough? We must examine them more closely before we can judge.

A civilized country depends on the circulation of its money as much as a living animal depends on the circulation of its blood. A general confiscation of private property and its incomes would produce an unprecedented congestion in London, where the national Treasury is, of money from all over the kingdom; and it would become a matter of life or death for the Government to pump that congested money promptly back again to the extremities of the land. Remember that the total sum congested would be much larger than under the capitalist system, because, as the capitalists spend much more of their incomes than they save, the huge amount of this expenditure would be saved and added to the Government revenue from the confiscated property.

Now for the safety valves. A prodigious quantity of the congested money would come from the confiscated ground rents of our cities and towns. The present proprietors spend these rents where they please; and they seldom please to spend them in the places where they were produced by the work of the inhabitants. A plutocrat does not decide to live in Bootle when he is free to live in Biarritz. The inhabitants of Bootle do not get the benefit of his expenditure, which goes to the west end of London and to the pleasure resorts and sporting grounds of all the world, though perhaps a little of it may come back if the town manufactures first class boots and riding breeches and polo mallets. The dwellers in the town enjoy a good deal of municipal communism; but they have to pay for it in rates which are now oppressively heavy everywhere. And they would be heavier still if the Government did not make what are called Grants-in-Aid to the municipalities.

An obvious safety valve, and a popular one with the ratepayers, would be the payment of the rates by the Treasury through greatly increased grants. If you are a ratepaying householder, and your landlord were suddenly to announce that in future he would pay the rates, you would rejoice in the prospect of having that much more money to spend on yourself. A similar announcement by the Chancellor of the Exchequer would be equally welcome. It would relieve the congestion at the Treasury, and send a flood of money back from the heart to the extremities.

Then there is the combination of raised wages in the confiscated industries with a flood of cheap capital pumped to all the business centres through the confiscated banks. The raised wages would check the flow of income to the Treasury by reducing dividends; and the cheapening of capital would enable new businesses to be started and old ones re-equipped to meet the demand created by the increased purchasing power (pocket money) of the wage workers and the disburdened ratepayers.

And there is always a good deal to be done in the way of public expenditure on roads; on reclamations of land from the sea; on afforestation; on building great dams across valleys and barrages across rivers and tideways to concentrate waterflow on turbine engines; on stations for the distribution of the power thus gained; on the demolition of slum towns that should never have been built, and their replacement by properly planned, healthy and handsome garden cities; and on a hundred other things that Capitalism never dreams of doing because it is impossible to appropriate their advantages as commercial profit. The demand for labor created by such operations would absorb all the employable unemployed, and leave only the superannuated and the incurably unemployable on the dole, with, of course, the children, on whom much more money could and should be spent than at present, with great uncommercial profit to the next generation.

All this sounds very reassuring, and costs little to describe on paper. But a few minutes' reflection will dispel all hope that it could occur instantly and spontaneously through the uncompensated transfer of all existing shares and title-deeds to the Government. The Ministry of Health would have to produce a huge scheme for the grants-in-aid to the cities; and Parliament would wrangle for months over it. As to glutting the existing banks with spare money to lend without any further interference with them, the results would include an orgy of competitive enterprise, over-capitalization, overproduction, hopeless shops and businesses started by inexperienced or silly or rash people or people who are all three: in short, a boom followed by a slump, with the usual unemployment, bankruptcies, and so forth. To keep that part of the program under control, it would be necessary to set up a new department of the Treasury to replace the present boards of predatory company directors; to open banks wherever the post offices are doing substantial business; and to staff the new banks with specially trained civil servants. And all that would take longer than it takes a ruined citizen to starve.

As to raising industrial wages and reducing prices with the object of eliminating profit, that is so precisely the contrary of the policy which the existing managers of our industry have trained themselves to pursue, and which alone they understand, that their replacement by civil servants would be just as necessary as in the case of the banks. Such replacements could be effected only as part of an elaborate scheme requiring long preliminary cogitation and a practical preparation involving the establishment of new public departments of unprecedented magnitude.

Public works, too, cannot be set on foot offhand in the manner of Peter the Great, who, when asked to dictate the route to be taken by his new road from Moscow to Petrograd, took up a ruler and drew a straight line on the map from the word Moscow to the Neva. If Peter had had to get a proposal for a turbine barrage through a parliament with a fiery Welsh contingent determined that it should be across the Severn, and an equally touchy Scots contingent bent on having it across the Kyle of

Tongue, he would have found many months slipping by him before he could set the first gang of navvies to work.

I need not weary you by multiplying instances. Wholesale nationalization without compensation is catastrophic: the patient dies before the remedy has time to operate. If you prefer a mechanical metaphor, the boiler bursts because the safety valves jam. The attempted nationalization would produce a revolution. You may say "Well, why not? What I have read in this book has made me impatient for revolution. The fact that any measure would produce a revolution is its highest recommendation".

If that is your view, your feelings do you credit: they are or have been shared by many good citizens. But when you go thoroughly into the matter you will realize that revolutions do not nationalize anything, and often make it much more difficult to nationalize them than it would have been without the revolution if only the people had had some education in political economy. If a revolution were produced by unskilled Socialism (all our parliamentary parties are dangerously unskilled at present) in the teeth of a noisy and inveterate Capitalist Opposition, it would produce reaction instead of progress, and give Capitalism a new lease of life. The name of Socialism would stink in the nostrils of the people for a generation. And that is just the sort of revolution that an attempt to nationalize all property at a blow would provoke. You must therefore rule out revolution on this particular issue of out-and-out uncompensated and unprepared general nationalization versus a series of carefully prepared and compensated nationalizations of one industry after another.

Later on, we shall expatiate a little on what revolutions can do and what they cannot. Meanwhile, note as a canon of nationalization (economists like to call their rules for doing anything canons) that all nationalizations must be prepared and compensated. This will be found an effectual safeguard against too many nationalizations being attempted at a time. We might even say against more than one nationalization being attempted at a time; only we must not forget that industries are now so amalgamated before they are ripe for nationalization that it is practically impossible to nationalize one without nationalizing half a dozen others that are inextricably mixed up with it. You would be surprised to learn how many other things a railway company does besides running trains. And if you have ever gone to sea in a big liner you have perhaps sometimes looked round you and wondered whether the business of making it was called shipbuilding or hotel building, to say nothing of engineering.

62

WHY CONFISCATION HAS SUCCEEDED HITHERTO

NOW that I have impressed on you at such length as a canon of nationalization that Parliament must always buy the owners out and not simply tax them out, I am prepared to be informed that the canon is dead against the facts, because the direct attack on property by simple confiscation: that is, by the Government taking the money of the capitalists away from them by main force and putting it into the public treasury, has already, without provoking reaction or revolution, been carried by Conservative and Liberal Governments to lengths which would have seemed monstrous and incredible to nineteenth century statesmen like Gladstone, proving that you can introduce almost any measure of Socialism or Communism into England provided you call it by some other name. Propose Socialistic confiscation of the incomes of the rich, and the whole country will rise to repel such Russian wickedness. Call it income tax, supertax, and estate duties, and you can lift enough hundreds of millions from the pockets of our propertied class to turn the Soviet of Federated Russian Republics green with envy.

Take a case or two in figures. Gladstone thought it one of his triumphs as Chancellor of the Exchequer to reduce the income tax to twopence in the pound, and hoped to be able to abolish it altogether. Instead of which it went up to six shillings in 1920, and stopped at that only because it was supplemented by an additional income tax (Supertax or Surtax) on the larger incomes, and a partial abolition of inheritance which makes the nation heir to a considerable part of our property when we die possessed of any. Just imagine the fuss there would have been over this if it had been proposed by a Socialist Prime Minister as Confiscation, Expropriation, and Nationalization of Inheritance on the Communist principles of the prophet Marx! Yet we took it lying down.

You have perhaps not noticed how this taxation is arrived at in Parliament at present. The Chancellor of the Exchequer is the Minister who has to arrange the national housekeeping for the year, and screw out of a reluctant House of Commons its consent to tax us for the housekeeping money; for with the negligible exception of the interest on certain shares in the Suez Canal and in some ten companies who had to be helped to keep going during the war the nation has no income from property. Whom he will be allowed to tax depends on the sort of members who have been returned to Parliament. Without their approval his Budget, as he calls his proposals for taxation, cannot become law; and until it becomes law nobody can be compelled to pay the taxes. In Gladstone's time Parliament consisted practically of landlords and capitalists and employers, the handful of working class members being hopelessly outvoted by the other three sections combined, or even single. Each of these sections naturally tried to throw as much of the burden of taxation as possible on the others; but all three were heartily agreed in throwing on the working class as much of it as they could without losing too many working class votes at the next election. Therefore the very last tax they wished to sanction was the income tax, which all of them had to pay directly, and which the wage workers escaped, as it does not apply to small incomes. Thus the income tax became a sort of residual tax or last resort: an evil to be faced only when every other device for raising money had been found insufficient. When Gladstone drove it down from sixpence to fourpence, and from fourpence to twopence, and expressed his intention of doing without it altogether, he was considered a very great Chancellor of the Exchequer indeed. To do this he had to raise money by putting taxes on food and drink and tobacco, on legal documents of different kinds, from common receipts and cheques and contracts to bills of exchange, share certificates, marriage settlements, leases and the like. Then there were the customs, or duties payable on goods sent into the country from abroad. The industrial employers, who were great importers of raw materials, and wanted food to be cheap because cheap food meant low wages, said "Let them come in free, and tax the landlords". The country gentlemen said "Tax imports, especially corn, to encourage agriculture". This created the great Free Trade controversy on which the Tories fought the Liberals for so many years. But both parties always agreed that income tax should not be imposed until every other means of raising the money had been exhausted, and that even then it should be kept down to the lowest possible figure.

When Socialism became Fabianized and began to influence Parliament through a new proletarian Labor Party, budgeting took a new turn. The Labor Party demanded that the capitalists should be the first to pay, and not the last, and that the taxation should be higher on unearned than on earned incomes. This involved a denial of the need for keeping Government expenditure and taxation down to the lowest possible figure. When taxation consists in taking money away from people who have not earned it and restoring it to its real earners by providing them with schools, better houses, improved cities, and public benefits of all sorts, then clearly the more the taxation the better for the nation. Where Gladstone cried "I have saved the income tax payers of the country another million. Hurrah!" a Labor Chancellor will cry "I have wrung another million from the supertaxed idlers, and spent it on the welfare of our people! Hooray!"

Thus for the last fifteen years we have had a running struggle in Parliament between the Capitalist and Labor parties: the former trying to keep down the income tax, the supertax, the estate duties, and public expenditure generally, and the latter trying to increase them. The annual debates on the Budget always turn finally on this point, though it is seldom frankly faced; and the capitalists have been losing bit by bit until now (in the nineteen-twenties) we have advanced from Gladstone's income tax of 2d. in the pound to rates of from four to six shillings, with, on incomes exceeding £2000, surtaxes that range from eighteen pence to six shillings according to the amount of the income; whilst on the death of a property owner his heirs have to hand over to the Government a share of the estate ranging from one per cent of its fictitious capital value when it is a matter of a little over £100, to forty per cent when it exceeds a couple of millions.

That is to say, if your uncle leaves you five guineas a year you have to pay the Government seventy-three days income. If he leaves you a hundred thousand a year you pay eight years income, and starve for the eight years unless you can raise the money by mortgaging your future income, or have provided for it by insuring your life at a heavy premium for the nation's benefit.

Now suppose this income of a hundred thousand a year belongs to an aristocratic family in which military service as an officer is a tradition which is practically obligatory. In a war it may easily happen, as it did sometimes during the late war, that the owner of such a property and his two brothers next in succession are killed within a few months. This would bring the income of £100,000 a year down to £12,000, the difference having been confiscated by the Government. If we were to read in The Morning Post that the Russian Soviet had taken £78,000 a year from a private family without paying a penny of compensation, most of us would thank heaven that we were not living in a country where such Communistic monstrosities are possible. Yet our British anti-Socialist Governments, both Liberal and Conservative, do it as a matter of routine, though their Chancellors of the Exchequer go on making speeches against Socialistic confiscation as if nobody outside Russia ever dreamt of such a thing!

That is just like us. All the time we are denouncing Communism as a crime, every street lamp and pavement and water tap and police constable is testifying that we could not exist for a week without it. Whilst we are shouting that Socialistic confiscation of the incomes of the rich is robbery and must end in red revolution, we are actually carrying it so much further than any other fully settled country that many of our capitalists have gone to live in the south of France for seven months in the year to avoid it, though they affirm their undying devotion to their native country by insisting that our national anthem shall be sung every Sunday on the Riviera as part of the English divine service, whilst the Chancellor of the Exchequer at home implores heaven to "frustrate their knavish tricks" until he can devise some legal means of defeating their evasions of his tax collectors.

But startling from the Victorian point of view as are the sums taken annually from the rich, they have not in the lump gone beyond what the property owners can pay in cash out of their incomes, nor what the Government is prepared to throw back into circulation again by spending it immediately. They have transferred purchasing power from the rich to the poor, producing minor commercial crises here and there, and often seriously impoverishing the old rich; but they have been accompanied by such a development of capitalism that there are more rich, and richer rich, than ever; so that the luxury trades have had to expand instead of contract, giving more employment instead of less. And they have proved that you may safely confiscate income derived from property provided you can immediately redistribute it. But you cannot tax it to extinction at a single mortal blow. You have always to consider most carefully how far and how fast you can go without crashing. The rule that the Government must not tax at all until it has an immediate use for the money it takes is fundamental: it holds in every case. The rule that if it uses it to nationalize an already established commercial industry or service it must have a new public department ready to take the business over, and must compensate the owners from whom it takes it, is also invariable. When the object is not nationalization, but simple redistribution of income within the capitalist system by transferring purchasing power from one set of people to another, usually from a richer set to a poorer set, thus changing the demand in the shops from dear luxuries to comparatively cheap necessities, then the process must go no faster than the capitalist shops can adapt themselves to this change. Else it may produce enough bankruptcies to make the Government very unpopular at the next election.

Let us study a sensational instance in which we have incurred a heavy additional burden of unearned income, so strongly resented by the mass of the people that our Governments, whether Labor or Conservative, may not long be able to resist the demand for its redistribution.

63

HOW THE WAR WAS PAID FOR

IN 1914 we went to war. War is frightfully expensive and frightfully destructive: it results in a dead loss as far as money is concerned. And everything has to be paid for on the nail; for you cannot kill Germans with promissory notes or mortgages or national debts: you must have actual stores of food, clothing, weapons, munitions, fighting men, and nursing, car driving, munition making women of military age. When the army has worn out the clothes and eaten up the food, and fired off the munitions, and shed its blood in rivers, there is nothing eatable, drinkable, wearable, or livable-in left to shew for it: nothing visible or tangible but ruin and desolation. For most of these military stores the Government in 1914-18 went heavily into debt. It took the blood and work of the young men as a matter of course, compelling them to serve whether they liked it or not, and breaking up their businesses, when they had any, without compensation of any kind. But being a Capitalist Government it did not take all the needed ready money from the capitalists in the same way. It took some of it by taxation. But in the main, it borrowed it.

Naturally the Labor Party objected very strongly to this exemption of the money of the rich from the conscription that was applied ruthlessly to the lives and livelihoods and limbs of the poor. Its protests were disregarded. The spare subsistence needed to support the soldiers and the workers who were producing food and munitions for them, instead of being all taken without compensation by taxation, was for the most part hired from capitalists, their price being the right to take without working, for every hundred pounds worth of spare subsistence lent, five pounds a year out of the future income of the country for waiting until the hundred pounds they put down was repaid to them in full.

Roughly, and in round figures, what happened was that the National Debt of 660 millions owing in 1914 from former wars was increased by the new war to over 7000 millions. Until we are able to repay this in full we have to pay more than 350 millions a year to the lenders for waiting; and as the current expenses of our civil services (300 millions), with our army, our navy, our air force, and all the other socialized national establishments, come to more than as much again, the Chancellor of the Exchequer has now to budget for more than two millions a day, and get that out of our pockets as best he can. And as it is no use asking the proletarians for it at a time when perhaps a million or so of them are unemployed, and have to be supported out of the taxes instead of paying any, he has to make the property holders contribute, in income tax, supertax, and estate duties, over 380 millions a year: that is, a million and fifty thousand a day, or more than half the total taxation. This is confiscation with a vengeance.

Does it strike you that there is something funny about this business of borrowing most of the 7000 millions from our own capitalists by promising to pay them, say 325 millions a year whilst they are waiting for repayment, and then taxing them to the tune of 382 millions a year to pay not only their own waiting money but that of the foreign lenders as well? They are paying over 50 millions a year more than they are getting, and are therefore, as a class, losing by the transaction. The Government pays them with one hand, and takes the money back again, plus over 17 per cent interest, with the other. Why do they put up with it so tamely?

The explanation is easy. If the Government took back from each holder of War Loan exactly what it had paid him plus three and sixpence in the pound, all the holders would very promptly cry "Thank you for worse than nothing: we will cancel the debt; and much good may it do you". But that is not what happens. The holders of War Loan Stock are only a part of the general body of property owners; but all the property owners have to pay income tax and death duties, and, when their income exceeds £2000, supertax. Those who did not lend money to the Government for the war get nothing from it. Those who did lend get the 325 millions a year all to themselves; but their liability for the taxation out of which it is paid is shared with all the other property owners. Therefore, though the property owners as a whole lose by the transaction, those property owners who hold War Loan Stock gain by it at the expense of those who do not. The Government not only robs capitalist Peter to pay capitalist Paul, but robs both of more than it pays to Paul; yet though Peter and Paul taken together are poorer, Paul taken by himself is richer, and therefore supports the Government in the arrangement, whilst Peter complains that the burden of taxation is intolerable.

To illustrate, my wife and I are capitalists, but I hold some War Loan stock, whilst all her money is in bank, railway, and other stocks. We are both taxed equally to pay me the interest on my War Loan; but as the Government pays me that interest and does not pay her anything, I gain by the transaction at her expense; so that if we were not, as it happens, on the communal footing of man and wife, we should never agree about it. Most capitalists do not understand the deal, and are in effect humbugged by it; but those who do understand it will never be unanimous in resisting it; consequently it is voteproof at the parliamentary elections.

This quaint state of things enables the Labor Party to demonstrate that it would pay the propertied class, as a whole, to cancel the National Debt, and put an end to the absurdity of a nation complaining that it is staggering under an intolerable burden of debt when as a matter of fact it owes most of the money to itself. The cancellation of the debt (except the fraction due to foreigners) would be simply a redistribution of income between its citizens without costing the nation, as a whole, a single farthing.

The plan of raising public money by borrowing money from capitalists instead of confiscating it by direct taxation is called funding; and lending money to the Government used to be called putting it in the Funds. And as the terms of the borrowing are that the lender is to have an income for nothing by waiting until his money is repaid, we get the queer phenomenon of lenders who, instead of being anxious to get their money back, dread nothing more; so that the Government, in order to get the loans, has actually to promise that it will not pay back the loan before a certain date, the further off the better. According to Capitalist morality people who live on their capital instead of on interest (as the payment for waiting is called) are spendthrifts and wasters. The capitalist must never consume his spare subsistence himself even when it is of a kind that will keep until he is hungry again. He must use it to purchase an income; and if the purchaser stops paying the income and repays the sum lent him, the lender must not spend that sum, but must immediately buy another income with it, or, as we say, invest it.

This is not merely a matter of prudence: it is a matter of necessity; for as investing capital means lending it to be consumed before it rots, it can never really be restored to the investor. Investing it means, as we have seen, allowing a body of workmen to eat it up whilst they are engaged in preparing some income producing concern like a railway or factory; and when it is once consumed no mortal power can bring it back into existence. If you do a man or a company or a Government the good turn of letting them use up what you can spare this year, he or she or they may do you the good turn of letting you have an equivalent if they can spare it twenty years hence, and pay you for waiting meanwhile; but they cannot restore what you actually lend them.

The war applied our spare money, not to a producing concern but to a destroying one. In the books of the Bank of England are written the names of a number of persons as the owners of capital to the value of 7000 million pounds. They are said in common speech to be "worth 7000 millions". Now they are in fact "worth" nothing at all. Their 7000 millions have long since been eaten, drunk, worn out, or blown to smithereens, along with much other valuable property and precious lives, on battle-fields all over the world. We are therefore in the ridiculous position of pretending that our country is enriched by property to the value of 7000 millions when as a matter of fact it is impoverished by having to find 350 fresh millions a year for people who are not doing a stroke of work for her in return: that is, who are consuming a huge mass of wealth without producing any. It is as if a bankrupt, asked if he has any assets, should reply proudly, "Oh no: I have made ducks and drakes of all my assets; but then I have a tremendous lot of debts". The 7000 millions of capital standing in the names of the stockholders in the Bank of England is not wealth, it is debt. If we flatly repudiated it, the nation would be richer not only by 350 millions a year, but by the work the stockholders would have to do to support themselves when their incomes were cut off. The objection to repudiating it is not that it would make the nation poorer, but that repudiation would seem a breach of contract after which nobody would ever lend money to the Government again. Besides, the United States, which lent us a thousand millions of it, might distrain on us for that amount by force of arms. Therefore we protest that nothing would induce us to commit such an act of cynical dishonesty. But that does not prevent us, as far as the debt is due to our own capitalists, from paying them honestly with one hand, and forcibly taking back the money plus seventeen per cent interest with the other.

By the way, lest somebody should come along and assure you that these figures are inaccurate, and that I am not to be trusted, I had better warn you that the figures are in round numbers; that they vary from year to year through paying off and fluctuation of values; that the thousand millions borrowed from America were lent by us to allies of whom some cannot afford to pay us at all, and others, who can, are trying how little we can be induced to take; that the rest of the money was raised through the banks in such a way that indignant statisticians have proved that we accepted indebtedness for nearly twice what we actually spent; that the rise in the market price of hiring spare money must have enriched the capitalists more than the war taxation impoverished them: in short, that the simplicity of the case can be addled by a hundred inessential circumstances when the object is to addle and not to elucidate. My object being elucidatory, I have left them all out, as I want to shew you the nest, not the hedge.

The point is that the war has produced an enormous consumption of capital; and instead of this consumption leaving behind it an addition to our industrial plant and means of communication and other contrivances for increasing our output of wealth, it has effected a wholesale destruction of such things, leaving the world with less income to distribute than before. The fact that it has swept away three empires, and substituted republicanism for monarchy as the prevalent form of government in Europe, thus bringing Europe into line with America as a republican continent, may seem to you to be worth the money; or, as this is not in the least what was intended by the British or any other of the belligerent Powers, it may seem to you a scandalous disaster. But that is a matter of sentiment, not of economics. Whether you regard the political result with satisfaction or dismay, the cost of the war remains the same, and so does the effect of our way of paying it on the distribution of our national income. We are all heavily taxed to enable that section of the capitalist class which

formerly imposed to pay the home War Loan interest, and use the dividends of the confiscated shares to pay the interest on our war debt to America, taking off also the taxation that now pays that interest. If it were a Conservative Government it would take it off in the form of a reduction of income tax, supertax, excess profits tax (if any), death duties, and other taxes on property and big business. A Labor Government would leave these taxes untouched, and take taxes off food, or increase its contributions to the unemployed fund, its grants-in-aid to the municipalities for public work, or anything else that would benefit the proletariat and make for equality of income. Thus the levy could be manipulated to make the rich richer as easily as to raise the general level of well-being; and this is why it is just as likely to be done by a Capitalist as by a Labor Government until the domestic war debt is—shall we say liquidated, as repudiated sounds so badly?

The special objection to such practicable levies is that they are raids on private property rather than orderly and gradual conversions of it into public property. The objection to raids is that they destroy the sense of security which induces the possessors of spare money to invest it instead of spreeing it. Insecurity discourages saving among those who can afford to save, and encourages reckless expenditure. If you have a thousand pounds to spare, and have not the slightest doubt that by investing it you can secure a future income of £50 a year, subject only to income tax, you will invest it. If you are led to think it just as likely as not that if you invest it the Government will presently take it or some considerable part of it from you under pretext of a Debt Redemption Levy, you will probably conclude that you may as well spend it while you are sure of it. It would be much better for the country and for yourself if you could feel sure that if the Government took your property it would buy it from you at full market price, or, if that were for any reason impracticable, compensate you fully for it. It is true that, as we found when we went into the question of compensation, this apparently conservative way of doing it is really as expropriative as the direct levy, because the Government raises the purchase money or compensation by taxing property; so that the proprietors buy each other out and are not as a body compensated at all; but the sense of insecurity created by the raiding method is demoralizing, as you will understand if you read the description by Thucydides of the plague at Athens, which applies to all plagues, pathological or financial. Plagues destroy the sense of security of life: people come to feel that they will probably be dead by the end of the week, and throw their characters away for a day's pleasure just as capitalists throw their money away when it is no longer safe. A raid on property, as distinguished from a regular annual income tax, is like a plague in this respect. Also it forms a bad precedent and sets up a raiding habit. Thus domestic debt redemption levies, though physically practicable, are highly injudicious.

65

THE CONSTRUCTIVE PROBLEM SOLVED

YOU may now stop for breath, as you are at last in possession not only of the object of Socialism, which is simply equality of income, but of the methods by which it can be attained. You know why coal mining and banking should be nationalized, and how the expropriation of the coalowners and bankers can be compensated so as to avoid injustice to individuals or any shock to the sense of security which is necessary to prevent the continued investment of spare money as capital. Now when you have the formula for these two nationalizations, one of a material industry involving much heavy manual work, and the other a service conducted by sedentary brain work, you have a formula for all nationalizations. And when you have the formula for the constitutional compensated expropriation of the coalowners and bankers by taxation you have the formula for the expropriation of all proprietors. Knowing how to nationalize industry you know how to place the Government in control of the distribution of the income produced by industry. We have not only found these formulas, but seen them tested in practice in our existing institutions sufficiently to have no more doubt that they would work than we have that next year's budget will work. Therefore we need no longer be worried by demands for what people call a constructive program. There it is for them; and what will surprise them most about it is that it does not contain a single novelty. The difficulties and the novelty are not, as they imagine, in the practical part of the business, which turns out to be quite plain sailing, but in the metaphysical part: that is, in the will to equality. We know how to take the distribution of the national income out of the hands of the private owners of property and place it under the control of the Government. But the Government can distribute it unequally if it decides to do so. Instead of destroying the existing inequality it can intensify it. It can maintain a privileged class of idlers with huge incomes, and give them State security for the continuance of those incomes.

It is this possibility that may enlist and to a certain extent has already enlisted the most determined opponents of Socialism on the side of nationalization, expropriative taxation, and all the constructive political machinery of Socialism, as a means of redistributing income, the catch in it being that the redistribution at which they aim is not an equal distribution, but a State-guaranteed unequal one. John Bunyan, with his queer but deep insight, pointed out long ago that there is a way to hell even from the gates of heaven; that the way to heaven is therefore also the way to hell; and that the name of the gentleman who goes to hell by that road is Ignorance. The way to Socialism, ignorantly pursued, may land us in State Capitalism. Both must travel the same road; and this is what Lenin, less inspired than Bunyan, failed to see when he denounced the Fabian methods as State Capitalism. What is more, State Capitalism, plus Capitalist Dictatorship (Fascism), will compete for approval by cleaning up some of the dirtiest of our present conditions: raising wages; reducing death rates; opening the career to the talents; and ruthlessly cashiering inefficiency, before in the long run succumbing to the bane of inequality, against which no civilization can finally stand out.

This is why, though you are now equipped with a complete answer to those who very properly demand from Socialists constructive plans, practical programs, a constitutional parliamentary routine, and so forth, you are still not within eight score pages of the end of this book. We have still to discuss not only the pseudo-Socialism against which I have just warned you, but other things which I cannot omit without leaving you more or less defenceless against the alarmist who, instead of being sensibly anxious about constructive methods, is quite convinced that the world can be turned upside down in a day by an unwashed Russian in a red tie and an uncombed woman with a can of petrol if only they are wicked enough. These poor scared things will ask you what about revolution? what about marriage? what about children? what about sex? when, as they assume, Socialism will have upset all our institutions and substituted for our present population of sheep a raving pack of mad dogs. No doubt you can tell them to go away, or to talk about such matters as they are capable of understanding; but you will find that they are only the extreme instances of a state of mind that is very common. Not only will plenty of your most sensible friends want to discuss these subjects in connection with Socialism, but you yourself will be as keen about them as they. So now that we know exactly what Socialism aims at and how it can be done, let us leave all that as settled, and equip ourselves for general conversation on or around the subject.

66

SHAM SOCIALISM

THE example of the war shews how easy it is for a government to confiscate the incomes of one set of citizens, and hand them over to another without any intention of equalizing distribution or effecting any nationalization of industries or services. If any class or trade or clique can obtain control of Parliament, it can use its power to plunder any other class or trade or clique, to say nothing of the nation as a whole, for its own benefit. Such operations are of course always disguised as reforms of one kind or another, or as political necessities; but they are really intrigues to use the State for selfish ends. They are not on that account to be opposed as pernicious: rogues with axes to grind must use popular reforms as bait to catch votes for Acts of Parliament in which they have some personal interest. Besides, all reforms are lucrative to somebody. For instance, the landlords of a city may be the warmest supporters of street improvements, and of every public project for making the city more attractive to residents and tourists, because they hope to reap the whole money value of the improvements in raised rents. When a public park is opened, the rents of all the houses looking on that park go up. When some would-be public benefactor endows a great public school for the purpose of making education cheap, he unintentionally makes all the private houses within reach of it dear. In the long run the owners of the land take from us as rent in one form or another everything that we can do without. But the improvements are none the less improvements. Nobody would destroy the famous endowed schools of Bedford because rents are higher there than in towns which possess no such exceptional advantage. When Faust asked Mephistopheles what he was, Mephistopheles answered that he was part of a power that was always willing evil and always doing good; and though our landlords and capitalists are certainly not always either willing evil or doing good, yet Capitalism justifies itself and was adopted as an economic principle on the express ground that it provides selfish motives for doing good, and that human beings will do nothing except for selfish motives. Now though the best things have to be done for the greater glory of God, as some of us say, or for the enlargement of life and the bettering of humanity, as others put it, yet it is very true that if you want to get a philanthropic measure enacted by a public body, parliamentary or municipal, you may find it shorter to give the rogues an axe to grind than to stir up the philanthropists to do anything except preach at the rogues. Rogues, by which perhaps rather invidious name I designate persons who will do nothing unless they get something out of it for themselves, are often highly effective persons of action, whilst idealist talkers only sow the wind, leaving the next generation of men of action to reap the whirlwind.

It is already a well-established method of Capitalism to ask the Government to provide for some private enterprise on the ground of its public utility. Some good has been done in this way: for instance, some of our modern garden cities and suburbs could not have been built if the companies that built them had not been enabled, under the Industrial and Provident Societies Act, to borrow a large share of their capital from the Government on the understanding that the shareholders were poor people holding no more than £200 capital apiece. But this limitation is quite illusory, because, though the companies may not issue more than

£200 in shares to any individual, they may and do borrow unlimited sums by creating what is called Loan Stock; and the very same person who is not allowed to have more than £200 in shares may have two hundred millions in Loan Stock if the company can use them. Consequently these garden cities, which are most commendable enterprises in their way, are nevertheless the property of rich capitalists. As I hold a good deal of stock in them myself I am tempted to claim that their owners are specially philanthropic and public-spirited men, who have voluntarily invested their capital where it will do the most good and not where it will make the most profit for them; but they are not immortal; and we have no guarantee that their heirs will inherit their disinterestedness. Meanwhile the fact remains that they have built up their property largely with public money: that is, by money raised by taxing the rest of the community, and that this does not make the nation the owner of the garden city, nor even a shareholder in it. The Government is simply a creditor who will finally be paid off, leaving the cities in the hands of their capitalist proprietors. The tenants, though led to expect a share in the surplus profits of the city, find such profits practically always applied to extending the enterprise for the benefit of fresh investors. The garden cities and suburbs are an enormous improvement on the manufacturing towns produced by unaided private enterprise; but as they do not pay their proprietors any better than slum property, nor indeed as well, it is quite possible that this consideration may induce the future owners to abolish their open spaces and overcrowd them with houses until they are slums. To guarantee the permanence of the improvement it would be safer for the Government to buy out the shareholders than for the shareholders to pay off the Government, though even that would fail if the Government acted on Capitalist principles by selling the cities to the highest bidders.

A more questionable development of this exploitation of the State by Capitalism and Trade Unionism is the subsidy of £10,000,000 paid by the Government to the coalowners in 1925 to avoid a strike. The coal miners said they would not work unless they got such and such wages. The employers vowed they could not afford to keep their mines open unless the men would accept less; and a great press campaign was set up to persuade us that the country was on the verge of ruin through excessive wages when as a matter of fact the country was in a condition that at many earlier periods would have been described as cheerfully prosperous. Finally the Government, to avert a strike which would have paralyzed the main industries of the country, had either to make up out of the taxes the wages offered by the employers to the wages demanded by the men, or else nationalize the mines. Being a Capitalist Government, pledged not to nationalize anything, it chose to make up the wages out of the taxes. When the £10,000,000 was exhausted, the trouble began again. The Government refused to renew the subsidy; the employers refused to go on without it unless the miners worked eight hours a day instead of seven; the miners refused to work more or take less; there was a big strike, in which the workers in several other industries at first took part "sympathetically" until they realized that by using up the funds of the Trade Unions on strike pay they were hindering the miners instead of helping them; and many respectable people were, as usual on such occasions, frightened out of their wits and into the belief that the country was on the verge of revolution. And there was this excuse for them: that under fully-developed Capitalism civilization is always on the verge of revolution. We live as in a villa on Vesuvius.

During the strike the taxpayer was no longer exploited by the owners; but the ratepayer was exploited by the workers. A man on strike has no right to outdoor relief; but his wife and children have. Consequently a married miner with two children could depend on receiving a pound a week at the expense of the ratepayers whilst he was refusing to work. This development of parochial Communism really knocks the bottom out of the Capitalist system, which depends on the ruthless compulsion of the proletariat to work on pain of starvation or imprisonment under detestable conditions in the workhouse. Thus you have had the Government first giving outdoor relief (the ten million subsidy) to the owners at the expense of the taxpayers, and then the local authorities giving outdoor relief to the proletariat at the expense of the ratepayers, the Government being manned mostly by capitalists and the local authorities by proletarians.

It was in the proletarian quarters of London, notably in Poplar, that the Poor Law Guardians first claimed the right to give outdoor relief at full subsistence rates to all unemployed persons, thereby freeing their proletarian constituents from "the lash of starvation", and enabling them to hold out for the highest wages their trades could afford. The mining districts followed suit during the coal strike of 1926. This right was contested by the Government, which tried to supplant the parochial authorities by the central Ministry of Health. The Ministry, through the auditors of public accounts, surcharged the Guardians with the part of the outdoor relief which they considered excessive; but as the Guardians could not have paid the surcharge even if the proceedings taken against them had not failed, the Government took the administration of the Poor Law into its own hands, and passed Acts to confirm its powers to do so. This was essentially an attempt by the Capitalist central Government to recover the weapon of starvation which the proletarian local authorities had taken out of the owners' hands. But the day had gone by for the ultra-capitalist relief rules of the nineteenth century, when, as I well recollect, the Registrar-General's returns of the causes of the deaths during the year always included starvation as a matter of course. The lowest scale of relief which the Government ventured to propose would have seemed ruinously extravagant and demoralizing to the Gradgrinds and Bounderbys denounced by Dickens in 1854.

As to the demoralization, they would not have been very far wrong. If mine-owners, or any other sort of owners, find that when they get into difficulties through being lazy, or ignorant, or too grasping, or behind the times, or all four, they can induce the Government to confiscate the taxpayers' incomes for subsidies to get them out of their difficulties, they will go from bad to worse. If miners, or any other sort of workers, find that the local authorities will confiscate the incomes of the ratepayers to feed them when they are idle, their incentive to pay their way by their labor will be, to say the least, perceptibly slackened. Yet it is no use simply refusing to make these confiscations. If the nation will not take its industries out of the hands of private owners it must enable them to carry them on, whether they can make them pay or not. If the owners will not pay subsistence wages the nation must; for it cannot afford to have its children undernourished and its civil and military strength weakened, though it was fool enough to think it could in Queen Victoria's time. Subsidies and doles are demoralizing, both for employers and proletarians; but they stave off Socialism, which people seem to consider worse than pauperized insolvency, Heaven knows why!

Still, governments need not be so shamelessly unbusinesslike as they are when subsidies are in question. The subsidizing habit was acquired by the British Government during the war, when certain firms had to be kept going at all costs, profit or no profit, because their activities were indispensable. It was against all Capitalist principles; but in war economic principles are thrown to the wind like Christian principles; and the habits of war are not cured instantly by armistices. In 1925, when the Government was easily blackmailed into paying the mine-owners ten millions of the money of the general taxpayer (your money and mine), it might at least have secured for us an equivalent interest in the mines. It might have obliged the owners to mortgage their property to the nation for the means to carry on, as they would have had to do if they had raised the money in the ordinary commercial way. As to the miners, they felt no responsibility, because, as the owners bought labor in the market exactly as they bought pit props, there was no more excuse for asking the miners to admit indebtedness for the subsidy than the dealers in pit props. On every principle of Capitalism the Government should either have refused to interfere, and have let the comparatively barren mines which could not afford to pay the standard wage for the standard working day go smash, or else it should have advanced the millions by way of mortgage, not on the worthless security of the defaulting mines, but on that of all the coal mines, good and bad. The interest on the mortgage would in that case have been paid to the nation by the good mines, which would thus have been compelled to make up the deficits of the bad ones; and if the interest had not been paid, the Government could finally have nationalized the mines by simple foreclosure instead of by purchase.

But capitalists are by no means in favor of having Capitalist principles applied to themselves in their dealings with the State. Besides, why should the fortunate owners of solvent mines subsidize the owners of insolvent ones? If the Government chooses to subsidize bad mines, let it be content with the security of the bad mines. It ended in the Government making the owners a present of the ten millions. The owners had to pass it on to the miners as wages: at least that was the idea; and it was more or less the fact also. But whether we regard it as a subsidy to the miners or to the owners or to both, it was none the less confiscated from the general taxpayer and handed as alms to favored persons.

The people who say that such subsidies are Socialistic, whether with the object of discrediting them or recommending them, are talking nonsense: they might as well say that the perpetual pensions conferred by Charles II on his illegitimate children were Socialistic. They are frank exploitations of the taxpayer by bankrupt Capitalism and its proletarian dependents. Socialist agitators, far from supporting such subsidies, will shout at you that you are paying part of the men's wages whilst the mine-owners take all the profits; that if you will stand that, you will stand anything; that you are paying for nationalization and not getting it; that you are being saddled with a gigantic system of outdoor relief for the rich in addition to their rents, their dividends, and the doles they have left you to pay to their discarded employees; that the capitalists, having plundered everything else, land, capital, and labor, are now plundering the Treasury; that, not content with overcharging you for every article you buy, they are now taxing you through the Government collector; and that as they will have to hand over a share of what they take from you in this way as wages, the Trade Unions are taking good care to make the Labor Party support the subsidies in Parliament.

Meanwhile you hear from all quarters angry denunciations of Poplarism as a means by which the rate collector robs you of your possibly hardearned money, often to the tune of twentyfour shillings for every pound of the value of your house, to keep idle ablebodied laborers eating their heads off at a higher rate of expenditure than you, perhaps, can afford in your own house.

All this, with due allowance for platform rhetoric, is true. The attempt to maintain a failing system by subsidies plus Poplarism burns the candle at both ends, and makes straight for industrial bankruptcy. But you will not, if you are wise, waste your forces in resentful indignation. The capitalists are not making a conscious attempt to rob you. They are the flies on the wheel of their own system, which they understand as little as you did before we sat down to study it. All they know is that Trade Unionism is playing their own game against them with such success that more and more of the overcharges (to you) that formerly went to profit are now going to wages. They cry to the Government to save them, and it saves them (at your expense) partly because it is afraid of a big strike; partly because it wants to put off the alternative of nationalization as long as possible; partly because it has to consider the proletarian vote at the next general election; and mostly because it can think of nothing better to do in the rare moments when it has time to think at all. The British employers, the British Trade Unionists, and the British Government have no deep designs: so far it is just hand to mouth with them; and you need not waste any moral indignation on them. But please note the word British, thrice repeated in the last sentence, and also the words "so far". The American employers and financiers are far more self-conscious than our business men and working men are; and the Americans are teaching our people their methods. Modern scientific discoveries have set them dreaming of enormously increased production; and they have found out that as the world depends on the people who work, whether with head or hand, they can by combining prevent idle and incapable owners of land and capital from getting too much of the increase. They know that they can neither realize their dream nor combine properly by using their own brains; and they are now paying large salaries to clever persons whose sole business is to think for them. Suppose you were the managing head of a big business, and that you were determined not to tolerate Trade Unionism among your workpeople, and therefore had to treat them well enough to prevent them feeling the want of a union. In England your firm would be called "a rat house", in America simply a non-union house. Imagine yourself visited by a well-dressed lady or gentleman with the pleasant nonchalance of a person of proved and conscious ability and distinction. She (we will assume that she is a lady) has called to suggest that you should order all your workpeople to join the union of their trade, of which she is the pampered representative. You gasp, and would order her out if you dared; but how can one shew the door to a superior and perfectly self-confident person. She proceeds to explain whilst you are staring at her. She says it will be worth your while: that her union is prepared to put some new capital into your business, and that it will come to a friendly arrangement with you as to the various trade restrictions to which you so much object. She points out that if instead of working to increase the dividends of your idle shareholders you were just to give them what they are accustomed to expect, and use the rest of the profit for bettering the condition of the people who are doing the work (including yourself), the business would receive a fresh impulse, and you and all the really effective people in it make much more money. She suggests ways of doing it that you have never dreamt of. Can you see any reason except stupid conservatism for refusing such a proposal?

This is not a fancy picture. It has actually occurred in America as the result of the Trade Unions employing first-rate business brains to think for them, and not grudging them salaries equal to the wages of a dozen workmen. When English Trade Unions become Americanized as English big business is becoming Americanized they will do the same. Our big businesses are already picking out brainy champions from the universities and the public services to do just such jobs for them. Both big business and skilled labor will presently be managing their affairs scientifically, instead of dragging heavily and unimaginatively through the old ruts. And when this is accomplished they will enslave the unskilled, unorganized proletariat, including, as we have seen, the middle-class folk who have no aptitude for money making. They will enslave the Government. And they will do it mostly by the methods of Socialism, effecting such manifest improvements in the condition of the masses that it will be inhuman to stop them. The organized workers will live, not in slums, but in places like Port Sunlight, Bournville, and the Garden Cities. Employers like Mr Ford, Lord Leverhulme and Mr Cadbury will be the rule and not the exception; and the sense of helpless dependence on them will grow at the expense of individual adventurousness. The old communal cry of high rates and a healthy city will be replaced by Mr Ford's cry of high wages and colossal profits.

Those profits are the snag in the stream of prosperity. If they are unequally distributed they will wreck the system that has produced them, and involve the nation in the catastrophe. In spite of all the apparent triumphs of increased business efficiency the Socialists will still have to insist on public control of distribution and equalization of income. Without that, capitalist big business, in league with the aristocracy of Trade Unionism, will control the Government for its private ends; and you may find it very difficult, as a voter, to distinguish between the genuine Socialism that changes private into public ownership of our industries, and the sham Socialism that confiscates the money of one set of citizens without compensation only to hand it over to another set, not to make our incomes more equal, but to give more to those who have already too much.

67

CAPITALISM IN PERPETUAL MOTION

AND now, learned lady reader (for by this time you know much more about the vital history and present social problems of your country and of the world than an average Capitalist Prime Minister), do you notice that in these ceaseless activities which keep all of us fed and clothed and lodged, and some of us even pampered, NOTHING STAYS PUT? Human society is like a glacier: it looks like an immovable and eternal field of ice; but it is really flowing like a river; and the only effect of its glassy rigidity is that its own unceasing movement splits it up into crevasses that make it frightfully dangerous to walk on, all the more as they are beautifully concealed by natural whitewash in the shape of snow. Your father's bankruptcy, your husband's, or your own may precipitate you at any moment into a little crevasse. A big one may suddenly swallow a whole empire, as three of them were swallowed in 1918. If, as is most likely, you have been brought up to believe that the world is a place of permanent governments, settled institutions, and unchangeable creeds in which all respectable people believe, to which they all conform, and which are unalterable because they are founded for all eternity on Magna Carta, the Habeas Corpus Act, the Apostles' Creed, and the Ten Commandments, what you have gathered here of the continual and unexpected changes and topsy-turvy developments of our social order, the passing of power from one class to another, the changes of opinion by which what was applauded as prosperity and honor and piety at the beginning of the nineteenth century came to be execrated as greedy villainy at the end of it, and what were prosecuted as criminal conspiracies under George IV are legalized and privileged combinations, powerful in Parliament, under George V, may have driven you to ask, what is the use of your drudging through all these descriptions and explanations if by the time you have reached the end of the book everything will have changed? I can only assure you that the way to understand the changes that are going on is to understand the changes that have gone before, and warn you that many women have spoilt their whole lives and misled their children disastrously by not understanding them.

Besides, the things I have been describing have not passed wholly away. There are still old-fashioned noblemen who lord it over the countryside as their ancestors have done for hundreds of years, sometimes benevolently, sometimes driving the inhabitants out to make room for sheep or deer at their pleasure. There are still farmers, large and small. There are still many petty employers carrying on small businesses singly or in firms of two or three partners. There are still joint stock companies that have not been merged in Trusts. There are still multitudes of employees who belong to no Trade Union, and are as badly sweated as the woman who sat in unwomanly rags and sang the Song of the Shirt. There are still children and young persons who are cruelly over-worked in spite of the Acts of Parliament that reach only the factories and workshops. The world at large, though it contains London and Paris and New York, also contains primitive villages where gas, electric light, tap water and main drainage are as unknown as they were to King Alfred. Our famous universities and libraries and picture galleries are within travelling distance of tribes of savages and cannibals, and of barbarian empires. Thus you can see around you living examples of all the stages of the Capitalist System I have described. Indeed, if you come, or your parents came (like mine) from one of those families of more than a dozen children in the genteel younger-son class which were to come from. I repeat, capitalists as such need no special ability, and lose nothing by the lack of it. If they seem able to feed Peter the Laborer it is only because they have taken the food from Paul the Farmer; and even this they have not done with their own hands: they have paid Matthew the Agent to do it, and had his salary from Mark the Shopkeeper. And when Peter is a navvy, Paul an engineer, Matthew the manager of a Trust, and Mark a banker, the situation remains essentially unchanged. Peter and Paul, Matthew and Mark, do all the work: the capitalist does nothing but take as much of what they make as she can without starving them (killing the goose that lays the golden eggs).

Therefore you may disregard both the Capitalist papers which claim all the glories of our history as the fruit of Capitalist virtue and talent, and the anti-Capitalist papers which ascribe all our history's shames and disgraces to the greed of the capitalists. Waste neither your admiration nor your indignation. The more you understand the system, the better you will see that the most devout personal righteousness cannot evade it except by political changes which will rescue the whole nation from it.

But though the capitalist as such does nothing but invest her money, Capitalism does a great deal. When it has filled the home markets with all the common goods the people can afford to pay for out of their wages, and all the established fashionable luxuries the rich will buy, it must apply its fresh accumulations of spare money to more out-of-the-way and hazardous enterprises. It is then that Capitalism becomes adventurous and experimental; listens to the schemes of hungry men who are great inventors or chemists or engineers; and establishes new industries and services like telephones, motor charabancs, air services, wireless concerts, and so forth. It is then that it begins to consider the question of harbors, which, as we saw, it would not look at whilst there was still room for new distilleries. At the present moment an English company has undertaken to build a harbor at a cost of a million pounds for a Portuguese island in the Atlantic, and even to make it a free port (that is, charge no harbor dues) if the Government of the island lets it collect and keep the customs duties.

The capitalists, though they are very angry when the hungry ask for Government help of any kind, have no scruples about asking it for themselves. The railways ask the Government to guarantee their dividends; the air services ask for large sums from the Government to help them to maintain their aeroplanes and make money out of them; the coalowners and the miners between them extort subsidies from the Government by threatening a strike if they do not get it; and the Government, under the Trades Facilities Acts, guarantees loans to private capitalists without securing any share in their enterprises for the nation, which provides them with capital cheaply, but has to pay profiteering prices for their goods and services all the same. In the end there is hardly any conceivable enterprise that can be made to pay dividends that Capitalism will not undertake as long as it can find spare money; and when it cannot it is quite ready to extract money from the Government—that is, to take it forcibly from the people by taxes—by assuring everyone that the Government can do nothing itself for the people, who must always come to the capitalists to get it done for them in return for substantial profits, dividends, and rents. Its operations are so enormous that it alters the size and meaning of what we call our country. Trading companies of capitalists have induced the Government to give them charters under which they have seized large and populous islands like Borneo, whole empires like India, and great tracts of country like Rhodesia, governing them and maintaining armies in them for the purpose of making as much money out of them as possible. But they have taken care to hoist the British flag, and make use directly or indirectly, of the British army and navy at the cost of the British taxpayers to defend these conquests of theirs; and in the end the British Commonwealth has had to take over their responsibilities and add the islands and countries they have seized to what is called the British Empire, with the curious result, quite unintended by the British people, that the centre of the British Empire is now in the East instead of in Great Britain, and out of every hundred of our fellow subjects only eleven are whites, or even Christians. Thus Capitalism leads us into enterprises of all sorts, at home and abroad, over which we have no control, and for which we have no desire. The enterprises are not necessarily bad: some of them have turned out well; but the point is that Capitalism does not care whether they turn out well does not feel his responsibility enough to be frightened out of his wits by it. But in the long run civilization depends on our governments gaining an intelligent control of the forces that are running away with Capitalism; and for that an understanding of them is necessary. Mere character and energy, much as we admire them, are positively mischievous without intellect and knowledge.

Our present difficulty is that nobody understands except a few students whose books nobody else reads, or here and there a prophet crying in the wilderness and being either ignored by the press or belittled as a crank. Our rulers are full of the illusions of the money market, counting £5 a year as £100. Our voters have not got even so far as this, because nine out of ten of them, women or men, have no more experience of capital than a sheep has of a woollen mill, though the wool comes off its own back.

But between the government and the governed there is a very important difference. The governments do not know how to govern; but they know that government is necessary, and that it must be paid for. The voters regard government as a tyrannical interference with their personal liberty, and taxation as the plunder of the private citizen by the officials of a tyrannous state. Formerly this did not matter much, because the people had no votes. Queen Elizabeth, for instance, told the common people, and even the jurymen and the Knights of the Shires who formed the Parliament in her time, that affairs of State were not their business, and that it was the grossest presumption on their part to have any opinion of their own on such matters. If they attempted to argue with her she threw them into prison without the smallest hesitation. Yet even she could not extract money enough from them in taxes to follow up her political successes. She could barely hold her own by being quite right about the incompetence of the commoners and knights, and being herself the most competent person of her time. These two advantages made her independent of the standing armies by which other despots maintained themselves. She could depend on the loyalty of her people because she was able, as we say, to deliver the goods. When her successors attempted to be equally despotic without being able to deliver the goods, one of them was beheaded, and the other driven out of the country. Cromwell rivalled her in ability; but though he was a parliament man, he was finally driven to lay violent hands on Parliament, and rule by armed force.

As to the common people, the view that their poverty and political ignorance disqualified them for any share in the government of the country was accepted until within my own lifetime. Within my father's lifetime the view that to give every man a vote (to say nothing of every woman) was ridiculous and, if acted on, dangerous, seemed a matter of course not only to Tories like the old Duke of Wellington, but to extreme revolutionaries like the young poet Shelley. It seems only the other day that Mr Winston Churchill declared that Labor is not fit to govern.

Now you probably agree with Queen Elizabeth, Cromwell, Wellington, Shelley, and Mr Winston Churchill. At all events if you do you are quite right. For although Mr Ramsay MacDonald easily convinced the country that a Labor Government can govern at least as well as either the Liberal or Conservative Governments who have had the support of Mr Churchill, the truth is that none of them can govern: Capitalism runs away with them all. The hopes that we founded on the extension of the franchise, first to working men and finally to women, which means in effect to all adults, have been disappointed as far as controlling Capitalism is concerned, and indeed in most other respects too. The first use the women made of their votes was to hurl Mr MacDonald out of Parliament and vote for hanging the Kaiser and making Germany pay for the war, both of them impossibilities which should not have imposed on even a male voter. They got the vote mainly by the argument that they were as competent politically as the men; and when they got it they at once used it to prove that they were just as incompetent. The only point they scored at the election was that the defeat of Mr MacDonald by their vote in Leicester shewed that they were not, as the silliest of their opponents had alleged, sure to vote for the best-looking man.

What the extension of political power to the whole community (Democracy, as they call it) has produced is a reinforcement of the popular resistance to government and taxation at a moment when nothing but a great extension of government and taxation can hope to control the Gadarene rush of Capitalism towards the abyss. And this has produced a tendency which is the very last that the old Suffragists and Suffragettes dreamt of, or would have advocated if they had dreamt of it: namely, a demand for the abandonment of parliamentary government and the substitution of a dictatorship. In desperation at the failure of Parliament to rescue industry from the profiteers, and currency from the financiers (which means rescuing the livelihood of the people from the purely predatory side of Capitalism), Europe has begun to clamor for political disciplinarians to save her. Victorious France, with her currency in the gutter, may be said to be advertising for a Napoleon or a political Messiah. Italy has knocked its parliament down and handed the whip to Signor Mussolini to thrash Italian democracy and bureaucracy into some sort of order and efficiency. In Spain the king and the military commander-in-chief have refused to stand any more democratic nonsense, and taken the law into their own hands. In Russia a minority of devoted Marxists maintain by sheer force such government as is possible in the teeth of an intensely recalcitrant peasantry. In England we should welcome another Cromwell but for two considerations. First, there is no Cromwell. Second, history teaches us that if there were one, and he again ruled us by military force after trying every sort of parliament and finding each worse than the other, he would be worn out or dead after a few years; and then we should return like the sow to her wallowing in the mire and leave the restored profiteers to wreak on the corpse of the worn-out ruler the spite they dared not express whilst he was alive. Thus our inability to govern ourselves lands us in such a mess that we hand the job over to any person strong enough to undertake it; and then our unwillingness to be governed at all makes us turn against the strong person, the Cromwell or Mussolini, as an intolerable tyrant, and relapse into the condition of Bunyan's Simple, Sloth, and Presumption the moment his back is turned or his body buried. We clamor for a despotic discipline out of the miseries of our anarchy, and, when we get it, clamor out of the severe regulation of our law and order for what we call liberty. At each blind rush from one extreme to the other we empty the baby out with the bath, learning nothing from our experience, and furnishing examples of the abuses of power and the horrors of liberty without ascertaining the limits of either.

Let us see whether we cannot clear up this matter of government versus liberty a little before we give up the human race as politically hopeless.

69

THE NATURAL LIMIT TO LIBERTY

ONCE for all, we are not born free; and we never can be free. When all the human tyrants are slain or deposed there will still be the supreme tyrant that can never be slain or deposed, and that tyrant is Nature. However easygoing Nature may be in the South Sea Islands, where you can bask in the sun and have food for the trouble of picking it up, even there you have to build yourself a hut, and, being a woman, to bear and rear children with travail and trouble. And, as the men are handsome and quarrelsome and jealous, and, having little else to do except make love, combine exercise with sport by killing one-another, you have to defend yourself with your own hands.

But in our latitudes Nature is a hard taskmaster. In primitive conditions it was only by working strenuously early and late that we could feed and clothe and shelter ourselves sufficiently to be able to survive the rigors of our climate. We were often beaten by famine and flood, wolves and untimely rain and storms; and at best the women had to bear large families to make up for the deaths of children. They had to make the clothes of the family and bake its bread as well as cook its meals. Such leisure as a modern woman enjoys was not merely reprehensible: it was impossible. A chief had to work hard for his power and privileges as lawgiver, administrator, and chief of police; and had even his most pampered wife attempted to live as idly and wastefully as thousands of ordinary ladies now do with impunity, he would certainly have corrected her with a stick as thick as his thumb, and been held not only guiltless, but commendably active in the discharge of his obvious social duty. And the women were expected to do the like by their daughters instead of teaching them, as Victorian ladies did, that to do anything useful is disgraceful, and that if, as inevitably happens, something useful has to be done, you must ring for a servant and by no means do it yourself.

Now commercial civilization has been at root nothing more

than the invention of ways of doing Nature's tasks with less labor. Men of science invent because they want to discover Nature's secrets; but such popular inventions as the bow and spear, the spade and plough, the wheel and arch, come from the desire to make work easier out of doors. Indoors the spinning wheel and loom, the frying-pan and poker, the scrubbing brush and soap, the needle and safety pin, make domestic work easier. Some inventions make the work harder, but also much shorter and more intelligent, or else they make operations possible that were impossible before: for instance, the alphabet, Arabic numerals, ready reckoners, logarithms, and algebra. When instead of putting your back into your work you put the horse's or ox's back into it, and later on set steam and explosive spirits and electricity to do the work of the strained backs, a state of things is reached in which it becomes possible for people to have less work than is good for them instead of more. The needle becomes a sewing machine, the sweeping brush becomes a vacuum cleaner, and both are driven from a switch in the wall by an engine miles away instead of being treadled and wielded by foot and hand. In Chapter 42 we had a glance at the way in which we lost the old manual skill and knowledge of materials and of buying and selling, first through division of labor (a very important invention), and then through machinery. If you engage a servant today who has been trained at a first-rate institution in the use of all the most modern domestic machinery, and take her down to a country house, I will not go quite so far yet as to warn you that though she knows how to work the buttons on an automatic electric lift or step on and off an escalator without falling on her nose, she cannot walk up or downstairs; but it may come to that before long. Meanwhile you will have on your hands a supercivilized woman whom you will be glad to replace by a girl from the nearest primitive village, if any primitive villages are left in your neighborhood.

Let us, however, confine ourselves to the bearing of all this on that pet topic of the leisured class, our personal liberty.

What is liberty? Leisure. What is leisure? Liberty. If you can at any moment in the day say "I can do as I please for the next hour" then for that hour you are at liberty. If you say "I must now do such and such things during the next hour whether I like it or not" then you are not at liberty for that hour in spite of Magna Carta, the Declaration of Rights (or of Independence), and all the other political title-deeds of your so-called freedom.

May I, without being too intrusive, follow you throughout your daily routine? You are wakened in the morning, whether you like it or not, either by a servant or by that nerve-shattering abomination an alarum clock. You must get up and light the fire and wash and dress and prepare and eat your breakfast. So far, no liberty. You simply must. Then you have to make your bed, wash up the breakfast things, sweep and tidy-up the place, and tidy yourself up, which means that you must more or less wash and re-dress your person until you are presentable enough to go out and buy fresh supplies of food and do other necessary shopping. Every meal you take involves preparation, including cooking, and washing up afterwards. In the course of these activities you will have to travel from place to place, which even in the house often means treadmill work on the stairs. You must rest a little occasionally. And finally you must go to sleep for eight hours.

In addition to all this you must earn the money to do your shopping and pay your rent and rates. This you can do in two main ways. You can work in some business for at least eight hours a day, plus the journeys to and from the place where you work. Or you can marry, in which case you will have to do for your husband and children all the preparation of meals and marketing that you had to do for yourself, to wash and dress the children until they are able to wash and dress themselves, and to do all the other things that belong to the occupation of wife and mother, including the administration of most of the family income. If you add up all the hours you are forced to spend in these ways, and subtract them from the twenty-four hours allowed you by Nature to get through them in, the remainder will be your daily leisure: that is, your liberty. Historians and journalists and political orators may assure you that the defeat of the Armada, the cutting off of King Charles's head, the substitution of Dutch William for Scottish James on the throne, the passing of the Married Women's Property Acts, and the conquest by the Suffragettes of Votes for Women, have set you free; and in moments of enthusiasm roused by these assurances you may sing fervently that Britons never never will be slaves. But though all these events may have done away with certain grievances from which you might be suffering if they had not occurred, they have added nothing to your leisure and therefore nothing to your liberty. The only Acts of Parliament that have really increased liberty: that is, added to the number of minutes in which a woman's time is her own, are the Factory Acts which reduced her hours of industrial labor, the Sunday Observance Acts which forbid commercial work on every seventh day, and the Bank Holiday Acts.

You see, then, that the common trick of speaking of liberty as if we were all either free or slaves, is a foolish one. Nature does not allow any of us to be wholly free. In respect of eating and drinking and washing and dressing and sleeping and the other necessary occasions of physical life, the most incorrigible tramp, sacrificing every decency and honesty to freedom, is as much a slave for at least ten or eleven hours a day as a constitutional king, who has to live an almost entirely dictated life. An enslaved negress who has six hours a day to herself has more liberty than a "free" white woman who has only three. The white woman is free to go on strike, and the negress is not; but the negress can console herself by her freedom to commit suicide (fundamentally much the same thing), and by pitying the Englishwoman because, having so much less liberty, she is only poor white trash.

Now in our desire for liberty we all sympathize with the tramp. Our difference from him, when we do differ, is that some of us want leisure so that we may be able to work harder at the things we like than slaves, except under the most brutal compulsion, work at the things they must do. The tramp wastes his leisure and is miserable: we want to employ our leisure and be happy. For leisure, remember, is not rest. Rest, like sleep, is compulsory. Genuine leisure is freedom to do as we please, not to do nothing.

As I write, a fierce fight between the miners and the mineowners has culminated in the increase of the miners' daily working hours from seven to eight. It is said that the miners want a seven hours working day. This is the wrong way to put it. What the miners want is not seven hours mining but seventeen hours off, out of which Nature will take at least ten for her occasions, and locomotion another. Thus the miner, by rigidly economizing his time, cutting out all loafing, and being fortunate in the weather and season, might conceivably manage to have six hours of effective leisure out of the twenty-four on the basis of seven hours earning and eleven hours for sleep, recreation, loafing and locomotion. And it is this six hours of liberty that he wants to increase. Even when the immediate object of his clamor for shorter hours of work is only a mask for his real intention of working as long as before but receiving overtime pay (half as much again) for the last hour, his final object is to obtain more money to spend on his leisure. The pieceworker, the moment the piecework rate enables him to earn as much in three or four days as he has been accustomed to earn in a week, is as likely as not to take two or three days off instead of working as long as before for twice as much money. He wants leisure more than money.

But the conclusive instance is that of property. Women desire to be women of property because property secures to them the maximum of leisure. The woman of property need not get up at six in the morning to light the fire. She need not prepare her husband's breakfast nor her own. She need not wash-up nor empty the slops nor make the beds. She need not do the marketing, nor any shopping except the sort she enjoys. She need not bother more about her children than she cares to. She need not even brush her own hair; and if she must still eat and sleep and wash and move from place to place, these operations are made as luxurious as possible. She can count on at least twelve hours leisure every day. She may work harder at trying on new dresses, hunting, dancing, visiting, receiving, bridge, tennis, mountain climbing, or any other hobby she may have, than a laborer's wife works at her compulsory housekeeping; but she is doing what she likes all the time, and not what she must. And so, having her fill of liberty, she is usually an ardent supporter of every political movement that protects her privilege, and a strenuous and sometimes violently abusive opponent of every political movement that threatens to curtail her leisure or reduce the quantity of money at her disposal for its enjoyment. She clings to her position because it gives her the utmost possible liberty; and her grievance is that she finds it difficult to obtain and retain domestic servants because, though she offers them higher wages and better food and lodging and surroundings than they can secure for themselves as industrial employees, she also offers them less freedom. Their time, as they say, is never their own except for occasional evenings out. Formerly women of all classes, from governesses to scullery maids, went into domestic service because the only alternative was rough work in unbearably coarse company, and because, with comparatively gentle dispositions, they were for the most part illiterate and ignorant. Nowadays, being imprisoned in schools daily for at least nine years, they are no longer illiterate; and there are many occupations open to them (for instance, in city offices) that were formerly reserved for men. Even in rough employment the company is not so rough as it used to be; besides, women of gentle nurture are no longer physically disabled for them by the dress and habits that made the Victorian woman half an invalid. A hundred years ago a housemaid was so different from a herring-gutter or a ragpicker that she was for all business purposes an animal of another species. Today they are all "young ladies" in their leisure hours; and the single fact that a housemaid has less leisure than an industrial employee makes it impossible to obtain a housemaid who is not half imbecile in a factory town, and not easy to get one in a fishing port.

It is the same with men. But do not conclude that every woman and every man desires freedom above all things. Some people are very much afraid of it. They are so conscious that they cannot fend for themselves either industrially or morally that they feel that the only safe condition for them is one of tutelage, in which they will always have someone to tell them not only what to do but how to behave. Women of this kind seek domestic service, and men military service, not in spite of the forfeiture of their freedom but because of it. Were it not for this factor in the problem it would be harder to get domestic servants and soldiers than it is. Yet the ideal of the servant and soldier is not continual tutelage and service: it is tutelage relieved by an occasional spree. They both want to be as free as they dare. Again, the very last thing the ordinary industrial male worker wants is to have to think about his work. That is the manager's job. What he wants to think about is his play. For its sake he wants his worktime to be as short, and his playtime as long, as he can afford. Women, from domestic necessity and habit, are more accustomed to think about their work than men; for a housewife must both work and manage; but she also is glad when her work is over.

The great problem of the distribution of the national income thus becomes also a problem of the distribution of necessary work and the distribution of leisure or liberty. And this leisure or liberty is what we all desire: it is the sphere of romance and infinite possibilities, whilst worktime is the sphere of cut and dried compulsory reality. All the inventions and expedients by which labor is made more productive are hailed with enthusiasm, and called progress, because they make more liberty possible for us. Unfortunately, we distribute the leisure gained by the invention of the machines in the most absurd way that can be conceived. Take your woman of property whom we have just discussed, with her fifteen hours leisure out of the twenty-four. How does she obtain that leisure? Not by inventing anything, but by owning machines invented by somebody else and keeping the leisure they produce all to herself, leaving those who actually work the machines with no more leisure than they had before. Do not blame her: she cannot help herself, poor lady! that is Capitalist law.

Look at it in the broader case of the whole nation. Modern methods of production enable each person in the nation to produce much more than they need consume to keep themselves alive and reproduce themselves. That means that modern methods produce not only a national fund of wealth but a national fund of leisure or liberty. Now just as you can distribute the wealth so as to make a few people monstrously rich whilst leaving all the rest as poor as before, you can distribute the leisure in such a way as to make a few people free for fifteen hours a day whilst the rest remain as they were, with barely four hours to dispose of as they please. And this is exactly what the institution of private property has done, and why a demand for its abolition and for the equal distribution of the national leisure or liberty among the whole population has arisen under the banner of Socialism.

Let us try to make a rough picture of what would happen if leisure, and consequently productive work, were equally distributed. Let us pretend that if we all worked four hours a day for thirtyfive years each of us could live as well as persons with at least a thousand a year do now. Let us assume that this state of things has been established by general agreement, involving a compromise between the people who want to work only two hours and live on a five-hundred-a-year scale and those who want to work four hours and live twice as expensively!

The difficulty then arises that some kinds of work will not fit themselves into instalments of four hours a day. Suppose you are married, for example. If your husband is in business there is no trouble for him. He does every day what he now does on Saturday: that is, begins at nine and knocks off at one. But what about your work? The most important work in the world is that of bearing and rearing children; for without that the human race would presently be extinct. All women's privileges are based on that fact. Now a woman cannot be pregnant for four hours a day, and normal for the rest of it. Nor can she nurse her infant for four hours and neglect it until nine next morning. It is true that pregnancy does not involve complete and continuous disablement from every other productive activity: indeed, no fact is better established by experience than that any attempt to treat it as such is morbid and dangerous. As some writers inelegantly express it, it is not a whole time job. Nursing is much more continuously exacting, as children in institutions who receive only what ignorant people call necessary attention mostly die, whilst home children who are played with and petted and coddled and tossed and sung-to survive with a dirty rag or two for clothing, and a thatched cabin with one room and a clay floor for habitation.

A four hours working day, then, does not mean that everybody can begin work at nine and leave off at one. Pregnancy and nursing are only items in the long list of vitally important occupations that cannot be interrupted and resumed at the sound of a hooter. It is possible in a factory to keep a continuous process going by having six shifts of workers to succeed oneanother during the twentyfour hours, so that each shift works no more than four hours; but a ship, being a home as well as a workplace, cannot accommodate six crews. Even if we built warships big enough to hold 5000 and carry food for them, the shifts could not retire from Jutland battles at the end of each spell of four hours. Nor is such leisure as is possible on board ship the equivalent of shore leisure, as the leisured passengers, with their silly deck games, and their agonized scamperings fore and aft for exercise know only too well.

Then there are the jobs that cannot be done in shifts because they must be done by the same person throughout with a continuance that stretches human endurance to the utmost limit. A chemist or physicist watching an experiment, an astronomer watching an eclipse, a doctor or nurse watching a difficult case, a Cabinet minister dealing with news from the front during a war, a farmer saving his hay in the face of an unfavorable weather forecast, or a body of scavengers clearing away a snowfall, must go on if necessary until they drop, four hours or no four hours. Handel's way of composing an oratorio was to work at it night and day until it was finished, keeping himself awake as best he might. Explorers are lucky if they do not die of exhaustion, as many of them have, from prolonged effort and endurance.

A four hour working day therefore, though just as feasible as an eight hour day is now, or the five day week which is the latest cry, is in practice only a basis of calculation. In factory and office work, and cognate occupations out of doors, it can be carried out literally. It may mean short and frequent holidays or long and rare ones. I do not know what happens to you in this respect; but in my own case, in spite of the most fervent resolutions to order my work more sensibly, and of the fact that an author's work can as a rule quite well be divided into limited daily periods, I am usually obliged to work myself to the verge of a complete standstill and then go away for many weeks to recuperate. Eight or nine months overwork, and three or four months change and overleisure, is very common among professional persons.

Then there is a vital difference between routine work and what is called creative or original work. When you hear of a man achieving eminence by working sixteen hours a day for thirty years, you may admire that apparently unnatural feat; but you must not conclude that he has any other sort of ability: in fact you may quite safely put him down as quite incapable of doing anything that has not been done before, and doing it in the old way. He never has to think or invent. To him today's work is a repetition of yesterday's work. Compare him, for example, with Napoleon. If you are interested in the lives of such people you are probably tired of hearing how Napoleon could keep on working with fierce energy long after all the members of his council were so exhausted that they could not even pretend to keep awake. But if you study the less often quoted memoirs of his secretary Bourrienne you will learn that Napoleon often moodled about for a week at a time doing nothing but play with children or read trash or waste his time helplessly. During his enforced leisure in St Helena, which he enjoyed so little that he probably often exclaimed, after Cowper's Selkirk, "Better live in the midst of alarms than dwell in this horrible place", he was asked how long a general lasted. He replied, "Six years". An American president is not expected to last more than four years. In England, where there is no law to prevent a worn-out dotard from being Prime Minister, even so imposing a parliamentary figure as Gladstone had to be practically superannuated when he tried to continue into the eighteen-nineties the commanding activities which had exhausted him in the seventies. To descend to more commonplace instances you cannot make an accountant work as long as a bookkeeper, nor a historian as continuously as a scrivener or typist, though they are performing the same arithmetical and manual operations. One will be tired out in three hours: the other can do eight without turning a hair with the help of a snack or a cup of tea to relieve her boredom occasionally. In the face of such differences you cannot distribute work equally and uniformly in quantities measured by time. What you can do is to give the workers, on the whole, equal leisure, bearing in mind that rest and recuperation are not leisure, and that periods of necessary recuperation in idleness must be counted as work, and often very irksome work, to those who have been prostrated by extraordinary efforts excessively prolonged.

The long and short of it is that freedom with a large F, general and complete, has no place in nature. In practice the questions that arise in its name are, first, how much leisure can we afford to allow ourselves? and second, how far can we be permitted to do what we like when we are at leisure? For instance, may we hunt stags on Dartmoor? Some of us say no; and if our opinion becomes law, the liberty of the Dartmoor Hunt will be curtailed to that extent. May we play golf on Sundays during church hours? Queen Elizabeth would not only have said no, but made churchgoing compulsory, and thereby have made Sunday a half-holiday instead of a whole one. Nowadays we enjoy the liberty of Sunday golf. Under Charles II, on the other hand, women were not allowed to attend Quaker meetings, and were flogged if they did. In fact attendance at any sort of religious service except that of the Church of England was a punishable offence; and though it was not possible to enforce this law fully against Roman Catholics and Jews, its penalties were ruthlessly inflicted on George Fox and John Bunyan, though King Charles himself sympathized with them. It cost us a revolution to establish comparative "liberty of conscience"; and we can now build and attend handsome temples of The Church of Christ Scientist, and form fantastic Separatist sects by the score if it pleases us.

On the other hand many things that we were free to do formerly we may not do now. In England until quite lately, as in Italy to this day, when a woman married, all her property became her husband's; and if she had the ill luck to marry a drunken blackguard, he could leave her to make a home for herself and her children by her own work, and then come back and seize everything she possessed and spend it in drink and debauchery. He could do it again and again, and sometimes did. Attempts to remedy this were denounced by happily married pious people as attacks on the sanctity of the marriage tie; and women who advocated a change were called unwomanly; but at last commonsense and decency prevailed; and in England a married woman is now so well protected from plunder and rapine committed by her husband that a Married Men's Rights agitation has begun.

Outside the home a factory owner might and did work little children to death with impunity, and do or leave undone anything he liked in his factory. Today he can no more do what he likes there than you can do what you like in Westminster Abbey. He is compelled by law to put up in a conspicuous place a long list of the things he must do and the things he may not do, whether he likes it or not. And when he is at leisure he is still subject to laws that restrict his freedom and impose duties and observances on him. He may not drive his motor car faster than twenty miles an hour (though he always does), and must drive on the left and pass on the right in England, and drive to the right and pass on the left in France. In public he must wear at least some clothing, even when he is taking a sunbath. He may not shoot wild birds or catch fish for sport except during certain seasons of the year; and he may not shoot children for sport at all. And the liberty of women in these respects is limited as the liberty of men is.

I need not bother you with more instances: you can think of dozens for yourself. Suffice it that without leisure there is no liberty, and without law there is no secure leisure. In an ideal free State, the citizen at leisure would find herself headed off by a police officer (male or female) whenever she attempted to do something that her fellow citizens considered injurious to them, or even to herself; but the assumption would be that she had a most sacred right to do as she pleased, however eccentric her conduct might appear, provided it was not mischievous. It is the contrary assumption that she must not do anything that she is not expressly licensed to do, like a child who must come to its mother and ask leave to do anything that is not in the daily routine, that destroys liberty. There is in British human nature, and I daresay in human nature in general, a very strong vein of pure inhibitiveness. Never forget the children in Punch, who, discussing how to amuse themselves, decided to find out what the baby was doing and tell it it mustnt. Forbiddance is an exercise of power; and we all have a will to personal power which conflicts with the will to social freedom. It is right that it should be jealously resisted when it leads to acts of irresponsible tyranny. But when all is said, the people who shout for freedom without understanding its limitations, and call Socialism or any other advance in civilization slavery because it involves new laws as well as new liberties, are as obstructive to the extension of leisure and liberty as the more numerous victims of the Inhibition Complex who, if they could, would handcuff everybody rather than face the risk of having their noses punched by somebody.

70
RENT OF ABILITY

HAVING cleared up the Liberty question by a digression (which must have been a relief) from the contemplation of capital running away with us, perhaps another digression on the equally confused question of the differences in ability between one person and another may not be out of place; for the same people who are in a continual scare about losing the liberty which they have mostly not got are usually much troubled about these differences. Years ago I wrote a small book entitled Socialism and Superior Brains which I need not repeat here, as it is still accessible. It was a reply to the late William Hurrell Mallock, who took it as a matter of course, apparently, that the proper use of cleverness in this world is to take advantage of stupid people to obtain a larger share than they of the nation's income. Rascally as this notion is, it is too common to be ignored. The proper social use of brains is to increase the amount of wealth to be divided, not to grab an unfair share of it; and one of the most difficult of our police problems is to prevent this grabbing, because it is a principle of Capitalism that everyone shall use not only her land and capital, but her cunning, to obtain as much money for herself as possible. Capitalism indeed compels her to do so by making no other provision for the clever ones than what they can make out of their cleverness.

Let us begin by taking the examples which delight and dazzle us: that is, the possessors of some lucrative personal talent. A lady with a wonderful voice can hire a concert room to sing in, and admit nobody who does not pay her. A gentleman able to paint a popular picture can hang it in a gallery with a turnstile at the door, passable only on payment. A surgeon who has mastered a dangerous operation can say to his patient, in effect, "Your money or your life". Giants, midgets, Siamese twins, and two-headed singers exhibit themselves for money as monsters. Attractive ladies receive presents enough to make them richer than their plainer or more scrupulous neighbors. So do fascinating male dancing partners. Popular actresses sometimes insist on being pampered and allowed to commit all sorts of follies and extravagances on the ground that they cannot keep up their peculiar charm without them; and the public countenances their exactions fondly.

These cases need not worry us. They are very scarce: indeed if they became common their power to enrich would vanish. They do not confer either industrial power or political privilege. The world is not ruled by prima donnas and painters, two-headed nightingales and surgical baronets, as it is by financiers and industrial organizers. Geniuses and monsters may make a great deal of money; but they have to work for it: I myself, through the accident of a lucrative talent, have sometimes made more than a hundred times as much money in a year as my father ever did; but he, as an employer, had more power over the lives of others than I. A practical political career would stop my professional career at once. It is true that I or any other possessor of a lucrative talent or charm can buy land and industrial incomes with our spare money, and thus become landlords and capitalists. But if that resource were cut off, by Socialism or any other change in the general constitution of society, I doubt whether anyone would grudge us our extra spending money. An attempt by the Government to tax it so as to reduce us to the level of ordinary mortals would probably be highly unpopular, because the pleasure we give is delightful and widespread, whilst the harm we do by our conceit and tantrums and jealousies and spoiltness is narrowly limited to the unfortunate few who are in personal contact with us. A prima donna with a rope of pearls ten feet long and a coronet of Kohinoors does not make life any worse for the girl with a string of beads who, by buying a five shilling ticket, helps to pay for the pearls: she makes it better by enchanting it.

Besides, we know by our own experience, not only of prima donnas but of commercial millionaires, that regular daily personal expenditure cannot be carried beyond that of the richest class to be found in the community. Persons richer than that, like Cecil Rhodes, Andrew Carnegie, and Alfred Nobel, the inventor of dynamite (to name only the dead), cannot spend their incomes, and are forced to give away money in millions for galleries and museums which they fill with magnificent collections and then leave to the public, or for universities, or churches, or prizes, or scholarships, or any sort of public object that appeals to them.

If equality of income were general, a freak income here and there would not enable its possessor to live differently from the rest. A popular soprano might be able to fill the Albert Hall for 100 nights in succession at a guinea a head for admission; but she could not obtain a lady's maid unless ladies' maids were a social institution. Nor could she leave a farthing to her children unless inheritance were a social institution, nor buy an unearned and as yet unproduced income for them unless Capitalism were a social institution. Thus, though it is always quite easy for a Government to checkmate any attempt of an individual to become richer than her neighbors by supertaxing her or directly prohibiting her methods, it is unlikely that it will ever be worth while to do so where the method is the exercise of a popular personal talent.

But when we come to that particular talent which makes its money out of the exercise of other people's talents, the case becomes gravely different. To allow Cleopatra to make money out of her charms is one thing: to allow a trader to become enormously rich by engaging five hundred Cleopatras at ten pounds a week or less, and hiring them out at ten pounds a day or more, is quite another. We may forgive a burglar in our admiration of his skill and nerve; but for the fence who makes money by purchasing the burglar's booty at a tenth of its value it is impossible to feel any sympathy. When we come to reputable women and honest men we find that they are exploited in the same way. Civilization makes matters worse in this respect, because civilization means division of labor. Remember the pin makers and pin machines. In a primitive condition of society the maker of an article saves the money to buy the materials, selects them, purchases them, and, having made the article out of these materials, sells it to the user or consumer. Today the raising of the money to buy the materials is a separate business; the selection and purchasing is another separate business; the making is divided between several workers or else done by a machine tended by a young person; and the marketing is yet another separate business. Indeed it is much more complicated than that, because the separate businesses of buying materials and marketing products are themselves divided into several separate businesses; so that between the origin of the product in raw material from the hand of Nature and its final sale across the counter to you there may be dozens of middlemen, of whom you complain because they each take a toll which raises the price to you, and it is impossible for you to find out how many of them are really necessary agents in the process and how many mere intercepters and parasites.

The same complication is found in that large part of the world's work which consists, not in making things, but in service. The woman who once took the wool that her husband had just shorn from their sheep, and with her own hands transformed it into a garment and sold it to the wearer, or clothed her family with it, is now replaced by a financier, a shipper, a woolbroker, a weaving mill, a wholesaler, a shopkeeper, a shop assistant, and Heaven knows how many others besides, each able to do her own bit of the process but ignorant of the other bits, and unable to do even her own bit until all the others are doing their bits at the same time. Any one of them without the others would be like an artillery man without a cannon or a shop assistant with nothing to sell.

Now if you go through all these indispensable parties to any industry or service, you will come on our question of exceptional ability in its most pressing and dangerous form. You will find, for instance, that whereas any ablebodied normal woman can be trained to become a competent shop assistant, or a shorthand typist and operator of a calculating machine (arithmetic is done by machines nowadays), or a factory hand, or a teacher, hardly five out of every hundred can manage a business or administer an estate or handle a large capital. The number of persons who can do what they are told is always greatly in excess of the number who can tell others what to do. If an educated woman asks for more than four or five pounds a week in business, nobody asks whether she is a good woman or a bad one: the question is, is there a post for her in which she will have to make decisions, and if so, can she be trusted to make them. If the answer is yes, she will be paid more than a living wage: if not, no.

Even when there is no room for original decisions, and there is nothing to do but keep other people hard at their allotted work, and maintain discipline generally, the ability to do this is an exceptional gift and has a special value. It may be nothing more admirable than the result of a combination of brute energy with an unamiable indifference to the feelings of others; but its value is unquestionable: it makes its possessor a forewoman or foreman in a factory, a wardress in a prison, a matron in an institution, a sergeant in the army, a mistress in a school, and the like. Both the managing people and the mere disciplinarians may be, and often are, heartily detested; but they are so necessary that any body of ordinary persons left without what they call superiors, will immediately elect them. A crew of pirates, subject to no laws except the laws of nature, will elect a boatswain to order them about and a captain to lead them and navigate the ship, though the one may be the most insufferable bully and the other the most tyrannical scoundrel on board. In the revolutionary army of Napoleon an expeditionary troop of dragoons, commanded by an officer who became terrified and shammed illness, insisted on the youngest of their number, a boy of sixteen, taking command, because he was an aristocrat, and they were accustomed to make aristocrats think for them. He afterwards became General Marbot: you will find the incident recorded in his memoirs. Every woman knows that the most strongminded woman in the house can set up a domestic tyranny which is sometimes a reign of terror. Without directors most of us would be like riderless horses in a crowded street. The philosopher Herbert Spencer, though a very clever man, had the amiable trait in his character of an intense dislike to coercion. He could not bring himself even to coerce his horse; and the result was that he had to sell it and go on foot, because the horse, uncoerced, could do nothing but stop and graze. Tolstoy, equally a professed humanitarian, tamed and managed the wildest horses; but he did it by the usual method of making things unpleasant for the horse until it obeyed him.

However, horses and human beings are alike in that they very seldom object to be directed: they are usually only too glad to be saved the trouble of thinking and planning for themselves. Ungovernable people are the exception and not the rule. When authority is abused and subordination made humiliating, both are resented; and anything from a mutiny to a revolution may ensue; but there is no instance on record of a beneficially and tactfully exercised authority provoking any reaction. Our mental laziness is a guarantee of our docility: the mother who says

"How dare you go out without asking my leave?" presently finds herself exclaiming "Why cant you think for yourself instead of running to me for everything?" But she would be greatly astonished if a rude motor car manufacturer said to her, "Why cant you make a car for yourself instead of running to me for it?"

I am myself by profession what is called an original thinker, my business being to question and test all the established creeds and codes to see how far they are still valid and how far worn out or superseded, and even to draft new creeds and codes. But creeds and codes are only two out of the hundreds of useful articles that make for a good life. All the other articles I have to take as they are offered to me on the authority of those who understand them; so that though many people who cannot bear to have an established creed or code questioned regard me as a dangerous revolutionary and a most insubordinate fellow, I have to be in most matters as docile a creature as you could desire to meet. When a railway porter directs me to number ten platform I do not strike him to earth with a shout of "Down with tyranny!" and rush violently to number one platform. I accept his direction because I want to be directed, and want to get into the right train. No doubt if the porter bullied and abused me, and I, after submitting to this, found that my train really started from number seven platform and that the number ten train landed me in Portsmouth when my proper destination was Birmingham, I should rise up against that porter and do what I could to contrive his downfall; but if he had been reasonably civil and had directed me aright I should rally to his defence if any attempt were made to depose him. I have to be housekept-for, nursed, doctored, and generally treated like a child in all sorts of situations in which I do not know what to do; and far from resenting such tutelage I am only too glad to avail myself of it. The first time I was ever in one of those electric lifts which the passengers work for themselves instead of being taken up and down by a conductor pulling at a rope, I almost cried, and was immensely relieved when I stepped out alive.

You may think I am wandering from our point; but I know too well by experience that there is likely to be at the back of your mind a notion that it is in our nature to resent authority and subordination as such, and that only an unpopular and stern coercion can maintain them. Have I not indeed just been impressing on you that the miseries of the world today are due in great part to our objection, not merely to bad government, but to being governed at all? But you must distinguish. It is true that we dislike being interfered with, and want to do as we like when we know what to do, or think we know. But when there is something that obviously must be done, and only five in every hundred of us know how to do it, then the odd ninetyfive will not merely be led by the five: they will clamor to be led, and will, if necessary, kill anyone who obstructs the leaders. That is why it is so easy for ambitious humbugs to get accepted as leaders. No doubt competent leadership may be made unpopular by bad manners and pretension to general superiority; and subordination may be made intolerable by humiliation. Leaders who produce these results should be ruthlessly cashiered, no matter how competent they are in other respects, because they destroy self-respect and happiness, and create a dangerous resentment complex which reduces the competence and upsets the tempers of those whom they lead. But you may take it as certain that authority and subordination in themselves are never unpopular, and can be trusted to re-establish themselves after the most violent social convulsion. What is to be feared is less their overthrow than the idolization of those who exercise authority successfully. Nelson was idolized by his seamen; Lenin was buried as a saint by revolutionary Russia; Signor Mussolini is adored in Italy as The Leader (Il Duce); but no anarchist preaching resistance to authority as such has ever been popular or ever will be.

Now it is unfortunately one of the worst vices of the Capitalist system that it destroys the social equality that is indispensable to natural authority and subordination. The very word subordination, which is properly co-ordination, betrays this perversion. Under it directing ability is sold in the market like fish; and, like sturgeon, it is dear because it is scarce. By paying the director more than the directee it creates a difference of class between them; and the difference of class immediately changes a direction or command which naturally would not only not be resented but desired and begged for, into an assertion of class superiority which is fiercely resented. "Who are you that you should order

In socialized services no difficulty arises. The civil servant, the judge, the navy captain, the field marshal, the archbishop, however extraordinary able, gets no more than any routineer of his rank and seniority. A real gentleman is not supposed to sell himself to the highest bidder: he asks his country for a sufficient provision and a dignified position in return for the best work he can do for it. A real lady can say no less. But in capitalist commerce they are both forced to be cads: that is, to hold up to ransom those to whom their services are indispensable, and become rich at their expense. The mere disciplinarian cannot extort very much because disciplinarians of one sort or another are not very scarce. But the organizer and financier is in a strong position. The owner of a big business, if his employees ask for anything more than a subsistence wage as their share of its product, can always say "Well, if you are not satisfied, take the business and work it yourself without me". This they are unable to do. The Trade Union to which his employees belong may be tempted to take him at his word; but it soon finds itself unable to carry on, that sort of management not being its job. He says in effect, and often in so many words, "You cannot do without me; so you must work on my terms". They reply with perfect truth "Neither can you do without us: let us see you organize without any workers to organize". But he beats them; and the reason is not that he can do without them any more than they can do without him (or her), but that his bargain for the use of his ability is not really made with them but with the landlords whose land he is using and the capitalists who have lent him the capital for his enterprise. It is to them that he can say unanswerably "You cannot do without me". They may say "Yes we can. We can tell the workers that unless they give up everything they can make out of our land and capital to us except what is enough to keep them alive and renew themselves from generation to generation they shall starve; because they cannot produce without land and capital, and we own all there is available of both". "That is true" retorts the able organizer and financier; "but please to remember that without an elaborate scientific organization of their labor they can produce no more than a mob of allotment holders, or of serfs on a tenth century manor, whereas if I organize them for you industrially and financially I can multiply their product a thousandfold. Even if you have to pay me a large share of the increase due to my ability you are still far richer than if you did without me." And to this there is no reply. In this way there arises under Capitalism not only a rent of land and a rent of capital (called interest), but a rent of ability (called profit); and just as in order to secure equality of income it becomes necessary to nationalize land and capital, so it becomes necessary to nationalize ability. We already do this in part by taxing profits. But we do it completely only when, as in the public services, we give it direct national or municipal employment.

Note that rent of ability is a form of rent of labor. Rent is a word that it is very necessary to understand, and that very few people do understand: they think it is only what they have to pay to their landlord. But technically rent is a price that arises whenever there are differences in the yield of any particular source of wealth. When there is a natural difference between the yield of one field and another, or one coal-mine and another, or between the advantages of one building site and another, people will pay more for the better than for the worse; and that extra price is rent. Similarly, when there is a difference between the business ability of one person and another, the price of that difference is rent. You cannot abolish rent, because you cannot abolish the natural difference between one cornfield and another, one coal-field and another, or one person and another; but you can nationalize it by nationalizing the land, the mines, and the labor of the country either directly or by national appropriation of their product by taxation, as to which latter method, as we have seen, there are limits. Until this is done, rent of ability in profiteering will make its possessors rich enough to make their children idle landlords and capitalists and destroy economic equality. Great astronomers, chemists, mathematicians, physicists, philosophers, explorers, discoverers, teachers, preachers, sociologists, and saints may be so poor that their wives are worn-out in a constant struggle to keep up appearances and make both ends meet; but the business organizers pile millions on millions whilst their unfortunate daughters carry about diamonds and sables to advertize their parent's riches, and drink cocktails until they feel so bad inside that they pay large sums to surgeons to cut them open and find out what is the matter with them. If you reproach these organizers for their inordinate gains, they tell you—or they would tell you if they understood their own position and could express it intelligibly—that every penny they make is made by making money for other people as well; that before they can spend a farthing on themselves they must provide rent for the landlord, interest for the capitalist, and wages for the proletarian on a scale that would be impossible without them; and that England can support five times the number of people she could a hundred years ago because her industries are better organized and more amply financed by them and their like. This is true; but you need not be abashed by it; for which of us has not to provide rent for the landlord, interest for the capitalist, and wages for the laborer before we can spend a penny on ourselves? And why should the organizer and financier be paid more for the exercise of his particular faculty than we who have to co-operate with him by the exercise of our particular faculties before he can produce a loaf of bread or a glass of milk? It is not natural necessity but the capitalist system that enables him to snatch more than his fellow workers from the welter of competitive commerce; and while this lasts we shall have the financier's daughter saying to the scavenger's daughter "What would your common dirty father do without my father, who is going to be made a lord?" and the scavenger's daughter retorting "What would your greedy robber of a father do if my father did not keep the streets clean for him?" Of course you have never heard a lady or a young person talk like that. And probably you never will. They are too polite and too thoughtless to discuss their father's positions. Besides, they never speak to oneanother. But if they did, and anything upset their tempers, their last words before they came to blows would be just those which I have imagined. If you doubt it, read what the capitalist papers say about Trade Unionists and Socialists, and what the proletarian papers say about landlords and capitalists and bosses. Do you suppose that the charwoman, who has worked in her own necessary way all her life as hard as or harder than any financier, and in the end has nothing to leave to her daughter but her pail and scrubbing brush, really believes, or ever will believe, that Lady Billionham, inheriting a colossal income from her father the financier, has any moral right to her money? Or, if your father had discovered and worked out the theory of relativity, and was acknowledged throughout the world to have the greatest mind since Newton's, would you consider it morally satisfactory to be obliged to jump at an offer of marriage from a Chicago pork king to enable your illustrious parent to have more than one presentable suit of clothes, knowing all the time that if it had not been for the work of men like your father in pure science not a wheel in the whole vast machinery of modern production would be turning, nor a bagman be able to travel faster than Marco Polo? Privately appropriated rent, whether of land, capital, or ability, makes bad blood; and it is of bad blood that civilizations die. That it is why it is our urgent business to see that Lord Billionham gets no more than Einstein, and neither of them more than the charwoman. You cannot equalize their abilities, but fortunately you can equalize their incomes. Billionham's half-crown is as good as Einstein's two-and-sixpence; and the charwoman's thirty pennies will buy as much bread as either. Equalize them in that respect, and their sons and daughters will be intermarriageable, which will be a very good thing for them, and lead to an enormous improvement of our human stock, the quality of which is the most important thing in the world.

71

PARTY POLITICS

YOU are now in possession of enough knowledge of Socialism and Capitalism to enable you to understand what is going on in the world industrially and politically. I shall not advise you to discuss these matters with your friends. They would listen in distressed silence and then tell the neighborhood that you are what they imagine a Bolshevik to be.

It is possible, however, that you may be interested in current party politics yourself, even to the extent of attending party meetings, applauding party candidates, canvassing for party votes, and experiencing all the emotions of party enthusiasm, party loyalty, and party conviction that the other party and its candidate are enemies of the human race. In that case I must give you a warning.

Do not rush to the conclusion that Socialism will be established by a Socialist party and opposed by an anti-Socialist party. Within my lifetime I have seen the Conservatives, when in opposition, vehemently opposing and denouncing a measure proposed by the Liberals, and, when they had defeated the Liberals and come into power, pass that very measure themselves in a rather more advanced form. And I have seen the Liberals do the same, and this, too, not in matters of no great consequences, but in such far-reaching social changes as Free Trade, the enfranchisement of the working classes, the democratization of local government, and the buying-out of the Irish landlords. The Spanish lady in Byron's poem, who, "swearing she would ne'er consent, consented", was a model of consistency compared to our party governments. We have at present a Capitalist party opposed by a Labor party; but it is quite possible that all the legislative steps towards Socialism will be taken when the anti-Socialist party is in power, and pretty certain that at least half of them will. When they are proposed by a Capitalist Government they will be opposed by the Labor Opposition, and when they are proposed by a Labor Government they will be opposed by the Capitalist Opposition, because "it is the business of an Opposition to oppose".

There is another possibility which may disappoint your expectation. The Labor Party is growing rapidly. Twenty years ago it did not exist officially in Parliament. Today it is the official Opposition. If it continues to grow at this rate the time is not very far off when it will take practically complete possession of the House of Commons. The Conservatives and Liberals left will, even in coalition, be too few to constitute an effective Opposition, much less form a Government. But beware of assuming that the result will be a unanimous House of Commons with an unopposed Labor Government carrying everything before it. Do not even assume that the Labor Party will split into two parties, one Conservative and the other Progressive. That would be the happiest of the possibilities. The danger is that it may split into half a dozen or more irreconcilable groups, making parliamentary government impossible. That is what happened in the Long Parliament in the seventeenth century, when men were just what they are now, except that they had no telephones nor airplanes. The

Long Parliament was united at first by its opposition to the King. But when it cut off the King's head, it immediately became so disunited that Cromwell, like Signor Mussolini today, had at last to suppress its dissensions by military force, and rule more despotically than ever the King had dared. When Cromwell died, it reassembled and split up again worse than ever, bringing about such a hopeless deadlock in government that there was no way out of the mess but to send for the dead King's son and use him, under his father's title, as the figurehead of a plutocratic oligarchy exercising all the old kingly powers and greatly extending them.

If six hundred Labor members were returned at the next General Election history might repeat itself. The Socialists, the Trade Unionists who are not Socialists, the Communists who are not Communists but only pseudo-Bolshevists, the Republicans, the Constitutional-Monarchists, the old Parliamentary hands who are pure Opportunists, and the uncompromising Idealists, to say nothing of the Churchmen and Anti-clericals (Episcopalians and Separatists), the Deists and Atheists, would come to loggerheads at once. As far as I can see, nothing could avert a repetition of the seventeenth century catastrophe, or the modern Italian and Spanish ones, except a solid Socialist majority of members who really know what Socialism means and are prepared to subordinate all their traditional political and religious differences to its establishment. Unfortunately most of the people who call themselves Socialists at present do not know what Socialism means, and attach its name to all sorts of fads and faiths and resentments and follies that have nothing to do with it. A Labor electoral triumph may end either in another Cromwell or Napoleon III or Mussolini or General Primo di Rivera if there happens to be one at hand, or in the passing of power to any party that is solid enough to keep together and vote together, even though its solidarity be the solidarity of sheepish stupidity or panic-stricken retreat. Stupidity and cowardice never lose this advantage. You must have noticed among your acquaintances that the very conventional ones have all the same old opinions, and are quite impervious to new ones, whilst the unconventional ones are all over the shop with all sorts of opinions, and disagree with and despise oneanother furiously. That is why, though all progress depends on the unconventional people who want to change things, they have so little influence politically. They pull hard; but they do not pull together; and they pull in different directions. The people whom in your moments of impatience with their dullness you call stick-in-the-muds either pull all together and in the same direction (generally backwards), or, more formidably still, stand together solid and foursquare, refusing to move in any direction. Against stupidity, said Schiller, the gods themselves fight in vain. Long before Schiller, Solomon said "Let a bear robbed of her whelps meet a man, rather than a fool in his folly". They were both right.

Yet it is a mistake to vote for stupidity on the ground that stupid people do not quarrel among themselves. Within the limits of their conservatism they quarrel more irreconcilably, because more unreasonably, than comparatively clever people. That is why we call them pigheaded. If six hundred of them were returned at the next General Election, so that they had no longer anything to fear from Labor or Liberalism or any other section, it would be just as impossible to keep them together as if they were proletarians. In 1924 the country was stampeded by a ridiculous anti-Russian scare into returning anti-Socialists in a majority of more than two to one. The result was, not a very solid Government, but a very fragmentary one. It soon split up into reckless Diehard Coercionists, timid Compromisers, cautious Opportunists, Low Church Protestants, Anglican Catholics, Protectionists from the Midlands, Free Traders from the ports, country gentlemen, city bosses, Imperialists, Little Englanders, innocents who think that Trade Unions ought to be exterminated like nests of vipers, and practical business men who know that big business could not be carried on without them, advocates of high expenditure on the fighting forces as Empire Insurance, blind resisters of taxation as such, Inflationists, Gold Bugs, High Tories who would have Government authority and interference everywhere, Laisser-faire doctrinaires who would suffer it as nearly as possible nowhere, and Heaven knows how many others, all pulling the Cabinet different ways, paralyzing it and neutralizing oneanother, whilst the runaway car of Capitalism kept rushing them into new places and dangerous situations all the time.

During the first half of my own lifetime: that is, during the latter half of the nineteenth century, the Conservative and Liberal parties were much more equally balanced than at present. The Governments were on their good behavior because their majorities were narrow. The House of Commons was then respected and powerful. With the South African war a period of large majorities set in. Immediately the House of Commons began to fall into something very like contempt in comparison with its previous standing. The majorities were so large that every Government felt that it could do what it liked. That quaint conscience which was invented by English statesmen to keep themselves honest, and called by everybody Public Opinion, was overthrown as an idol, and the ignorance, forgetfulness, and follies of the electorate were traded on cynically until the few thinkers who read the speeches of the political leaders and could remember for longer than a week the pledges and statements they contained, were amazed and scandalized at the audacity with which the people were humbugged. The specific preparations for war with Germany were concealed, and finally, when suspicion became acute, denied; and when at last we floundered into the horror of 1914-18, which left the English Church disgraced, and the great European empires shattered into struggling Republics (the very last thing that the contrivers of the war intended), the world had lost faith in parliamentary government to such an extent that it was suspended and replaced by dictatorship in Italy, Spain, and Russia without provoking any general democratic protest beyond a weary shrug of the shoulders. The old parliamentary democrats were accomplished and endless talkers; but their unreal theory that nothing political must be done until it was understood and demanded by a majority of the people (which meant in effect that nothing political must ever be done at all) had disabled them as men of action; and when casual bodies of impatient and irresponsible proletarian men of action attempted to break up Capitalism without knowing how to do it, or appreciating the nature and necessity of government, a temper spread in which it was possible for Signor Mussolini to be made absolute managing director (Dictator or Duce) of the Italian nation as its savior from parliamentary impotence and democratic indiscipline.

Socialism, however, cannot perish in these political storms and changes. Socialists have courted Democracy, and even called Socialism Social-Democracy to proclaim that the two are inseparable. They might just as plausibly argue that the two are incompatible. Socialism is committed neither way. It faces Caesars and Soviets, Presidents and Patriarchs, British Cabinets and Italian Dictators or Popes, patrician oligarchs and plebeian demagogues, with its unshaken demonstration that they cannot have a stable and prosperous State without equality of income. They may plead that such equality is ridiculous. That will not save them from the consequences of inequality. They must equate or perish. The despot who values his head and the crowd that fears for its liberty are equally concerned. I should call Socialism not Democratic but simply Catholic if that name had not been taken in vain so often by so many Churches that nobody would understand me.

72

THE PARTY SYSTEM

OUR Party System does not mean, as many people suppose, that differences of opinion always divide human beings into parties. Such differences existed ages before the Party System was ever dreamt of.

What it means is that our monarchs, instead of choosing whom they please to advise them as Cabinet Ministers in ruling the realm (to form a Government, as we say), must choose them all from whatever party has a majority in the House of Commons, however much they may dislike them or mistrust their ability, or however obvious it may be that a more talented Cabinet could be formed by selecting the ablest men from both parties.

This system carries with it some quaint consequences. Not only must the King appoint to high offices persons whom he may privately regard as disastrous noodles, or whose political and religious principles he may abhor: the ordinary member of Parliament and the common voter are placed in a similar predicament, because every vote given in the House or at a parliamentary election becomes a vote on the question whether the Party in office is to remain there or not. For instance, a Bill is introduced by the Government to allow women to vote at the same age as men, or to put a tax on bachelors, or to institute pensions for widowed mothers, or to build ten more battleships, or to abolish or extend divorce, or to raise the age for compulsory school attendance, or to increase or diminish taxation, or anything else you please. Suppose this Bill is brought in by a Conservative Government, and you are a Conservative member of Parliament! You may think it a most detestable and mischievous Bill. But if you vote against it, and the Bill is thrown out, the Conservative Government will no longer be in a majority, or, as we say, it will no longer possess the confidence of the House. Therefore it must go to the King and resign, whereupon the King will dissolve Parliament; and there will be a General Election at which you will have to stand again (which will cost you a good deal of money and perhaps end in your defeat) before anything else can be done. Now if you are a good Conservative you always feel that however much you may dislike this Bill or that Bill, yet its passing into law would be a less evil than an overthrow of the Conservative Government, and the possible accession to power of the Labor Party. Therefore you swallow the Bill with a wry face, and vote just as the Government Whips tell you to, flatly against your convictions.

But suppose you are a member of the Labor Party instead, and think the Bill a good one. Then you are in the same fix: you must vote against it and against your convictions, because however good you may think the Bill, you think that a defeat of the Government and a chance for the Labor Party to return to power would be still better. Besides, if the Bill is good, the Labor Party can bring it in again and pass it when Labor wins a majority.

If you are only a voter you are caught in the same cleft stick. It may be plain to you that the candidate of your Party is a political imbecile, a pompous snob, a vulgar ranter, a conceited self-seeker, or anything else that you dislike, and his opponent an honest, intelligent, public-spirited person. No matter: you must vote for the Party candidate, because, if you do not, your Party may be defeated, and the other Party come into power. And, anyhow, however disagreeable your candidate may be personally, when he gets into the House he will have to vote as the Party Whips tell him to; so his personal qualities do not matter.

The advantage of this system is that a House of Commons consisting of about a dozen capable ministers and their opponents: say twenty-five effectives all told, and 590 idiots with just enough intelligence to walk into the lobby pointed out to them by the Whips and give their names at the door, can carry on the government of the country quite smoothly, when 615 independents, with opinions and convictions of their own, voting according to those opinions and convictions, would make party government impossible. It was not, however, on this ground that the party system was introduced, though it has a great deal to do with its maintenance. It was introduced because our Dutch king William the Third, of glorious, pious, and immortal memory, discovered that he could not fight the French king, Louis XIV, *le Roi Soleil,* with a House of Commons refusing him supplies and reducing the army just as each member thought fit. A clever statesman of that time named Robert Spencer, second Earl of Sunderland, pointed out to him that if he chose his ministers always from the strongest party in the House of Commons, which happened just then to be the Whig party, that party would have to back him through the war and make its followers do the same, just as I have described. King William hated the Whigs, being a strong Tory himself; and he did not like Sunderland's advice. But he took it, and thereby set up the Party System under which we are ruled.

Is there any practicable alternative to the Party System? Suppose, for instance, that there was a general revolt against being compelled to vote for dummies and nincompoops, and that independent candidates became so popular that all party candidates were defeated by them, or, if you think that is going too far, suppose independent candidates returned in such numbers that they could defeat any Government by casting their votes in the House against it, like the old Irish Nationalist Party! Such a revolt already exists and always will exist. The upshot of the General Elections is determined, not by the voters who always vote for their party right or wrong, but by a floating body of independent electors who vote according to their interests and preferences, and often support one party at one election and the opposite party at the next. It is these unattached people who win the odd trick which decides which party shall govern. They either know nothing about the Party System, or snap their fingers at it and vote just as they please. It is probable that they outnumber the party voters, and return party members to Parliament only because, as no others are selected as candidates by the party organizations, there is seldom any independent candidate to vote for.

It is conceivable that the King might some day find himself confronted by a House of Commons in which neither party had a majority, the effective decision resting with members belonging to no party. In that case His Majesty might appeal in vain to the party leaders to form a Government. This situation has occurred several times of late in France, where it has been brought about by the existence in the French Chamber of so many parties that none of them is in a majority; so that a leader can form a Government only by inducing several of these parties to combine for the moment, and thus make what is called a Block. But this is not always easy; and even when it is accomplished, and the Blockmaker forms a Government, it is so hard to keep the Block together that nobody expects it to last for five years, as our party governments do: its lifetime is anything from a week to six months. There have been moments lately in France when we did not know from one day to another who was Prime Minister there, M. Briand, M. Herriot, M. Painlevé, or M. Poincaré. And what has happened in France may happen here, either through an overwhelming party majority causing the party to split up into hostile groups and thus substitute half a dozen parties, all in a minority, for the two parties which are necessary to the working of the Party System, or through the return of enough independent members to make any Party Government dependent on them. You will therefore be justified if you ask me rather anxiously whether Parliament can not be worked on some other than the Party System.

As a matter of fact in this country we have, beside the House of Commons, parliaments all over the place. We have the great city Corporations, the County Councils, the Borough Councils, the District Councils, and so on down to the Parish meetings in the villages; and not one of them is worked on the Party System. They get on quite well without it. If you mention this, you will be at once contradicted, because on many of these bodies party feeling is intense. The members hold party meetings. The elections are fought on party cries. Votes are taken on party lines, and members of the party which is in the minority are sometimes excluded from the committee chairmanships, which are the nearest things to ministerial offices available, though such exclusion is considered sharp practice if pushed too far. But all this does not involve the Party System any more than a pot of jam and a pound of flour constitute a roly-poly pudding. There is no Prime Minister and no Cabinet. The King does not meddle in the business: he does not send for the most prominent men and ask them to form a Government. There is no Government in the House of Commons sense of the word, though the city or county is nevertheless governed, and often governed with an efficiency which puts the House of Commons to shame. Every member can vote as he thinks best without the slightest risk of throwing his party out of power and bringing on a General Election. If a motion is defeated, nobody resigns: if it is carried, nobody's position is changed. Things are not done in that very puzzling way.

The way they are done is simple enough. The Council is elected for three years; and until the three years are up there can be no general election. Its business is conducted by committees: Public Health Committees, Electric Lighting Committees, Finance Committees, and so forth. These committees meet separately, and set forth their conclusions as to what the Council ought to do in their departments in a series of resolutions. When the whole Council meets, these strings of resolutions are brought up as the reports of the Committees, and are confirmed or rejected or amended by the general vote. Many of our Labor members of the House of Commons have served their parliamentary apprenticeship on local bodies under this straightforward system.

The two systems, though widely different today, spring from the same root. Before Sunderland prompted William III to introduce the Party System, the King used to appoint committees, which were then all called cabinets, to deal with the different departments of government. These cabinets were committees of his Council; and in this stage they were the model of the municipal committees I have just described. The secretaries of the cabinets, called Secretaries of States, met to concert their activities. The activities thus concerted formed their policy; and they themselves, being all cabinet ministers, came to be called THE Cabinet, after which the word was no longer applied to other bodies. In politics it now means nothing else, the old cabinets being called Offices (Home Office, War Office, Foreign Office, etc.), Boards, Chanceries, Treasuries, or anything except cabinets.

The rigidity of the Party System, as we have seen, depends on the convention that whenever the Government is defeated on a division in the House, it must "appeal to the country": that is, the Cabinet Ministers must resign their offices, and the King dissolve the Parliament and have a new one elected. But this leads to such absurd consequences when the question at issue is unimportant and the vote taken when many members are absent, and at all times it reduces the rank and file of the members to such abject voting machines, that if it were carried out to the bitter end members might as well stay at home and vote by proxy on postcards to the Whips, as shareholders do at company meetings. Such slavery is more than even parliamentary flesh and blood, to say nothing of brains, can stand; consequently Governments are forced to allow their followers some freedom by occasionally declaring that the measure under discussion is "not a Party Question", and "taking off the Whips", which means that members may vote as they please without fear of throwing their Party out of office and bringing on a General Election. This practice is bound to grow as members become more independent and therefore more apt to split up into groups. The tendency already is for Governments to resign only when they are defeated on an explicit motion that they possess or have forfeited the confidence of the House, except, of course, when the division is on one of those cardinal points of policy which, if decided against the Government, would involve an appeal to the country in any case. No doubt the Whips will continue to threaten weak-minded members that the slightest exercise of independence will wreck the Government; and those whose election expenses are paid out of party funds will find that when the Party pays the piper the Whips call the tune; but I think you may take it (in case you should think of going into Parliament) that the House of Commons is becoming less and less like a stage on which an opera chorus huddles round a few haughty soloists, never opening its hundred mouths except to echo these principals and give them time to breathe. It is already evident that the more women there are in the House, the more refractory it will be to the logical extremes of party discipline, and the sooner party questions will become the exceptions and open questions the rule.

Here, however, I must warn you of another possibility. The two Houses of Parliament are as much out of date as instruments for carrying on the public business of a modern community as a pair of horses for drawing an omnibus. In 1920 two famous Socialist professors of political science, Sidney and Beatrice Webb, published a Constitution for the Socialist Commonwealth of Great Britain. In that Constitution the notion of going on with our ancient political machinery at Westminster is discarded as impracticable, and its present condition described as one of creeping paralysis. Instead, it is proposed that we should have two parliaments, one political and the other industrial, the political one maintaining the cabinet system, and the industrial one the municipal system. I cannot go into the details of such a change here: you will find them in the book. I mention it just to prepare you for such happenings. Certain it is that if our old Westminster engine is left as it is to cope with the modern developments of Capitalism, Capitalism will burst it; and then something more adequate must be devised and set up, whether we like it or not.

73

DIVISIONS WITHIN THE LABOR PARTY

YOU now see how essential it is to the working of our parliamentary system, under a Labor or any other Government, that the Cabinet should have a united party behind it, large enough to outvote any other party in the House. You see also that whereas a party only barely large enough to do this is held together by the fear of defeat, a party so large that the whole House belongs to it ceases to be a party at all, and is sure to split up into groups which have to be combined into blocks of groups before a Cabinet can be formed and government effectively carried on. In the nineteenth century we were all sure that this could never occur. In the twentieth it is as certain as anything of the kind can be that the Proletariat will extend its present invasion of Parliament until it achieves in effect complete conquest. Therefore we had better examine a few questions on which the apparent unanimity in the Labor Party is quite delusive.

To interest you I am tempted to begin with the question of the virtual exclusion of women from certain occupations. This morning I received a letter from the Government College of Lahore in the Punjab which contains the following words: "The number of people in India speaking Urdu of one kind or another is about 96,000,000. Out of this number 46,000,000 are women who are mostly in purdah and do not go out." Now I dare not tell you, even if I knew, how many members of the Labor Party believe that the proper place for women is in purdah. There are enough, anyhow, to start a very pretty fight with those who would remove all artificial distinctions between men and women. But I must pass over this because, vital as it is, it will not split the Labor Party more than it has split the older parties. If men were the chattel slaves of women in law (as some of them are in fact), or women the chattel slaves of men in fact (as married women used to be in law), that would not affect the change from Capitalism to Socialism. Let us confine ourselves to cases that would affect it.

It is fundamental in Socialism that idleness shall not be tolerated on any terms. And it is fundamental in Trade Unionism that the worker shall have the right at any moment to down tools and refuse to do another stroke until his demands are satisfied. It is impossible to imagine a flatter contradiction. And the question of the right to strike is becoming more acute every year. We have seen how the little businesses have grown into big businesses, and the big businesses into Trusts that control whole industries. But the Trade Unions have kept up with this growth. The little unions have grown into big unions; and the big unions have combined into great federations of unions; consequently the little strikes have become terribly big strikes. A modern strike of electricians, a railway strike, or a coal strike can bring these industries, and dozens of others which depend on them, to a dead stop, and cause unbearable inconvenience and distress to the whole nation.

To make strikes more effective, a new sort of Trade Union has developed, called an Industrial Union to distinguish it from the old Craft Unions. The Craft Union united all the men who lived by a particular craft or trade: the carpenters, the masons, the tanners and so on. But there may be men of a dozen different crafts employed in one modern industry: for instance, the building industry employs carpenters, masons, bricklayers, joiners, plumbers, slaters, painters, and various kinds of laborers, to say nothing of the clerical staffs; and if these are all in separate unions a strike by one of them cannot produce the effect that a strike of all of them would. Therefore unions covering the whole industry without regard to craft (Industrial Unions) have been formed. We now have such bodies as the Transport Workers' Union and the National Union of Railway Workers, in which workers from dozens of different trades are combined. They can paralyze the whole industry by a strike. In the nineteenth century very few strikes or lock-outs were big enough to be much noticed by the general public. In the twentieth there have already been several which were national calamities. The Government has been forced to interfere either by trying to buy the disputants off with subsidies, or to persuade the employers and the strikers to come to some agreement. But as the Government has no power either to force the men to go back to work or the employers to grant their demands, its intervention is not very effective, and never succeeds until a great deal of mischief has been done. It has been driven at last to attempt a limitation of the magnitude of strikes by an Act of 1927 forbidding "sympathetic" strikes and lock-outs, lock-outs being included to give the Act an air of fair play. But as this Act does not forbid the formation of industrial unions, nor take away the right to strike or lock-out when a grievance can be established (as of course it always can), it is only a gesture of impotent rage, useless as a remedy, but significant of the growing indisposition of the nation to tolerate big strikes. They are civil wars between Capital and Labor in which the whole country suffers.

The Socialist remedy for this dangerous nuisance is clear. Socialism would impose compulsory social service on all serviceable citizens, just as during the war compulsory military service was imposed on all men of military age. When we are at war nowadays no man is allowed to plead that he has a thousand a year of his own and need not soldier for a living. It does not matter if he has fifty thousand: he has to "do his bit" with the rest. In vain may he urge that he is a gentleman, and does not want to associate with common soldiers or be classed with them. If he is not a trained officer he has to become a private, and possibly find that his sergeant has been his valet, and that his lieutenant, his major, his colonel, and his brigadier are respectively his tailor, his bootmaker, his solicitor, and the manager of his favourite golfing hotel. The penalty of neglect to discharge his duties precisely and punctually even at the imminent risk of being horribly wounded or blown to bits, is death. Now the righteousness of military service is so questionable that the man who conscientiously refuses to perform it can justify himself by the test proposed by the philosopher Kant: that is, he can plead that if everybody did the same the world would be much safer, happier, and better.

A refusal of social service has no such excuse. If everybody refused to work, nine-tenths of the inhabitants of these islands would be dead within a month; and the rest would be too weak to bury them before sharing their fate. It is useless for a lady to plead that she has enough to live on without work: if she is not producing her own food and clothing and lodging other people must be producing them for her; and if she does not perform some equivalent service for them she is robbing them. It is absurd for her to pretend that she is living on the savings of her industrious grandmother; for not only is she alleging a natural impossibility, but there is no reason on earth why she should be allowed to undo by idleness the good that her grandmother did by industry. Compulsory social service is so unanswerably right that the very first duty of a government is to see that everybody works enough to pay her way and leave something over for the profit of the country and the improvement of the world. Yet it is the last duty that any government will face. What governments do at present is to reduce the mass of the people by armed force to a condition in which they must work for the capitalists or starve, leaving the capitalists free from any such obligation, so that capitalists can not only be idle but produce artificial overpopulation by withdrawing labor from productive industry and wasting it in coddling their idleness or ministering to their vanity. This our Capitalist Governments call protecting property and maintaining personal liberty; but Socialists believe that property, in that sense, is theft, and that allowable personal liberty no more includes the right to idle than the right to murder.

Accordingly, we may expect that when a Labor House of Commons is compelled to deal radically with some crushing national strike, the Socialists in the Labor Party will declare that the remedy is Compulsory Social Service for all ablebodied persons. The remnants of the old parties and the non-Socialist Trade Unionists in the Labor Party will at once combine against the proposal, and clamor for a subsidy to buy off the belligerents instead. Subsidy or no subsidy, the Trade Unionists will refuse to give up the right to strike, even in socialized industries. The strike is the only weapon a Trade Union has. The employers will be equally determined to maintain their right to lock-out. As to the landlords and capitalists, their dismay can be imagined. They will be far more concerned than the employers and financiers, because employers and financiers are workers: to have to work is no hardship to them. But the real ladies and gentlemen, who know no trade, and have been brought up to associate productive work with social inferiority, imprisonment in offices and factories, compulsory early rising, poverty, vulgarity, rude manners, roughness and dirt and drudgery, would see in compulsory social service the end of the world for them and their class, as indeed it happily will be, in a sense. The condition of many of them would be so pitiable (or at least they would imagine it to be so) that they would have to be provided with medical certificates of disability until they died out; for, after all, it is not their fault that they have been brought up to be idle, extravagant, and useless; and when that way of life (which, by the way, they often make surprisingly laborious) is abolished, they may reasonably claim the same consideration as other people whose occupation is done away with by law. We can afford to be kind to them.

However that may be, it is certain that the useless classes will join the Trade Unionists in frantic opposition to Compulsory Social Service. If the Labor ministers, being, as they now mostly are, Socialists, attempt to bring in a Compulsory Service Bill, they may be defeated by this combination, in which case there would be a general election on the question; and at this general election the contest would not be between the Labor Party and the Capitalists, but between the Conservative or Trade Unionist wing of the Labor Party, which would be called the Right, and the Socialist wing, which would be called the Left. So that even if the present Conservatives be wiped out of Parliament there may still be two parties contending for power; and the Intelligent Woman may be canvassed to vote Right or Left, or perhaps White or Red, just as she is now canvassed to vote Conservative or Labor.

74

RELIGIOUS DISSENSIONS

HOWEVER, two parties would not hurt the House of Commons, as it is worked by the division of the members into two sets, one carrying on the government and the other continually criticizing it and trying to oust it and become itself the Government. This two-division system is not really a two-party system in the sense that the two divisions represent different policies: they may differ about nothing but the desire for office. From the proletarian point of view the difference between Liberals and Conservatives since 1832 has been a difference between Tweedledum and Tweedledee. But this did not matter, because the essence of the arrangement is that the Government shall be unsparingly and unceasingly criticized by a rival set of politicians who are determined to pick every possible hole in its proceedings. Government and Opposition might be called Performance and Criticism, the performers and critics changing places whenever the country is convinced that the critics are right and the performers wrong.

The division of the House of Commons into two parties with different policies suits this situation very well. But its division into half a dozen parties would not suit it at all, and might, as we have seen, deadlock parliamentary government altogether. Now there is abundant material for a dozen parties in the British proletariat. Take the subject of religion, inextricably bound up with the parliamentary question of education in public elementary schools. It is unlikely that a Proletarian House of Commons will suffer the nation's children to go on being taught Capitalist and

Imperialist morality in the disguise of religion; and yet, the moment the subject is touched, what a hornet's nest is stirred up! Parents are inveterate proselytizers: they take it as a matter of course that they have a right to dictate their children's religion. This right was practically undisputed, unless the parents were professed atheists, when all children who had any schooling went either to Biblical private schools or to public schools and universities where the established religion was the State religion. Nowadays Unitarian schools, Quaker schools, Roman Catholic schools, Methodist schools, Theosophist schools, and even Communist schools may be chosen by parents and guardians (not by the children) to suit their own private religious eccentricities.

But when schooling is made a national industry, and the Government sets up schools all over the country, and imposes daily attendance on the huge majority of children whose parents cannot afford to send their children to any but the State school, a conflict arises over the souls of the children. What religion is to be taught in the State school? The Roman Catholics try to keep their children out of the State school (they must send them to some school or other) by subscribing money themselves to maintain Roman Catholic schools alongside the State schools; and the other denominations, including the Church of England, do the same. But unless they receive State aid: that is, money provided by taxing and rating all citizens indiscriminately, they cannot afford to take in all the children, or to keep up to a decent standard the schooling of those whom they do take in. And the moment it is proposed to give them money out of the rates and taxes, the trouble begins. Rather than pay rates to be used in making Roman Catholics or even Anglo-Catholics of little English children, Nonconformist Protestant ratepayers will let themselves be haled before the magistrates and allow their furniture to be sold up. They would go to the stake if that were the alternative to paying Peter's Pence to the Scarlet Woman and setting children's feet in the way to eternal damnation. For it is not in Ireland alone that Protestants and Roman Catholics believe each that the other will spend eternity immersed in burning brimstone. Church of England zealots hold that belief even more convincedly about village Dissenters than about Roman Catholics.

The opinions of the parties are so irreconcilable, and the passion of their hostility so fierce, that the Government, when it is once committed to general compulsory education, either directly in its own schools or by subsidies to other schools, finds itself driven to devise some sort of neutral religion that will suit everybody, or else forbid all mention of the subject in school. An example of the first expedient is the Cowper-Temple clause in the Education Act of 1870, which ordains that the Bible shall be read in schools without reference to any creed or catechism peculiar "to any one denomination". The total prohibition expedient is known as Secular Education, and has been tried extensively in Australia.

The Cowper-Temple plan does not meet the case of the Roman Catholics, who do not permit indiscriminate access to the Bible, nor of the Jews, who can hardly be expected to accept the reading of the New Testament as religious instruction. Besides, if the children are to learn anything more than the three Rs, they must be taught Copernican astronomy, electronic physics, and evolution. Now it is not good sense to lead a child at ten o'clock to attach religious importance to the belief that the earth is flat and immovable, and the sky a ceiling above it in which there is a heaven furnished like a king's palace, and, at eleven, that the earth is a sphere spinning on its axis and rushing round the sun in limitless space with a multitude of other spheres. Nor can you reasonably order that during the religious instruction hour the children are to be informed that all forms of life were created within six days, including the manufacture of a full-grown woman out of a man's rib, and, when the clock strikes, begin explaining that epochs of millions of years were occupied in experiments in the production of various forms of life, from prodigious monsters to invisibly small creatures, culminating in a very complicated and by no means finally satisfactory form called Woman, who specialized a variety of herself, in some respects even less satisfactory, called Man. This would not matter if the teacher might explain that as the astronomy and biology of the Bible are out of date, and we think we know better nowadays, they have been discarded like the barbarous morality of the Israelitish kings and the idol to which they made human sacrifices. But such explanations would frustrate the Cowper-Temple clause, under which the children were to be left to make what they could of the contradictions between their religious and secular instruction. They usually solve it by not thinking about it at all, provided their parents let them alone on the subject, which is not always the case.

As to the alternative of giving no religious instruction, and confining school teaching to what is called Secular or Matter-of-Fact Education, it is not really a possible plan, because children must be taught conduct as well as arithmetic, and the ultimate sanctions of conduct are metaphysical, by which imposing phrase I mean that from the purely matter-of-fact point of view there is no difference between a day's thieving and a day's honest work, between placid ignorance and the pursuit of knowledge for its own sake, between habitual lying and truth-telling: they are all human activities or inactivities, to be chosen according to their respective pleasantness or material advantages, and not to be preferred on any other grounds. When you find your children acting, as they often do (like their elders), quite secularly, and lying, stealing, or idling, you have to give them either a matter-of-fact or a religious reason for ceasing to do evil and learning to do well. The matter-of-fact reason is temptingly easy to manufacture. You can say "If I catch you doing that again I will clout your head, or smack your behind, or send you to bed without your supper, or injure you in some way or other that you will not like". Unfortunately these secular reasons, though easy to devise and apply, and enjoyable if you have a turn that way, always seem avoidable by cunning concealment and a little additional lying. You know what becomes of the pseudo-morality produced by whipping the moment your back is turned. And what is your own life worth if it has to be spent spying on your children with a cane in your hand? Hardly worth living, I should say, unless you are one of the people who love caning as others love unnatural sensualities, in which case you may fall into the hands of the Society for the Prevention of Cruelty to Children, which will make short work of your moral pretensions. In any case you will find yourself strongly tempted to whack your children, not really to compel them to conduct themselves for their own good, but to conduct themselves in the manner most convenient to yourself, which is not always nor even often the same thing.

Finally, if you are not selfish and cruel, you will find that you must give the children some reason for behaving well when no one is looking, and there is no danger of being found out, or when they would rather do the forbidden thing at the cost of a whacking than leave it undone with impunity. You may tell them that God is always looking, and will punish them inevitably when they die. But you will find that posthumous penalties are not immediate enough nor real enough to deter a bold child. In the end you must threaten it with some damage to a part of it called its soul, of the existence of which you can give it no physical demonstration whatever. You need not use the word soul: you can put the child "on its honor". But its honor also is an organ which no anatomist has yet succeeded in dissecting out and preserving in a bottle of spirits of wine for the instruction of infants. When it transgresses you can resort to scolding, calling it a naughty, dirty, greedy little thing. Or you may lecture it, telling it solemnly that "it is a sin to steal a pin" and so forth. But if you could find such a monster as an entirely matter-of-fact child, it might receive both scoldings and lectures unmoved, and ask you "What then? What is a sin? What do you mean by naughty, greedy? I understand dirty; but why should I wash my hands if I am quite comfortable with them dirty. I understand greedy; but if I like chocolates why should I give half of them to Jane?" You may retort with "Have you no conscience, child?"; but the matter-of-fact reply is "What is conscience?" Faced with this matter-of-fact scepticism you are driven into pure metaphysics, and must teach your child that conduct is a matter, not of fact, but of religious duty. Good conduct is a respect which you owe to yourself in some mystical way; and people are manageable in proportion to their possession of this self-respect. When you remonstrate with a grown-up person you say "Have you no self-respect?" But somehow one does not say that to an infant. If it tells a lie, you do not say "You owe it to yourself to speak the truth", because the little animal does not feel any such obligation, though it will later on. If you say "You must not tell lies because if you do nobody will believe what you say", you are conscious of telling a thundering lie yourself, as you know only too well that most lies are quite successful, and that human society would be impossible without a great deal of goodnatured lying. If you say "You must not tell lies because if you do you will find yourself unable to believe anything that is told to you", you will be much nearer the truth; but it is a truth that a child cannot understand: you might as well tell it the final truth of the matter, which is, that there is a mysterious something in us called a soul, which deliberate wickedness kills, and without which no material gain can make life bearable. How can you expect a naughty child to take that in? If you say "You must not tell a lie because it will grieve your dear parents", the effect will depend on how much the child cares whether its parents are grieved or not. In any case to most young children their parents are as gods, too great to be subject to grief, as long as the parents play up to that conception of them. Also, as it is not easy to be both loved and feared, parents who put on the majesty of gods with their children must not allow the familiarity of affection, and are lucky if their children do not positively hate them. It is safer and more comfortable to invent a parent who is everybody's Big Papa, even Papa's papa, and introduce it to the child as God. And it must be a god that children can imagine. It must not be an abstraction, a principle, a vital impulse, a life force, or the Church of England god who has neither body, parts, nor passions. It must be, like the real papa, a grown-up person in Sunday clothes, very very good, terribly powerful, and all-seeing: that is, able to see what you are doing when nobody is looking. In this way the child who is too young to have a sufficiently developed self-respect and intelligent sense of honor: in short, a conscience, is provided with an artificial, provisional, and to a great extent fictitious conscience which tides it over its nonage until it is old enough to attach a serious meaning to the idea of God.

In this way it was discovered in the nursery, long before Voltaire said it, that "if there were no God it would be necessary to invent Him". After Voltaire's death, when the government of France fell into the hands of a set of very high-principled professional and middle-class gentlemen who had no experience of government, and ended by making such a mess of it that France would have been ruined if they had not fortunately all cut oneanother's heads off on the highest principles, the most high-principled of them all, an intensely respectable lawyer named

Robespierre, who had tried to govern without God because a good many of the stories told to children about God were evidently not strictly true, found that governments dealing with nations could no more do without God than parents dealing with their families. He, too, declared, echoing Voltaire, that if there were no God it would be necessary to invent one. He had previously, by the way, tried a goddess whom he called the Goddess of Reason; but she was no use at all, not because she was a goddess (for Roman Catholic children have a Big Mamma, or Mamma's mamma, who is everybody's mamma, and makes the boys easier to manage, as well as a Big Papa), but because good conduct is not dictated by reason but by a divine instinct that is beyond reason. Reason only discovers the shortest way: it does not discover the destination. It would be quite reasonable for you to pick your neighbor's pocket if you felt sure that you could make a better use of your money than she could; but somehow it would not be honorable; and honor is a part of divinity: it is metaphysics: it is religion. Some day it may become scientific psychology; but psychology is as yet in its crudest infancy; and when it grows up it will very likely be too difficult not only for children but for many adults, like the rest of the more abstruse sciences.

Meanwhile we must bear in mind that our beliefs are continually passing from the metaphysical and legendary into the scientific stage. In China, when an eclipse of the sun occurs, all the intelligent and energetic women rush out of doors with pokers and shovels, trays and saucepan lids, and bang them together to frighten away the demon who is devouring the sun; and the perfect success of this proceeding, which has never been known to fail, proves to them that it is the right thing to do. But you, who know all about eclipses, sit calmly looking at them through bits of smoked glass, because your belief about them is a scientific belief and not a metaphysical one. You probably think that the women who are banging the saucepans in China are fools; but they are not: you would do the same yourself if you lived in a country where astronomy was still in the metaphysical stage.

You must also beware of concluding, because their conduct seems to you ridiculous, and because you know that there is no demon, that there is no eclipse. You may say that nobody could make a mistake like that; but I assure you that a great many people, seeing how many childish fables and ridiculous ceremonies have been attached to the conception of divinity, have rushed to the conclusion that no such thing as divinity exists. When they grow out of believing that God is an old gentleman with a white beard, they think they have got rid of everything that the old gentleman represented to their infant minds. On the contrary, they have come a little nearer to the truth about it.

Now the English nation consists of many million parents and children of whom hardly any two are in precisely the same stage of belief as to the sanctions of good conduct. Many of the parents are still in the nursery stage: many of the children are in the comparatively scientific stage. Most of them do not bother much about it, and just do what their neighbors do and say they believe what most of their neighbors say they believe. But those who do bother about it differ very widely and differ very fiercely. Take those who, rejecting the first article of the Church of England, attach to the word God the conception of a Ruler of the universe with the body, parts, and passions of man, but with unlimited knowledge and power. Here at least, you might think, we have agreement. But no. There are two very distinct parties to this faith. One of them believes in a God of Wrath, imposing good conduct on us by threats of casting us for ever into an inconceivably terrible hell. Others believe in a God of Love, and openly declare that if they could be brought to believe in a God capable of such cruelty as hell implies, they would spit in his face. Others hold that conduct has nothing to do with the matter, and that though hell exists, anyone, however wicked, can avoid it by believing that God accepted the cruel death of his own son as an expiation of their misdeeds, whilst nobody, however virtuous, can avoid it if she has the slightest doubt on this point. Others declare that neither conduct nor belief has anything to do with it, as every person is from birth predestined to fall into hell or mount into heaven when they die, and that nothing that they can say or do or believe or disbelieve can help them. Voltaire described us as a people with thirty religions and only one sauce; and though this was a great compliment to the activity and independence of our minds, it held out no hope of our ever agreeing about religion.

Even if we could confine religious instruction to subjects which are supposed to have passed from the metaphysical to the scientific stage, which is what the advocates of secular education mean, we should be no nearer to unanimity; for not only do our scientific bigots differ as fiercely as those of the sects and churches, and try to obtain powers of ruthless persecution from the Government, but their pretended advances from the metaphysical to the scientific are often disguised relapses into the pre-metaphysical stage of crude witchcraft, ancient augury, and African "medicine".

Roughly speaking, governments in imposing education on the people have to deal with three fanaticisms: first, that which believes in a God of Wrath, and sees in every earthquake, every pestilence, every war: in short, every calamity of impressive or horrifying magnitude, a proof of God's terrible power and a warning to sinners; second, that which believes in a God of Love in conflict with a Power of Evil personified as the Devil; and third, that of the magicians and their dupes, believing neither in God nor devil, claiming that the pursuit of knowledge is absolutely free from moral law, however atrocious its methods, and pretending to work miracles (called "the marvels of science") by which they hold the keys of life and death, and can make mankind immune from disease if they are given absolute control over our bodies.

A good many women are still so primitive and personal in religious matters that their first impulse on hearing them discussed at all is to declare that their beliefs are the only true beliefs, and must of course be imposed on everyone, all other beliefs to be punished as monstrous blasphemies. They do not regard Jehovah, Allah, Brahma, as different names for God: if they call God Brahma they regard Allah and Jehovah as abominable idols, and all Christians and Moslems as wicked idolaters whom no repectable person would visit. Or if Jehovah, they class Moslems and Indians as "the heathen", and send out missionaries to convert them. But this childish self-conceit would wreck the British Empire if our rulers indulged it. Only about 11 per cent of British subjects are Christians: the enormous majority of them call God Allah or Brahma, and either do not distinguish Jesus from any other prophet or have never even heard of him. Consequently when a woman goes into Parliament, central or local, she should leave the sectarian part of her religion behind her, and consider only that part of it which is common to all the sects and Churches, however the names may differ. Unfortunately this is about the last thing that most elected persons ever dream of doing. They all strive to impose their local customs, names, institutions, and even languages on the schoolchildren by main force.

Now there is this to be said for their efforts, that all progress consists in imposing on children nobler beliefs and better institutions than those at present inculcated and established. For instance, as every Socialist believes that Communism is more nobly inspired and better in practice than private property and competition, her object in entering Parliament is to impose that belief on her country by having it taught to the children in the public schools so that they may grow up to regard it as the normal obvious truth, and to abhor Capitalism as a disastrous idolatry. At present she finds herself opposed by statesmen who quite lately spent a hundred millions of English public money in subsidizing military raids on the Russian Government because it was a Socialist Government. To such statesmen Socialist, Communist, Bolshevist, are synonyms for Scoundrel, Thief, Assassin. In opposition to them the Socialists compare Labor exploited by landlords and capitalists to Christ crucified between two thieves. They both say that we no longer persecute in the name of religion; but this means only that they refuse to call the creeds they are persecuting religions, whilst the beliefs they do call religions have become comparatively indifferent to them. To put down sedition, rebellion, and attacks on property, or, on the other hand, to make an end of the robbery of the poor, suppress shameless idleness, and restore the land of our country, which God made for us all, to the whole people, seems simple enforcement of the moral law, and not persecution; therefore those who do it are not, they think, persecutors, to prove which they point to the fact that they allow us all to go to church or not as we please, and to believe or disbelieve in transubstantiation according to our fancy. Do not be deceived by modern professions of toleration. Women are still what they were when the Tudor sisters sent Protestants to the stake and Jesuits to the rack and gallows; when the defenders of property and slavery in Rome set up crosses along the public roads with the crucified followers of the revolted gladiator slave Spartacus dying horribly upon them in thousands; and when the saintly Torquemada burnt alive every Jew he could lay hands on as piously as he told his beads. The difference between the Socialist versus Capitalist controversy and the Jew versus Christian controversy or the Roman Catholic versus Protestant controversy is not that the modern bigot is any more tolerant or less cruel than her ancestors, nor even that the proletarians are too numerous and the proprietors too powerful to be persecuted. If the controversy between them could be settled by either party exterminating the other, they would both do their worst to settle it in that way. History leaves us no goodnatured illusions on this point. From the wholesale butcheries which followed the suppression of the Paris Commune of 1871 to the monstrous and quite gratuitous persecution of Russians in the United States of America after the war of 1914-18, in which girls were sentenced to frightful terms of imprisonment for remarks that might have been made by any Sunday School teacher, there is abundant evidence that modern diehards are no better than medieval zealots, and that if they are to be restrained from deluging the world in blood and torture in the old fashion it will not be by any imaginary advance in toleration or in humanity. At this moment (1927) our proprietary classes appear to have no other conception of the Russian Soviet Government and its sympathizers than as vermin to be ruthlessly exterminated; and when the Russian Communist and his western imitators speak of the proprietors and their political supporters as "bourgeois", they make no secret of regarding them as enemies of the human race. The spirit of the famous manifesto of 1792, in which the Duke of Brunswick, in the name of the monarchs of Europe, announced that he meant to exterminate the French Republican Government and deliver up the cities which tolerated it to "military execution and total subversion", is reflected precisely in the speeches made by our own statesmen in support of the projected expedition against the Union of Soviet Republics which was countermanded a few years ago only because the disapproval of the British proletarian voters became so obvious that the preparations for the Capitalist Crusade had to be hastily dropped.

It is therefore very urgently necessary that I should explain to you why it is that a Labor Party can neither establish Socialism by exterminating its opponents, nor its opponents avert Socialism by exterminating the Socialists.

75

REVOLUTIONS

YOU must first grasp the difference between revolutions and social changes. A revolution transfers political power from one party to another, or one class to another, or even one individual to another, just as a conquest transfers it from one nation or race to another. It can be and often is effected by violence or the threat of violence. Of our two revolutions in the seventeenth century, by which political power in England was transferred from the throne to the House of Commons, the first cost a civil war; and the second was bloodless only because the King ran away. A threat of violence was sufficient to carry the nineteenth century revolution of 1832, by which the political power was transferred from the great agricultural landowners to the industrial urban employers. The South American revolutions which substitute one party or one President for another are general elections decided by shooting instead of by voting.

Now the transfer of political power from our capitalists to our proletariat, without which Socialist propaganda would be suppressed by the Government as sedition, and Socialist legislation would be impossible, has already taken place in form. The proletarians can outvote the capitalists overwhelmingly whenever they choose to do so. If on the issue of Socialism versus Capitalism all the proletarians were for Socialism and all the capitalists for Capitalism, Capitalism would have had to capitulate to overwhelming numbers long ago. But the proletarians who live upon the incomes of the capitalists as their servants, their tradesmen, their employees in the luxury trades, their lawyers and doctors and so on, not to mention the troops raised, equipped, and paid by them to defend their property (in America there are private armies of this kind) are more violently Conservative than the capitalists themselves, many of whom, like Robert Owen and

William Morris, not to mention myself, have been and are ardent Socialists. The Countess of Warwick is a noted Socialist; so you have seen a Socialist Countess (or at least her picture); but have you ever seen a countess's dressmaker who was a Socialist? If the capitalists refused to accept a parliamentary decision against them, and took to arms, like Charles I, they would have in many places a majority of the proletariat on their side.

If you are shocked by the suggestion that our capitalists would act so unconstitutionally, consider the case of Ireland, in which after thirty years of parliamentary action, and an apparently final settlement of the Home Rule question by Act of Parliament, the establishment of the Irish Free State was effected by fire and slaughter, the winning side being that which succeeded in burning the larger number of the houses of its opponents.

Parliamentary constitutionalism holds good up to a certain point: the point at which the people who are outvoted in Parliament will accept their defeat. But on many questions people feel so strongly, or have such big interests at stake, that they leave the decision to Parliament only as long as they think they will win there. If Parliament decides against them, and they see any chance of a successful resistance, they throw Parliament over and fight it out. During the thirty years of the parliamentary campaign for Irish Home Rule there were always Direct Action men who said "It is useless to go to the English Parliament: the Unionists will never give up their grip of Ireland until they are forced to; and you may as well fight it out first as last". And these men, though denounced as wanton incendiaries, turned out to be right. The French had to cut off the heads of both king and queen because the king could not control the queen, and the queen would not accept a constitutional revolution, nor stop trying to induce the other kings of Europe to march their armies into France and slaughter the Liberals for her. In England we beheaded our king because he would not keep faith with the Liberal Parliament even after he had fought it and lost. In Spain at this moment the King and the army have suppressed Parliament, and are ruling by force of arms on the basis of divine right, which is exactly what Cromwell did in England after he had cut off King Charles's head for trying to do the same. Signor Mussolini, a

Socialist, has overridden parliament in Italy, his followers having established what is called a reign of terror by frank violence.

These repudiations of constitutionalism in Spain and Italy have been made, not to effect any definite social change, but because the Spanish and Italian governments had become so unbearably inefficient that the handiest way to restore public order was for some sufficiently energetic individuals to take the law into their own hands and just break people's heads if they would not behave themselves. And it may quite possibly happen that even if the most perfect set of Fabian Acts of Parliament for the constitutional completion of Socialism in this country be passed through Parliament by duly elected representatives of the people; swallowed with wry faces by the House of Lords; and finally assented to by the King and placed on the statute book, the capitalists may, like Signor Mussolini, denounce Parliament as unpatriotic, pernicious, and corrupt, and try to prevent by force the execution of the Fabian Acts. We should then have a state of civil war, with, no doubt, the Capitalist forces burning the co-operative stores, and the proletarians burning the country houses, as in Ireland, in addition to the usual war routine of devastation and slaughter.

As we have seen, the capitalists would be at no loss for proletarian troops. The war would not be as the Marxist doctrinaires of the Class War seem to imagine. In our examination of the effect of unequal distribution of income we found that it is not only the rich who live on the poor, but also the servants and tradesmen who live on the money the rich spend, and who have their own servants and tradesmen. In the rich suburbs and fashionable central quarters of the great cities, and all over the South of England where pleasant country houses are dotted over the pleasantest of the English counties, it is as hard to get a Labor candidate into Parliament as in Oxford University. If the unearned incomes of the rich disappeared, places like Bournemouth would either perish like the cities of Nineveh and Babylon, or else the inhabitants would have, as they would put it, to cater for a different class of people; and many of them would be ruined before they could adapt themselves to the new conditions. Add to these the young men who are out of employment, and will fight for anyone who will pay them well for an exciting adventure, with all the people who dread change of any sort, or who are duped by the newspapers into thinking Socialists scoundrels, or who would be too stupid to understand such a book as this if they could be persuaded to read anything but a cheap newspaper; and you will see at once that the line that separates those who live on rich customers from those who live on poor customers: in other words which separates those interested in the maintenance of Capitalism from those interested in its replacement by Socialism, is a line drawn not between rich and poor, capitalist and proletarian, but right down through the middle of the proletariat to the bottom of the very poorest section. In a civil war for the maintenance of Capitalism the capitalists would therefore find masses of supporters in all ranks of the community; and it is their knowledge of this that makes the leaders of the Labor Party so impatient with the extremists who talk of such a war as if it would be a Class War, and echo Shelley's very misleading couplet "Ye are many: they are few". And as the capitalists know it too, being reminded of it by the huge number of votes given for them by the poor at every election, I cannot encourage you to feel too sure that their present denunciations of Direct Action by their opponents mean that when their own sooner-or-later inevitable defeat by Labor in Parliament comes, they will take it lying down.

But no matter how the government of the country may pass from the hands of the capitalists into those of the Socialist proletarians, whether by peaceful parliamentary procedure or the bloodiest conceivable civil war, at the end of it the survivors will be just where they were at the beginning as far as practical Communism is concerned. Returning a majority of Socialists to Parliament will not by itself reconstruct the whole economic system of the country in such a way as to produce equality of income. Still less will burning and destroying buildings or killing several of the opponents of Socialism, and getting several Socialists killed in doing so. You cannot wave a wand over the country and say "Let there be Socialism": at least nothing will happen if you do.

The case of Russia illustrates this. After the great political revolution of 1917 in that country, the Marxist Communists were so completely victorious that they were able to form a Government far more powerful than the Tsar had ever really been. But as the Tsar had not allowed Fabian Societies to be formed in Russia to reduce Socialism to a system of law, this new Russian Government did not know what to do, and, after trying all sorts of amateur experiments which came to nothing more than pretending that there was Communism where there was nothing but the wreck of Capitalism, and giving the land to the peasants, who immediately insisted on making private property of it over again, had to climb down hastily and leave the industry of the country to private employers very much as the great ground landlords of our cities leave the work of the shops to their tenants, besides allowing the peasant farmers to hold their lands and sell their produce just as French peasant proprietors or English farmers do.

This does not mean that the Russian Revolution has been a failure. In Russia it is now established that capital was made for Man, and not Man for Capitalism. The children are taught the Christian morality of Communism instead of the Mammonist morality of Capitalism. The palaces and pleasure seats of the plutocrats are used for the recreation of workers instead of for the enervation of extravagant wasters. Idle ladies and gentlemen are treated with salutary contempt, whilst the worker's blouse is duly honored. The treasures of art, respected and preserved with a cultural conscientiousness which puts to shame our own lootings in China, and our iconoclasms and vandalisms at home, are accessible to everyone. The Greek Church is tolerated (the Bolsheviks forbore to cut off their Archbishop's head as we cut off Archbishop Laud's) ; but it is not, as the Church of England is, allowed without contradiction to tell little children lies about the Bible under pretence of giving them religious instruction, nor to teach them to reverence the merely rich as their betters. That sort of doctrine is officially and very properly disavowed as Dope.

All this seems to us too good to be true. It places the Soviet Government in the forefront of cultural civilization as far as good intention goes. But it is not Socialism. It still involves sufficient inequality of income to undo in the long run enough of its achievements to degrade the Communist Republic to the level of the old Capitalist Republics of France and America. In short, though it has made one of those transfers of political power which are the object of revolutions, and are forced through by simple slaughter and terror, and though this political transfer has increased Russian self-respect and changed the moral attitude of the Russian State from pro-Capitalist to anti-Capitalist, it has not yet established as much actual Communism as we have in England, nor even raised Russian wages to the English level.

The explanation of this is that Communism can spread only as Capitalism spread: that is, as a development of existing economic civilization and not by a sudden wholesale overthrow of it. What it proposes is not a destruction of the material utilities inherited from Capitalism, but a new way of managing them and distributing the wealth they produce. Now this development of Capitalism into a condition of ripeness for Socialization had not been reached in Russia; consequently the victorious Communist Bolsheviks in 1917 found themselves without any highly organized Capitalistic industry to build upon. They had on their hands an enormous agricultural country with a population of uncivilized peasants, ignorant, illiterate, superstitious, cruel, and land-hungry. The cities, few and far between, with their relatively insignificant industries, often managed by foreigners, and their city proletariats living on family wages of five and threepence a week, were certainly in revolt against the misdistribution of wealth and leisure; but they were so far from being organized to begin Socialism that it was only in a very limited sense that they could be said to have begun urban civilization. There were no Port Sunlights and Bournvilles, no Ford factories in which workmen earn £9 in a five-day week and have their own motor cars, no industrial trusts of national dimensions, no public libraries, no great public departments manned by picked and tested civil servants, no crowds of men skilled in industrial management and secretarial business looking for employment, no nationalized and municipalized services with numerous and competent official staffs, no national insurance, no great Trade Union organization representing many millions of workmen and able to extort subsidies from Capitalist governments by threatening to stop the railways and cut off the coal supply, no fifty years of compulsory schooling supplemented by forty years of incessant propaganda of political science by Fabian and other lecturers, no overwhelming predominance of organized industry over individualist agriculture, no obvious breakdown of Capitalism under the strain of the war, no triumphant rescue by Socialism demonstrating that even those public departments that were bywords for incompetence and red tape were far more efficient than the commercial adventurers who derided them. Well may Mr Trotsky say that the secret of the completeness of the victory of the Russian Proletarian Revolution over Russian Capitalist civilization was that there was virtually no Capitalist civilization to triumph over, and that the Russian people had been saved from the corruption of bourgeois ideas, not by the famous metaphysical dialectic inherited by Marx from the philosopher Hegel, but by the fact that they are still primitive enough to be incapable of middle class ideas. In England, when Socialism is consummated it will plant the red flag on the summit of an already constructed pyramid; but the Russians have to build right up from the sand. We must build up Capitalism before we can turn it into Socialism. But meanwhile we must learn how to control it instead of letting it demoralize us, slaughter us, and half ruin us, as we have hitherto done in our ignorance.

Thus the fact that the Soviet has had to resort to controlled Capitalism and bourgeois enterprise, after denouncing them so fiercely under the Tsardom in the phrases used by Marx to denounce English Capitalism, does not mean that we shall have to recant in the same way when we complete our transfer of political power from the proprietary classes and their retainers to the Socialist proletariat. The Capitalism which the Russian Government is not only tolerating but encouraging would be for us, even now under Capitalism, an attempt to set back the clock. We could not get back to it if we tried, except by smashing our machinery, breaking up our industrial organization, burning all the plans and documents from which it could be reconstructed, and substituting an eighteenth for a twentieth century population.

The moral of all this is that though a political revolution may be necessary to break the power of the opponents of Socialism if they refuse to accept it as a Parliamentary reform, and resist it violently either by organizing what is now called Fascism or a *coup d'état* to establish a Dictatorship of the Capitalists, yet neither a violent revolution nor a peacefully accepted series of parliamentary reforms can by themselves create Socialism, which is neither a battle cry nor an election catchword, but an elaborate arrangement of our production and distribution of wealth in such a manner that all our incomes shall be equal. This is why Socialists who understand their business are always against bloodshed. They are no milder than other people; but they know that bloodshed cannot do what they want, and that the indiscriminate destruction inseparable from civil war will retard it. Mr Sidney Webb's much quoted and in some quarters much derided "inevitability of gradualness" is an inexorable fact. It does not, unfortunately, imply inevitability of peacefulness. We can fight over every step of the gradual process if we are foolish enough. We shall come to an armed struggle for political power between the parasitic proletariat and the Socialist proletariat if the Capitalist leaders of the parasitic proletariat throw Parliament and the Constitution over, and declare for a blood and iron settlement instead of a settlement by votes. But at the end of the fighting we shall all be the poorer, none the wiser, and some of us the deader. If the Socialists win, the road to Socialism may be cleared; but the pavement will be torn up and the goal as far off as ever.

All the historical precedents illustrate this. A monarchy may be changed into a republic, or an oligarchy into a democracy, or one oligarchy supplanted by another, if the people who favor the change kill enough of the people who oppose it to intimidate the rest; and when the change is made you may have factions fighting instead of voting for the official posts of power and honor until, as in South America in the nineteenth century, violent revolutions become so common that other countries hardly notice them; but no extremity of fighting and killing can alter the distribution of wealth or the means of producing it. The guillotining of 4000 people in eighteen months during the French Revolution left the people poorer than before; so that when the Public Prosecutor who had sent most of the 4000 to the guillotine was sent there himself, and the people cursed him as he passed to his death, he said, "Will your bread be any cheaper tomorrow, you fools?" That did not affect the Capitalist makers of the French Revolution, because they did not want to make the bread of the poor cheaper: they wanted to transfer the government of France from the King and the nobles to the middle class. But if they had been

Socialists, aiming at making everything much cheaper except human life, they would have had to admit that the laugh was with Citizen Fouquier Tinville. And if William Pitt and the kings of Europe had let the French Revolution alone, and it had been as peaceful and parliamentary as our own revolutionary Reform Bill of 1832, it would have been equally futile as far as putting another pennorth of milk into baby's mug was concerned.

Whenever our city proletarians, in the days before the dole (say 1885 for instance), were driven by unemployment to threaten to burn down the houses of the rich, the Socialists said "No: if you are foolish enough to suppose that burning houses will put an end to unemployment, at least have sense enough to burn down your own houses, most of which are unfit for human habitation. The houses of the rich are good houses, of which we have much too few." Capitalism has produced not only slums but palaces and handsome villas, not only sweaters' dens but first-rate factories, shipyards, steamships, ocean cables, services that are not only national but international, and what not. It has also produced a great deal of Communism, without which it could not exist for a single day (we need not go over all the examples already given: the roads and bridges and so forth). What Socialist in his senses would welcome a civil war that would destroy all or any of this, and leave his party, even if it were victorious, a heritage of blackened ruins and festering cemeteries? Capitalism has led up to Socialism by changing the industries of the country from petty enterprises conducted by petty proprietors into huge Trusts conducted by employed proletarians directing armies of workmen, operating with millions of capital on vast acreages of land. In short, Capitalism tends always to develop industries until they are on the scale of public affairs and ripe for transfer to public hands. To destroy them would be to wreck the prospects of Socialism. Even the proprietors who think that such a transfer would be robbery have at least the consolation of knowing that the thief does not destroy the property of the man he intends to rob, being as much interested in it as the person from whom he means to steal it. As to managing persons, Socialism will need many more of them than there are at present, and will give them much greater security in their jobs and dignity in their social standing than most of them can hope for under Capitalism.

And now I think we may dismiss the question whether the return of a decisive majority of Socialists to Parliament will pass without an appeal to unconstitutional violence by the capitalists and their supporters. Whether it does or not may matter a good deal to those unlucky persons who will lose their possessions or their lives in the struggle if there be a struggle; but when the shouting and the killing and the house burning are over the survivors must settle down to some stable form of government. The mess may have to be cleared up by a dictatorship like that of Napoleon the Third, King Alfonso, Cromwell, Napoleon, Mussolini, or Lenin; but dictatorial strong men soon die or lose their strength, and kings, generals, and proletarian dictators alike find that they cannot carry on for long without councils or parliaments of some sort, and that these will not work unless they are in some way representative of the public, because unless the citizens co-operate with the police the strongest government breaks down, as English government did in Ireland.

In the long run (which nowadays is a very short run) you must have your parliament and your settled constitution back again; and the risings and *coups d'état,* with all their bloodshed and burnings and executions, might as well have been cut out as far as the positive constructive work of Socialism is concerned. So we may just as well ignore all the battles that may or may not be fought, and go on to consider what may happen to the present Labor Party if its present constitutional growth be continued and consummated by the achievement of a decisive Socialist majority in Parliament, and its resumption of office, not, as in 1923-24, by the sufferance of the two Capitalist parties and virtually under their control, but with full power to carry out a proletarian policy, and, if it will, to make Socialism the established constitutional order in Britain.

CHANGE MUST BE PARLIAMENTARY

LET us assume, then, that we have resigned ourselves, as we must sooner or later, to a parliamentary settlement of the quarrels between the Capitalists and the Socialists. Mind: I cannot, women and men being what they are, offer you any sincere assurances that this will occur without all the customary devilments. Every possible wrong and wicked way may be tried before their exhaustion drives us back into the right way. Attempts at a general strike, a form of national suicide which sane people are bound to resist by every extremity of violent coercion, may lead to a proclamation of martial law by the Government, whether it be a Labor or a Capitalist Government, followed by slaughtering of mobs, terroristic shelling of cities (as in the case of Dublin), burning and looting of country houses, shooting of police officers at sight as uniformed enemies of the people, and a hectic time for those to whom hating and fighting and killing are a glorious sport that makes life worth living and death worth dying. Or if the modern machine gun, the bombing aeroplane, and the poison gas shell make military coercion irresistible, or if the general strikers have sufficient sense shot into them to see that blockade and boycott are not good tactics for the productive proletariat because they themselves are necessarily the first victims of it, still Parliament may be so split up into contending groups as to become unworkable, forcing the nation to fall back on a dictatorship. The dictator may be another Bismarck ruling in the name of a royal personage, or a forceful individual risen from the ranks like Mahomet or Brigham Young or Signor Mussolini, or a general like Cæsar or Napoleon or Primo di Rivera.

In the course of these social convulsions you and I may be outraged, shot, gas poisoned, burnt out of house and home, financially ruined, just as anyone else may. We must resign ourselves to such epidemics of human pugnacity and egotism just as we have to resign ourselves to epidemics of measles. Measles are less bitter to us because we have at least never done anything to encourage them, whereas we have recklessly taught our children to glorify pugnacity and to identify gentility and honor with the keeping down of the poor and the keeping up of the rich, thus producing an insanitary condition of public morals which makes periodic epidemics of violence and class hatred inevitable.

But sooner or later, the irreconcilables exterminate oneanother like the Kilkenny cats; for when the toughest faction has exterminated all the other factions it proceeds to exterminate itself. And the dictators die as Cromwell died, or grow old and are sent to the dustbin by ambitious young monarchs as Bismarck was; and dictators and ambitious monarchs alike find that autocracy is not today a practical form of government except in little tribes like Brigham Young's Latter Day Saints, nor even complete there. The nearest thing to it that will now hold together is the presidency of the United States of America; and the President, autocrat as he is for his four years of office, has to work with a Cabinet, deal with a Congress and a Senate, and abide the result of popular elections. To this parliamentary complexion we must all come at last. Every bumptious idiot thinks himself a born ruler of men; every snob thinks that the common people must be kept in their present place or shot down if society is to be preserved; every proletarian who resents his position wants to strike at something or somebody more vulnerable than the capitalist system in the abstract; but when they have all done their worst the dead they have slain must be buried, the houses they have burned rebuilt, and the hundred other messes they have left cleared up by women and men with sense enough to take counsel together without coming to blows, and business ability enough to organize the work of the community. These sensible ones may not always have been sensible: some of them may have done their full share of mischief before the necessary sanity was branded into them by bitter experience or horrified contemplation of the results of anarchy; but between the naturally sensible people and the chastened ones there will finally be some sort of Parliament to conduct the nation's business, unless indeed civilization has been so completely wrecked in the preliminary quarrels that there is no nation worth troubling about left, and consequently no national business to transact. That has often happened.

However, let us put all disagreeable possibilities out of our heads for the moment, and consider how Socialism is likely to advance in a Parliament kept in working order by the establishment of two main parties competing for office and power: one professing to resist the advance and the other to further it, but both forced by the need for gaining some sort of control of the runaway car of Capitalism to take many steps when in power which they vehemently denounced when in opposition, and in the long run both contributing about equally (as hitherto) to the redistribution of the national income and the substitution of public for private property in land and industrial organization.

Do not fear that I am about to inflict a complete program on you. Even if I could foresee it I know better than to weary you to that extent. All I intend is to give you a notion of the sort of legislation that is likely to be enacted, and of the sort of opposition it is likely to provoke; so that you may be better able to judge on which side you should vote when an election gives you the chance, or when a seat on some parliamentary body, local or central, calls you to more direct action. You must understand that my designs on you do not include making you what is called a good party woman. Rather do I seek to add you to that floating body of openminded voters who are quite ready to vote for this party today and for the opposite party tomorrow if you think the balance of good sense and practical ability has changed (possibly by the ageing of the leaders) or that your former choice has taken a wrong turn concerning some proposed measure of cardinal importance. Good party people think such openmindedness disloyal; but in politics there should be no loyalty except to the public good. If, however, you prefer to vote for the same side every time through thick and thin, why not find some person who has made the same resolution in support of the opposite party? Then, as they say in Parliament, you can pair with her: that is, you can both agree never to vote at all, which will have the same effect as if you voted opposite ways; and neither of you need ever trouble to vote again.

We are agreed, I take it, that practical Socialism must proceed by the Government nationalizing our industries one at a time by a series of properly compensated expropriations, after an elaborate preparation for their administration by a body of civil servants, who will consist largely of the old employees, but who will be controlled and financed by Government departments manned by public servants very superior in average ability, training, and social dignity to the commercial profiteers and financial gamblers who now have all our livelihoods at their mercy.

Now this preparation and nationalization will hardly be possible unless the voters have at least a rough notion of what the Government is doing, and approve of it. They may not understand Socialism as a whole; but they can understand nationalization of the coal mines quite well enough to desire it and vote for its advocates, if not for the sake of the welfare of the nation, at least for the sake of getting their coal cheaper. Just so with the railways and transport services generally: the most prejudiced Conservatives may vote for their nationalization on its merits as an isolated measure, for the sake of cheaper travelling and reasonable freights for internal produce. A few big nationalizations effected with this sort of popular support will make nationalization as normal a part of our social policy as old age pensions are now, though it seems only the other day that such pensions were denounced as rank Communism, which indeed they are.

There is therefore no hope for Capitalism in the difficulty that baffled the Soviet in dealing with the land: that is, that the Russian people were not Communists, and would not work the Communist system except under a compulsion which it was impossible to apply on a sufficiently large scale, because if a system can be maintained only by half the ablebodied persons in the country being paid to do nothing but stand over the other half, rifle in hand, then it is not a practicable system and may as well be dropped first as last. But a series of properly prepared nationalizations may not only be understood and voted for by people who would be quite shocked if they were called Socialists, but would fit in perfectly with the habits of the masses who take their bread as it comes and never think about anything of a public nature. To them the change would be only a change of masters, to which they are so accustomed that it would not strike them as a change at all, whilst it would be also a change in the remuneration, dignity, and certainty of employment, which is just what they are always clamoring for. This overcomes the difficulty, familiar to all reformers, that it is much easier to induce people to do things in the way to which they are accustomed, even though it is detestably bad for them, than to try a new system, even though it promises to be millennially good for them.

Socialistic legislation, then, will be no mere matter of forbidding people to be rich, and calling a policeman when the law is broken. It means an active interference in the production and distribution of the nation's income; and every step of it will require a new department or extension of the civil service or the municipal service to execute and manage it. If we had sense enough to make a law that every baby, destitute or not, should have plenty of bread and milk and a good house to shelter it, that law would remain a dead letter until all the necessary bakeries and dairies and builders' yards were ready. If we made a law that every ablebodied adult should put in a day's work for his or her country every day, we could not carry out that law until we had a job ready for everybody. All constructive and productive legislation is quite different from the Ten Commandments: it means the employment of masses of men, the establishing of offices and works, the provision of large sums of money to start with, and the services of persons of special ability to direct. Without these, all the Royal or Dictatorial Proclamations, all the Commandments, and all the Communist Manifestoes are waste paper as far as the estabishment of practical Socialism is concerned.

You may therefore take it that the change from inequality to equality of income, though it will be made by law and cannot be made in any other way, will not be made by simply passing a single Act of Parliament ordering everybody to have the same income, with arithmetical exactness in every case. Dozens of extensions of the civil and municipal services, dozens of successive nationalizations, dozens of annual budgets, all warmly contested on one ground or another, will take us nearer and nearer to Equality of Income until we are so close that the evil of such trifling inequalities as may be left is no longer serious enough to be worth bothering about. At present, when one baby has a hundred thousand a year, and a hundred other babies are dying of insufficient nourishment, equality of income is something to be fought for and died for if necessary. But if every baby had its fill, the fact that here and there a baby's father or mother might get hold of an extra five shillings or five pounds would not matter enough to induce anyone to cross the street to prevent it.

All social reforms stop short, not at absolute logical completeness or arithmetical exactness, but at the point at which they have done their work sufficiently. To a poor woman the difference between a pound a week and a guinea a week is very serious, because a shilling is a large sum of money to her. But a woman with twenty pounds a week would not engage in a civil war because some other woman had twenty guineas. She would not feel the difference. Therefore we need not imagine a state of society in which we should call the police if somebody made a little extra money by singing songs or selling prize chrysanthemums, though we might come to consider such conduct so sordidly unladylike that even the most impudent woman would not dare do it openly. As long as we were all equally well off, so that anybody's daughter could marry anybody else's son without any question of marrying above or beneath her, we should be contented enough not to haggle over halfpence in the division of the national income. For all that, equality of income should remain a fundamental principle, any noticeable departure from which would be jealously watched, and tolerated, if at all, with open eyes. There are no limits to the possibility of its enforcement.

This does not mean that there are no limits to any device of Socialism: for example, to the process of nationalizing industry and turning private employees into Government employees. We could not nationalize everything even if we went mad on nationalization and wanted to. There will never be a week in which the Sunday papers will report that Socialism was established in Great Britain last Wednesday, on which occasion the Queen wore a red silk scarf fastened on the shoulder with a circlet of rubies consecrated and presented to her by the Third International, and containing a portrait of Karl Marx with the famous motto, "Proletarians of All Lands: Unite". It is far more likely that by the time nationalization has become the rule, and private enterprise the exception, Socialism (which is really rather a bad name for the business) will be spoken of, if at all, as a crazy religion held by a fanatical sect in that darkest of dark ages, the nineteenth century. Already, indeed, I am told that Socialism has had its day, and that the sooner we stop talking nonsense about it and set to work, like the practical people we are, to nationalize the coal mines and complete a national electrification scheme, the better. And I, who said forty years ago that we should have had Socialism already but for the Socialists, am quite willing to drop the name if dropping it will help me to get the thing.

What I meant by my jibe at the Socialists of the eighteen-eighties was that nothing is ever done, and much is prevented, by people who do not realize that they cannot do everything at once.

77

SUBSIDIZED PRIVATE ENTERPRISE

WHILST we are nationalizing the big industries and the wholesale businesses we may have to leave a good many unofficial retailers to carry on the work of petty distribution much as they do at present, except that we may control them in the matter of prices as the Trusts do, whilst allowing them a better living than the landlords and capitalists allow them, and relieving them from the continual fear of bankruptcy inseparable from the present system. We shall nationalize the mines long before we nationalize the village smithy and make the village blacksmith a public official. We shall have national or municipal supplies of electric power laid on from house to house long before we meddle with the individual artists and craftsmen and scientific workers who will use that power, to say nothing of the housemaids who handle the vacuum cleaners. We shall nationalize land and large-scale farming without simultaneously touching fancy fruit farming and kitchen gardening. Long after Capitalism as we know it shall have passed away more completely than feudalism has yet passed away there may be more men and women working privately in businesses of their own than there ever can be under our present slavish conditions.

The nationalization of banking will make it quite easy for private businesses to be carried on under Socialism to any extent that may be found convenient, and will in fact stimulate them vigorously. The reduction of the incomes derived from them to the common level could be effected by taxing them if they were excessive. But the difficulty is more likely to be the other way:

that is, the people in the private businesses might find themselves, as most of them do at present, poorer than they would be in public employment. The immense fortunes that are made in private businesses to-day are made by the employment of workers who, as they cannot live without access to the products of land and capital, must either starve or consent to work for the landlords and capitalists for much less than their work creates. But when everybody could get a job in one of the nationalized industries, and receive an income which would include his or her share of the rent of the nationalized land, and the interest on the nationalized capital, no private employer could induce anyone to come and work for wages unless the wages were big enough to be equivalent to the advantages of such public employment; therefore private employment could not create poverty, and would in fact become bankrupt unless the employers were either clever and useful enough to induce the public to pay them handsomely for their products or services, or else were content, for the sake of doing things in their own way, to put up with less than they could make in some national establishment round the corner. To maintain their incomes at the national level some of them might actually demand and receive subsidies from the Government. To take a very simple instance: in an out-of-the-way village or valley, where there was not enough business to pay a carrier, the Government or local authority might find that the most economical and sensible plan was to pay a local farmer or shopkeeper or innkeeper a contribution towards the cost of keeping a motor lorry on condition that he undertook the carrying for the district.

In big business, as we have seen, this process has actually begun. When Trade Unionism forced up the wages of the coal miners to a point at which the worst coal mines could not afford to continue working, the owners, though devout opponents of Socialism, demanded and obtained from a Conservative Government a subsidy of £10,000,000 to enable them to make both ends meet. But it was too ridiculous to tax the general public to keep a few bad mines going, and incidentally to keep up the monstrous prices charged for coal, when the mines as a whole were perfectly well able to pay a decent living wage, which was all the Trade Unions asked for. The subsidy was stopped; and a terrific lock-out ensued. All this could have been prevented by nationalizing the coal mines and thus making it possible to keep up wages and reduce the price of coals to the public simultaneously. However, that is not our point at present. What comes in here is that the capitalists themselves have established the Socialistic practice of subsidizing private businesses when they do not yield sufficient profit to support those engaged in them, though they are too useful to be dispensed with. The novelty, by the way, is only in subsidizing common industries. Scientific research, education, religion, popular access to rare books and pictures, exploration, carriage of mails oversea, and the like are partly dependent on Government grants, which are subsidies under another name.

What is more, capitalists are now openly demanding subsidies to enable them to start their private enterprises. The aeroplane lines, for instance, boldly took it as a matter of course that the Government should help them, just as it had helped the dye industry during the war (and been sorry for it afterwards). I draw your attention specially to this new capitalistic method because by it you are not only invited to throw over the Capitalist principle of trusting to unaided competitive private enterprise for the maintenance of our industries, but taxed to take all the risks of it whilst the capitalists take all the profits and keep prices as high as possible against you, thus fleecing you both ways. They cannot consistently object (though they do object) when workmen ask the Government to guarantee them a living wage as well as guaranteeing profits and keeping up prices for their employers.

When Socialism is the order of the day these capitalistic exploitations of the taxpayer will have provided plenty of precedents for subsidizing experimental private ventures in new industries or inventions and new methods, or, as in the case of the village carrier, making it worth somebody's while to undertake some necessary service that is not for the moment worth nationalizing. In fact this will be the most interesting part of Socialism to clever business people. Direct and complete nationalizations will be confined mostly to well established routine services.

There are doctrinaire Socialists who will be shocked at the suggestion that a Socialist Government should not only tolerate private enterprise, but actually finance it. But the business of

Socialist rulers is not to suppress private enterprise as such, but to attain and maintain equality of income. The substitution of public for private enterprise is only one of several means to that end; and if in any particular instance the end can be best served for the moment by private enterprise, a Socialist Government will tolerate private enterprise, or subsidize private enterprise, or even initiate private enterprise. Indeed Socialism will be more elastic and tolerant than Capitalism, which would leave any district without a carrier if no private carrier could make it pay.

Note, however, that when a private experiment in business has been financed by the State, and has been successful in establishing some new industry or method or invention as part of the routine of national production and service, it will then be nationalized, leaving private enterprise to return to its proper business of making fresh experiments and discovering new services, instead of, as at present, wallowing in the profits of industries which are no longer experimental. For example, it has for many years past been silly to leave railways in the hands of private companies instead of nationalizing them, especially as the most hidebound bureaucrat could not have been more obsoletely reactionary, uninventive, and obstructive than some of our most pretentious railway chairmen have been. Everything is known about railway locomotion that need be known for nationalization purposes. But the flying services are still experimenting, and may be treated as State-aided private enterprises until their practice becomes as well established and uniform as railway practice.

Unfortunately this is so little understood that the capitalists, through their agents the employers and financiers, are now persuading our Conservative governments into financing them at the taxpayers' expense without retaining the taxpayers' interest in the venture. For instance, the £10,000,000 subsidy to the coalowners should clearly have been given by way of mortgage on the mines. For every £100 granted to private enterprise the Government should demand a share certificate. Otherwise, if and when it subsequently nationalizes the enterprise, it will be asked to compensate the proprietors for the confiscation of its own capital; and though this, as we have seen in our study of compensation, does not really matter, it does matter very seriously that the State should not have at least a shareholder's control. To make private adventurers an unconditional present of public money is to loot the Treasury and plunder the taxpayer.

So, you see, the difference between Capitalist and Socialist governments is not as to whether nationalization should be tolerated; for neither could get on for a day without it: the difference is as to how far it should be carried and how fast pushed. Capitalist governments regard nationalization and municipalization as evils to be confined to commercially unprofitable works; so as to leave everything profitable to the profiteers. When they acquire land for some temporary public purpose, they sell it to a private person when they have done with it, and use the price to reduce the income tax. Thereby a piece of land which was national property becomes private property; and the unearned incomes of the income taxpayers are increased by the relief from taxation. Socialist governments, on the other hand, push the purchase of land for the nation at the expense of the capitalists as hard and as fast as they can, and oppose its resale to private individuals fiercely. But they are often held back and even thrown back, just as the Russian Soviet was, by the inexorable necessity for keeping land and capital in constant and energetic use. If the Government takes an acre of fertile land or a ton of spare subsistence (capital) that it is not prepared instantly to cultivate or feed productive labor with, then, whether it likes or not, it must sell it back again into private hands and thus retrace the step towards Socialism which it took without being sufficiently prepared for it. During the war, when private enterprise broke down hopelessly, and caused an appalling slaughter of our young soldiers in Flanders by leaving the army without shells, the munitions had to be made in national factories. When the war was over, the Capitalist Government of 1918 sold off these factories as fast as it possibly could for an old song, in spite of the protests of the Labor Party. Some of the factories were unsaleable, either because they were in such out-of-the-way places (lest they should be bombarded) that private enterprise thought it could do better elsewhere, or because private enterprise was so wretchedly unenterprising. Yet when a Labor Government took office it, too, had to try to sell these remaining war factories because it could not organize enough new public enterprises to employ them for peace purposes.

This was another object-lesson in the impossibility of taking over land from the landlords and capital from the capitalists merely because doing so is Socialistic, without being ready to employ it productively. If you do, you will have to give it back again, as the Moscow Soviet had. You must take it only when you have some immediate use for it, and are ready to start on the job next morning. If a Capitalist Government were forced by a wave of successful Socialist propaganda to confiscate more property than it could administer, it might quite easily be forced to reissue it (not at all unwillingly, and with triumphant cries of "I told you so") to private employers on much worse terms for the nation than those on which it is held at present.

78

HOW LONG WILL IT TAKE?

THEN as to the rate at which the change can take place. If it be put off too long, or brought about too slowly, there may be a violent revolution which may produce a dismal equality by ruining everybody who is not murdered. But equality produced in that way does not last. Only in a settled and highly civilized society with a strong Government and an elaborate code of laws can equality of income be attained or maintained. Now a strong Government is not one with overwhelming fighting forces in its pay: that is rather the mark of a panicky Government. It is one that commands the moral approval of an overwhelming majority of the people. To put it more particularly, it is one in which the police and the other executive officers of the Government can always count on the sympathy and, when they need it, the co-operation of the citizens. A morally shocking Government cannot last, and cannot carry out such changes as the change from our present system to Socialism, which are matters of long business arrangements and extensions of the Civil Service. They must be made thoughtfully, bit by bit; and they must be popular enough to establish themselves too solidly for changes of Government to shake them, like our postal system or our Communism in roads, bridges, police, drainage, and highway lighting.

It is a great pity that the change cannot be made more quickly; but we must remember that when Moses delivered the Israelites from their bondage in Egypt, he found them so unfitted for freedom, that he had to keep them wandering round the desert for forty years, until those who had been in bondage in Egypt were mostly dead. The trouble was not the distance from Egypt to the Promised Land, which was easily walkable in forty weeks, but the change of condition, and habit, and mind, and the reluctance of those who had been safe and well treated as slaves to face danger and hardship as free adventurers. We should have the same trouble if we attempted to impose Socialism all in a lump on people not brought up to it. They would wreck it because they could not understand it nor work its institutions; and some of them would just hate it. The truth is, we are at present wandering in the desert between the old Commercialism and the new Socialism. Our industries and our characters and our laws and our religions are partly commercialized, partly nationalized, partly municipalized, partly communized; and the completion of the change will take place like the beginning of it: that is, without the unintelligent woman knowing what is happening, or noticing anything except that some ways of life are getting harder and some easier, with the corresponding exclamations about not knowing what the world is coming to, or that things are much better than they used to be. Mark Twain said "It is never too late to mend: there is no hurry"; and those who dread the change may comfort themselves by the assurance that there is more danger of its coming too slowly than too quickly, even though the more sloth the more suffering. It is well that we who are hopelessly unfitted for Socialism by our bringing-up will not live for ever. If only it were possible for us to cease corrupting our children our political superstitions and prejudices would die with us; and the next generation might bring down the walls of Jericho. Fortunately, the advantages to be gained by Socialism for the proletariat, and the fact that proletarian parents are a huge majority of the electorate, may be depended on to bias moral education more and more in favor of the movement towards Socialism.

I purposely avoid anticipating any moral pressure of public opinion against economic selfishness. No doubt that will become part of the national conscience under Socialism, just as under Capitalism children are educated to regard success in life as meaning more money than anyone else and no work to do for it. But I know how hard it is for you to believe that public opinion could change so completely. You may have observed that at present, although people do not always choose the occupation at which they can make the most money, and indeed will give up lucrative jobs to starve at more congenial ones, yet, when they have chosen their job, they will take as much as they can get for it; and the more they can get the better they are thought of. So I have assumed that they will continue to do so as far as they are allowed (few of them have any real liberty of this kind now), though I can quite conceive that in a Socialist future any attempt to obtain an economic advantage over one's neighbors, as distinguished from an economic advantage for the whole community, might come to be considered such exceedingly bad form that nobody could make it without losing her place in society just as a detected card-sharper does at present.

79

SOCIALISM AND LIBERTY

THE dread of Socialism by nervous people who do not understand it, on the ground that there would be too much law under it, and that every act of our lives would be regulated by the police, is more plausible than the terrors of the ignorant people who think it would mean the end of all law, because under Capitalism we have been forced to impose restrictions that in a socialized nation would have no sense, in order to save the proletariat from extermination, or at least from extremities that would have provoked it to rebellion. Here is a little example. A friend of mine who employed some girls in an artistic business in which there was not competition enough to compel him to do his worst in the way of sweating them, took a nice old riverside house, and decorated it very prettily with Morris wall-papers, furnishing it in such a way that the girls could have their tea comfortably in their workrooms, which he made as homelike as possible. All went well until one day a gentleman walked in and announced himself to my friend as the factory inspector. He looked round him, evidently much puzzled, and asked where the women worked. "Here" replied my friend, with justifiable pride, confident that the inspector had never seen anything so creditable in the way of a factory before. But what the inspector said was "Where is the copy of the factory regulations which you are obliged by law to post up on your walls in full view of your employees?" "Surely you dont expect me to stick up a beastly ugly thing like that in a room furnished like a drawing room" said my friend. "Why, that paper on the wall is a Morris paper: I cant disfigure it by pasting up a big placard on it." "You are liable to severe penalties" replied the inspector "for having not only omitted to post the regulations, but for putting paper on your walls instead of having them limewashed at the intervals prescribed by law." "But hang it all!" my friend remonstrated, "I want to make the place homely and beautiful. You forget that the girls are not always working. They take their tea here." "For allowing your employees to take their meals in the room where they work you have incurred an additional penalty" said the inspector. "It is a gross breach of the Factory Acts." And he walked out, leaving my friend an abashed criminal caught redhanded.

As it happened, the inspector was a man of sense. He did not return; the penalties were not exacted; the Morris wall-papers remained; and the illicit teas continued; but the incident illustrates the extent to which individual liberty has been cut down under Capitalism for good as well as for evil. Where women are concerned it is assumed that they must be protected to a degree that is unnecessary for men (as if men were any more free in a factory than women); consequently the regulations are so much stricter that women are often kept out of employments to which men are welcomed. Besides the factory inspector there are the Commissioners of Inland Revenue inquiring into your income and making you disgorge a lot of it, the school attendance visitors taking possession of your children, the local government inspectors making you build and drain your house not as you please but as they order, the Poor Law officers, the unemployment insurance officers, the vaccination officers, and others whom I cannot think of just at present. And the tendency is to have more and more of them as we become less tolerant of the abuses of our capitalist system. But if you study these interferences with our liberties closely you will find that in practice they are virtually suspended in the case of people well enough off to be able to take care of themselves: for instance, the school attendance officer never calls at houses valued above a certain figure, though the education of the children in them is often disgracefully neglected or mishandled. Poor Law officers would not exist if there were no poor, nor unemployment insurance officers if we all got incomes whether we were employed or not. If nobody could make profits by sweating, nor compel us to work in uncomfortable, unsafe, insanitary factories and workshops, a great deal of our factory regulations would become not only superfluous but unbearably obstructive.

Then consider the police: the friends of the honest woman and the enemies and hunters of thieves, tramps, swindlers, rioters, confidence tricksters, drunkards, and prostitutes. The police officer, like the soldier who stands behind him, is mainly occupied today in enforcing the legalized robbery of the poor which takes place whenever the wealth produced by the labor of a productive worker is transferred as rent or interest to the pockets of an idler or an idler's parasite. They are even given powers to arrest us for "sleeping out", which means sleeping in the open air without paying a landlord for permission to do so. Get rid of this part of their duties, and at the same time of the poverty which it enforces, with the mass of corruption, thieving, rioting, swindling, and prostitution which poverty produces as surely as insanitary squalor produces smallpox and typhus and you get rid of the least agreeable part of our present police activity, with all that it involves in prisons, criminal courts, and jury duties.

By getting rid of poverty we shall get rid of the unhappiness and worry which it causes. To defend themselves against this, women, like men, resort to artificial happiness, just as they resort to artificial insensibility when they have to undergo a painful operation. Alcohol produces artificial happiness, artificial courage, artificial gaiety, artificial self-satisfaction, thus making life bearable for millions who would otherwise be unable to endure their condition. To them alcohol is a blessing. Unfortunately, as it acts by destroying conscience, self-control, and the normal functioning of the body, it produces crime, disease, and degradation on such a scale that its manufacture and sale are at present prohibited by law throughout the United States of America, and there is a strong movement to introduce the same prohibition here.

The ferocity of the resistance to this attempt to abolish artificial happiness shows how indispensable it has become under Capitalism. A famous American Prohibitionist was mobbed by medical students in broad daylight in the streets of London, and barely escaped with the loss of one eye, and his back all but broken. If he had been equally famous for anything else, the United States Government would have insisted on the most ample reparation, apology, and condign punishment of his assailants; and if this had been withheld, or even grudged, American hotheads would have clamored for war. But for the enemy of the anæsthetic that makes the misery of the poor and the idleness of the rich tolerable, turning it into a fuddled dream of enjoyment, neither his own country nor the public conscience of ours could be moved even to the extent of a mild censure on the police. It was evident that had he been torn limb from limb the popular verdict would have been that it served him jolly well right.

Alcohol, however, is a very mild drug compared with the most effective modern happiness producers. These give you no mere sodden self-satisfaction and self-conceit: they give you ecstasy. It is followed by hideous wretchedness; but then you can cure that by taking more and more of the drug until you become a living horror to all about you, after which you become a dead one, to their great relief. As to these drugs, not even a mob of medical students, expressly educated to make their living by trading in artificial health and happiness, dares protest against strenuous prohibition, provided they may still prescribe the drug; nevertheless the demand is so great in the classes who have too much money and too little work that smuggling, which is easy and very profitable, goes on in spite of the heaviest penalties. Our efforts to suppress this trade in artificial happiness has already landed us in such interferences with personal liberty that we are not allowed to purchase many useful drugs for entirely innocent purposes unless we first pay (not to say bribe) a doctor to prescribe it.

Still, prohibition of the fiercer drugs has the support of public opinion. It is the prohibition of alcohol that rouses such opposition that the strongest governments shrink from it in spite of overwhelming evidence of the increase in material well-being produced by it wherever it has been risked. You prove to people that as teetotallers they will dwell in their own houses instead of in a frowsy tenement, besides keeping their own motor car, having a bank account, and living ten years longer. They angrily deny it; but when you crush their denials by unquestionable American statistics they tell you flatly that they had rather be happy for thirty years in a tenement without a car or a penny to put in the bank than be unhappy for forty years with all these things. You find a wife distracted because her husband drinks and is ruining her and her children; yet when you induce him to take the pledge, you find presently that she has tempted him to drink again because he is so morose when he is sober that she cannot endure living with him. And to make his drunkenness bearable she takes to drink herself, and lives happily in shameless degradation with him until they both drink themselves dead.

Besides, the vast majority of modern drinkers do not feel any the worse for it, because they do not miss the extra efficiency they would enjoy on the water waggon. Very few people are obliged by their occupations to work up to the extreme limit of their powers. Who cares whether a lady gardener or a bookkeeper or a typist or a shop assistant is a teetotaller or not, provided she always stops well short of being noticeably drunk? It is to the motorist or the aeroplane pilot that a single glass of any intoxicant may make the difference between life and death. What would be sobriety for a billiard marker would be ruinous drunkenness for a professional billiard player. The glass of stimulant that enlivens a routine job is often dropped because when the routineer plays golf "to keep herself fit" she finds that it spoils her putting. Thus you find that you can sometimes make a worker give up alcohol partly or wholly by giving her more leisure. She finds that a woman who is sober enough to do her work as well as it need be done is not sober enough to play as well as she would like to do it. The moment people are in a position to develop their fitness, as they call it, to the utmost, whether at work or at play, they begin to grudge the sacrifice of the last inch of efficiency which alcohol knocks off, and which in all really fine work makes the difference between first rate and second rate. If this book owed any of its quality to alcohol or to any other drug, it might amuse you more; but it would be enormously less conscientious intellectually, and therefore much more dangerous to your mind.

If you put all this together you will see that any social change which abolishes poverty and increases the leisure of routine workers will destroy the need for artificial happiness, and increase the opportunities for the sort of activity that makes people very jealous of reducing their fitness by stimulants. Even now we admit that the champion athlete must not drink whilst training; and the nearer we get to a world in which everyone is in training all the time the nearer we shall get to general teetotalism, and to the possibility of discarding all those restrictions on personal liberty which the prevalent dearth of happiness and consequent resort to pernicious artificial substitutes now force us to impose.

As to such serious personal outrages as compulsory vaccination and the monstrous series of dangerous inoculations which are forced on soldiers, and at some frontiers on immigrants, they are only desperate attempts to stave off the consequences of bad sanitation and overcrowding by infecting people with disease when they are well and strong in the hope of developing their natural resistance to it by exercise sufficiently to prevent them from catching it when they are ailing and weak. The poverty of our doctors forces them to support such practices in the teeth of all experience and disinterested science; but if we get rid of poor doctors and overcrowded and insanitary dwellings we get rid of the diseases which terrify us into these grotesque witch rituals; and no woman will be forced to expose her infant to the risk of a horrible, lingering, hideously disfiguring death from generalized vaccinia lest it should catch confluent smallpox, which, by the way, is, on a choice between the two evils, much to be preferred. Dread of epidemics: that is, of disease and premature death, has created a pseudo-scientific tyranny just as the dread of hell created a priestly tyranny in the ages of faith. Florence Nightingale, a sensible woman whom the doctors could neither humbug nor bully, told them that what was wrong with our soldiers was dirt, bad food, and foul water: in short, the conditions produced by war in the field and poverty in the slum. When we get rid of poverty the doctors will no longer be able to frighten us into imposing on ourselves by law pathogenic inoculations which, under healthy conditions, kill more people than the diseases against which they pretend to protect them. And when we get rid of Commercialism, and vaccines no longer make dividends for capitalists, the fairy tales by which they are advertized will drop out of the papers, and be replaced, let us hope, by disinterested attempts to ascertain and publish the scientific truth about them, which, by the way, promises to be much more hopeful and interesting.

As to the mass of oppressive and unjust laws that protect property at the expense of humanity, and enable proprietors to drive whole populations off the land because sheep or deer are more profitable, we have said enough about them already. Naturally we shall get rid of them when we get rid of private property.

Now, however, I must come to one respect in which official interference with personal liberty would be carried under Socialism to lengths undreamed of at present. We may be as idle as we please if only we have money in our pockets; and the more we look as if we had never done a day's work in our lives and never intend to, the more we are respected by every official we come in contact with, and the more we are envied, courted, and deferred to by everybody. If we enter a village school the children all rise and stand respectfully to receive us, whereas the entrance of a plumber or carpenter leaves them unmoved. The mother who secures a rich idler as a husband for her daughter is proud of it: the father who makes a million uses it to make rich idlers of his children. That work is a curse is part of our religion: that it is a disgrace is the first article in our social code. To carry a parcel through the streets is not only a trouble, but a derogation from one's rank. Where there are blacks to carry them, as in South Africa, it is virtually impossible for a white to be seen doing such a thing. In London we condemn these colonial extremes of snobbery; but how many ladies could we persuade to carry a jug of milk down Bond Street on a May afternoon, even for a bet?

Now it is not likely, human laziness being what it is, that under Socialism anyone will carry a parcel or a jug if she can induce somebody else (her husband, say) to carry it for her. But nobody will think it disgraceful to carry a parcel because carrying a parcel is work. The idler will be treated not only as a rogue and a vagabond, but as an embezzler of the national funds, the meanest sort of thief. The police will not have much trouble in detecting such offenders. They will be denounced by everybody, because there will be a very marked jealousy of slackers who take their share without "doing their bit". The real lady will be the woman who does more than her bit, and thereby leaves her country richer than she found it. Today nobody knows what a real lady is; but the dignity is assumed most confidently by the women who ostentatiously take as much and give as nearly nothing as they can.

The snobbery that exists at present among workers will also disappear. Our ridiculous social distinctions between manual labor and brain work, between wholesale business and retail business, are really class distinctions. If a doctor considers it beneath his dignity to carry a scuttle of coals from one room to another, but is proud of his skill in performing some unpleasantly messy operation, it is clearly not because the one is any more or less manual than the other, but solely because surgical operations are associated with descent through younger sons from the propertied class, and carrying coals with proletarian descent. If the petty ironmonger's daughter is not considered eligible for marriage with the ironmaster's son, it is not because selling steel by the ounce and selling it by the ton are attributes of two different species, but because petty ironmongers have usually been poor and ironmasters rich. When there are no rich and no poor, and descent from the proprietary class will be described as "criminal antecedents", people will turn their hands to anything, and indeed rebel against any division of labor that deprives them of physical exercise. My own excessively sedentary occupation makes me long to be a half-time navvy. I find myself begging my gardener, who is a glutton for work, to leave me a few rough jobs to do when I have written myself to a standstill; for I cannot go out and take a hand with the navvies, because I should be taking the bread out of a poor man's mouth; nor should we be very comfortable company for oneanother with our different habits and speech and bringing-up, all produced by differences in our parents' incomes and class. But with all these obstacles swept away by Socialism I could lend a hand at any job within my strength and skill, and help my mates instead of hurting them, besides being as good company for them as I am now for professional persons or rich folk. Even as it is a good deal of haymaking is done for fun; and I am persuaded (having some imagination, thank Heaven!) that under Socialism open air workers would have plenty of voluntary help, female as well as male, without the trouble of whistling for it. Laws might have to be made to deal with officiousness. Everything would make for activity and against idleness: indeed it would probably be much harder to be an idler than it is now to be a pickpocket. Anyhow, as idleness would be not only a criminal offence, but unladylike and ungentlemanly in the lowest degree, nobody would resent the laws against it as infringements of natural liberty.

Lest anyone should at this point try to muddle you with the inveterate delusion that because capital can increase wealth people can live on capital without working, let me go back just for a moment to the way in which capital becomes productive.

Let us take those cases in which capital is used, not for destructive purposes, as in war, but for increasing production: that is, saving time and trouble in future work. When all the merchandise in a country has to be brought from the makers to the users on packhorses or carts over bad roads the cost in time and trouble and labor of man and beast is so great that most things have to be made and consumed on the spot. There may be a famine in one village and a glut in another a hundred miles off because of the difficulty of sending food from one to the other. Now if there is enough spare subsistence (capital) to support gangs of navvies and engineers and other workers whilst they cover the country with railways, canals, and metalled roads, and build engines and trains, barges and motor cars to travel on them, to say nothing of aeroplanes, then all sorts of goods can be sent long distances quickly and cheaply; so that the village which formerly could not get a cartload of bread and a few cans of milk from a hundred miles off to save its life is able to buy quite cheaply grain grown in Russia or America and domestic articles made in Germany or Japan. The spare subsistence will be entirely consumed in the operation: there will be no more left of it than of the capital lent for the war; but it will leave behind it the roadways and waterways and machinery by which labor can do a great deal more in a given time than it could without them. The destruction of these aids to labor would be a very different matter from our annual confiscations of the National Debt by taxation. It would leave us much poorer and less civilized: in fact most of us would starve, because big modern populations cannot support themselves without elaborate machinery and railways and so forth.

Still, roadways and machines can produce nothing by themselves. They can only assist labor. And they have to be continually repaired and renewed by labor. A country crammed with factories and machines, traversed in all directions by roadways, tramways and railways, dotted with aerodromes and hangars and garages, each crowded with aeroplanes and airships and motor cars, would produce absolutely nothing at all except ruin and rust and decay if the inhabitants ceased to work. We should starve in the midst of all the triumphs of civilization because we could not breakfast on the clay of the railway embankments, lunch on boiled aeroplanes, and dine on toasted steam-hammers. Nature inexorably denies to us the possibility of living without labor or of hoarding its most vital products. We may be helped by past labor; but we must live by present labor. By telling off one set of workers to produce more than they consume, and telling off another set to live on the surplus while the first set makes roads and machines, we may make our labor much more productive, and take out the gain either in shorter hours of work or bigger returns from the same number of hours of work as before; but we cannot stop working and sit down and look on while the roads and machines make and fetch and carry for us without anyone lifting a finger. We may reduce our working hours to two a day, or increase our income tenfold, or even conceivably do both at once; but by no magic on earth can any of us honestly become an idler. When you see a person who does no productive or serviceable work, you may conclude with absolute certainty that she or he is spunging on the labor of other people. It may or may not be expedient to allow certain persons this privilege for a time: sometimes it is; and sometimes it is not. I have already described how we offer at present, to anyone who can invent a labor-saving machine, what is called a patent: that is, a right to take a share of what the workers produce with the help of that machine for fourteen years. When a man writes a book or a play, we give him, by what is called copyright, the power to make everybody who reads the book or sees the play performed pay him and his heirs something during his lifetime and fifty years afterwards. This is our way of encouraging people to invent machines and to write books and plays instead of being content with the old handiwork, and with the Bible and Shakespear; and as we do it with our eyes open and with a definite purpose, and the privilege lasts no longer than enough to accomplish its purpose, there is a good deal to be said for it. But to allow the descendants of a man who invested a few hundred pounds in the New River Water Company in the reign of James I to go on for ever and ever living in idleness on the incessant daily labor of the London ratepayers is senseless and mischievous. If they actually did the daily work of supplying London with water, they might reasonably claim either to work for less time or receive more for their work than a water-carrier in Elizabeth's time; but for doing no work at all they have not a shadow of excuse. To consider Socialism a tyranny because it will compel everyone to share the daily work of the world is to confess to the brain of an idiot and the instinct of a tramp.

Speaking generally, it is a mistake to suppose that the absence of law means the absence of tyranny. Take, for example, the tyranny of fashion. The only law concerned in this is the law that we must all wear something in the presence of other people. It does not prescribe what a woman shall wear: it only says that in public she shall be a draped figure and not a nude one. But does this mean that a woman can wear what she likes? Legally she can; but socially her slavery is more complete than any sumptuary law could make it. If she is a waitress or a parlormaid there is no question about it: she must wear a uniform or lose her employment and starve. If she is a duchess she must dress in the fashion or be ridiculous. In the case of the duchess nothing worse than ridicule is the penalty of unfashionable dressing. But any woman who has to earn her living outside her own house finds that if she is to keep her employment she must also keep up appearances, which means that she must dress in the fashion, even when it is not at all becoming to her, and her wardrobe contains serviceable dresses a couple of years out of date. And the better her class of employment the tighter her bonds. The ragpicker has the melancholy privilege of being less particular about her working clothes than the manageress of a hotel; but she would be very glad to exchange that freedom for the obligation of the manageress to be always well dressed. In fact the most enviable women in this respect are nuns and policewomen, who, like gentlemen at evening parties and military officers on parade, never have to think of what they will wear, as it is all settled for them by regulation and custom.

This dress question is only one familiar example of the extent to which the private employment of today imposes regulations on us which are quite outside the law, but which are none the less enforced by private employers on pain of destitution. The husband in public employment, the socialized husband, is much freer than the unsocialized one in private employment. He may travel third class, wearing a lounge suit and soft hat, living in the suburbs, and spending his Sundays as he pleases, whilst the others must travel first class, wear a frock coat and tall hat, live at a fashionable address, and go to church regularly. Their wives have to do as they do; and the single women who have escaped from the limitations of the home into independent activity find just the same difference between public work and private: in public employment their livelihood is never at the mercy of a private irresponsible person as it is in private. The lengths to which women are sometimes forced to go to please their private employers are much more revolting than, for instance, the petty dishonesties in which clerks are forced to become accomplices.

Then there are estate rules: that is to say, edicts drawn up by private estate owners and imposed on their tenants without any legal sanction. These often prohibit the building on the estate of any place of worship except an Anglican church, or of any public house. They refuse houses to practitioners of the many kinds that are now not registered by the General Medical Council. In fact they exercise a tyranny which would lead to a revolution if it were attempted by the King, and which did actually provoke us to cut off a king's head in the seventeenth century. We have to submit to these tyrannies because the people who can refuse us employment or the use of land have powers of life and death over us, and can therefore make us do what they like, law or no law. Socialism would transfer this power of life and death from private hands to the hands of the constitutional authorities, and regulate it by public law. The result would be a great increase of independence, self-respect, freedom from interference with our tastes and ways of living, and, generally, all the liberty we really care about.

Childish people, we saw, want to have all their lives regulated for them, with occasional holiday outbursts of naughtiness to relieve the monotony; and we admitted that the ablebodied ones make good soldiers and steady conventional employees. When they are left to themselves they make laws of fashions, customs, points of etiquette, and "what other people will say", hardly daring to call their souls their own, though they may be rich enough to do as they please. Money as a means of freedom is thrown away on these people. It is funny to hear them declaring, as they often do, that Socialism would be unendurable because it would dictate to them what they should eat and drink and wear, leaving them no choice in the matter, when they are cowering under a social tyranny which regulates their meals, their clothes, their hours, their religion and politics, so ruthlessly that they dare no more walk down a fashionable street in an unfashionable hat, which there is no law to prevent them doing, than to walk down it naked, which would be stopped by the police. They regard with dread and abhorrence the emancipated spirits who, within the limits of legality and cleanliness and convenience, do not care what they wear, and boldly spend their free time as their fancy dictates.

But do not undervalue the sheepish wisdom of the conventional. Nobody can live in society without conventions. The reason why sensible people are as conventional as they can bear to be is that conventionality saves so much time and thought and trouble and social friction of one sort or another that it leaves them much more leisure for freedom than unconventionality does. Believe me, unless you intend to devote your life to preaching unconventionality, and thus make it your profession, the more conventional you are, short of being silly or slavish or miserable, the easier life will be for you. Even as a professional reformer you had better be content to preach one form of unconventionality at a time. For instance, if you rebel against high-heeled shoes, take care to do it in a very smart hat.

80

SOCIALISM AND MARRIAGE

WHEN promising new liberties, Socialists are apt to forget that people object even more strongly to new liberties than to new laws. If a woman has been accustomed to go in chains all her life and to see other women doing the same, a proposal to take her chains off will horrify her. She will feel naked without them, and clamor to have any impudent hussy who does not feel about them exactly as she does taken up by the police. In China the Manchu ladies felt that way about their crippled feet. It is easier to put chains on people than to take them off if the chains look respectable.

In Russia marriage under the Tsars was an unbreakable chain. There was no divorce; but on the other hand there was, as with us, a widespread practice of illicit polygamy. A woman could live with a man without marrying him. A man could live with a woman without marrying her. In fact each might have several partners. In Russia under the Communist Soviet this state of things has been reversed. If a married couple cannot agree, they can obtain a divorce without having to pretend to disgrace themselves as in Protestant England. That shocks many English ladies, married or unmarried, who take the Book of Common Prayer literally. But the Soviet does not tolerate illicit relations. If a man lives with a woman as husband with wife he must marry her, even if he has to divorce another wife to do it. The woman has the right to the status of a wife, and must claim it. This seems to many English gentlemen an unbearable tyranny: they regard the Soviet legislators as monsters for interfering with male liberty in this way; and they have plenty of female sympathizers.

In countries and sects where polygamy is legal, the laws compelling the husband to pay equal attention to all his wives are staggering to a British husband, who is not now, as he was formerly, legally obliged to pay any attention to his one wife, nor she to him.

Now marriage institutions are not a part of Socialism. Marriage, of which we speak as if it were one and the same thing all the world over, differs so much from sect to sect and from country to country that to a Roman Catholic or a citizen of the State of South Carolina it means strict monogamy without the possibility of divorce; whilst to our high caste fellow-subjects in India it means unlimited polygamy, as it did to the Latter Day Saints of Salt Lake City within my recollection. Between these extremes there are many grades. There are marriages which nothing can break except death or annulment by the Pope; and there are divorces that can be ordered at a hotel like a bottle of champagne or a motor car. There is English marriage, Scottish marriage, and Irish marriage, all different. There is religious marriage and civil marriage, civil marriage being a recent institution won from the Churches after a fierce struggle, and still regarded as invalid and sinful by many pious people. There is an established celibacy, the negation of marriage, among nuns, priests, and certain Communist sects. With all this Socialism has nothing directly to do. Equality of income applies impartially to all the sects, all the States, and all the communities, to monogamists, polygamists, and celibates, to infants incapable of marriage and centenarians past it.

Why, then, is it that there is a rooted belief that Socialism would in some way alter marriage, if not abolish it? Why did quite respectable English newspapers after the Russian revolution of 1917 gravely infer that the Soviet had not only nationalized land and capital, but proceeded, as part of the logic of Socialism, to nationalize women? No doubt the main explanation of that extravagance is that the highly respectable newspapers in question still regard women as property, nationalizable like any other property, and were consequently unable to understand that this very masculine view is inconceivable to a Communist. But the truth under all such nonsense is that Socialism must have a tremendous effect on marriage and the family. At present a married woman is a female slave chained to a male one; and a girl is a prisoner in the house and in the hands of her parents. When the personal relation between the parties is affectionate, and their powers not abused, the arrangement works well enough to be bearable by people who have been brought up to regard it as a matter of course. But when the parties are selfish, tyrannical, jealous, cruel, envious, with different and antagonistic tastes and beliefs, incapable of understanding oneanother: in short, antipathetic and incompatible, it produces much untold human unhappiness.

Why is this unhappiness endured when the door is not locked, and the victims can walk into the street at any moment? Obviously because starvation awaits them at the other side of the door. Vows and inculcated duties may seem effective in keeping unhappy wives and revolting daughters at home when they have no alternative; but there must be an immense number of cases in which wives and husbands, girls and boys, would walk out of the house, like Nora Helmer in Ibsen's famous play, if they could do so without losing a single meal, a single night's protection and shelter, or the least loss of social standing in consequence.

As Socialism would place them in this condition it would infallibly break up unhappy marriages and families. This being obviously desirable we need not pretend to deplore it. But we must not expect more domestic dissolutions than are likely to happen. No parent would tyrannize as some parents tyrannize now if they knew that the result would be the prompt disappearance of their children, unless indeed they disliked their children enough to desire that result, in which case so much the better; but the normal merely hasty parent would have to recover the fugitives by apologies, promises of amendment, or bribes, and keep them by more stringent self-control and less stringent parental control. Husbands and wives, if they knew that their marriage could only last on condition of its being made reasonably happy for both of them, would have to behave far better to oneanother than they ever seem to dream of doing now. There would be such a prodigious improvement in domestic manners all round that a fairly plausible case can be made out for expecting that far fewer marriages and families will be broken up under Socialism than at present. Still, there will be a difference, even though the difference be greatly for the better. When once it becomes feasible for a wife to leave her husband, not for a few days or weeks after a tiff because they are for the moment tired of oneanother, but without any intention of returning, there must be prompt and almost automatic divorce, whether they like it or not. At present a deserted wife or husband, by simply refusing to sue for divorce, can in mere revenge or jealousy or on Church grounds, prevent the deserter from marrying again. We should have to follow the good example of Russia in refusing to tolerate such situations. Both parties must be either married or unmarried. An intermediate state in which each can say to the other "Well, if I cannot have you nobody else shall" is clearly against public morality.

It is on marriage that the secular State is likely to clash most sensationally with the Churches, because the Churches claim that marriage is a metaphysical business governed by an absolute right and wrong which has been revealed to them by God, and which the State must therefore enforce without regard to circumstances. But to this the State will never assent, except in so far as clerical notions happen to be working fairly well and to be shared by the secular rulers. Marriage is for the State simply a licence to two citizens to beget children. To say that the State must not concern itself with the question of how many people the community is to consist of, and, when a change is desired, at what rate the number should be increased or reduced, is to treat the nation as no sane person would dream of treating a ferryman. If the ferryman's boat will hold only ten passengers, and you tell him that it has been revealed to you by God that he must take all who want to cross over, even though they number a thousand, the ferryman will not argue with you, he will refuse to take more than ten, and will smite you with his oar if you attempt to detain his boat and shove a couple more passengers into it. And, obviously, the ten already aboard will help him for their own sakes.

When Socialism does away with the artificial overpopulation which Capitalism, as we have seen, produces by withdrawing workers from productive employments to wasteful ones, the State will be face to face at last with the genuine population question: the question of how many people it is desirable to have in the country. To get rid of the million or so for whom our capitalists fail to find employment, the State now depends on a high death-rate, especially for infants, on war, and on swarming like the bees. Africa, America, and Australasia have taken millions of our people from us in bee swarms. But in time all places comfortable enough to tempt people to emigrate get filled up; and their inhabitants, like the Americans and Australians today, close their gates against further immigration. If we find our population still increasing, we may have to discuss whether we should keep it down, as we keep down the cat population, by putting the superfluous babies into the bucket, which would be no wickeder than the avoidable infant mortality and surgical abortion resorted to at present. The alternative would be to make it a severely punishable crime for married couples to have more than a prescribed number of children. But punishing the parents would not dispose of the unwanted children. The fiercest persecution of the mothers of illegitimate children has not prevented illegitimate children from being born, though it has made most of them additionally undesirable by afflicting them with the vices and infirmities of disgrace and poverty. Any State limiting the number of children permitted to a family would be compelled not only to tolerate contraception, but to inculcate it and instruct women in its methods. And this would immediately bring it into conflict with the Churches. Whether under such circumstances the State would simply ignore the Churches or pass a law under which their preachers could be prosecuted for sedition would depend wholly on the gravity of the emergency, and not on the principles of liberty, toleration, freedom of conscience, and so forth which were so stirringly trumpeted in England in the eighteenth century when the boot was on the other foot.

In France at present the State is striving to increase the population. It is thus in the position of the Israelites in the Promised Land, and of Joseph Smith and his Mormons in the State of Illinois in 1843, when only a rapid increase in their numbers could rescue them from a condition of dangerous numerical inferiority to their enemies. Joseph Smith did what Abraham did: he resorted to polygamy. We, not being in any such peril ourselves, have seen nothing in this but an opportunity for silly and indecent jocularity; but there are not many political records more moving than Brigham Young's description of the horror with which he received Joseph's revelation that it was the will of God that they should all take as many wives as possible. He had been brought up to regard polygamy as a mortal sin, and did sincerely so regard it. And yet he believed that Smith's revelations were from God. In his perplexity, he tells us, he found himself, when a funeral passed in the street, envying the corpse (another mortal sin); and there is not the slightest reason to doubt that he was perfectly sincere. After all, it is not necessary for a married man to have any moral or religious objection to polygamy to be horrified at the prospect of having twenty additional wives "sealed" to him. Yet Brigham Young got over his horror, and was married more than thirty times. And the genuinely pious Mormon women, whose prejudices were straiter than those of the men, were as effectively and easily converted to polygamy as Brigham.

Though this proves that western civilization is just as susceptible to polygamy as eastern when the need arises, the French Government, for very good reasons, has not ventured to propose it as a remedy for underpopulation in France. The alternatives are prizes and decorations for the parents of large families (families of fifteen have their group portraits in the illustrated papers, and are highly complimented on their patriotism), bounties, exemptions from taxation, vigorous persecution of contraception as immoral, facilities for divorce amounting to successive as distinguished from simultaneous polygamy, all tending towards that State endowment of parentage which seems likely to become a matter of course in all countries, with, of course, encouragement to desirable immigrants. To these measures no Church is likely to object, unless indeed it holds that celibacy is a condition of salvation, a doctrine which has never yet found enough practising converts to threaten a modern nation with sterility. Compulsory parentage is as possible as compulsory military service; but just as the soldier who is compelled to serve must have his expenses paid by the State, a woman compelled to become a mother can hardly be expected to do so at her own expense.

But the maintenance of monogamy must always have for its basis a practical equality in numbers between men and women. If a war reduced the male population by, say, 70 per cent, and the female population by only one per cent, polygamy would immediately be instituted, and parentage made compulsory, with the hearty support of all the really popular Churches.

Thus, it seems, the State, Capitalist or Socialist, will finally settle what marriage is to be, no matter what the Churches say. A Socialist State is more likely to interfere than a Capitalist one, because Socialism will clear the population question from the confusion into which Capitalism has thrown it. The State will then, as I have said, be face to face with the real population question; but nobody yet knows what the real population question will be like, because nobody can now settle how many persons per acre offer the highest possibilities of living. There is the Boer ideal of living out of sight of your neighbors' chimneys. There is the Bass Rock ideal of crowding as many people on the earth as it can support. There is the bungalow ideal and the monster hotel ideal. Neither you nor I can form the least notion of how posterity will decide between them when society is well organized enough to make the problem practical and the issues clear.

81

SOCIALISM AND CHILDREN

IN the case of young children we have gone far in our interference with the old Roman rights of parents. For nine mortal years the child is taken out of its parents' hands for most of the day, and thus made a State school child instead of a private family child. The records of the Society for the Prevention of Cruelty to Children are still sickening enough to shew how necessary it is to protect children against their parents; but the bad cases are scarce, and shew that it is now difficult for the worst sort of parent to evade for long the school attendance officer, the teacher, and the police. Unfortunately the proceedings lead to nothing but punishment of the parents: when they come out of prison the children are still in their hands. When we have beaten the cat for cruelty we give it back its mouse. We have now, however, taken a step in the right direction by passing an Act of Parliament by which adoptive parents have all the rights of real parents. You can now adopt a child with complete security against the parents coming to claim the child back again whenever it suits them. All their rights pass to you by the adoption. Bad natural parents can be completely superseded by adoptive ones: it remains only to make the operation compulsory where it is imperative. Compulsory adoption is already an old established institution in the case of our Poor Law Guardians. Oliver Twist was a compulsory adopted child. His natural parents were replaced by very unnatural ones. Mr Bumble is being happily abolished; but there must still be somebody to adopt Oliver. When equality of income makes an end of his social disadvantages there will be no lack of childless volunteers.

Our eyes are being opened more and more to the fact that in our school system education is only the pretext under which parents get rid of the trouble of their children by bundling them off into a prison or child farm which is politely called a school. We also know, or ought to know, that institutional treatment of children is murderous for infants and bad for all children. Homeless infants can be saved from that by adoption; but the elder children are forcing us to face the problem of organizing child life as such, giving children constitutional rights just as we have had to give them to women, and ceasing to shirk that duty either by bundling the children off to Bastilles called schools or by making the child the property of its father (in the case of an illegitimate child, of its mother) as we have ceased to shirk women's rights by making the woman the property of her husband. The beginnings of such organization are already visible in the Girl Guides and the Boy Scouts. But the limits to liberty which the State has to set and the obligations which it has to impose on adults are as imperative for children as for adults. The Girl Guide cannot be always guiding nor the Boy Scout always scouting. They must qualify themselves for adult citizenship by certain acquirements whether they like it or not. That is our excuse for school: they must be educated.

Education is a word that in our mouths covers a good many things. At present we are only extricating ourselves slowly and, as usual, reluctantly and ill humoredly, from our grossest stupidities about it. One of them is that it means learning lessons, and that learning lessons is for children, and ceases when they come of age. I, being a septuagenarian, can assure you confidently that we never cease learning to the extent of our capacity for learning until our faculties fail us. As to what we have been taught in school and college, I should say roughly that as it takes us all our lives to find out the meaning of the small part of it that is true and the error of the large part that is false, it is not surprising that those who have been "educated" least know most. It is gravely injurious both to children and adults to be forced to study subjects for which they have no natural aptitude even when some ulterior object which they have at heart gives them a fictitious keenness to master it. Mental disablement caused in this way is common in the modern examination-passing classes. Dickens's Mr Toots is not a mere figure of fun: he is an authentic instance of a sort of imbecility that is dangerously prevalent in our public school and university products. Toots is no joke.

Even when a natural aptitude exists it may be overcome by the repulsion created by coercive teaching. If a girl is unmusical, any attempt to force her to learn to play Beethoven's sonatas is torture to herself and to her teachers, to say nothing of the agonies of her audiences when her parents order her to display her accomplishment to visitors. But unmusical girls are as exceptional as deaf girls. The common case of a rooted loathing for music, and a vindictive hope that Beethoven may be expiating a malevolent life in eternal torment, is that of the normally musical girl who, before she had ever heard a sonata or any other piece of music played well enough to seem beautiful to her, has been set to practise scales in a cold room, rapped over the knuckles when she struck a wrong note, and had the Pathetic Sonata rapped and scolded and bullied into her bar by bar until she could finger it out without a mistake. That is still what school-taught music means to many unfortunate young ladies whose parents desire them to have accomplishments, and accordingly pay somebody who has been handled in the same way to knock this particular accomplishment into them. If these unhappy victims thought that Socialism meant compulsory music they would die in the last ditch fighting against it; and they would be right.

If I were writing a book for men I should not speak of music: I should speak of verses written in literary Latin (meaning a sort of Latin that nobody ever spoke), of Greek, and of algebra. Many an unhappy lad who would have voluntarily picked up enough Latin and Greek to read Virgil, Horace, and Homer, or to whom Descartes, Newton, and Einstein would be heroes such as Handel, Mozart, Beethoven, and Wagner are to unspoilt musicians, loathes every printed page except in a newspaper or detective story, and shrinks from an algebraic symbol or a diagram of the parallelogram of forces as a criminal from a prison. This is the result of our educational mania. When Eton was founded, the idea was that the boys should be roused at six in the morning and kept hard at their Latin without a moment's play until they went to bed. And now that the tendency is to keep them hard at play instead, without a moment for free work, their condition is hardly more promising. Either way an intelligent woman, remembering her own childhood, must stand aghast at the utter disregard of the children's ordinary human rights, and the classing of them partly as animals to be tamed and broken in, for which, provided the methods are not those of the trainer of performing animals, there is something to be said, and partly as inanimate sacks into which learning is to be pourèd *ad libitum*, for which there is nothing to be said except what can be said for the water torture of the Inquisition, in which the fluid was poured down the victims' throats until they were bloated to death. But there was some method in this madness. I have already hinted to you what you must have known very well, that children, unless they are forced into a quiet, sedentary, silent, motionless, and totally unnatural association with adults, are so troublesome at home that humane parents who would submit to live in a bear-garden or a monkey-house rather than be cruelly repressive, are only too glad to hand them over to anyone who will profess to educate them, whilst the desperate struggle of the genteel disendowed younger son and unmarried daughter class to find some means of livelihood produces a number of persons who are willing to make a profession of child farming under the same highly plausible pretext.

Socialism would abolish this class by providing its members with less hateful and equally respectable employment. Nobody who had not a genuine vocation for teaching would adopt teaching as a profession. Sadists, female and male, who now get children into their power so as to be able to torture them with impunity, and child fanciers (who are sometimes the same people) of the kind that now start amateur orphanages because they have the same craze for children that some people have for horses and dogs, although they often treat them abominably, would be checkmated if the children had any refuge from them except the homes from which they had been practically turned out, and from which they would be promptly returned to their tyrants with the assurance that if they were punished it served them right for being naughty. Within a few days of writing this I have read as part of the day's news of a case in which a mother summoned a schoolmaster because he had first caned her boy for hiccuping, which is not a voluntary action, and then, because the boy made light of the punishment, fell on him in a fury and thrashed him until he raised wheals on him that were visible eight days afterwards. Magistrates are usually as lenient in dealing with these assaults as with similar assaults by husbands on their wives (assaults by wives are laughed out of court): indeed they usually dismiss the case with a rebuke to the victim for being an unmanly little coward and not taking his licking in good part; but this time they admitted that the punishment, as they called it, was too severe; and the schoolmaster had to pay the mother's costs, though nobody hinted at any unfitness on his part for the duties he had assumed. And, in fairness, it did not follow that the man was a savage or a Sadist, any more than it follows that married people who commit furious assaults on oneanother have murderous natural dispositions. The truth is that just as married life in a one-room tenement is more than human nature can bear even when there are no children to complicate it, life in the sort of prison we call a school, where the teacher who hates her work is shut in with a crowd of unwilling, hostile, restless children, sets up a strain and hatred that explodes from time to time in onslaughts with the cane, not only for hiccuping, but for talking, whispering, looking out of the window (inattention), and even moving. Modern psychological research, even in its rather grotesque Freudian beginnings, is forcing us to recognize how serious is the permanent harm that comes of this atmosphere of irritation on the one side and suppression, terror, and reactionary naughtiness on the other. Even those who do not study psychology are beginning to notice that chaining dogs makes them dangerous, and is a cruel practice. They will presently have misgivings about chained children too, and begin to wonder whether thrashing and muzzling them is the proper remedy.

As a general result we find that what we call education is a failure. The poor woman's child is imprisoned for nine years under pretext of teaching it to read, write, and speak its own language: a year's work at the outside. And at the end of the nine years the prisoner can do none of these things presentably. In 1896, after twenty-six years of compulsory general education, the secretary of the Union of Mathematical Instrument Makers told me that most of his members signed with a mark. Rich male children are kept in three successive prisons, the preparatory school, the public school (meaning a very exclusive private school malversating public endowments), and the university, the period of imprisonment being from twelve to fourteen years, and the subjects taught including classical languages and higher mathematics. Rich female children, formerly imprisoned in the family dungeon under a wardress called a governess, are now sent out like their brothers. The result is a slightly greater facility in reading and writing, the habits and speech of the rich idle classes, and a moral and intellectual imbecility which leaves them politically at the mercy of every bumptious adventurer and fluent charlatan who has picked up their ways and escaped their education, and morally on the level of medieval robber barons and early capitalist buccaneers. When they are energetic and courageous, in spite of their taming, they are public dangers: when they are mere sheep, doing whatever their class expects them to do, they will follow any enterprising bell-wether to the destruction of themselves and the whole community. Fortunately humanity is so recuperative that no system of suppression and perversion can quite abort it; but as far as our standard lady's and gentleman's education goes the very least that can be said against it is that most of its victims would be better without it.

It is, however, incidentally advantageous. The university student who is determined not to study, gains from the communal life of the place a social standing that is painfully lacking in the people who have been brought up in a brick box in ill mannered intercourse with two much older people and three or four younger ones, all keeping what they call their company manners (meaning an affectation which has no desirable quality except bare civility) for the few similarly reared outsiders who are neither too poor to be invited in nor too rich to condescend to enter the box. Nobody can deny that these middle class families which cannot afford the university for their sons, and must send them out as workers at fifteen or so, appear utterly unpresentable vulgarians compared to our university products. The woman from the brick box maintains her social position by being offensive to the immense number of people whom she considers her inferiors, reserving her civility for the very few who are clinging to her own little ledge on the social precipice; for inequality of income takes the broad, safe, and fertile plain of human society and stands it on edge so that everyone has to cling desperately to her foothold and kick off as many others as she can. She would cringe to her superiors if they could be persuaded to give her the chance, whereas at a university she would have to meet hundreds of other young women on equal terms, and to be at least commonly civil to everybody. It is true that university manners are not the best manners, and that there is plenty of foundation for the statement that Oxford and Cambridge are hotbeds of exclusiveness, university snobs being perhaps the most incorrigible of all snobs. For all that, university snobbery is not so disabling as brick box snobbery. The university woman can get on without friction or awkwardness with all sorts of people, high or low, with whom the brick box woman simply does not know how to associate. But the university curriculum has nothing to do with this. On the contrary, it is the devoted scholar who misses it, and the university butterfly, barely squeezing through her examinations, who acquires it to perfection. Also, it can now be acquired and greatly improved on by young people who break loose from the brick box into the wider social life of clubs and unofficial cultural associations of all kinds. The manners of the garden city and the summer school are already as far superior to the manners of the university college as these are to the manners of the brick box. There is no word that has more sinister and terrible connotations in our snobbish society than the word promiscuity; but if you exclude its special and absurd use to indicate an imaginary condition of sexual disorder in which every petticoat and every coat and trousers fall into oneanother's embraces at sight, you will see that social promiscuity is the secret of good manners, and that it is precisely because the university is more promiscuous than the brick box, and the Theosophical or Socialist summer school more promiscuous than the college, that it is also the better mannered.

Socialism involves complete social promiscuity. It has already gone very far. When the great Duke of Wellington fell ill, he said "Send for the apothecary", just as he would have said "Send for the barber"; and the apothecary no doubt "your Graced" him in a very abject manner: indeed I can myself remember famous old physicians, even titled ones, who took your fee exactly as a butler used to take your tip. In the seventeenth century a nobleman would sometimes admit an actor to an intimate friendship; but when he wrote to him he began his letter, not "My dear So and So", but "To Betterton the player". Nowadays a duke who went on like that would be ridiculed as a Pooh Bah. Everybody can now travel third class in England without being physically disgusted by their fellow-travellers. I can remember when second class carriages, now extinct, were middle class necessities.

The same process that has levelled the social intercourse between dukes and doctors or actors can level it between duchesses and dairymaids, or, what seems far less credible, between doctors' wives and dairymaids. But whilst Socialism makes for this sort of promiscuity it will also make for privacy and exclusiveness. At present the difference between a dairymaid and any decent sort of duchess is marked, not by a wounding difference between the duchess's address to the dairymaid and her address to another duchess, but by a very marked difference between the address of a dairymaid to the duchess and her address to another dairymaid. The decent duchess's civility is promiscuous; but her intimate friendship and society is not. Civility is one thing, familiarity quite another. The duchess's grievance at present is that she is obliged by her social and political position to admit to her house and table a great many people whose tastes and intellectual interests are so different from her own that they bore her dreadfully, whilst her income cuts her off from familiar intercourse with many poor people whose society would be delightful to her, but who could not afford her expensive habits. Equality would bring to the duchess the blessing of being able to choose her familiars as far as they were willing to respond. She would no longer have to be bored by men who could talk about nothing but fox hunting or party politics when she wanted to talk about science or literature, dressmaking or gardening, or, if her tastes were more curious, the morbidities of psycho-analysis. Socialism, by steam-rollering our class distinctions (really income distinctions) would break us up into sets, cliques, and solitaries. The duchess would play golf (if people could still find no more interesting employment for their leisure) with any charwoman, and lunch with her after; but the intimate circle of the duchess and the charwoman would be more exclusive and highly selected than it can possibly be now. Socialism thus offers the utmost attainable society and the utmost attainable privacy. We should be at the same time much less ceremonious in our public relations and much more delicate about intruding on oneanother in our private ones.

You may say, what has all this to do with education? Have we not wandered pretty far from it? By no means: a great part of our education comes from our social intercourse. We educate oneanother; and we cannot do this if half of us consider the other half not good enough to talk to. But enough of that side of the subject. Let us leave the social qualifications which children, like adults, pick up from their surroundings and from the company they keep, and return to the acquirements which the State must impose on them compulsorily, providing the teachers and schools and apparatus; testing the success of the teaching; and giving qualifying certificates to those who have passed the tests.

It is now evident in all civilized States that there are certain things which people must know in order to play their part as citizens. There are technical things that must be learned, and intellectual conceptions that must be understood. For instance, you are not fit for life in a modern city unless you know the multiplication table, and agree that you must not take the law into your own hands. That much technical and liberal education is indispensable, because a woman who could not pay fares and count change, and who flew at people with whom she disagreed and tried to kill them or scratch their eyes out, would be as incapable of civilized life as a wild cat. In our huge cities reading is necessary, as people have to proceed by written directions. In a village or a small country town you can get along by accosting the police officer, or the railway porter or station-master, or the post-mistress, and asking them what to do and where to go; but in London five minutes of that would bring business and locomotion to a standstill: the police and railway officials, hard put to it as it is answering the questions of foreigners and visitors from the country, would be driven mad if they had to tell everybody everything. The newspapers, the postal and other official guides, the innumerable notice boards and direction posts, do for the London citizen what the police constable or the nearest shopkeeper rather enjoys doing for the villager, as a word with a stranger seems an almost exciting event in a place where hardly anything else happens except the motion of the earth.

In the days when even the biggest cities were no bigger than our country towns, and all civilized life was conducted on what we should call village lines, "clergy", or the ability to read and write, was not a necessity: it was a means of extending the mental culture of the individual for the individual's own sake, and was quite exceptional. This notion still sticks in our minds. When we force a girl to learn to read, and make that an excuse for imprisoning her in a school, we pretend that the object of it is to cultivate her as an individual, and open to her the treasures of literature. That is why we do it so badly and take so long over it. But our right to cultivate a girl in any particular way against her will is not clear, even if we could claim that sitting indoors on a hard seat and being forbidden to talk or fidget or attend to anything but the teacher cultivated a girl more highly than the free activities from which this process cuts her off. The only valid reason for forcing her at all costs to acquire the technique of reading, writing, and arithmetic enough for ordinary buying and selling is that modern civilized life is impossible without them. She may be said to have a natural right to be taught them just as she has a natural right to be nursed and weaned and taught to walk.

So far the matter is beyond argument. It is true that in teaching her how to write you are also teaching her how to forge cheques and write spiteful anonymous letters, and that in teaching her to read you are opening her mind to foul and silly books, and putting into her hands those greatest wasters of time in the world, the novels that are not worth reading (say ninetynine out of every hundred). All such objections go down before the inexorable necessity for the accomplishments that make modern life possible: you might as well object to teaching her how to use a knife to cut her food on the ground that you are also teaching her how to cut the baby's throat. Every technical qualification for doing good is a technical qualification for doing evil as well; but it is not possible to leave our citizens without any technical qualifications for the art of modern living on that account.

But this does not justify us in giving our children technical education and damning the consequences. The consequences would damn us. If we teach a girl to shoot without teaching her also that thou shalt not kill, she may send a bullet through us the first time she loses her temper; and if we proceed to hang her, she may say, as so many women now say when they are in trouble, "Why did nobody tell me?" This is why compulsory education cannot be confined to technical education. There are parts of liberal education which are as necessary in modern social life as reading and writing; and it is this that makes it so difficult to draw the line beyond which the State has no right to meddle with the child's mind or body without its free consent. Later on we may make conditions: for instance, we may say that a surveyor must learn trigonometry, a sea captain navigation, and a surgeon at least as much dexterity in the handling of saws and knives on bones and tissues as a butcher acquires. But that is not the same thing as forcing everybody to be a qualified surveyor, navigator, or surgeon. What we are now considering is how much the State must force everyone to learn as the minimum qualification for life in a civilized city. If the Government forces a woman to acquire the art of composing Latin verses, it is forcing on her an accomplishment which she can never need to exercise, and which she can acquire for herself in a few months if she should nevertheless be cranky enough to want to exercise it. There is the same objection to forcing her to learn the calculus. Yet somewhere between forcing her to learn to read and put two and two together accurately, and forcing her to write sham Horace or learn the calculus, the line must be drawn. The question is, where to draw it.

On the liberal side of education it is clear that a certain minimum of law, constitutional history, and economics is indispensable as a qualification for a voter even if ethics are left entirely to the inner light. In the case of young children, dogmatic commandments against murder, theft, and the more obvious possibilities of untutored social intercourse, are imperative; and it is here that we must expect fierce controversy. I need not repeat all that we have already been through as to the impossibility of ignoring this part of education and calling our neglect Secular Education. If on the ground that the subject is a controversial one you leave a child to find out for itself whether the earth is round or flat, it will find out that it is flat, and, after blundering into many mistakes and superstitions, be so angry with you for not teaching it that it is round, that when it becomes an adult voter it will insist on its own children having uncompromising positive guidance on the point.

What will not work in physics will not work in metaphysics either. No Government, Socialist or anti-Socialist or neutral, could possibly govern and administer a highly artificial modern State unless every citizen had a highly artificial modern conscience: that is, a creed or body of beliefs which would never occur to a primitive woman, and a body of disbeliefs, or negative creed, which would strike a primitive woman as fantastic blasphemies that must bring down on her tribe the wrath of the unseen powers. Modern governments must therefore inculcate these beliefs and disbeliefs, or at least see that they are inculcated somehow; or they cannot carry on. And the reason we are in such a mess at present is that our governments are trying to carry on with a set of beliefs and disbeliefs that belong to bygone phases of science and extinct civilizations. Imagine going to Moses or Mahomet for a code to regulate the modern money market!

If we all had the same beliefs and disbeliefs, we could go smoothly on, whether to our destruction or the millennium. But the conflicts between contradictory beliefs, and the progressive repudiations of beliefs which must continue as long as we have different patterns of mankind in different phases of evolution, will necessarily produce conflicts of opinion as to what should be taught in the public schools under the head of religious dogma and liberal education. At the present moment there are many people who hold that it is absolutely necessary to a child's salvation from an eternity of grotesque and frightful torment in a lake of burning brimstone that it should be baptized with water, as it is born under a divine curse and is a child of wrath and sin, and that as it grows into a condition of responsibility it must be impressed with this belief, with the addition that all its sins were atoned for by the sacrifice of Christ, the Son of God, on the cross, this atonement being effectual only for those who believe in it. Failing such belief the efficacy of the baptism is annulled, and the doom of eternal damnation reincurred. This is the official and State-endowed religion in our country today; and there is still on the statute book a law decreeing heavy punishments for anyone who denies its validity, which no Cabinet dares repeal.

Now it is not probable that a fully developed Socialist State will either impress these beliefs on children or permit any private person to do so until the child has reached what is called in another connection the age of consent. The State has to protect the souls of the children as well as their bodies; and modern psychology confirms common experience in teaching that to horrify a young child with stories of brimstone hells, and make it believe that it is a little devil who can only escape from that hell by maintaining a sinless virtue to which no saint or heroine has ever pretended, is to injure it for life more cruelly than by any act of bodily violence that even the most brutal taskmaster would dare to prescribe or justify. To put it quite frankly and flatly, the Socialist State, as far as I can guess, will teach the child the multiplication table, but will not only not teach it the Church Catechism, but if the State teachers find that the child's parents have been teaching it the Catechism otherwise than as a curious historical document, the parents will be warned that if they persist the child will be taken out of their hands and handed over to the Lord Chancellor, exactly as the children of Shelley were when their maternal grandfather denounced his son-in-law as an atheist.

Further, a Socialist State will not allow its children to be taught that polygamy, slaughter of prisoners of war, and blood sacrifices, including human sacrifices, are divinely appointed institutions; and this means that it will not allow the Bible to be introduced in schools otherwise than as a collection of old chronicles, poems, oracles, and political fulminations, on the same footing as the travels of Marco Polo, Goethe's Faust, Carlyle's Past and Present and Sartor Resartus, and Ruskin's Ethics of the Dust. Also the doctrine that our life in this world is only a brief preliminary episode in preparation for an all-important life to come, and that it does not matter how poor or miserable or plague ridden we are in this world, as we shall be gloriously compensated in the next if we suffer patiently, will be prosecuted as seditious and blasphemous.

Such a change would not be so great as some of us fear, though it would be a cataclysm if our present toleration and teaching of these doctrines were sincere. Fortunately it is not. The people who take them seriously, or even attach any definite meaning to the words in which they are formulated, are so exceptional that they are mostly marked off into little sects which are popularly regarded as not quite sane. It may be questioned whether as much as one per cent of the people who describe themselves as members of the Church of England, sending their children to its baptismal fonts, confirmation rite, and schools, and regularly attending its services, either know or care what they are committed to by its dogmas or articles, or read and believe them as they read and believe the morning paper. Possibly the percentage of Nonconformists who know the Westminster Confession and accept it may be slightly larger, because Nonconformity includes the extreme sects; but as these sects play the most fantastic variations on the doctrine of the Catechism, Nonconformity covers views which have been violently persecuted by the Church as blasphemous and atheistic. I am quite sure that unless you have made a special study of the subject you have no suspicion of the variety and incompatibility of the British religions that come under the general heading of Christian. No Government could possibly please them all. Queen Elizabeth, who tried to do it by drawing up thirtynine articles alternately asserting and denying the disputed doctrines, so that every woman could find her own creed affirmed there and the other woman's creed denounced, has been a complete failure except as a means of keeping tender consciences and scrupulous intellects out of the Church. Ordinary clergymen subscribe them under duress because they cannot otherwise obtain ordination. Nobody pretends that they are all credible by the same person at the same moment; and few people even know what they are or what they mean. They could all be dropped silently without any shock to the real beliefs of most of us.

A Capitalist Government must inculcate whatever doctrine is

best calculated to make the common people docile wage slaves; and a Socialist Government must equally inculcate whatever doctrine will make the sovereign people good Socialists. No Government, whatever its policy may be, can be indifferent to the formation of the inculcated common creed of the nation. Society is impossible unless the individuals who compose it have the same beliefs as to what is right and wrong in commonplace conduct. They must have a common creed antecedent to the Apostles' creed, the Nicene creed, the Athanasian creed, and all the other religious manifestoes. Queen Mary Tudor and Queen Elizabeth, King James the Second and King William the Third, could not agree about the Real Presence; but they all agreed that it was wrong to rob, murder, or set fire to the house of your neighbor. The sentry at the gate of Buckingham Palace may disagree with the Royal Family on many points, ranging from the imperial policy of the Cabinet, or the revision of the Prayer Book, to which horse to back for the Derby; but unless there were perfect harmony between them as to the proper limits to the use of his rifle and bayonet their social relation could not be maintained: there could be neither king nor sentry. We all deprecate prejudice; but if all of us were not animated sacks of prejudices, and at least nine-tenths of them were not the same prejudices so deeply rooted that we never think of them as prejudices but call them common sense, we could no more form a community than so many snakes.

This common sense is not all inborn. Some of it is: for instance, a woman knows without being told that she must not eat her baby, and that she must feed it and rear it at all hazards. But she has not the same feeling about paying her rates and taxes, although this is as necessary to the life of society as the rearing of infants to the life of humanity. A friend of mine who was a highly educated woman, the head of a famous college in the north of London, fiercely disputed the right of the local authority to have the drainage of the college examined by a public sanitary inspector. Her creed was that of a jealously private lady brought up in a private house; and it seemed an outrage to her that a man with whom she was not on visiting terms should be legally privileged to walk into the most private apartments of her college otherwise than at her invitation. Yet the health of the community depends on a general belief that this privilege is salutary and reasonable. The enlargement of the social creed to that extent is the only way to get rid of cholera epidemics. But this very able and highly instructed lady, though still in the prime of life, was too old to learn.

The social creed must be imposed on us when we are children; for it is like riding, or reading music at sight: it can never become a second nature to those who try to learn it as adults; and the social creed, to be really effective, must be a second nature to us. It is quite easy to give people a second nature, however unnatural, if you catch them early enough. There is no belief, however grotesque and even villainous, that cannot be made a part of human nature if it is inculcated in childhood and not contradicted in the child's hearing. Now that you are grown up, nothing could persuade you that it is right to lame every woman for life by binding her feet painfully in childhood on the ground that it is not ladylike to move about freely like an animal. If you are the wife of a general or admiral nothing could persuade you that when the King dies you and your husband are bound in honor to commit suicide so as to accompany your sovereign into the next world. Nothing could persuade you that it is every widow's duty to be cremated alive with the dead body of her husband. But if you had been caught early enough you could have been made to believe and do all these things exactly as Chinese, Japanese, and Indian women have believed and done them. You may say that these were heathen Eastern women, and that you are a Christian Western. But I can remember when your grandmother, also a Christian Western, believed that she would be disgraced for ever if she let anyone see her ankles in the street, or (if she was "a real lady") walk there alone. The spectacle she made of herself when, as a married woman, she put on a cap to announce to the world that she must no longer be attractive to men, and the amazing figure she cut as a widow in crape robes symbolic of her utter desolation and woe, would, if you could see or even conceive them, convince you that it was purely her luck and not any superiority of western to eastern womanhood that saved her from the bound feet, the suttee, and the hara-kiri. If you still doubt it, look at the way in which men go to war and commit frightful atrocities because they believe it is their duty, and also because the women would spit in their faces if they refused, all because this has been inculcated upon them from their childhood, thus creating the public opinion which enables the Government not only to raise enthusiastic volunteer armies, but to enforce military service by heavy penalties on the few people who, thinking for themselves, cannot accept wholesale murder and ruin as patriotic virtues.

It is clear that if all female children are to have their minds formed as the mind of Queen Victoria was formed in her infancy, a Socialist State will be impossible. Therefore it may be taken as certain that after the conquest of Parliament by the proletariat, the formation of a child's mind on that model will be prevented by every means within the power of the Government. Children will not be taught to ask God to bless the squire and his relations and keep us in our proper stations, nor will they be brought up in such a way that it will seem natural to them to praise God because he makes them eat whilst others starve, and sing while others do lament. If teachers are caught inculcating that attitude they will be sacked: if nurses, their certificates will be cancelled, and jobs found for them that do not involve intercourse with young children. Victorian parents will share the fate of Shelley. Adults must think what they please subject to their being locked up as lunatics if they think too unsocially; but on points that are structural in the social edifice, constitutional points as we call them, no quarter will be given in infant schools. The child's up-to-date second nature will be an official second nature, just as the obsolete second nature inculcated at our public schools and universities is at present.

When the child has learnt its social creed and catechism, and can read, write, reckon, and use its hands: in short, when it is qualified to make its way about in modern cities and do ordinary useful work, it had better be left to find out for itself what is good for it in the direction of higher cultivation. If it is a Newton or a Shakespear it will learn the calculus or the art of the theatre without having them shoved down its throat: all that is necessary is that it should have access to books, teachers, and theatres. If its mind does not want to be highly cultivated, its mind should be let alone on the ground that its mind knows best what is good for it. Mentally, fallow is as important as seedtime. Even bodies can be exhausted by overcultivation. Trying to make people champion athletes indiscriminately is as idiotic as trying to make them Ireland Scholars indiscriminately. There is no reason to expect that Socialist rule will be more idiotic than the rule which has produced Eton and Harrow, Oxford and Cambridge, and Squeers.

82

SOCIALISM AND THE CHURCHES

HOW far a Socialist State will tolerate a Church in our sense at all is a pretty question. The quarrel between Church and State is an old one. In speculating on it we must for the moment leave our personal churchgoings and persuasions out of account, and try to look at the question from the outside as we look at the religions of the east; or, to put it bookishly, objectively, not subjectively. At present, if a woman opens a consulting room in Bond Street, and sits there in strange robes professing to foretell the future by cards or crystals or revelations made to her by spirits, she is prosecuted as a criminal for imposture. But if a man puts on strange robes and opens a church in which he professes to absolve us from the guilt of our misdeeds, to hold the keys of heaven and hell, to guarantee that what he looses or binds on earth shall be loosed and bound in heaven, to alleviate the lot of souls in purgatory, to speak with the voice of God, and to dictate what is sin and what is not to all the world (pretensions which, if you look at them objectively, are far more extravagant and dangerous than those of the poor sorceress with her cards and tea leaves and crystals), the police treat him with great respect; and nobody dreams of prosecuting him as an outrageous impostor. The objective explanation of his immunity is that a great many people do not think him an impostor: they believe devoutly that he can do all these things that he pretends to do; and this enables him and his fellow priests to organize themselves into a powerful and rich body calling itself The Church, supported by the money, the votes, and the resolution to die in its defence, of millions of citizens. The priest can not only defy the police as the common sorceress cannot: he has only to convince a sufficient number of people of his divine mission to thrust the Government aside; assume all its functions except the dirty work that he does not care to soil his hands with and therefore leaves to "the secular arm"; take on himself powers of life and death, salvation and damnation; dictate what we shall all read and think; and place in every family an officer to regulate our lives in every particular according to his notions of right and wrong.

This is not a fancy picture. History tells us of an emperor crawling on his knees through the snow and lying there all night supplicating pardon from the head of a Church, and of a king of England flogging himself in the cathedral where a priest had been murdered at his suggestion. Citizens have been stripped of all their possessions, tortured, mutilated, burned alive, by priests whose wrath did not spare even the dead in their graves, whilst the secular rulers of the land were forced, against their own interest and better sense, to abet them in their furious fanaticism.

You may say that this was far off or long ago; that I am raking up old tales of Canossa, of Canterbury in the middle ages, of Spain in the fifteenth century, of Orange bogies like Bloody Mary and Torquemada; that such things have not been done in England since the British parliamentary government cut off Archbishop Laud's head for doing them; and that popes are now in greater danger of being imprisoned, and priests and monks of being exiled, by emperors and republicans alike, than statesmen of being excommunicated. You may add that the British State burnt women alive for coining and for rebellion, and pressed men to death under heavy weights for refusing for their wives' and children's sake to plead to charges of felony, long after priests had dropped such methods of dealing with heretics.

But even if women were still burnt at the stake as ruthlessly as negroes are today by lynching mobs in America, there would still be a struggle between Church and State as to which of them had the right and power to burn. Who is to be allowed to exercise the great powers that the Government of a modern civilized State must possess if its civilization is to endure? The kings have subjugated the barons; the parliaments have subjugated the kings; democracy has been subjugated by plutocracy; and plutocracy is blindly provoking the subjugated Demos to set up the proletarian State and make an end of Capitalist Oligarchy. But there is a rival power which has persisted and will persist through all these changes; and that is Theocracy, the power of priests (sometimes called parsons) organized into Churches professing to derive their authority from God. Crushed in one form it arises in another. When it was organized as the Church of Rome its abuses provoked the Reformation in England and Northern Europe, and in France the wrath of Voltaire and the French revolution. In both cases it was disarmed until its power to overrule the State was broken, and it became a mere tool of Plutocracy.

But note what followed. The reaction against the priests went so far in Britain, Switzerland, Holland, and America that at the cry of No Popery every Roman Catholic trembled for his house and every priest for his life. Yet under Laud and the Star Chamber in England, and Calvin in Geneva, Theocracy was stronger than ever; for Calvin outpoped all the popes, and John Knox in Scotland made her princes tremble as no pope had ever done. But perhaps you will say again "This was long ago: we have advanced since them". So you have always been told; but look at the facts within my own recollection. Among my contemporaries I can remember Brigham Young, President Kruger, and Mrs Eddy. Joseph Smith, Junior, was martyred only twelve years before I was born. You may never have heard of Joseph; but I assure you his career was in many respects, up to the date of his martyrdom, curiously like that of Mahomet, the obscure Arab camel driver whose followers conquered half the world, and are still making the position of the British Empire in Asia very difficult. Joseph claimed direct revelation from God, and set up a Theocracy which was carried on by Brigham Young, a Mormon Moses, one of the ablest rulers on record, until the secular Government of the United States became convinced that Mormon Theocracy was not compatible with American Democracy, and took advantage of the popular prejudice against its "plurality of wives" (polygamy) to smash it. It is by no means dead yet; but for the moment its teeth, which were sharp, are drawn; and its place in the struggle is occupied by The Church of Christ Scientist, founded by an American lady (who might have been yourself) named Mrs Eddy. I often pass two handsome churches of hers in London; and for all I know there may be others that are out of my beat there. Now unless you happen to be a Mormon or a Christian Scientist, it is probable that you think about Mrs Eddy exactly as a Roman lady in the second century A.D. thought about the mother of Christ, and about Joseph Smith as an English lady in the Middle Ages thought about "the accurst Mahound". You may be right or you may be wrong; but for all you know Mrs Eddy a thousand years hence may be worshipped as the Divine Woman by millions of civilized people, and Joseph Smith may be to millions more what Mahomet now is to Islam. You never can tell. People begin by saying "Is not this the carpenter's son?" and end by saying "Behold the Lamb of God!"

The secular Governments, or States, of the future, like those of the present and past, will find themselves repeatedly up against the pretensions of Churches, new and old, to exercise, as Theocracies, powers and privileges which no secular Government now claims. The trouble becomes serious when a new Church attempts to introduce new political or social institutions, or to revive obsolete ones. Joseph Smith was allowed to represent himself as having been directed by an angel to a place where a continuation of the Bible, inscribed on gold plates, was buried in the earth, and as having direct and, if necessary, daily revelations from God which enabled him to act as an infallible lawgiver. When he found plenty of able business women and men to believe him, the Government of the United States held that their belief was their own business and within their own rights as long as Joseph's laws harmonized with the State laws. But when Joseph revived Solomonic polygamy the monogamic secular Government had to cross swords with him. Not for many years did it get the upper hand; and its adversary is not dead yet.

Mrs Eddy did the opposite: she did not introduce a new institution; but she challenged one of the standing institutions of the secular State. The secular State prescribed pathogenic inoculations as preventives of disease, and bottles of medicine and surgical operations, administered and performed by its registered doctors and surgeons, as cures; and anyone who left a child or an invalid for whom she was responsible undoctored was punished severely for criminal neglect. Some governments refused to admit uninoculated persons into their territories. Mrs Eddy revived the practice prescribed by St James in the New Testament, instructing her disciples to have nothing to do with bottles and inoculations; and immediately the secular government was at war with Christian Science and began to persecute its healers.

This case is interesting because it illustrates the fact that new Churches sometimes capture the secular government by denying that they are Churches. The conflict between Mrs Eddy and the secular governments was really a conflict between the Church of Christ Scientist and the new Church of Jenner and Pasteur Scientists, which has the secular governments in its pocket exactly as the Church of Rome had Charlemagne. It also incidentally illustrates the tendency of all Churches to institute certain rites to signalize the reception of children and converts into the Church. The Jews prescribe a surgical operation, fortunately not serious nor harmful. The Christian Churches prescribe water baptism and anointing: also quite harmless. The babies object vociferously; but as they neither foresee the rite nor remember it they are none the worse. But the inoculations of the modern Churches which profess Science, with their lists of miracles, their biographies of their saints, their ruthless persecutions, their threats of dreadful plagues and horrible torments if they are disobeyed, their claims to hold the keys of mortal life and death, their sacrifices and divinations, their demands for exemption from all moral law in their researches and all legal responsibility in their clinical practice, leave the pretensions of the avowed priests and prophets nowhere, are dangerous and sometimes deadly; and it is round this disguised Church that the persecutions and fanaticisms of today rage. There is very little danger of a British Parliament persecuting in the name of Christ, and none at all of its persecuting in the name of Mahomet in the west; but it has persecuted cruelly for a century in the name of Jenner; and there is a very serious danger of its persecuting the general public as it now persecutes soldiers in the name of Pasteur, whose portrait is already on the postage stamps of the resolutely secularist (as it imagines) French Republic. In the broadest thoroughfare of fashionable London we have erected a startling brazen image of the famous Pasteurite surgeon Lord Lister, who, when the present age of faith in scientific miracles has passed, will probably be described as a high priest who substituted carbolic acid for holy water and consecrated oil as a magic cure for festering wounds. His methods are no longer in fashion in the hospitals; and he has been left far behind as a theorist; but when the centenary of his birth was celebrated in 1927, the stories of his miracles, told with boundless credulity and technical ignorance in all the newspapers, shewed that he was really being worshipped as a saint.

From this, I invite you to note how deceptive history may be. The continual springing up of new Churches has always forced secular governments to make and administer laws to deal with them, because, though some of them are reasonable and respectable enough to be left alone, and others are too strongly represented in Parliament and in the electorate to be safely interfered with, a good many of which you have never heard defy the laws as to personal decency and violate the tables of consanguinity to such an extent that if the authorities did not suppress them the people would lynch them. That is why tribunals like the Inquisition and the Star Chamber had to be set up to bring them to justice. But as these were not really secular tribunals, being in fact instruments of rival Churches, their powers were abused, the new prophets and their followers being restrained or punished, not as offenders against the secular law, but as heretics: that is, as dissenters from the Church which had gained control of the secular government: the Church of Rome in the case of the Inquisition, and the Church of England in the case of the Star Chamber.

The difficulty, you see, is that though there is a continual rivalry between Churches and States for the powers of government, yet the States do not disentangle themselves from the Churches, because the members of the secular parliaments and Cabinets are all Churchmen of one sort or another. In England this muddle is illustrated by the ridiculous fact that the bishops of the Church of England have seats as such in the House of Lords whilst the clergy are excluded as such from the House of Commons. The Parliaments are the rivals of the Churches and yet become their instruments; so that the struggle between them is rather as to whether the Churches shall exercise power directly, calling in the secular arm merely to enforce their decisions without question, or whether they shall be mere constituents of the Parliaments like any other society of citizens, leaving the ultimate decisions to the

State. If, however, any particular Church is powerful enough to make it a condition of admission to Parliament, or of occupation of the throne or the judicial bench, or of employment in the public services or the professions, that the postulant shall be one of its members, that Church will be in practice, if not in theory, stronger than it could be as a Theocracy ruling independently of the secular State. This power was actually achieved by the Church of England; but it broke down because the English people would not remain in one Church. They broke away from the Church of England in all directions, and formed Free Churches. One of these, called the Society of Friends (popularly called Quakers), carried its repudiation of Church of England ecclesiasticism to the length of denouncing priests as impostors, set prayers as an insult to God ("addressing God in another man's words"), and church buildings as "steeple houses"; yet this body, by sheer force of character, came out of a savage persecution the most respected and politically influential of religious forces in the country. When the Free Churches could no longer be kept out of Parliament, and the Church of England could not be induced to grant any of them a special privilege, there was nothing for it but to admit everybody who was a Christian Deist of any denomination. The line was still drawn at Jews and Atheists; but the Jews soon made their way in; and finally a famous Atheist, Charles Bradlaugh, broke down the last barrier to the House of Commons by forcing the House to accept, instead of the Deist oath, a form of affirmation which relieved Atheists from the necessity of perjuring themselves before taking their seats. We are now accustomed to Jewish Prime Ministers; and we do not know whether our Gentile Prime Ministers are Atheists or not, because it never occurs to us to ask the question. The King alone remains bound by a coronation oath which obliges him to repudiate the Church of many of his subjects, though he has to maintain that Church and several others, some not even Christian, in parts of the Empire where the alternative would be no Church at all.

When Parliament is open to all the Churches, including the Atheist Churches (for the Positivist Societies, the Ethical Societies, the Agnostics, the Materialists, the Darwinian Natural Selectionists, the Creative Evolutionists, and even the Pantheists are all infidels and Atheists from the strict Evangelical or Fundamentalist point of view), it becomes impossible to attach religious rites to our institutions, because none of the Churches will consent to make any rites but their own legally obligatory. Parliament is therefore compelled to provide purely civil formalities as substitutes for religious services in the naming of children, in marriage, and in the disposal of the dead. Today the civil registrar will marry you and name your children as legally as an archbishop or a cardinal; and when there is a death in the family you can have the body cremated either with any sort of ceremony you please or no ceremony at all except the registration of the death after certification of its cause by a registered doctor.

As, in addition, you need not now pay Church rates unless you want to, we have arrived at a point at which, from one end of our lives to the other, we are not compelled by law to pay a penny to the priest unless we are country landlords, nor attend a religious service, nor concern ourselves in any way with religion in the popular sense of the word. Compulsion by public opinion, or by our employers or landlords, is, as we have seen, another matter; but here we are dealing only with State compulsion. Delivered from all this, we are left face to face with a body of beliefs calling itself Science, now more Catholic than any of the avowed Churches ever succeeded in being (for it has gone right round the world), demanding, and in some countries obtaining, compulsory inoculation for children and soldiers and immigrants, compulsory castration for dysgenic adults, compulsory segregation and tutelage for "mental defectives", compulsory sanitation for our houses, and hygienic spacing and placing for our cities, with other compulsions of which the older Churches never dreamt, at the behest of doctors and "men of science". In England we are still too much in the grip of the old ways to have done either our best or our worst in this direction; but if you care to know what Parliaments are capable of when they have ceased to believe what oldfashioned priests tell them and lavish all their natural childish credulity on professors of Science you must study the statute books of the American State Legislatures, the "crowned republics" of our own Dominions, and the new democracies of South America and Eastern Europe. When all the States are captured by the proletariat in the names of Freedom and Equality, the cry may arise that the little finger of Medical Research (calling itself Science) is thicker than the loins of Religion.

Now what made the oldfashioned religion so powerful was that at its best (meaning in the hands of its best believers) there was much positive good in it, and much comfort for those who could not bear the cruelty of nature without some explanation of life that carried with it an assurance that righteousness and mercy will have the last word. This is the power of Science also: it, too, at its best has done enormous positive good; and it also at its highest flight gives a meaning to life which is full of encouragement, exultation, and intense interest. You may yourself be greatly concerned as to whether the old or the new explanation is the true one; but looking at it objectively you must put aside the question of absolute truth, and simply observe and accept the fact that the nation is made up of a relatively small number of religious or scientific zealots, a huge mass of people who do not bother about the business at all, their sole notion of religion and morality being to do as other people in their class do, and a good many Betwixt-and-Betweens. The neutrals are in one sense the important people, because any creed may be imposed on them by inculcation during infancy, whereas the believers and unbelievers who think for themselves will let themselves be burnt alive rather than conform to a creed imposed on them by any power except their own consciences. It is over the inculcation, involving the creation of that official second nature which we discussed in the preceding chapter, that the State finds itself at loggerheads with the Churches which have not captured it.

Take a typical example or two. If any society of adults, calling itself a Church or not, preaches the old doctrine of the resurrection of the body at a great Last Judgment of all mankind, there is no likelihood of the municipality of a crowded city objecting. But if a survival of the childish idea that a body can be preserved for resurrection by putting it into a box and burying it in the earth, whereas reducing it to ashes in two hours in a cremation furnace renders its resurrection impossible, leads any sect or Church or individual to preach and practise intramural interment as a religious duty, then it is pretty certain that the municipality will not only keep such preaching out of its schools, but see to it that the children are taught to regard cremation as the proper way of disposing of the dead in towns, and forcibly prevent intramural interment whether pious parents approve of it or not.

If a Church, holding that animals are set apart from human beings by having no souls, and were created for the use of mankind and not for their own sakes, teaches that animals have no rights, and women and men no duties to them, their teaching on that point will be excluded from the schools and their members prosecuted for cruelty to animals by the secular authority.

If another Church wants to set up an abattoir in which animals will be killed in a comparatively cruel manner instead of by a humane killer in the municipal abattoir, it will not be allowed to do it nor to teach children that it ought to be done, unless, indeed, it commands votes enough to control the municipality to that extent; and if its members refuse to eat humanely slaughtered meat they will have to advance, like me, to vegetarianism.

When the question is raised, as it will be sooner or later, of the reservation of our cathedrals for the sermons of one particular Church, it will not be settled on the assumption that any one Church has a monopoly of religious truth. It is settled at present on the Elizabethan assumption that the services of the Church of England ought to please everybody; and it is quite possible that if the services of the Church of England were purified from its grosser sectarian superstitions, and a form of service arrived at containing nothing offensive to anyone desiring the consolation or stimulus of a religious ritual, the State might very well reserve the cathedrals for that form of service exclusively, provided that, as at present, the building were available most of the time for free private meditation and prayer. (You may not have realized that any Jew, any Mahometan, any Agnostic, any woman of any creed or no creed, may use our cathedrals daily to "make her soul" between the services.) To throw open the cathedrals to the rituals of all the Churches is a physical impossibility. To sell them on capitalist principles to the highest bidders to do what they like with is a moral impossibility for the State, though the Church has sold churches often enough. To simply make of them show places like Stonehenge, and charge for admission, as the Church of England sometimes does in the choir, would destroy their value for those who cannot worship without the aid of a ritual.

There is also the Russian plan of the State taking formal possession of the material property of the national Church, and then letting it go on as before, with the quaint difference that the statesmen and officials, instead of posing as devout Churchmen, sincerely or not, as in England, solemnly warn the people that the whole business is a superstitious mummery got up to keep them in submissive slavery by doping them with promises of bliss after death if only they will suffer poverty and slavery patiently before it. This, however, cannot last. It is only the reaction of the victorious proletariat against the previous unholy alliance of the Church with their former oppressors. It is mere anti-clericalism; and when clericalism as we know it disappears, and Churches can maintain themselves only as Churches of the people and not as spiritual fortresses of Capitalism, the anti-clerical reaction will pass away. The Russian Government knows that a purely negative attitude towards religion is politically impossible; accordingly, it teaches the children a new creed called Marxism, of which more presently. Even in the first flush of the reaction the Soviet was more tolerant than we were when our hour came to revolt. We frankly robbed the Church of all it possessed and gave the plunder to the landlords. Long after that we deliberately cut off our Archbishop's head. Certainly the Soviet made it quite clear to the Russian archbishop that if he did not make up his mind to accept the fact of the revolution and give to the Soviet the allegiance he had formerly given to the Tsar, he would be shot. But when he very sensibly and properly made up his mind accordingly, he was released, and is now presumably pontificating much more freely than the Archbishop of Canterbury.

So far, I have dealt with the Churches objectively and not with religion subjectively. It is an old saying: the nearer the Church the farther from God. But we must cross the line just for a paragraph or two. A live religion alone can nerve women to overcome their dread of any great social change, and to face that extraction of dead religions and dead parts of religions which is as necessary as the extraction of dead or decaying teeth. All courage is religious: without religion we are cowards. Men, because they have been specialized for fighting and hunting whilst women, as the child-bearers, have had to be protected from such risks, have got into the way of accepting the ferocities of war and the daring emulations of sportsmanship as substitutes for courage; and they have imposed that fraud to some extent on women. But women know instinctively, even when they are echoing male glory stuff, that communities live not by slaughter and by daring death, but by creating life and nursing it to its highest possibilities. When Ibsen said that the hope of the world lay in the women and the workers he was neither a sentimentalist nor a demagogue. You cannot have read this far (unless you have skipped recklessly) without discovering that I know as well as Ibsen did, or as you do, that women are not angels. They are as foolish as men in many ways; but they have had to devote themselves to life whilst men have had to devote themselves to death; and that makes a vital difference in male and female religion. Women have been forced to fear whilst men have been forced to dare: the heroism of a woman is to nurse and protect life, and of a man to destroy it and court death. But the homicidal heroes are often abject cowards in the face of new ideas, and veritable Weary Willies when they are asked to think. Their heroism is politically mischievous and useless. Knowing instinctively that if they thought about what they do they might find themselves unable to do it, they are afraid to think. That is why the heroine has to think for them, even to the extent of often having no time left to think for herself. She needs more and not less courage than a man; and this she must get from a creed that will bear thinking of without becoming incredible.

Let me then assume that you have a religion, and that the most important question you have to ask about Socialism is whether it will be hostile to that religion. The reply is quite simple. If your religion requires that incomes shall be unequal, Socialism will do all it can to persecute it out of existence, and will treat you much as the government of British India treated the Thugs in 1830. If your religion is compatible with equality of income, there is no reason on earth to fear that a Socialist Government will treat it or you any worse than any other sort of government would; and it would certainly save you from the private persecution, enforced by threats of loss of employment, to which you are subject under

Capitalism today if you are in the employment of a bigot.

There is, however, a danger against which you should be on your guard. Socialism may be preached, not as a far-reaching economic reform, but as a new Church founded on a new revelation of the will of God made by a new prophet. It actually is so preached at present. Do not be misled by the fact that the missionaries of Church Socialism do not use the word God, nor call their organization a Church, nor decorate their meeting-places with steeples. They preach an inevitable, final, supreme category in the order of the universe in which all the contradictions of the earlier and lower categories will be reconciled. They do not speak, except in derision, of the Holy Ghost or the Paraclete; but they preach the Hegelian Dialectic. Their prophet is named neither Jesus nor Mahomet nor Luther nor Augustine nor Dominic nor Joseph Smith, Junior, nor Mary Baker Glover Eddy, but Karl Marx. They call themselves, not the Catholic Church, but the Third International. Their metaphysical literature begins with the German philosophers Hegel and Feuerbach, and culminates in Das Kapital, the literary masterpiece of Marx, described as "The Bible of the working classes", inspired, infallible, omniscient. Two of their tenets contradict oneanother as flatly as the first two paragraphs of Article 27 of the Church of England. One is that the evolution of Capitalism into Socialism is predestined, implying that we have nothing to do but sit down and wait for it to occur. This is their version of Salvation by Faith. The other is that it must be effected by a revolution establishing a dictatorship of the proletariat. This is their version of Salvation by Works.

The success of the Russian revolution was due to its leadership by Marxist fanatics; but its subsequent mistakes had the same cause. Marxism is not only useless but disastrous as a guide to the practice of government. It gets no nearer to a definition of Socialism than as a Hegelian category in which the contradictions of Capitalism shall be reconciled, and in which political power shall have passed to the proletariat. Germans and Clydeside Scots find spiritual comfort in such abstractions; but they are unintelligible and repulsive to Englishwomen, and could not by themselves qualify anyone, English, Scotch, or German, to manage a whelkstall for five minutes, much less to govern a modern State, as Lenin very soon found out and very frankly confessed.

But Lenin and his successors were not able to extricate the new Russian national State they had set up from this new Russian international (Catholic) Church any more than our Henry II or the Emperor who had come to Canossa were able to extricate the English State and the medieval Empire from the Church of Rome. Nobody can foresee today whether the policy of Russia in any crisis will be determined on secular and national grounds by the Soviet or by the Third International on Marxist grounds. We are facing the Soviet as Queen Elizabeth faced Philip of Spain, willing enough to deal with him as an earthly king, but not as the agent of a Catholic Theocracy. In Russia the State will sooner or later have to break the temporal power of the Marxist Church and take politics out of its hands, exactly as the British and other Protestant States have broken the temporal power of the Roman Church, and been followed much more drastically by the French and Italian States. But until then the Church of Marx, the Third International, will give as much trouble as the Popes did formerly. It will give it in the name of Communism and Socialism, and be resisted not only by Capitalists but by the Communists and Socialists who understand that Communism and Socialism are matters for States and not for Churches to handle. King John was no less Christian than the Pope when he said that no Italian priest should tithe and toll in his dominions; and our Labor leaders can remain convinced Socialists and Communists whilst refusing to stand any foreign or domestic interference from the Third International or to acknowledge the divinity of Marx.

Still, our Protestant repudiation of the authority of the new Marxist Church should not make us forget that if the Marxist Bible cannot be taken as a guide to parliamentary tactics, the same may be said of those very revolutionary documents the Gospels. We do not on that account burn the Gospels and conclude that the preacher of The Sermon on the Mount has nothing to teach us; and neither should we burn Das Kapital and ban Marx as a worthless author whom nobody ought to read. Marx did not get his great reputation for nothing: he was a very great teacher; and the people who have not yet learnt his lessons make most dangerous stateswomen and statesmen. But those who have really learnt from him instead of blindly worshipping him as an infallible prophet are not Marxists any more than Marx himself was a Marxist. I myself was converted to Socialism by Das Kapital; and though I have since had to spend a good deal of time pointing out Marx's mistakes in abstract economics, his total lack of experience in the responsible management of public affairs, and the unlikeness at close quarters of his typical descriptions of the proletariat to any earthly working woman or of the bourgeoisie to any real lady of property, you may confidently set down those who speak contemptuously of Karl Marx either as pretenders who have never read him or persons incapable of his great mental range. Do not vote for such a person. Do not, however, vote for a Marxist fanatic either, unless you can catch one young enough or acute enough to grow out of Marxism after a little experience, as Lenin did. Marxism, like Mormonism, Fascism, Imperialism, and indeed all the would-be Catholicisms except Socialism and Capitalism, is essentially a call to a new Theocracy. Both Socialism and Capitalism certainly do what they can to obtain credit for representing a divinely appointed order of the universe; but the pressure of facts is too strong for their pretensions: they are forced to present themselves at last as purely secular expedients for securing human welfare, the one advocating equal distribution of income, and the other private property with free contract, as the secret of general prosperity.

83

CURRENT CONFUSIONS

I COULD go on like this for years; but I think I have now told you enough about Socialism and Capitalism to enable you to follow the struggle between them intelligently. You will find it irritating at first to read the newspapers and listen to the commonplaces of conversation on the subject, knowing all the time that the writers and talkers do not know what they are writing and talking about. The impulse to write to the papers, or intervene in the conversation to set matters right, may be almost irresistible. But it must be resisted, because if you once begin there will be no end to it. You must sit with an air of placid politeness whilst your neighbors, by way of talking politics, denounce the people they do not like as Socialists, Bolshevists, Syndicalists, Anarchists, and Communists on the one side, and Capitalists, Imperialists, Fascists, Reactionaries, and Bourgeois on the other, none of them having an idea of the meaning of these words clear enough to be called without flattery the ghost of a notion. A hundred years ago they would have called one another Jacobins, Radicals, Chartists, Republicans, Infidels, and even, to express the lowest depth of infamy, Co-operators; or, contrariwise, Tories, Tyrants, Bloated Aristocrats, and Fundholders. None of these names hurt now: Jacobins and Chartists are forgotten; republics are the rule and not the exception in Europe as well as in America; Co-operators are as respectable as Quakers; Bloated Aristocracy is the New Pauperism; and the proletariat, with its millions invested in Savings Certificates and Savings Bank deposits, would not at all object to being described as having money "in the funds", if that expression were still current. But the names in the mouths of the factions mean nothing anyhow. They are mere electioneering vituperation. In France at elections the Opposition posters always exhort the electors to vote against Assassins and Thieves (meaning the Cabinet); and the Government posters "feature" precisely the same epithets, whilst the candidates in their own homes call their pet dogs Bandits when pretending to scold them. It all means nothing. They had much better call each other Asses and Bitches (they sometimes do, by the way), because everyone knows that a man is not an ass nor a woman a bitch, and that calling them so is only a coarse way of insulting them; whereas most people do not know what the words Bolshevik, Anarchist, Communist, and so forth mean, and are too easily frightened into believing that they denote every imaginable extremity of violence and theft, rapine and murder. The Russian word Bolshevik, which has such a frightful sound to us, means literally nothing more than a member of a parliamentary majority; but as an English epithet it is only the political form of Bogey or Blackguard or the popular Bloody, denoting simply somebody or something with whom the speaker disagrees.

But the names we hurl at oneanother are much less confusing than the names we give ourselves. For instance, quite a lot of people, mostly a very amiable mild sort of people, call themselves Communist-Anarchists, which Conservatives interpret as Double-Dyed Scoundrels. This is very much as if they called themselves Roman Catholic Protestants, or Christian Jewesses, or undersized giantesses, or brunette blondes, or married maids, or any other flat contradiction in terms; for Anarchism preaches the obliteration of statute law and the abolition of Governments and States, whilst Communism preaches that all the necessary business of the country shall be done by public bodies and regulated by public law. Nobody could logically be in favor of both all the time. But there is a muddled commonsense in the name for all that. What the Communist-Anarchist really means is that she is willing to be a Communist as to the work and obedience to public law for everybody that is necessary to keep the community healthy and solvent, and that then she wants to be let go her own way. It is her manner of saying that she needs leisure and freedom as well as taskwork and responsibility: in short, as I have heard it expressed, that she does not want to be "a blooming bee". That is the attitude of all capable women; but to apply the term Communist-Anarchism to it is so confusing, and so often perversely adopted by the kind of muddler who, being against law and public enterprise because she wants to be free, and against freedom because freedom of contracts is a capitalist device for exploiting the proletariat, spends her life in obstructing both Socialism and Capitalism and never getting anywhere, that, on the whole, I should not call myself a Communist-Anarchist if I were you.

The truth is, we live in a Tower of Babel where a confusion of names prevents us from finishing the social edifice. The Roman Catholic who does not know what his Church teaches, the member of the Church of England who would repudiate several of the Thirty-Nine Articles if they were propounded to her without a hint of where they came from, the Liberal who has never heard of the principles of the Manchester School and would not have understood them if she had, and the Tory who is completely innocent of De Quincey's Logic of Political Economy: that is to say, the vast majority of Catholics, Protestants, Liberals, and Tories, have their counterparts in the Socialists, the Communists, the Syndicalists, the Anarchists, the Laborists, who denounce

Capitalism and middle class morality, and are saturated with both all the time. The Intelligent Woman, as she reads the newspapers, must allow for this as best she can. She must not only remember that every professing Socialist is not necessarily a Trade Unionist, and cannot logically be an Anarchist, but is sometimes so little a Socialist that, when entrusted with public business enough to bring her face to face with the Conservative or Liberal leaders she has been denouncing, she will be flattered to find that these eminent persons are quite of her real way of thinking, and vote with them enthusiastically every time.

The name Communist is at the present moment (1927) specially applied to and adopted by those who believe that Capitalism will never be abolished by constitutional parliamentary means in the Fabian manner, but must be overthrown by armed revolution and supplanted by the Muscovite Marxist Church. This is politely called the policy of Direct Action. Conservative Diehards who advocate a forcible usurpation of the government by the capitalists as such call it a *coup d'état*. But a proletarian may be an advocate of Direct Action without being a bit of a Communist. She may believe that the mines should belong to the miners, the railways to the railwaymen, the army to the soldiers, the churches to the clergymen, and the ships to the crews. She may even believe that the houses should belong to the housemaids, especially if she is a housemaid herself. Socialism will not hear of this. It insists that industries shall be owned by the whole community, and regulated in the interests of the consumer (or customer), who must be able to buy at cost price without paying a profit to anybody. A shop, for instance, must not belong to the shop assistants, nor be exploited by them for their profit: it must be run for the benefit of the customers, the shop assistant's safeguard against finding herself sacrificed to the customer being that she is herself a customer at the other shops, and the customer herself a worker in other establishments. When incomes are equal, and everyone is both a producer and a consumer, the producers and consumers may be trusted to treat each other fairly from self-love if from no more generous motive; but until then, to make any industry the property of the workers in it would be merely to replace the existing idle joint stock shareholders by working shareholders profiteering on a much larger scale, as they would appropriate the rent of their sites and make none of those contributions to a central exchequer for the benefit of the nation that now take place under parliamentary rule. The inequalities of income between, say, miners in the richest mines and farmers on the poorest soils would be monstrous. But I need not plague you with arguments: the arrangement is impossible anyhow; only, as several of the proletarian proposals, and cries of the day, including Trade Unionism, Producers' Co-operation, Workers' Control, Peasant Proprietorship, and the cruder misunderstandings of Syndicalism and Socialism, are either tainted or saturated with it to such an extent that it wrecked the proletarian movement in Italy after the war and led to the dictatorship of Signor Mussolini, and as it is often supposed to be part of Socialism, you had better beware of it; for it has many plausible pseudo-socialistic disguises. It is really only Poor Man's Capitalism, like Poor Man's Gout.

On their negative side the proletarian Isms are very much alike: they all bring the same accusations against Capitalism; and Capitalism makes no distinction between them because they agree in their hostility to it. But there is all the difference in the world between their positive remedies; and any woman who voted for Syndicalism or Anarchism or Direct Action disguised as Communism indiscriminately under the impression that she was voting for Socialism would be as mistaken as one who voted for Conservatism or Liberalism or Imperialism or the Union Jack or King and Country or Church and State indiscriminately under a general impression that she was voting against Socialism.

And so you have the curious spectacle of our Parliamentary Labor Party, led by Socialists who are all necessarily Communists in principle, and are advocating sweeping extensions of Communism, expelling the so-called Communist Party from its ranks, refusing to appear on the same platforms with its members in public, and being denounced by it as bourgeois reactionaries. It is most confusing until you know; and then you see that the issue just now between the rival proletarian parties in England is not Communism against Socialism: it is constitutional action, or Fabianism as it used to be called, against Direct Action followed by a dictatorship. And as Diehard Capitalism is now sorely tempted to try a British-Fascist *coup d'état* followed by a dictatorship, as opposed to Liberal constitutional Capitalism, the confusion and disunion are by no means all on the Labor side. The extremists of the Right and those of the Left are both propagandists of impatient disgust with parliament as an institution. There is a Right wing of the Right just as there is a Left wing of the Left; whilst the Constitutional Centre is divided between Capitalism and Socialism. You will need all your wits about you to find out where you are and keep there during the coming changes.

The proletarian party inherits from Trade Unionism the notion that the strike is the classic weapon and the only safeguard of proletarian labor. It is therefore dangerously susceptible to the widespread delusion that if instead of a coal strike here and a railway strike there, a lightning strike of waitresses in a restaurant today, and a lightning strike of match girls in a factory tomorrow, all the workers in all the occupations were to strike simultaneously and sympathetically, Capitalism would be brought to its knees. This is called The General Strike. It is as if the crew of a ship, oppressed by its officers, were advised by a silly-clever cabin boy to sink the ship until all the officers and their friends the passengers were drowned, and then take victorious command of it. The objection that the crew could not sail the ship without navigating officers is superfluous, because there is the conclusive preliminary objection that the crew would be drowned, cabin boy and all, as well as the officers. In a General Strike ashore the productive proletarians would be starved before the employers, capitalists, and parasitic proletarians, because these would have possession of the reserves of spare food. It would be national suicide.

Obvious as this is, the General Strike has been attempted again and again, notably on one occasion in Sweden, when it was very thoroughly tried out; and though it has always necessarily collapsed, it is still advocated by people who imagine that the remedy for Capitalism is to treat labor as the capital of the proletariat (that is, the spare money of those who have no money), and to hold up the Capitalists by threat of starvation just as the Capitalists have hitherto held up the proletariat. They forget that the capitalists have never yet been so absurd as to attempt a general lock-out. It would be much more sensible to support a particular strike by calling all other strikes off, thus isolating the particular employers aimed at, and enabling all the other workers to contribute to the strike fund. But we have already discussed the final impossibility of tolerating even particular strikes or lock-outs, much less general ones. They will pass away as duelling has passed away. Meanwhile be on your guard against propagandists of the General Strike; but bear in mind too that the term is now being used so loosely in the daily papers that we see it applied to any strike in which more than one trade is concerned.

A favorite plea of the advocates of the General Strike is that it could prevent a war. Now it may be admitted that the fear of an attempt at it does to some extent restrain governments from declaring unpopular wars. Unfortunately once the first fellow-countryman is killed or the first baby bombed, no war is unpopular: on the contrary, it is as well known to our Capitalist governments as it was to that clever lady the Empress Catherine of Russia that when the people become rebellious there is nothing like "a nice little war" for bringing them to heel again in a patriotic ecstasy of loyalty to the Crown. Besides, the fundamental objection to the general strike, that when everybody stops working the nation promptly perishes, applies just as fatally to a strike against war as to a strike against a reduction of wages. It is true that if the vast majority in the belligerent nations, soldiers and all, simultaneously became conscientious objectors, and the workers all refused to do military service of any kind, whether in the field or in the provisioning, munitioning, and transport of troops, no declaration of war could be carried out. Such a conquest of the earth by Pacifism seems millennially desirable to many of us; but the mere statement of these conditions is sufficient to shew that they do not constitute a general strike, and that they are so unlikely to occur that no sane person would act on the chance of their being realized. A single schoolboy militarist dropping a bomb from an aeroplane into a group of children will make an end of local pacifism in an instant until it becomes certain that the bomber and his employers will be called to account before a competent and dreaded tribunal. Meanwhile the fear of a so-called General Strike against war will never deter any bellicose Government from equipping and commissioning such adventurous young aces. But no Government dare send them if it knew that it would be blockaded by a combination of other nations sufficiently strong to intimidate the most bellicose single nation.

The formation of such a combination is the professed object of the present League of Nations; and though there is no sign so far of the leading military Powers even consulting it, much less obeying and supporting it, when they have any weighty military interests at stake, still even their military interests will force them sooner or later to take the League seriously, substitute supernational morality, law, and action, for the present international anarchism, according to which it is proper for nations, under certain forms, to murder and plunder foreigners, though it is a crime for them to murder and plunder oneanother. No other method of preventing war so far discovered is worth your attention. It is very improbable even that our quaint and illogical toleration of conscientious objection during the last war will ever be repeated; and in any case the experiment proved its futility as a preventive of war. The soldier in the trenches will always ask why he should be shot for refusing to go "over the top" when his brother at home is spared after refusing even to enter the trench. The General Strike is still more futile. War cannot be stopped by the refusal of individuals or even of whole trades to take part in it: nothing but combinations of nations, each subordinating what they call their sovereign rights to the world's good, or at least to the good of the combination, can prevail against it.

This subordination of nationalism is called supernationalism, and might be called catholicism if that word could be freed from misleading historical associations. It already exists in the United States of America, which are federated for certain purposes, including currency and a *pax Americana* which was established at the cost of a fierce war. There is no reason except pure devilment why the States of Europe, or, to begin with, a decisive number of them, should not federate to the same extent for the same purposes. The Empires are changing into Commonwealths, or voluntary federations, for common human purposes. Here, and not in local antipatriotic strikes, are the real hopes of peace.

You will find constitutional changes specially bothersome because of the continual clashing between the tightening-up of social discipline demanded by Socialism and the jealousy of official power and desire to do what we like which we call Democracy. Democracy has a very strong hold on organized labor. In the Trade Unions every device is tried to make the vote of the whole union supreme. When delegates vote at the Union Congresses they are allowed a vote for every member of their respective unions; and as far as possible the questions on which they cast their hundreds of thousands of votes are settled beforehand in the unions by the votes of the members; so that when the delegates go to Congress they are not representatives but mere spokesmen handing in the decisions of their unions. But these crude democratic precautions defeat their own object. In practice, a Trade Union secretary is the nearest thing on earth to an irremovable autocrat. The "card vote" is not called for except to decide questions on which the decisions could not be carried out unless the delegates of the Big Powers of trade unionism (that is, the unions whose membership runs into millions) could outvote the delegates of the Little Powers; and as in the ranks of Labor not only is "the career open to the talents" but absolutely closed to nonentities, the leaders are much more arbitrary than they would be in the House of Lords, where the hereditary peers may include persons of average or less than average ability. Even the humblest Trade Union secretary must have exceptional business ability and power of managing people; and if anyone but a secretary obtains a delegation to a Congress he must have at least a talent for self-assertion. He may be for all public purposes an idiot; but he must be a fairly blatant idiot, and to some extent a representative one, or he could never persuade large bodies of his equals to pick him out from the obscurity of his lot.

Now as this oligarchy of bureaucrats and demagogues is the result of the most jealous democracy, the oligarchs of labor are determined to maintain the system which has placed them in power. You must have noticed that some of the most imperiously wilful women, unable to bear a moment's contradiction, and tyrannizing over their husbands, daughters, and servants until nobody else in the house can call her soul her own, have been the most resolute opponents of Women's Rights. The reason is that they know that as long as the men govern they can govern the men. Just so a good many of the ablest and most arbitrary of the leaders of Trade Unionism are resolutely democratic in Labor politics because they know very well that as long as the workers can vote they can make the workers vote as they please. They are democrats, not because of their faith in the judgment, knowledge, and initiative of the masses, but because of their experience of mass ignorance, gullibility, and sheepishness. It is only the idealists of the propertied and cultivated middle classes who believe that the voice of the people is the voice of God: the typical proletarian leader is a cynic in this matter, believing secretly that the working folk will have to be born again and born differently before they can be safely allowed to have their own silly way in public affairs: indeed it is to make this rebirth possible that the leaders are Socialists. They have often been strongly anti-Socialist. Thus both the cynics and the idealists are strenuous defenders of democracy, and regard the series of enfranchisements of the people which began with the Conservative Act of 1867 and culminated in Votes for Women, as a glorious page in the history of the emancipation of mankind from tyranny and oppression, instead of a reduction to absurdity of the notion that giving slaves votes to defend their political rights and redress their wrongs is much wiser than giving razors to infants for the same purpose.

The naked truth is that democracy, or government by the people through votes for everybody, has never been a complete reality; and to the very limited extent to which it has been a reality it has not been a success. The extravagant hopes which have been attached to every extension of it have been disappointed. A hundred years ago the great Liberal Reform Bill was advocated as if its passage into law would produce the millennium. Only the other day the admission of women to the electorate, for which women fought and died, was expected to raise politics to a nobler plane and purify public life. But at the election which followed, the women voted for hanging the Kaiser; rallied hysterically round the worst male candidates; threw out all the women candidates of tried ability, integrity, and devotion; and elected just one titled lady of great wealth and singular demagogic fascination, who, though she justified their choice subsequently, was then a beginner. In short, the notion that the female voter is more politically intelligent or gentler than the male voter proved as great a delusion as the earlier delusions that the business man was any wiser politically than the country gentleman or the manual worker than the middle class man. If there were any disfranchised class left for our democrats to pin their repeatedly disappointed hopes on, no doubt they would still clamor for a fresh set of votes to jump the last ditch into their Utopia; and the vogue of democracy might last a while yet. Possibly there may be here and there lunatics looking forward to votes for children, or for animals, to complete the democratic structure. But the majority shows signs of having had enough of it. Discipline for Everybody and Votes for Nobody is the fashion in Spain and Italy; and for some years past in Russia the proletarian Government has taken no more notice of an adverse vote than the British Raj of an Indian jury's verdict, except when it turns the majority out of doors in the manner of Bismarck or Cromwell.

These reactions of disgust with democracy are natural enough where Capitalism, having first produced a huge majority of proletarians with no training in management, responsibility, or the handling of big money, nor any notion of the existence of such a thing as political science, gives this majority the vote for the sake of gaining party advantages by popular support. Even in ancient Greece, where our proletarians were represented by slaves, and only what we call the middle and upper classes voted, there was the same reaction, which is hardly surprising in view of the fact that one of the famous feats of Athenian democracy was to execute Socrates for using his superior brains to expose its follies.

Nevertheless, I advise you to stick to your vote as hard as you can, because though its positive effects may do you more harm than good, its negative effect may be of great value to you. If one candidate is a Socratic person and the other a fool who attracts you by echoing your own follies and giving them an air of patriotism and virtuous indignation, you may vote for the fool, that being as near as you can get to executing Socrates; and so far your vote is all to the bad. But the fact that your vote, though only one among many thousands, may conceivably turn the scale at an election, secures you a consideration in Parliament which it would be mad and cowardly for you to relinquish as long as inequality of income prevents you from being really represented by the members of the Government. Therefore cling to it tooth and nail, however unqualified you may be to make a wise use of it.

The Labor Party is in a continual dilemma on this point. At the election of 1918 the leader of the Labor Party, a steadfast supporter of votes for women, knew quite well that he would be defeated in his old constituency by the vote of the suburban ladies; and he was. The Labor Party, confronted by a scheme for making Parliament more representative of public opinion by securing due representation for minorities (called Proportional Representation), finds itself forced to oppose it lest it should break Parliament up into a host of squabbling groups and make parliamentary government impossible. All reformers who use democracy as a stepping stone to power find it a nuisance when they get there. The more power the people are given the more urgent becomes the need for some rational and well-informed superpower to dominate them and disable their inveterate admiration of international murder and national suicide. Voltaire said that there is one person wiser than Mrs Anybody, and that is Mrs Everybody; but Voltaire had not seen modern democracy at work: the democracy he admired in England was a very exclusive oligarchy; and the mixture of theocracy and hereditary autocracy that disgusted him in France was not a fair test of aristocracy, or government by the best qualified. We now know that though Mrs Everybody knows where the shoe pinches and must therefore have a say in the matter, she cannot make the shoe, and cannot tell a good shoemaker from a bad one by his output of hot air on a platform. Government demands ability to govern: it is neither Mrs Everybody's business nor Mrs Anybody's, but Mrs Somebody's. Mrs Somebody will never be elected unless she is protected from the competition of Mrs Noodle and Mrs Bounder and Mrs Noisy Nobody and Mrs King-and-Country and Mrs Class War and Mrs Hearth-and-Home and Mrs Bountiful and Mrs Hands-off-the-Church and Mrs Please-I-want-everybody-to-love-me. If democracy is not to ruin us we must at all costs find some trustworthy method of testing the qualifications of candidates before we allow them to seek election. When we have done that we may have great trouble in persuading the right people to come forward. We may even be driven to compel them; for those who fully understand how heavy are the responsibilities of government and how exhausting its labor are the least likely to shoulder them voluntarily. As Plato said, the ideal candidate is the reluctant one. When we discover such a test you will still have your electoral choice between several Mrs Somebodys, which will make them all respect you; but you will not be taken in by Mrs Noodle and Co. because they will not be eligible for election. Meanwhile, Heaven help us! we must do the best we can.

84

PERORATION

AND now a last word as to your own spiritual centre. All through this book we have been thinking of the public, and of our two selves as members of the public. This is our duty as citizens; but it may drive us mad if we begin to think of public evils as millionfold evils. They are nothing of the kind. What you yourself can suffer is the utmost that can be suffered on earth. If you starve to death you experience all the starvation that ever has been or ever can be. If ten thousand other women starve to death with you, their suffering is not increased by a single pang: their share in your fate does not make you ten thousand times as hungry, nor prolong your suffering ten thousand times. Therefore do not be oppressed by "the frightful sum of human suffering": there is no sum: two lean women are not twice as lean as one nor two fat women twice as fat as one. Poverty and pain are not cumulative: you must not let your spirit be crushed by the fancy that it is. If you can stand the suffering of one person you can fortify yourself with the reflection that the suffering of a million is no worse: nobody has more than one stomach to fill nor one frame to be stretched on the rack. Do not let your mind be disabled by excessive sympathy. What the true Socialist revolts against is not the suffering that is not cumulative, but the waste that is. A thousand healthy, happy, honorable women are not each a thousand times as healthy, happy, or honorable as one; but they can co-operate to increase the health, happiness, and honor possible for each of them. At present nobody can be healthy, happy, or honorable: our standards are so low that when we call ourselves so we mean only that we are not sick nor crying nor lying nor stealing (legally or illegally) oftener than we must agree to put up with under our Capitalist Constitution.

We have to confess it: Capitalist mankind in the lump is detestable. Class hatred is not a mere matter of envy on the part of the poor and contempt and dread on the part of the rich. Both rich and poor are really hateful in themselves. For my part I hate the poor and look forward eagerly to their extermination. I pity the rich a little, but am equally bent on their extermination. The working classes, the business classes, the professional classes, the propertied classes, the ruling classes, are each more odious than the other: they have no right to live: I should despair if I did not know that they will all die presently, and that there is no need on earth why they should be replaced by people like themselves. I do not want any human child to be brought up as I was brought up, nor as any child I have known was brought up. Do you?

And yet I am not in the least a misanthrope. I am a person of normal affections, as you probably are; but for that very reason I hate to be surrounded, not by people whose interests are the same as my own, whom I cannot injure without injuring myself, and who cannot injure me without injuring themselves, but by people whose interest it is to get as much out of me as they possibly can, and give me as little for it as possible (if anything). If I were poor, my relatives, now that I am old, would have to support me to keep me out of the workhouse, which means that they would have a strong interest in my death. As I am rich enough to leave some property, my children, if I had any, would be looking forward impatiently to my funeral and the reading of my will. The whole propertied class is waiting for dead men's shoes all the time. If I become ill and send for a doctor I know that if he does not prolong my illness to the utmost, and send me to expensive nursing homes to submit to still more expensive operations, he will be taking bread out of his children's mouths. My lawyer is bound by all his affections to encourage me in litigation, and to make it as protracted and costly as he can. Even my clergyman, partly State supported as he is, dare not if I belong to the Church of England rebuke me for oppressing the poor any more than he dare champion me against the oppression of the rich if I were poor. The teacher in the school where my neighbors' children have their morals formed would find herself in the gutter if she taught any child that to live on what is called an independent income without working is to live the life of a thief without the risks and enterprise that make the pirate and the burglar seem heroic to boys. My tradesmen's business is to overcharge me as much as they can without running too great a risk of being undersold by trade rivals. My landlord's business is to screw out of me the uttermost extractable farthing of my earnings for his permission to occupy a place on earth. Were I unmarried I should be pursued by hordes of women so desperately in need of a husband's income and position that their utmost efforts to marry me would be no evidence of their having the smallest personal regard for me. I cannot afford the friendship of people much richer than myself: those much poorer cannot afford mine. Between those who do the daily work of my house, and are therefore necessary partners in my work, and me there is a gulf of class which is nothing but a gulf of unequal distribution of wealth. Life is made lonely and difficult for me in a hundred unnecessary ways; and so few people are clever and tactful and sensible and self-controlled enough to pick their way through the world without giving or taking offence that the first quality of capitalistic mankind is quarrelsomeness. Our streets are fuller of feuds than the Highlands or the Arabian desert. The social friction set up by inequality of income is intense: society is like a machine designed to work smoothly with the oil of equality, into the bearings of which some malignant demon keeps pouring the sand of inequality. If it were not for the big pools of equality that exist at different levels, the machine would not work at all. As it is, the seizings-up, the smashings, the stoppages, the explosions, never cease. They vary in magnitude from a railway worker crushed in the shunting-yard to a world war in which millions of men with the strongest natural reasons for saving each others' lives destroy them instead in the cruellest manner, and from a squabble over a penny in a one-room tenement to a lawsuit lasting twenty years and reducing all the parties to it to destitution. And to outface this miserable condition we bleat once a year about peace on earth and good-will to men: that is, among persons to whom we have distributed incomes ranging from a starvation dole to several thousands a day, piously exhorting the recipients to love one-another. Have you any patience with it? I have none.

Now you may, for all I know, be a sharp, cynical sort of person; or you may be a nice, mushy, amiable, goodnatured one. If the latter you will tell me that people are not governed so much by money considerations as I make out: that your doctor hates to see you ill and does his best to cure you; that your solicitor keeps you out of litigation when you lose your temper and want to rush into it; that your clergyman calls himself a Christian Socialist and leads all the popular agitations against the oppression of the rich by the poor; that your children were heartbroken when their father died and that you never had a cross word with him about his property or yours; that your servants have been with you for forty years and have brought you up from your childhood more devotedly and affectionately than your own parents, and have remained part of the family when your children flew away from the nest to new nests of their own; that your tradesmen have never cheated you, and have helped you over hard times by giving you long and forbearing credit: in short, that in spite of all I may say, this Capitalist world is full of kindliness and love and good-fellowship and genuine religion. Dr Johnson, who described his life as one of wretchedness; Anatole France, who said he had never known a moment's happiness; Dean Swift, who saw in himself and his fellowmen Yahoos far inferior to horses; and Shakespear, to whom a man in authority was an angry ape, are known to have been admired, loved, petted, entertained, even idolized, throughout lives of honorable and congenial activity such as fall to the lot of hardly one man in a billion; yet the obscure billions manage to get on without unbearable discontent. William Morris, whose abhorrence of Capitalism was far deeper than that of persons of only ordinary mental capacity and sensibility, said, when he was told that he was mortally ill, "Well, I cannot complain: I have had a good time".

To all this consolation I have been able in this book to add that Capitalism, though it richly deserves the very worst that Karl Marx or even John Ruskin said of it and a good deal more that they never thought of, was yet, in its origin, thoroughly well intentioned. It was indeed much better intentioned than early Christianity, which treated this world as a place of punishment for original sin, of which the end was fortunately at hand. Turgot and Adam Smith were beyond all comparison more sincere guides to earthly prosperity than St Paul. If they could have foreseen the history of the practical application of their principles in the nineteenth century in England they would have recoiled in horror, just as Karl Marx would have recoiled if he had been foreshewn what happened in Russia from 1917 to 1921 through the action of able and devoted men who made his writings their Bible. Good people are the very devil sometimes, because, when their good-will hits on a wrong way, they go much further along it and are much more ruthless than bad people; but there is always hope in the fact that they mean well, and that their bad deeds are their mistakes and not their successes; whereas the evils done by bad people are not mistakes but triumphs of wickedness. And since all moral triumphs, like mechanical triumphs, are reached by trial and error, we can despair of Democracy and despair of Capitalism without despairing of human nature: indeed if we did not despair of them as we know them we should prove ourselves so worthless that there would be nothing left for the world but to wait for the creation of a new race of beings capable of succeeding where we have failed.

Nevertheless I must warn my amiable optimist and meliorist readers not only that all the virtues that comfort them are operating in spite of Capitalism and not as part of it, but that they are baffled by it in ways that are hidden from people who have not examined the situation with a good deal of technical knowledge and some subtlety. Take your honest and kindly doctor, and your guardian angel solicitor. I quite admit that there are plenty of them: the doctor who is a mercenary scoundrel and the lawyer who is a mischievous and heartless rascal is as exceptional as any other sort of criminal: I myself have never chanced to come across one, and most likely you have not either. But I have come across honest doctors whose treatment has been fatal, and honest lawyers whose advice has been disastrous. So have you, perhaps.

You know the very true saying that where there is a will there is a way. Unfortunately the good will does not necessarily find the right way. There are always dozens of ways, bad, good, and indifferent. You must know some bad women who are doing the right thing from bad motives side by side with good women who are doing the wrong thing from the best motives in the world. For instance, the number of children, especially first children, who are guarded and swaddled and drugged and doctored to death by the solicitude of their ignorantly affectionate mothers, must be greater than that of the children who die of maternal dislike and neglect. When silly people (writers, I regret to say, some of them) tell you that a loving heart is enough, remind them that fools are more dangerous than rogues, and that women with loving hearts are often pitiable fools. The finding of the right way is not sentimental work: it is scientific work, requiring observation, reasoning, and intellectual conscientiousness.

It is on this point of intellectual conscientiousness that we all break down under pecuniary temptation. We cannot help it, because we are so constituted that we always believe finally what we wish to believe. The moment we want to believe something, we suddenly see all the arguments for it, and become blind to the arguments against it. The moment we want to disbelieve anything we have previously believed, we suddenly discover not only that there is a mass of evidence against it, but that this evidence was staring us in the face all the time. If you read the account of the creation of the world in the book of Genesis with the eye of faith you will not perceive a single contradiction in it. If you read it with the eye of hostile critical science you will see that it consists of two successive accounts, so different that they cannot both be true. In modern books you will be equally baffled by your bias. If you love animals and have a horror of injustice and cruelty, you will read the books of wonderful discoveries and cures made by vivisectors with a sickened detestation of their callous cruelty, and with amazement that anyone could be taken in by such bad reasoning about lies which have been reduced to absurdity by force of flat fact every few years, only to be replaced by a fresh crop. If, however, you have only a dread of disease for yourself or your family, and feel that in comparison to relief from this terror the sufferings of a few dogs and guinea-pigs are not worth bothering about, you will find in the same books such authentic and convincing miracles, such marvellous cures for all diseases, such gospels of hope, monuments of learning, and infallible revelations of the deepest truths of Science, that your indignation at the derisive scepticism of the humanitarians may develop into an enmity (heartily reciprocated) that may end in persecutions and wars of science like the persecutions and wars of religion that followed the Reformation, and were not new then.

But, you will ask, what have Socialism and Capitalism to do with the fact that belief is mostly bias. It is very simple. If by inequality of income you give your doctors, your lawyers, your clergymen, your landlords, or your rulers an overwhelming economic interest in any sort of belief or practice, they will immediately begin to see all the evidence in favor of that sort of belief and practice, and become blind to all the evidence against it. Every doctrine that will enrich doctors, lawyers, landlords, clergymen, and rulers will be embraced by them eagerly and hopefully; and every doctrine that threatens to impoverish them will be mercilessly criticized and rejected. There will inevitably spring up a body of biassed teaching and practice in medicine, law, religion, and government that will become established and standardized as scientifically, legally, religiously, constitutionally, and morally sound, taught as such to all young persons entering these professions, stamping those who dare dissent as outcast quacks, heretics, sedition mongers, and traitors. Your doctor may be the honestest, kindliest doctor on earth; your solicitor may be a second father or mother to you; your clergyman may be a saint; your member of Parliament another Moses or Solon. They may be heroically willing to put your health, your prosperity, your salvation, and your protection from injustice before their interest in getting a few extra pounds out of you; but how far will that help you if the theory and practice of their profession, imposed on them as a condition of being allowed to pursue it, has been corrupted at the root by pecuniary interest? They can proceed only as the hospitals and medical schools teach them and order them to proceed, as the courts proceed, as the Church proceeds, as Parliament proceeds: that is their orthodoxy; and if the desire to make money and obtain privileges has been operating all the time in building up that orthodoxy, their best intentions and endeavors may result in leaving you with your health ruined, your pocket empty, your soul damned, and your liberties abrogated by your best friends in the name of science, law, religion, and the British constitution. Ostensibly you are served and protected by learned professions and political authorities whose duty it is to save life, minimize suffering, keep the public health as tested by vital statistics at the highest attainable pitch, instruct you as to your legal obligations and see that your legal rights are not infringed, give you spiritual help and disinterested guidance when your conscience is troubled, and make and administer, without regard to persons or classes, the laws that protect you and regulate your life. But the moment you have direct personal occasion for these services you discover that they are all controlled by Trade Unions in disguise, and that the high personal honor and kindliness of their individual members is subject to the morality of Trade Unionism, so that their loyalty to their union, which is essentially a defensive conspiracy against the public, comes first, and their loyalty to you as patient, client, employer, parishioner, customer or citizen, next. The only way in which you can set their natural virtues free from this omnipresent trade union and governing class corruption and tyranny is to secure for them all equal incomes which none of them can increase without increasing the income of everybody else to exactly the same amount; so that the more efficiently and economically they do their work the lighter their labor will be and the higher their credit.

Under such conditions you would find human nature good enough for all your reasonable purposes; and when you took up such books as Gulliver's Travels or Candide which under Capitalism are unanswerable indictments of mankind as the wickedest of all known species, you would see in them only terribly vivid clinical lectures on extinct moral diseases which were formerly produced by inequality as smallpox and typhus were produced by dirt. Such books are never written until mankind is horribly corrupted, not by original sin but by inequality of income.

Then the coveted distinction of lady and gentleman, instead of being the detestable parasitic pretension it is at present, meaning persons who never condescend to do anything for themselves that they can possibly put on others without rendering them equivalent service, and who actually make their religion centre on the infamy of loading the guilt and punishment of all their sins on an innocent victim (what real lady would do so base a thing?), will at last take on a simple and noble meaning, and be brought within the reach of every ablebodied person. For then the base woman will be she who takes from her country more than she gives to it; the common person will be she who does no more than replace what she takes; and the lady will be she who, generously overearning her income, leaves the nation in her debt and the world a better world than she found it.

By such ladies and their sons can the human race be saved, and not otherwise.

AYOT ST LAWRENCE,
16*th March* 1927.

APPENDIX

INSTEAD OF A BIBLIOGRAPHY

THIS book is so long that I can hardly think that any woman will want to read much more about Socialism and Capitalism for some time. Besides, a bibliography is supposed to be an acknowledgment by the author of the books from which his own book was compiled. Now this book is not a compilation: it is all out of my own head. It was started by a lady asking me to write her a letter explaining Socialism. I thought of referring her to the hundreds of books which have been written on the subject; but the difficulty was that they were nearly all written in an academic jargon which, though easy and agreeable to students of economics, politics, philosophy, and sociology generally, is unbearably dry, meaning unreadable, to women not so specialized. And then, all these books are addressed to men. You might read a score of them without ever discovering that such a creature as a woman had ever existed. In fairness let me add that you might read a good many of them without discovering that such a thing as a man ever existed. So I had to do it all over again in my own way and yours. And though there were piles of books about Socialism, and an enormous book about Capitalism by Karl Marx, not one of them answered the simple question, "What is Socialism?" The other simple question, "What is Capital?" was smothered in a mass of hopelessly wrong answers, the right one having been hit on (as far as my reading goes) only once, and that was by the British economist Stanley Jevons when he remarked casually that capital is spare money. I made a note of that.

However, as I know that women who frequent University Extension lectures will not be satisfied until they have choked their brains by reading a multitude of books on the subject; and as the history of Socialist thought is instructive, I will say just a word or two in the customary pedantic manner about the literary milestones on the road from Capitalism to Socialism.

The theory of Capitalism was not finally worked out until early in the nineteenth century by Ricardo, a Jewish stockbroker. As he had a curious trick of saying the opposite of what he meant whilst contriving somehow to make his meaning clear, his demonstration was elegantly and accurately paraphrased by a first rate literary artist and opium eater, Thomas De Quincey, who could write readably and fascinatingly about anything.

The theory was that if private property in land and capital, and sanctity of free contract between individuals, were enforced as fundamental constitutional principles, the proprietors would provide employment for the rest of the community on terms sufficient to furnish them with at least a bare subsistence in return for continuous industry, whilst themselves becoming rich to such excess that the investment of their superfluous income as capital would cost them no privation. No attempt was made to disguise the fact that the resultant disparity between the poverty of the proletarian masses and the riches of the proprietors would produce popular discontent, or that as wages fell and rents rose with the increase of population, the contrast between laborious poverty and idle luxury would provide sensational topics for Radical agitators. Austin's Lectures on Jurisprudence and Macaulay's forecasts of the future of America prove that the more clear-headed converts of the theory of Capitalism had no millennial illusions.

But they could see no practicable alternative. The Socialist alternative of State organization of industry was inconceivable, because, as industry had not yet finished the long struggle by which it extricated itself from the obsolete restrictions and oppressions of medieval and feudal society, State interference, outside simple police work, still seemed a tyranny to be broken, not a vital activity to be extended. Thus the new Capitalist economic policy was put forward in opposition, not to Socialism, but to Feudalism or Paternal Oligarchy. It was dogmatically called Political Economy absolute, complete, and inevitable; and the workers were told that they could no more escape or modify its operation than change the orbits of the planets.

In 1840 a French proletarian, Proudhon, published an essay with the startling title "What is Property? Theft". In it he demonstrated that a *rentier,* or person living, as we now put it, by owning instead of by working, inflicts on society precisely the same injury as a thief. Proudhon was a poor Frenchman; but a generation later John Ruskin, a rich Englishman of the most conservative education and culture, declared that whoever was not a worker was either a beggar or a robber, and published accounts of his personal activities and expenditure to prove that he had given good value for his rents and dividends. A generation later again Cecil Rhodes, an ultra-imperialist, made a famous will bequeathing his large fortune for public purposes, and attaching the condition that no idler should ever benefit by it. It may be said that from the moment when Capitalism established itself as a reasoned-out system to be taught at the universities as standard political economy, it began to lose its moral plausibility, and, in spite of its dazzling mechanical triumphs and financial miracles, steadily progressed from inspiring the sanguine optimism of Macaulay and his contemporaries to provoking a sentiment which became more and more like abhorrence among the more thoughtful even of the capitalists themselves.

All such moral revolutions have their literary prophets and theorists; and among them the first place was taken by Karl Marx, in the second half of the nineteenth century, with his history of Capital, an overwhelming exposure of the horrors of the industrial revolution and the condition to which it had reduced the proletariat. Marx's contribution to the abstract economic theory of value, by which he set much store, was a blunder which was presently corrected and superseded by the theory of Jevons; but as Marx's category of "surplus value" (Mehrwerth), meaning rent, interest, and profits, represented solid facts, his blunder in no way invalidated his indictment of the capitalist system, nor his historical generalization as to the evolution of society on economic lines. His so-called Historic Materialism is easily vulnerable to criticism as a law of nature; but his postulate that human society does in fact evolve on its belly, as an army marches, and that its belly biases its brains, is a safe working one. Buckle's much less read History of Civilization, also a work of the mind changing sort, has the same thesis but a different moral: to wit, that progress depends on the critical people who do not believe everything they are told: that is, on scepticism.

Even before Karl Marx the Capitalist economists had lost their confidence, and its ordinary exponents become disingenuously evasive. Not so the bigger men. John Stuart Mill began as a Ricardian and ended as an avowed Socialist. Cairnes still saw no practicable alternative to Capitalism; but his contempt for the "drones in the hive" who live by owning was as thorough and outspoken as Ruskin's. Their latest academic successor, Mr Maynard Keynes, dismisses Laisser-faire contemptuously as an exploded fallacy.

After Cairnes a school of British Socialist economists arose, notably Sidney and Beatrice Webb of the Fabian Society, who substituted the term Political Science for Political Economy. They gave historical consciousness to the proletarian movement by writing its history with the intimate knowledge and biographical vivacity needed to give substance to the abstract proletariat described by Marx. The evolution of Trade Unionism, Co-operation, and proletarian politics (Industrial Democracy) was reasoned out and documented by them. Their histories of English local government and of the Poor Law cover a huge part of the general field of British constitutional and administrative activity, past and present. They cured Fabianism of the romantic amateurishness which had made the older Socialist agitations negligible and ridiculous, and contributed most of the Fabian Society's practical proposals for the solution of pressing problems. They shattered the old Capitalist theory of the impotence of the State for anything but mischief in industry, and demonstrated not only that communal and collective enterprise has already attained a development undreamt of by Ricardo and his contemporaries, but that Capitalism itself is dependent for its existence on State guidance, and has evolved collective forms of its own which have taken it far beyond the control of the individual private investor, and left it ripe for transfer to national or municipal ownership. Their volume on the decay of Capitalism has completed Marx's work of driving Capitalism from its old pretension to be normal, inevitable, and in the long run always beneficial in modern society, to a position comparable to that of an army digging itself into its last ditch after a long series of surrenders and retreats. They estimate roughly that in its hundred years of supremacy Capitalism justified its existence, *faute de mieux,* for the first fifty years, and for the last fifty has been collapsing more and more on its crazy foundation.

Beatrice Webb's curious mixture of spiritual and technical autobiography, entitled My Apprenticeship, describes how an intelligent girl-capitalist, with a sensitive social conscience and a will of her own, critically impervious to mere persuasion, and impressible by first hand evidence and personal experience only, was led to Socialism by stubbornly investigating the facts of Capitalist civilization for herself. The Intelligent Woman with a turn for investigation or an interest in character study, or both, should read it.

Between Karl Marx and the Webbs came Henry George with his Progress and Poverty, which converted many to Land Nationalization. It was the work of a man who had seen that the conversion of an American village to a city of millionaires was also the conversion of a place where people could live and let live in tolerable comfort to an inferno of seething poverty and misery. Tolstoy was one of his notable converts. George's omission to consider what the State should do with the national rent after it had taken it into the public treasury stopped him on the threshold of Socialism; but most of the young men whom he had led up to it went through (like myself) into the Fabian Society and other Socialist bodies. Progress and Poverty is still Ricardian in theory: indeed it is on its abstract side a repetition of De Quincey's Logic of Political Economy; but whereas De Quincey, as a true-blue British Tory of a century ago, accepted the Capitalist unequal distribution of income, and the consequent division of society into rich gentry and poor proletarians, as a most natural and desirable arrangement, George, as an equally true-blue American republican, was revolted by it.

After Progress and Poverty the next milestone is Fabian Essays, edited by myself, in which Sidney Webb first entered the field as a definitely Socialist writer with Graham Wallas, whose later treatises on constitutional problems are important, and Sydney Olivier (Lord Olivier) whose studies of the phenomenon of the "poor white" in Africa and America, facing the competition of the black proletariats created by negro slavery, should be read by Colonial Ministers. In Fabian Essays Socialism is presented for the first time as a completely constitutional political movement, which the most respectable and least revolutionary citizen can join as irreproachably as he might join the nearest Conservative club. Marx is not mentioned; and his peculiar theory of value is entirely ignored, the economic theories relied on being Jevons' theory of value and Ricardo's theory of the rent of land, the latter being developed so as to apply to industrial capital and interests as well. In short, Socialism appears in Fabian Essays purged of all its unorthodox views and insurrectionary Liberal associations. This is what distinguished the volume at that time from such works as the England For All of Henry Mayers Hyndman, the founder of the Social-Democratic Federation, who, until 1918, when the Russian Marxists outraged his British patriotism by the treaty of Brest Litovsk, clung to Marx's value theory, and to the Marxian traditions of the barricade Liberalism of 1848, with a strong dash of the freethinking gentlemanly cosmopolitanism of the advanced republican *littérateurs* of the middle of the nineteenth century.

After Fabian Essays treatises on Socialism followed, first singly, then in dozens, then in scores, and now in such profusion that I never read them unless I know the writers personally, nor always, I confess, even then.

If you read Sociology, not for information but for entertainment (small blame to you!), you will find that the nineteenth-century poets and prophets who denounced the wickedness of our Capitalism exactly as the Hebrew prophets denounced the Capitalism of their time, are much more exciting to read than the economists and writers on political science who worked out the economic theory and political requirements of Socialism. Carlyle's Past and Present and Shooting Niagara, Ruskin's Ethics of the Dust and Fors Clavigera, William Morris's News from Nowhere (the best of all the Utopias), Dickens's Hard Times and Little Dorrit, are notable examples: Ruskin in particular leaving all the professed Socialists, even Karl Marx, miles behind in force of invective. Lenin's criticisms of modern society seem like the platitudes of a rural dean in comparison. Lenin wisely reserved his most blighting invectives for his own mistakes.

But I doubt whether nineteenth-century writers can be as entertaining to you as they are to me, who spent the first forty-four years of my life in that benighted period. If you would appreciate the enormous change from nineteenth-century self-satisfaction to twentieth-century self-criticism you can read The Pickwick Papers (jolly early Dickens) and then read Our Mutual Friend (disillusioned mature Dickens), after which you can try Dickens's successor H. G. Wells, who, never having had any illusions about the nineteenth century, is utterly impatient of its blunderings, and full of the possibilities of social reconstruction. When you have studied nineteenth-century county gentility in the novels of Anthony Trollope and Thackeray for the sake of understanding your more behindhand friends, you must study it up-to-date in the novels of John Galsworthy. To realize how ignorant even so great an observer as Dickens could be of English life outside London and the main coaching routes you can compare his attempt to describe the Potteries in Hard Times with Arnold Bennett's native pictures of the Five Towns; but to appreciate his much more serious and complete ignorance of working-class history and organization in his own day you would have to turn from fiction to the Webbs' History of Trade Unionism.

The earlier nineteenth-century literature, for all its invective, satire, derision and caricature, made amiable by its generous indignation, was not a literature of revolt. It was pre-Marxian. Post-Marxian literature, even in its most goodhumored pages by men who never read Marx, is revolutionary: it does not contemplate the survival of the present order, which Thackeray, for instance, in his bitterest moods seems never to have doubted.

For women the division is made by Marx's Norwegian contemporary Ibsen rather than by Marx. Ibsen's women are all in revolt against Capitalist morality; and the clever ladies who have since filled our bookshelves with more or less autobiographical descriptions of female frustration and slavery are all post-Ibsen. The modern literature of male frustration, much less copious, is post-Strindberg. In neither branch are there any happy endings. They have the Capitalist horror without the Socialist hope.

The post-Marxian, post-Ibsen psychology gave way in 1914-18 to the post-war psychology. It is very curious; but it is too young, and I too old, for more than this bare mention of its existence and its literature.

Finally I may mention some writings of my own, mostly in the form of prefaces to my published plays. One of the oddities of English literary tradition is that plays should be printed with prefaces which have nothing to do with them, and are really essays, or manifestoes, or pamphlets, with the plays as a bait to catch readers. I have exploited this tradition very freely, puzzling many good people who thought the prefaces must be part of the plays. In this guise I contended that poverty should be neither pitied as an inevitable misfortune, nor tolerated as a just retribution for misconduct, but resolutely stamped out and prevented from recurring as a disease fatal to human society. I also made it quite clear that Socialism means equality of income or nothing, and that under Socialism you would not be allowed to be poor. You would be forcibly fed, clothed, lodged, taught, and employed whether you liked it or not. If it were discovered that you had not character and industry enough to be worth all this trouble, you might possibly be executed in a kindly manner; but whilst you were permitted to live you would have to live well. Also you would not be allowed to have half a crown an hour when other women had only two shillings, or to be content with two shillings when they had half a crown. As far as I know I was the first Socialist writer to whom it occurred to state this explicitly as a necessary postulate of permanent civilization; but as nothing that is true is ever new I daresay it had been said again and again before I was born.

Two Fabian booklets of mine entitled Socialism and Superior Brains and The Common Sense of Municipal Trading are still probably worth reading, as they are written from personal experience of both.

INDEX

By BEATRICE WHITE, M.A.